CONJUNCTIONS

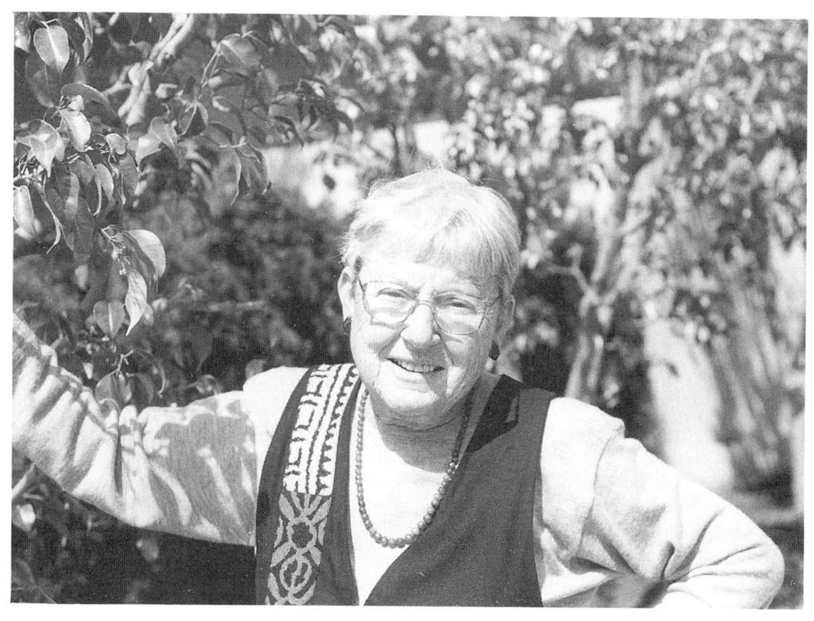

Renée Riese Hubert. Photo courtesy Candace Hubert.

CONJUNCTIONS:

VERBAL-VISUAL RELATIONS

(Essays in honor of Renée Riese Hubert)

Edited by
Laurie Edson

San Diego State University Press
1996

Georges Roque's "The Role of Language in Seeing an Image" first appeared in Spanish as "El Papel de lo verbal en la visión de las imágenes" in *XV Coloquio Internacional de Historia del Arte: Los Discursos sobre el arte*. Mexico City: Instituto de Investigaciones Estéticas, Universidad Nacional Autónoma de México, 1994, pp. 321-39.

Conjunctions: Verbal-Visual Relations is published by San Diego State University Press.

First Edition

ISBN 1-879691-45-0

Cover art by Michel Deguy/Bertrand Dorny, *Nous nous souvenons*, gravure manuscrite. Courtesy Bertrand Dorny.

Contents

Acknowledgments

I would like to thank all the authors and translators who contributed to this volume and helped make this idea a reality. We all, of course, are especially grateful to Renée Riese Hubert for her pioneering work in verbal-visual relations, work that continues to have a tremendous influence in the field. I would also like to thank Judd D. Hubert, who provided invaluable help throughout the process, and Harry Polkinhorn, Director of San Diego State University Press, for his excellent guidance and expert help in preparing the manuscript. Thanks, too, to Dean Paul Strand and the College of Arts and Letters Research and Professional Leaves Committee at San Diego State University for supporting this project with a grant, and to Carey Wall, Chair of the Department of English and Comparative Literature, for providing release time. Finally, I would like to thank my husband, Jim Carmody, for helping me locate so many elusive references.

Introduction

This volume of original essays by an international group of scholars investigates verbal-visual relations, broadly conceived, in the modern period. The book explores, through a wide variety of theoretical and critical approaches, how thinkers in various fields—aesthetics, poetry, visual art, philosophy, and book illustration—have approached the problematic relationship between the verbal and the visual.

As this collection of essays makes clear, interarts studies are richly diverse in their preoccupations, strategies, and techniques. What unites all the essays, however, is a commitment to perceiving and developing fertile crossovers between literature and the visual arts, as well as a desire to question the border that has traditionally separated the two fields. In this sense, this volume participates in a larger phenomenon taking place in contemporary culture: a re-evaluation of conventional habits of thinking and organizing knowledge.

I have gathered together a first group of essays under the heading "Stagings." The section begins with Michel Deguy's essay, in both French and English, on "La Scène de la Cène," a critical and poetic account of representation as a staging. Judd D. Hubert's article on "The Frame as Metaphor" treats metaphorical framing as a way of staging difference. As he puts it, "purposeful metaphorical framing in literary texts and inner framing in artifacts [is] a way of deliberately setting them apart, if not necessarily above, everyday apprehensions, whether verbal, visual, or auditory." In an essay on "Torn Pages of Deconstruction: The Palimpsests of Mireille W. Descombes," Claude Gandelman analyzes Descombes' artworks as stagings of violence in the context of deconstruction, a violence done with words and to words. Because her violence is done on paper, with words torn and scratched on paper, Gandelman compares it to the palimpsest. My own essay on "Excess, Transgression, and the Subversion of Form: Lautréamont and Dali" analyzes the analogous ways in which Dali and Lautréamont stage transgression and subversion. Finally, Marjorie Perloff's "'Writing Through' Wittgenstein: Joseph Kosuth's *Abridged in Ghent*" proposes that in his artist's book, Kosuth stages and refigures the meaning system of Wittgenstein's own art.

I have gathered a second group of essays together under the heading "Seeing"; these deal with the issue of what happens when we "see" an image. Georges Roque's essay, "The Role of Language in Seeing an Image," is a theoretical inquiry into the relationship between the verbal and the visual. While most studies of verbal-visual relations presuppose a radical difference between the visual image and language, Roque argues "the important role that verbal language plays not only in the interpretation of the image, but also in the mechanisms involved in the perception of the image, whether dealing with form or color." Sydney Lévy takes up a related issue in his essay on "Seeing and Knowing in Francis Ponge." Starting from Ponge's physical reaction upon seeing one of Braque's paintings, Lévy discusses Ponge's attention to a kind of knowledge for and of the body (embodied knowledge) that is unsayable: "[T]he visual experience imparts a knowledge other than its value as information [and] it is inscribed on the body. . . ." His essay thus addresses a cognitive process of the visual experience at work in Ponge's texts. Anne-Marie Christin, too, writes about the visual experience in her "Narration and Visual Thought: Philippe Clerc's *Revue-Images*." Christin theorizes visual thought and draws attention to the positive value of interspaces in her study of Clerc's *revue-images*, which she calls "a transformation of visual thought into spectacle."

The third group of essays I have gathered under the heading "Reading and Readings." Breon Mitchell's essay, "The Secret Life of the Book: The *Livre d'artiste* and the Act of Reading," is an exploration of the aesthetic experience of truly "reading" the *livre d'artiste*, and he cites Renée Riese Hubert's reading of Ania Staritsky's book as a model reading. As Mitchell puts it, Renée, in fact, "performed" Staritsky's book in a participatory way, actualizing the elements already built into it. For Steven

Winspur, too, the reader of Eluard's poetry is a necessary participant in the "performance" of the poem, already implicated in the poem through Eluard's poetic strategy of "strange loops." In his essay, "Ethical Loops in Eluard," Winspur examines the ethical thrust of Eluard's strategy of structuring his poems so that "readers understand that they are not only decoding signs of literary meaning but also signs of their own activity." The activity of art criticism itself is the subject of Roger Cardinal's "The Hanover *Merzbau*: Tracing a Lost Masterwork." Here, Cardinal discusses Kurt Schwitters' first *Merzbau* and concludes that "the density of this lost masterwork is to be the everlasting talking-piece of art criticism, the aggregate of all that it is possible to say about it, whether true or false." In other words, it is precisely the absence of the work of art that creates the infinite possibility of speaking about it.

In his "Spiritual Quest and Scriptural Inquiry: Pierre Jean Jouve's Art Criticism" Robert W. Greene explores some of Jouve's art criticism and locates the simultaneous double focus mentioned in his title. As he puts it, "Jouve's criticism, like the art it lovingly peruses and memorializes, faces up to death by moving through desire, merging a deeply spiritual quest with a meticulous scriptural inquiry." Eric T. Haskell's essay, "Painter Beholding Poet: Recent Illustrations for Rimbaud's 'Voyelles,'" analyzes August Ohm's and Abdallah Benanteur's illustrations for Rimbaud's poem "Voyelles" and locates their break with traditional methods of picturing poetry. Unlike their predecessors, suggests Haskell, Ohm and Benanteur succeed in matching, on the graphic plane, Rimbaud's invention on the verbal plane. In "Joan Miró and Composition of the *Livre de peintre*," Harriett Watts traces the evolution of Miró's form language from his first illustrated book in 1930 to the composition of Tristan Tzara's *Parler seul*, which appeared in 1950. Willard Bohn provides readings of two of Juliette Roche's verbal-visual compositions in his essay, "Juliette Roche and the Ideoplastic Method." And in "*Ralentir travaux*: The Second Surrealist Manifesto," Virginia A. La Charité reads *Ralentir travaux* as the second artistic manifesto of the Surrealist movement, a poetic counterattack against the Marxist leanings expressed in the *Deuxième Manifeste du Surréalisme*.

It is with great pleasure that we present these essays to our colleague and friend, Renée Riese Hubert.

—Laurie Edson

Trois Hommages

I

In the mid-fifties, Renée and Judd Hubert lived in a light-flooded apartment high above Massachusetts Avenue and looking out over Harvard Yard. On the ground floor of the same building the Grolier Book Shop offered a few select poetry volumes to pedestrians on Plympton Street, and hid the rest of its vast stock in exiguous back rooms. The Grolier always seemed an appropriate checkpoint because Renée was known to the rest of us primarily as a poet. Yes, she taught French too, in spite of her soft German accent in English. But Judd, Sphinx-like and patient, was the professor of the family. Renée wrote poems—both in French and German as I recall. When I discovered several I liked, my response was simply to translate. For instance.

Courant poétique

Faithful
       the blood circulates in the vein
on the grinding axle of routine

The reel of film unwinds without a whisper

The watch hand
forever behind
describes its vicious circle

> While the trackless train
> travels on and on
> drawn into the same circuit
>
> The earth is round and it turns

By "the rest of us" I mean four instructors who shared one barracks-like office in Little Hall right on Harvard Square, long since torn down to make way for larger commercial structures. Directing squads of graduate students, the four of us did the basic language and literature teaching at a period made exciting by the recent arrival of a great new secular faith called Existentialism. *La Nausée* and *L'Etranger* were publicly taught. We spent our nights trying to plough through *L'Etre et le néant*. Within a few years we had all moved on — the four instructors to the four winds, Renée and Judd all the way to the West Coast.

One summer this exotic couple loaned me their apartment while my family went off to Canada. For a couple of weeks I lived surrounded by choice volumes in French and German literature and — even more imposing and demanding — Renée's plants. Carefully trained tendrils reached yearningly across the dining room on stretched strings. Others framed the windows. Renée had evidently taken great pains to decorate the space with vines that thrived in the airy quarters. I remember no painstaking instructions, only considerable anxiety about how to care for them properly.

At that time Renée was an elusive presence, a beautiful poet married to a rising scholar of mysterious presence. Above all she was spontaneously friendly to us four horsemen. Almost no one else talked to us in the dim corridors of Little Hall where the representatives of the Romance Languages generally avoided one another. She came to see us. Renée, who seemed to have no office of her own, just a presence, was our elf and our muse. I find it very hard to imagine her anywhere else or in any other role.

—Roger Shattuck

II

It was March of 1976. The University of Indiana (Bloomington) was holding a large comparative literature conference on Literature and the Other Arts. I was giving a paper—on what, I don't even remember—and had flown into Indianapolis from Philadelphia, where I then lived. I was a novice at interarts conferences and knew hardly anyone who was going. Indeed, I was a greenhorn professor, having received my Ph.D. only a few years earlier—and at the unfashionable Catholic University of America in Washington.

In Indianapolis, I had to change planes to the tiny turbo-prop jet that flies from there to Bloomington. It was a short bumpy ride and I sat by myself. As we descended from the plane, I saw a group of people (students? young professors?) awaiting the arrival of someone who was evidently a celebrity—one of the keynote speakers. The group brushed past me, ignoring my existence. The person they were awaiting was Madame Renée Hubert. I had never met Renée but had heard a great deal about her and Judd from my very dear friend at Catholic University (where I had taught before moving to Maryland in 1972), Professor Gerda Blumenthal. Gerda had told me that both Huberts, who were her fellow graduate students in French and Comparative Literature at Columbia, were "brilliant" and "knew everything." And she had given me some of Renée's essays on Rimbaud and Mallarmé, Beckett and Valéry.

So I was naturally curious when "Madame Hubert" was welcomed by the little throng of "fidèles" and was about to be whisked into a car when, lo and behold, it turned out that her suitcase was missing. Somehow, it had not been transferred to the small plane. The faithful apologized profusely. Madame Hubert smiled graciously and said, "Well, as long as I can get a toothbrush, I shall be all right." And, walking tall and proud, she made her way to the waiting car. I tagged along behind and somehow got to go in the same car. I introduced myself. Renée was gracious but reserved; she had other things to think about besides some friend of Gerda's who was giving a paper at the conference.

That was my first meeting with Renée, and I was in awe of her. She had Aura. Not till I moved to California a year later did

I dare to contact her, and then only at Gerda's suggestion. And so began a friendship that was to be one of my greatest pleasures. "Madame Hubert" turned out to be the funniest, wittiest, most incisive, most delightfully malicious (when she wants to be) and endearing person imaginable. She is really quite shy, and small talk has never been her predilection. There is something quixotic about her presence. My husband Joseph refers to her as a Paul Klee figure: what he means is that there is such a marvelous disjunction between Renée's "serious" outward appearance and her wonderfully humorous "real" self.

And so, on her eightieth birthday, I want to salute this great woman, who still travels around the world calmly and bravely, not worrying too much whether her luggage has arrived, as long as there might be a toothbrush for her to buy. Her understanding of poetry and painting, fiction and drama, the artist's book and the installation is keener than ever. She is extremely demanding of herself, undemanding of others. And she is just as brilliant as Gerda Blumenthal had promised me she was.

—Marjorie Perloff

III

As a student in my first graduate seminar on modern French poetry, I watched Professor Renée Riese Hubert cast far and wide the most brilliant net of ideas imaginable. It was a magic sight, and I was spellbound, so much so that I do not recall uttering a word during the first few class meetings. I was irrevocably caught in that net, mesmerized by its multiple *puissances* and wanting to know more.

Renée had a crystalline way with words. She brought concepts into focus with clarity. She proposed critical approaches and theoretical discourses that glowed. And with all this, poetry remained poetic. Renée resisted tampering with its mystic tonalities. Art was unviolated, respected, often venerated.

When we learned weeks later that our professor was also an accomplished poet with several volumes of published verse, I rushed to the library, checked them out, and bathed in their beauty. These tomes have entrancing titles such as *La Cité borgne, Plumes et pinceaux, Enchaînement,* and *Natures mortes.* Their poetry explained at least in part why her approach to teaching was distinguished by such finesse and *savoir-faire* or, more appropriately, *savoir-dire.* It was all about surface and the layers of meaning below. In her treatment of a text, Renée would progress quickly past surfaces and façades. Moments later, we would be hard at work flushing out meaning that, like gold, was there in the strata beneath. When excavations seemed complete, Renée encouraged breaking through to yet another level and, there again, treasures awaited.

As a teacher, Renée was understated. Silences were often charged in such ways that they could mean as much as mountains of words. Things unsaid were frequently *sous-entendu,* and ideas often came into focus without an overkill of verbal prompts. Less was more in this regard, and a certain *rigueur* always characterized Renée's teaching style. It impressed me from the beginning. I found it sometimes intimidating, but it helped bring order to chaotic systems in some texts. Or, at least, it helped me to appreciate the chaos and to understand that disorders have their own order.

When Renée made a positive comment about your work, you felt certain that you had created something of value. Her judgement was impeccable. In a few words she would shore up the essential configurations of an essay or a thesis chapter and remedy whatever was not quite right. Loose ends were tailored in a flash.

Renée was committed to her students, to their graduate experience, and to their future as scholar-teachers. She provided us with a model of how to conjugate the often incongruous modes of scholarship, teaching, and service and to navigate the problematic straits of the profession. When I completed the Ph.D. and with Renée's help secured an assistant professorship at a time when they were few and far between, especially in California, I approached obstacles with Renée in mind and inevitably found solutions, again, with Renée in mind. Since then, we have collaborated on many projects — from co-authoring and co-editing to working on exhibitions and symposia — and each has been challenging, rewarding, and enriching quite beyond my expectations.

Renée has always had a penchant for Joseph Cornell's box compositions in which each compartment holds unexpected surprises. This *festschrift,* published due to the vision and persistence of Laurie Edson, is a frame for so many boxes, all authored by Renée's colleagues, and all united by their concern with verbal-visual relations. Together we celebrate the accomplishments of a woman whose thoughtful scholarship and teaching have redefined the physiognomy of verbal-visual inquiry and its relation to the illustrated book. Like so many of her students and colleagues, I am indebted to Renée. She has always been and will always be a professor *and* friend par excellence.

—Eric T. Haskell

La Scène de la Cène*/
The Scene of the Last Supper

Michel Deguy

(for Renée Riese Hubert)

It is rumored that "representation" will soon end its run. But how can we run from it? The difficulties are numerous and, I fear, inherently impossible. To see is always to show, to display, to stage. My remark here refers to the solidarity of representation and scene. There can be no representation without a staging of the representation, which includes the subject representing him or herself, spectator or reader or reader-quasi-spectator.

What does the scene represent? Answer: represented in the scene is self-representation.

We readers or spectators, visitors at art galleries or retrospective readers of history whose imagination accompanies our reading, we are represented in the scene at the same time that we regressively represent it. We surprise it; we peer at it from a distance while occupying this absolute, virtual, and utopian edge, like the eye of a hidden god who sees from within and from without; a point symmetrical to the vanishing point of perspective.

I call to mind the real or possible "illustration"[1] that punctuated romanesque scenes in nineteenth-century books. The "western scene" portrays (is this a constant?) a front line of white heroes, explorers, or Robinson Crusoes or GIs in commandos, or children of "the night of the hunter." The back of their heads

1

occupies—for us, who are always behind them and come upon the napes of their necks without their notice—the lower order or one side of the "picture," like some sort of donors. These heroes have crawled up onto a ledge *from which* they see, down below, a camp clearing where the prey, enemies, savages ignorant of the ethnologist, or Robinson or Rambo, philosophy or western god, or tourists, bustle about, oblivious to the fact that they are being watched. Let us call this scene the scene of the clearing. It is that of the viewed sacrifice, hunt, massacre—the spectacle of which is copied by a film or a cartoon strip.

The scene of the punishment of Tantalus. The scene at the threshold of the banquet where Socrates has remained for hours, and we are behind him and about to follow him right into Agathon's house. Scene of the Last Supper, which we come upon at the Museum: the twelve dining with the Rabbi. He's the one giving light. Sometimes the artist places the disciples in a semi-circle facing the faithful or the patron; sometimes he closes the circle of guests "in front of" the visitor. Can we date the moment in "art history" when the artist closes the *Cène* [scene/Supper] and sees—that is, shows us—certain disciples from the back, and does this "moment" mark a transition from the icon to modern "representation?"

Sixteenth-century "savages" have taken the place of "primitive" prey lower down, where I view them—if need be with my binoculars whose black ring forms the customary border, the frame (as in cartoon strips) of the scene that "is cut out"—some of them eating others (it is before the "colonizer," descended from the explorers, brought Christ, the abolisher of anthropophagy). Scene of that circular covetousness that the Last Supper intended to eliminate and atone? Scene of the "feast of life" represented by a "life of feasting," a Greek scene erased by the artistic Christian Last Supper?

Or furthermore: scene of the "Feast of Turin," where we read that Jean-Jacques, at the back among the man-servants—occupying the foreground for *us*, who have furtively approached, noiseless readers, the meal of the Masters, whose heads are partially blocked from our view—that Jean-Jacques, indeed, surprises the Masters, upsets their Supper centered around the seasoned prey illumined by candles, transforms the masters into natives, and plays ethnological tricks on them.

Scene of conviviality oblivious to its surroundings, in which each modern "subject" is simultaneously within the group scene and, like Rousseau, excluded and victorious.

And now as a spectating *philosophe*, hanging over Lethe where "the others" are steeped, the not-being-aware of "others." My observation consists in "staging" this implication of the subject representing itself in the representation by a kind of fable of the staging "representing" the Last Supper! . . . "Mise en Cène ". . .** that "unfathomable" play on words that loops the loop but whose reverberation does not shed light! This "closure of the representation," or entrapment by staging, closes in on the subject because there is no *retreating* from the position "for a better view" that could enable him to "get out of it." Is this a "western" staging? Thus, the "whites" have taken the place of the divine Voyeurs who encircled and watched over life. Like Olympian spectators, festive feast-lovers themselves, fashionable revelers on ambrosia. They open round eyes on the circularity of primitive life, which becomes their big "discovery"; afterwards, today's greedy pillaging tourists. And finally, in a retreat like a supplementary recess, an iteration of the withdrawal will not change this position of the voyeur of voyeurs, of "us," spectators of the film, of *history*—or perhaps at the theatre where we've arrived late, like Marcel, to occupy the *critic's* seat behind "the orchestra of the others," or like Mr. Teste, to observe the illumined scene where the Last Supper [*Cène*/Scene] is being rehearsed, "the vanishing clearing" (Badou)—since that "end of history" that we proclaim since no other Judgment could be more final, if I can say, than this one, ours, dying (all of them called to "leave the banquet") and at the same time immortal.

Finally, do I perceive a homothetic relationship between what I have just designated as the scene and the big backward zoom used so profusely in advertising, the one that "moves back" from the cell to the nebula, or that springs forth from the depths of the cosmos millions of light years away so as to accommodate, within the focal (American) hearth, everything from infinite-nothingness to total-infinity mixed up with "my life," according to the perspectivism of absolute ego-centrism that connects the big bang to ego?

How does one leave representation, where staging and fiction have wrapped around the "creator-subject?"

The myth of creation is that of a brusque mutation, of the fiat, of the "magic wand," of the leap, of the *all of a sudden.* . . . We could argue that the suddenness of the *appearance* (disappearance) is a requirement of our faith in *art,* in representation and in its representability, the scene and its staging. "Language must have its appearance suddenly," says Claude Lévi-Strauss.

At this rate, "science," in response to the "testing of facts," substitutes the frightening slowness of time, the slow motion of an inconceivable sequence in which every real genesis dissolves, where the possibility of *attending* a "phase" breaks down, *disappears*: that of the millions of years that need to be continually added *between* this and that; science cannot answer the *how did that happen,* which demands paraphrase, fable, narrative, staging.

Notes

[1]A cartoon strip only generalizes—continually carries out—the constant imagination of a reader wishing to "represent himself or herself" in terms of the scenic visibility of what is read. A continuous strip of "illustration."

—Translated by Georgette James

———

* Translator's note: *Scène* and *Cène* are homophones.

** Translator's note: *"mettre en scène"* to stage; a word play on *scène* and *Cène* (Last Supper), pronounced the same.

La Scène de la Cène

Michel Deguy

à Renée Riese Hubert

Il est bruit d'une "sortie de la représentation." Mais comment en sortir? Les difficultés sont nombreuses et je crains même que l'impossibilité soit de principe. Voir, c'est toujours montrer; montrer à; mettre en scène. Ma remarque ice vise la solidarité de la représentation et de la scène. Pas de représentation sans mise en scène de la représentation, qui inclut le sujet se représentant, spectateur ou lecteur-quasi-spectateur.

La scène représente quoi? Réponse: le se-représentant est représenté dans la scène.

Nous, spectateurs ou lecteurs, visiteurs de la galerie de tableaux ou lecteurs en retrait de l'histoire dont l'imagination accompagne la lecture, nous sommes à la fois représentés dans la scène et nous la représentons en retrait. Nous surprenons; nous supervisons, en recul, occupant ce point de surplomb absolu, virtuel et utopique comme l'oeil du dieu caché qui considère du dedans et du dehors; point symétrique du point de fuite de la perspective.

J'évoque "l'illustration,"[1] réelle ou possible, qui scandait les scènes romanesques dans les livres du 19e siècle. La "scène occidentale" représente (est-ce une constant?) une première rangée de héros blancs, explorateurs ou Robinsons, ou GI's en commandos, ou enfants de "la nuit du chasseur," dont les têtes de dos occupent — pour nous qui sommes toujours en arrière, et en surprenons les nuques sans qu'ils en soient avisés — le bord inférieur ou une marge latérale du "tableau," comme une espèce

5

de donateurs. Ces héros ont rampé jusqu'à un surplomb *d'où* ils voient en contrebas la clairière d'un camp où s'affairent, ne sachant pas qu'ils sont observés, la proie, les ennemis, les sauvages — ignorants de l'ethnologue, de Robinson ou de Rambo, du philosophe ou du dieu occidental, ou du touriste. Appelons cette scène la scène de la clairière. C'est celle du sacrifice, de la chasse, du massacre — observés, et dont l'observation est reproduite par le film ou la BD.

Scène de Tantale puni. Scène du banquet au bord duquel s'est retenu Socrate pendant des heures, et nous sommes dans son dos et nous allons pénétrer chez Agathon à sa suite. Scène de la Cène que nos surprenons au Musée: les douze sont à table avec le Rabbi, c'est lui qui éclaire. Tantôt le peintre dispose les disciples en demi-cercle face au fidèle ou à l'amateur; tantôt il ferme le cercle des convives "devant" le visiteur. Peut-on dater le moment en "histoire de l'art" où l'artiste ferme la Cène et voit — c'est-à-dire nous montre — certains disciples de dos, et ce "moment" marquerait-il un passage de l'icône à la "représentation" moderne?

Les "sauvages" au 16e siècle ont pris la place de la proie "primitive," en contrebas où je les aperçois — au besoin avec mes lunettes d'approche dont le cerne noir fait le bord, le cadre, conventionnel dans la BD, de la scène qui "se découpe" — se mangeant les uns les autres (c'est avant le Christ abolisseur de l'anthropophagie que leur apporte le "colonisateur," qui descend de l'explorateur). Scène de la convoitise en rond dont la Cène pensait être l'abolition et la réparation? Scène du "festin de la vie" représentée par la vie de festin, scène grecque oblitérée par la Cène artistique chrétienne?

Ou encore: scène du "repas de Turin": où nous lisons que Jean-Jacques en arrière parmi les valets — qui occupent le premier rang pour *nous* qui nous sommes rapprochés furtifs, silencieux lecteurs, du repas des Maîtres dont ils nous cachent un peu les têtes — que Jean-Jacques, donc, surprend les Maîtres, renverse leur Cène centrée sur les proies épicées que les chandelles éclairent; transforme les maîtres en natifs, leur fait le coup de l'ethnologue.

Scène de la convivialité oublieuse de son dehors, où chaque "sujet" moderne est à la fois dans la scène de groupe, et, pareil à Rousseau, exclu et vainqueur.

Et maintenant spectateur *philosophe,* surplombant le Léthê où trempent "les autres," le ne-pas-s'en-apercevoir des "autres." Ma remarque consiste à "mettre en scène" cette implication du sujet, se représentant dans la représentation par une sorte de fable de la mise en scène "représentant" la Cène! . . . "Mise en Cène." . . . Jeux de mots "abyssaux" où la boucle se boucle mais où la réverbération ne fait pas la clarté! Cette "clôture de la représentation," ou piège de la mise en scène, se referme sur le sujet parce qu'il n'y a pas de *recul* de sa position "pour mieux voir" qui puisse le faire "s'en sortir." Est-ce une mise en scène "occidentale?"

Ainsi: les "blancs" ont pris la place des Voyeurs divins qui entouraient et surplombaient la vie. Pareils aux Olympiens spectateurs, viveurs banqueteurs eux-mêmes, fêtards mondains de l'ambroisie. Ils ouvrent des yeux ronds sur le rond de la vie primitive, dont ils font la "grande découverte"; puis touristes rapaces pillards d'aujourd'hui. Et à la fin, dans un retrait tel qu'un retrait supplémentaire, une itération du recul ne changerait pas cette position de voyeur des voyeurs, "nous," spectateurs du film, de l'*histoire*—ou bien au théâtre où nous sommes arrivés en retard comme Marcel pour occuper la position de *critique* "derrière" "l'orchestre des autres," ou comme M. Teste, qui regardent la scène illuminée où se répète la Cène, "l'éclaircie disparaissante" (Badiou)—depuis cette "fin de l'histoire" que nous prononçons parce qu'aucun Jugement ne peut être davantage dernier, si je puis dire, que celui-ci, le nôtre, à la fois mourants (tous appelés à "quitter le banquet") et immortels.

Et à la fin je remarque une homothétie entre ce que je viens d'appeler la scène et ce grand zoom arrière que la publicité exploite, celui qui "recule" de la cellule à la nébuleuse, ou qui fond du fond du cosmos à des millions d'années lumières pour accommoder sur ce "foyer" (. . . américain), de l'infini-néant à l'infini-tout confondu avec "ma vie," dans le perspectivisme ego-centriste absolu qui relie le big-bang à ego?

Comment sortir de la représentation, où mise en scène et fiction se sont mises en boucle autour du "sujet créateur?"

Le mythe de la création est celui de la mutation brusque, du fiat, du "coup de baguette," du saut, du *d'un-coup.* . . . On dirait que la brusquerie de l'*apparition* (disparition) est un réquisit de la croyance en l'*art,* en la représentation et sa représentabilité, la scène et sa mise en scène. "Le langage a dû faire son apparition d'un coup," dit Claude Lévi-Strauss.

A ce rythme la "science," obéissante à "l'expérience des faits," substitue l'effrayante longueur du temps, le ralenti de la successivité inimaginable où toute genèse réelle se dissout, où la possibilité d'*assister* à une "phase" se décompose, *disparaît*: celle des millions d'années qu'il faut rajouter sans cesse *entre* ça et ça; la science ne peut répondre au *comment ça s'est passé*, qui exige du résumé, de la fable, du récit, de la mise en scène.

Notes

[1]La BD ne fait que généraliser — réaliser en continu — cette *imagination* constante d'un lecteur désireux de "se représenter" en termes de visibilité scénique ce qu'il lit. Bande continue de "l'illustration."

The Frame as Metaphor

Judd D. Hubert

Taking my cue from aesthetic as well as evolutionary theories, formulated by Henri Bergson, I assume that when we scrutinize works of art and decipher literary texts, we react perceptually to an environment in basically the same way that we deal with everyday sights and occurrences (Bergson 199 ff). The difference between aesthetic and ordinary perception may result from the perceiver's adaptation to, or attitude toward, her or his immediate surroundings. Aesthetic perception, which may depend on the possibility of leisurely detachment if not distanciation from a potentially if not inveterately threatening environment, can focus, for instance, on a set of objects deliberately segregated from whatever extraneous material may share their field of vision. In a sense, framing, even today, hardly precludes an expectancy of danger; witness the TV insurance commercial showing a commonplace and, so to speak, innocent traffic situation where the conditioned viewer ghoulishly searches for a collision. This kind of perception, so cleverly manipulated in the TV commercial, essentially consists in framing for the sake of heightened observation a segment carefully selected from an impinging environment. Such manipulation of a viewer's attention can involve not only a banal city sight, but also natural landscapes, figments of the imagination, abstract displays of color, and linear interplays. Whether in connection with viewing a TV screen, with ordinary perception, or with art, framed attentiveness seems to have assumed over the centuries Euclidean qualities, culminating, at least from an aesthetic point of view, in the perfecting of linear perspective by such Tuscan artists as Paolo Uccello and Piero della Francesca whose works feature precisely matched interior frames (Figure 1). The paintings of Lascaux or Altamira, apart from the protective enclosure of the cave, did not require framing of any sort, let alone the prepared flat two-dimensional surface taken for granted by artists of later and perhaps more leisurely periods, artists who could distance themselves more readily from an invasive environment, though hardly from hostile human intrusions. The Lascaux and other

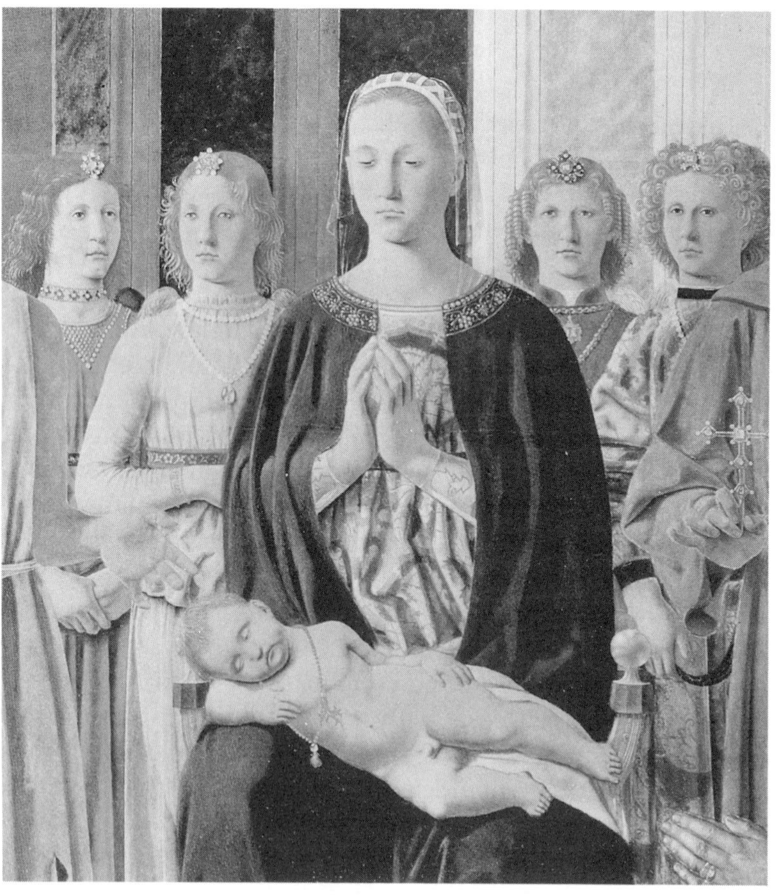

Figure 1. Piero della Francesca. *The Virgin and Child with Saints and Angels.* Circa 1483-91. 97 1/4" x 66 3/4". Milano, Brera.

prehistoric painters remained, in the relative safety of their caverns, more involved than city artists with the creatures they represented, usually taking care to show them in profile and in movement rather than in potentially more threatening and at the same time more static frontal positions. But perhaps the unevenness of the cavern walls lent itself more readily to a profiled rather than a frontal view. The naturalistic representations that covered prehistoric caves could hardly fit into the rigorously geometrical temples favored by such early civilizations as the Hittite, whose framed processional bas-reliefs express an unmistakable sense of hierarchy and order.[1]

The etymology of the word frame indicates purposeful activity, hence deliberation, from "framien," meant to make something useful or profitable and hence to improve it. The French word "cadre," etymologically designating a square, eventually developed quite different implications, for it can now refer to organization and hierarchy. Obviously, both English etymology and French semantic displacement hardly preclude artistic creativity. In any case, I propose to consider purposeful metaphorical framing in literary texts and inner framing in artifacts as a way of deliberately setting them apart from, if not necessarily above, everyday apprehensions whether verbal, visual, or auditory. Lyrical poetry, an essentially verbal production, and drama, where visual settings and performance often undermine verbal dominance, rely on quite different self-representational frames relating them to, and at the same time separating them from, an audience.

Such notions as adaptation to the environment and protective distanciation explain only in part, if at all, the frequent if not inevitable presence of framing, metaphorical or otherwise, in verbal and visual artifacts. Among other advantages, inner separations allow a graphic work to designate itself as a constructed artifact and thus enable the medium to assert itself, sometimes at the expense of content and referentiality. In short, framing devices tend to keep under control or even minimize the mimetic aspects of art. The presence of frames also puts into question that search for immediacy considered indispensable by many practitioners, theoreticians, and viewers. Framing thus appears to pertain to the intellect rather than to the sensibility. But how can we distinguish an emotion from a thought if not by superimposed classifications tantamount to framing?

Many lyrical poems, notably those of the Romantic period, feature a display of privacy whereby the persona ostentatiously isolates itself, more often than not within a purportedly natural setting. This device may appear paradoxical insofar as poets usually have a pervasive audience in mind, starting of course with themselves as readers. And poetry often provides a built-in reader as though to keep both in or out of tune with the entire poetic tradition and eventually secure a paginated emplacement and definitive framing within a perennial anthology. In addition to such obvious framing devices as typography and prosody, some sophisticated poems designate a frame and develop it thematically as well as structurally, for instance, Baudelaire's "Invitation au voyage" with its constant spatial allusions to Dutch painting, which some readers persist in identifying with Holland. In "Le Voyage," the poet deliberately uses the word "cadres": "Faites pour égayer l'ennui de nos prisons, / Passer sur nos esprits tendus comme une toile, / Vos souvenirs avec leurs cadres d'horizon" 'To cheer the boredom of our prison / On our mind stretched like a canvas, / Display your recollections with their framing horizons.'[2] Unfortunately, I cannot make use of a felicitous translation by James Huneker (in Laver), far more poetic than my prosaic rendition, because it bypasses my targeted metaphor. Here as elsewhere in "Le Voyage," allusions to painting play an important part. Moreover, Baudelaire's "operational," as opposed to confessional persona, by multiplying exchanges and reversals between inner and outer directed verbal perceptions, establishes flexible settings within the main frame of the poem. In his *Illuminations,* appropriately subtitled *Painted Plates,* Rimbaud ventures even further than his predecessors in frequently multiplying inner or metaphorical frames capable of giving coherence to otherwise episodic texts. In "Enfance," paradoxes, contradictions, and analogies, many of them spatial, give an inner coherence to deliberately discontinuous narratives, several of them parodying Romantic novels. I shall limit myself to the opening verses of the first part:[3]

> Cette idole, yeux noirs et crins jaunes, sans parents ni cour, plus noble que la fable, mexicaine et flamande: son domaine, azur et verdure insolents, court sur des plages nommées par des vagues sans vaisseaux de noms férocement grecs, slaves, celtiques.
>
> A la lisière de la forêt—les fleurs de rêve tintent, éclatent, éclairent—la fille à lèvre d'orange, les genoux croisés dans le clair

déluge qui sourd des prés, nudité qu'ombrent, traversent et habillent les arcs-en-ciel, la flore, la mer.

> That idol, black eyes and yellow mane, without parents or court, nobler than fables, Mexican and Flemish: her domain, insolent azure and verdure, runs along beaches to which shipless waves give names ferociously Greek, Slavic, Celtic.
> At the skirt of the forest — the dream flowers tinkle, burst, illuminate — the orange-lipped girl, her knees crossed in the clear deluge that springs from the fields, a nudity shaded, traversed, and dressed by rainbows, flora, and sea.

Whereas the idol appears isolated and immobilized, her domain arrogates the role of agent. Transformed into two brilliant and haughty colors, it transgresses margins by rushing along sandy stretches to rejoin the sea. Dispensing with ancestors, the idol's nobility manifests itself etymologically — fable, from "fari," also present in the title "Enfance" — as linguistic and fabulatory superiority. Nevertheless, it combines the contrasting coloration of the pre-Columbians and Flemings — just another infringement of spatial and chronological borders. Personified no less than the "domaine," the polyglot waves possess the power to name the beaches they so noisily assault. Liberated from all human presence, borders and frames, by systematic reversal, operate as agents while the idol, though a sort of unmoved mover, functions passively as décor.

Similar relationships prevail in the second paragraph where "la lisière" provides a frame separating the forest from the fields and the sea. And this border, by means of synesthesic puns: "éclatent" and "clair," establishes and transgresses limits within the dream world, for it simultaneously separates and joins together "tintent" and "éclairent." "Tintent" itself may even provide a corroborating homonymous pun, "teintent" 'tinge.' Although we can associate through juxtaposition but hardly identify her with the idol, "la fille à lèvre d'orange" strikes a similar ritualistic note by assuming the immobilizing position of a seated goddess. She marks, however, an obvious displacement and expansion toward the human. By virtue of another synesthesic pun, "clair," the "déluge" surrounding her brings more closely together "prés" and "mer." Thus, everything encroaches upon everything else, and Rimbaud multiplies borders only to transgress them. Once again, space generates all the movements whereas the nude girl passively lets rainbows—frames arising from the luminous "déluge"—flora, and the sea dress her or rather paint her. The poet has thus repeated the reversal of the first paragraph.

Prose poems, as Renée Riese Hubert discovered many years ago, take indeed their cue from painting rather than from music, so prevalent in rhyming verse ("Technique"). Similar framings, however, can transform a verse poem into a miniature play where personified objects function as actants. In Mallarmé's sonnet "Ses purs ongles très haut dédiant leur onyx" ("Her pure nails aloft dedicating their onyx") featuring a bourgeois salon from which the poet's persona, "le Maître," has departed, personified objects interact within interlocking spatial contexts and a rarefied rhyme scheme, joining together a domestic scene and a starry night as well as banal curios and ancient myths. But framing devices play an important part not only in French symbolism, but in poetry of other periods and other languages. In John Donne's "Canonization," the writing of poetry designates itself through metaphorical framing: "And if no peece of Chronicle wee prove, / We'll build in sonnets pretty roomes." The final stanza provides framing of an equally witty sort:

> You, to whom love was peace, that now is rage;
> Who did the whole world's soul contract, and drove
>   Into the glasses of your eyes
>   (So made such mirrors, and such spies,
> That they did all to you epitomize,)
>   Countries, Townes, Courts: Beg from above
>   A patterne of your love!

Donne has playfully combined the macrocosm of geographical entities with the microcosm of human desire. Anticipating Baudelaire's pictorial poetics, a later English poet, Blake, tellingly uses our key word in one of his most familiar texts, "The Tyger": "What immortal hand or eye / Could frame thy fearful symmetry?" Framing devices predominate, perhaps even more clearly, in modern poetry, for instance, in Hart Crane's "O Carib Isle": "And yet suppose / I count these nacreous frames of tropic death, / Brutal necklaces of shells around each grave / Squared off so carefully." And his most famous poetic suite depends on and thematizes a geometrical engineering construct: Brooklyn Bridge.

Some modern poets, however, have reacted against the inhuman and unnatural enclosing devices imposed by industrialization. Renée Riese Hubert has expressed this revolt in the terminology of framing:

Nature Morte

Elle se tortillait gentiment, cette route ancienne qui reliait toutes les demeures sans laisser personne au dehors. Tantôt sertie de coquilles ou de barbelés, tantôt d'une famille de pissenlits ou d'un chaînon de pêchers, mais toujours chargé de regards oisifs, elle était sujette à la pluie et au beau temps.

Comme on ne s'était attaché qu'à sa vieillesse, il a bien fallu la remplacer. La jeune reste alignée, n'importe où l'on se place. Rebelle à la poussière, elle tient à distance les maisons, et de part et d'autre maintient un chlorophylle qui ne tolère pas de mauvaises herbes. Des arbres géométriques aux ombres immaculées y accentuent l'évidence des frontières. Hier, pour la première fois, un oiseau survola cette route: une colombe sans doute. (*Berceau* 72)

Pleasantly adhering to its twisting ways, the old road connected all the dwellings without leaving anyone outside. Sometimes encrusted with shells or barbed wire, sometimes accompanied by a family of dandelions or a chain of peach trees, but always heaped with idle looks, it was a creature of rain and shine.

Because people saw only its decrepitude, it had to be replaced. The new one displays a perfect alignment whatever your vantage point. Impervious to dust, it keeps houses at a distance and maintains a chlorophyll scornful of weeds. Geometrical trees casting immaculate shadows make only too evident the presence of frontiers. Yesterday, for the first time, a bird flew over the road: a dove no doubt.

This prose poem with a punning title opposes antithetical kinds of framing and personification, the first as natural and familiar as a pet, the second artificial and forbidding, implying the death of nature. Moreover, the new aseptic road repulses memories of any sort even though the dove—an allusion to Noah's Ark—ironically promises a new kind of harmony.

Besides the obvious framing devices provided by staging, drama, which far from requiring a persona or encouraging privacy must function without a subject, frequently uses metaphorical framing in designating itself as theater. We might even claim that by combining the three unities with the single stage and interlocking scenes French classicism brought to a climax the theater's inevitable involvement with enclosures. Although *Twelfth Night* subscribes to a freer form of drama, it features both in plot and language a wealth of separating devices. Olivia wishes at first to sequester herself for seven long years within the confines of her own room. Later in the comedy, she unveils her face while comparing it to a painting until now concealed behind a curtain and later sends a framed miniature of herself to Viola. Finally, she imprisons the supposedly insane Malvolio, an exemplary victim of framing in both the American and the ordinary acceptation of the term. By thus metaphorizing various aspects of Elizabethan staging, Shakespeare overdetermines the medium, thus adding to the complexity of whatever narrative message his play may convey (J. D. Hubert 39-52). Seventeenth-century French playwrights did not, however, limit their framing to deliberate if sometimes grudging submission to the three unities. Baroque dramatists, including Corneille in his early plays, multiplied prison scenes to such an extent that it became a cliché of the period. In Racine's *Bajazet*, the seraglio, coinciding with the scene beheld by the audience, functions as an imprisoning enclosure even though hope of liberation provides the main theme of the tragedy:

> Songez-vous que je tiens les portes du Palais,
> Que je puis vous l'ouvrir ou fermer pour jamais,
> Que j'ai sur votre vie un empire suprême,
> Que vous ne respirez qu'autant que je vous aime?

> Remember that in my power I hold the Palace gates,
> That for you I can open or close it forever,
> That I have full control over your life,
> That you breathe only to the extent that I love you?

Enclosure predominates to such a degree that Roxane can express her passion for Bajazet in terms of framing. Although "respirez" means to remain alive, it can hardly preclude an allusion to breathing in the concrete sense of the word and even to smothering, all the more so because Roxane will have Bajazet strangled by her mute executioners.

When looked at not only closely but metaphorically, paintings reveal in various ways inner framing if only to structure their rhythmic qualities or give helpful directions to viewers by inducing their gaze to penetrate and recede (for instance Manet's *Le Balcon* [Figure 2]) without in any way discouraging the eye's rhythmic movement across the surface. In this work, the open

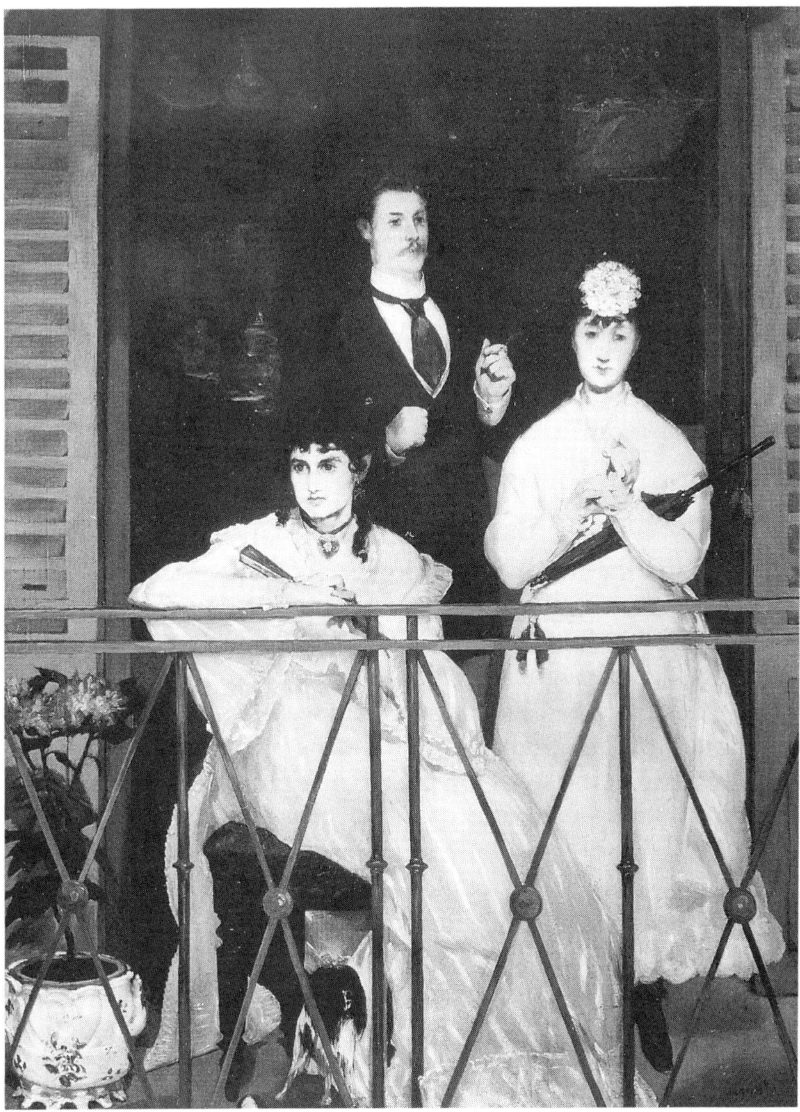

Figure 2. Edouard Manet. *The Balcony.* 1868-69. 66 1/4" x 48 1/2". Paris, Louvre.

window separating the dimly visible room from the open air, the green shutters on each side, the equally green forged iron balcony with its rectangular and triangular divisions, the chair framing the little dog but itself framed by the white dress of the woman seated on it, finally the clothing and gestures of the three people provide a multiplicity of inner borders that diversify the painting while perhaps expressing bourgeois possessiveness as opposed to Francesca's mathematical harmonies. No less than poetry, painting establishes varying relationships between the one and the many insofar as unity succeeds in asserting itself despite or by means of divisions and separations. For obvious reasons, cubist art immediately comes to mind because it divides analytically while striving toward a new kind of integration. Most early cubist canvases provide among other pictorial advantages an assemblage of frames by reason of the artist's systematic reduction of objects to selected shapes. Nonetheless, inner framing plays a less obvious but equally effective part in paintings from other schools both old and new. Manessier's crucifixions, particuarly an early version based on Saint Matthew's Gospel, shown at a recent retrospective in Paris, feature a set of interlocking frames, based on the form of the cross, which serve to impose an almost cubistic order on the intensely affective coloration of the whole (Figure 3). Stylization thus enhances by containment the canvas's overpowering emotional appeal. This mystical painting thus functions far more as an object of contemplation than of devotion. Kaspar Friedrich's famous *Landscape with Monk* (Figure 4) leads toward contemplation in a far more mimetic manner, for as viewers we place ourselves in the position of the religious man who turns his back to the painter while gazing at the sea. However, contagious mimetism would hardly suffice if sky, sea, and land did not function dynamically as interreacting frames. In this canvas, enclosure structures and enlarges the diminutive monk's invitation to transcend mere appearance and become, like himself, an incitement to vision. Artists who preceded Tuscan experimentation with perspective made a no less subtle use of inner frames, notably Simone Martini and Lippo Memmi in their *Annunciation* (Figure 5), where an inescapable architectural setting stabilizes the Angel's advance and the Virgin's timorous retreat. A generation later, an even more religious painter, Fra Angelico, will make full use of such

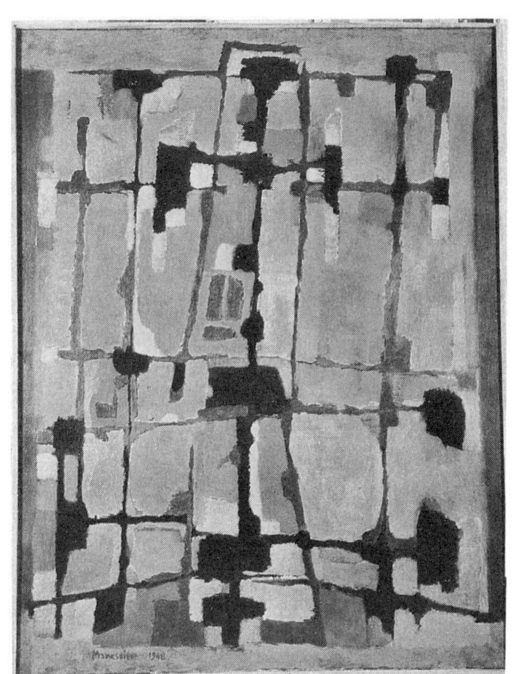

Figure 3. Alfred Manessier. *Gospel According to Saint Matthew.* 1948. 18 1/4" x 15". Private collection. © Artists Rights Society (ARS), 1995.

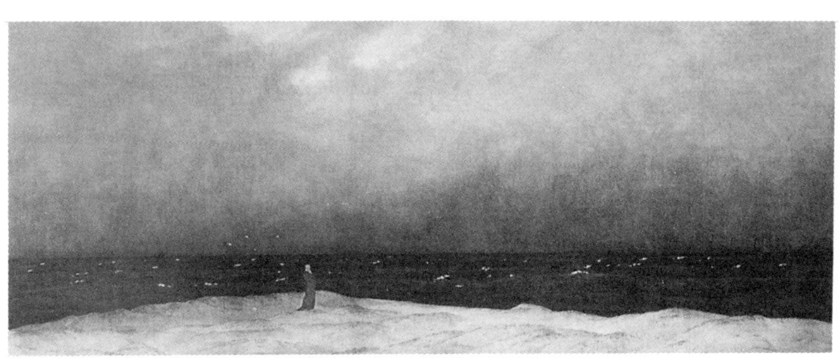

Figure 4. Kaspar David Friedrich. *Landscape with Monk.* 1809-10. Berlin. National Gallery.

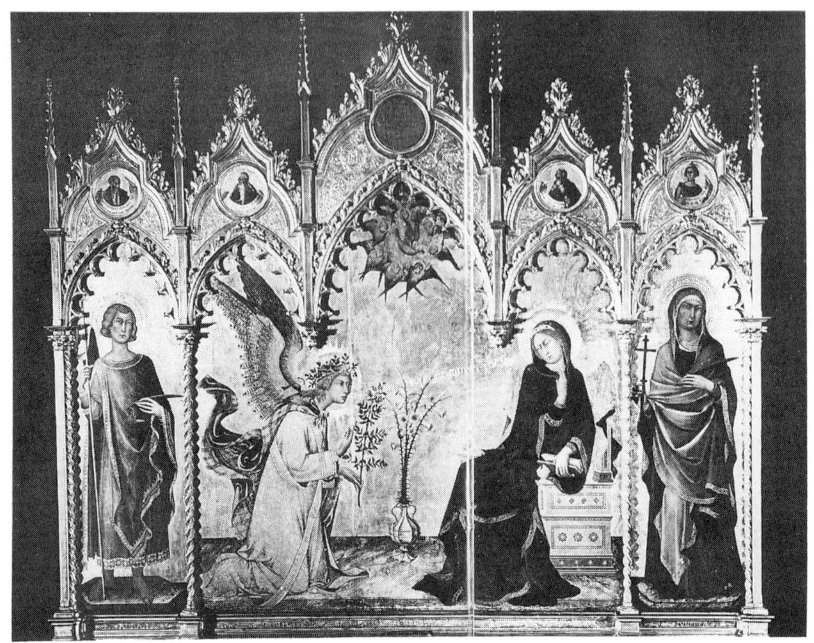

Figure 5. Simone Martini and Lippo Memmi. *Annunciation*. 1333. Florence. Uffizi.

sacred enclosures as chapels and altars, some of which repeat the position of hands joined in prayer, which provide a sort of *mise en abyme* of cathedral steeples. His Annunciation relies even more heavily on separating enclosures than the Sienese masterpiece (Figure 6).

In their attempts to challenge traditional practices and attitudes, some modern and especially postmodern artists have in various ways subverted the frame henceforth treated as a limiting and imprisoning enclosure. In so doing, they show a strong awareness of framing, for in many cases enclosure becomes a far greater issue in their works of art than, if any, referential content. Baldessari's photographs, as shown in a recent retrospective, often transgress their frames so as to establish tricky relationships with pictures located at considerable distances from them. Other artists, for instance, Man Ray in his *Self-Portrait* (Figure 7), establish ambiguous relationships between a painted frame and the enclosed picture by making it impossible to distinguish one from the other. In addition to ambiguous framing, Man Ray had recourse to intertextuality — another way to trans-

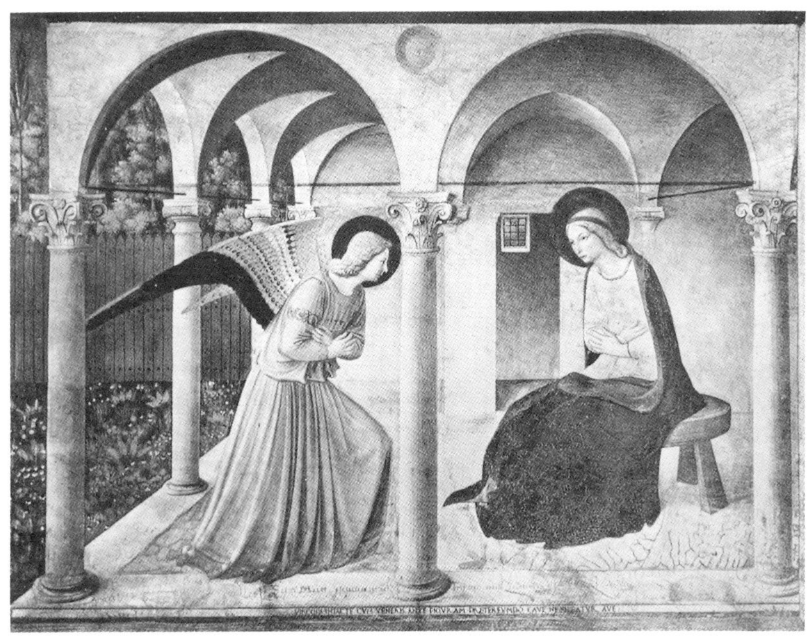

Figure 6. Fra Angelico. *Annunciation*. n.d. 63" x 70 3/4". Cortona. San Domenico.

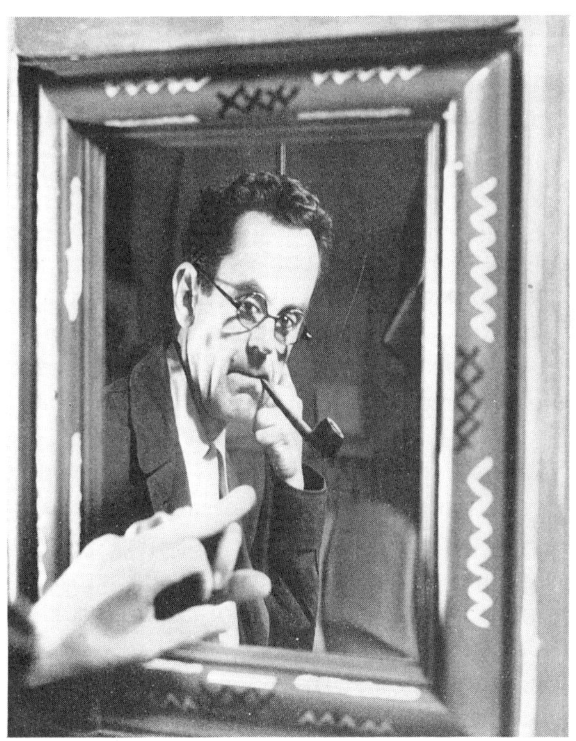

Figure 7. Man Ray. *Self-Portrait*. Aluminum mirror framed in wood. 1944. Private collection. © Artists Rights Society (ARS), 1995.

gress borders—by alluding to Chardin's *Self-Portrait*. In some of these works, a veritable exchange or reversal of characteristics seems to have taken place. In a sense, such practices bring into plastic art the collapsing, not infrequent in poetry since Baudelaire, of the outer and inner worlds.

Framing inevitably plays a preeminent part in book illustration where the page provides a primary, but in avant-garde books, a frequently transgressed enclosure. Strange as this may seem, one of the subtlest uses of framing occurred during the reign of Louis XV. In his rococo vignettes for Dorat's *Fables nouvelles* (1773), Marillier contrived constant interplays between intruding enclosures and narrative representations (Figures 8 and 9). In many instances, framing devices become artistically even more compelling than the charming scenes incompletely contained therein. We witness in many of the illustrations a playful duel between narrative scene and limiting structures as though to discover how playfully each one can encroach upon the other. Nevertheless, the entire vignette confines its activities to the top half of the page without ever daring to interfere with typographical space.

Such invasions and transgressions characterize, however, modern and especially postmodern *livres de peintre*. In Ponge and Fautrier's *L'Asparagus*, as Renée Riese Hubert has shown, zincographs and letterpress intermingle in incredible ways, sometimes at the expense of legibility ("Ponge"). In his handwritten lithographic rendition of *Un Coup de dés*, André Masson not only transgressed Mallarmé's highly meaningful typography, but the inner margin of the page, which the poet had respected, perhaps because its infringement would have stopped in their tracks even the most ingenious printers (Hubert and Hubert). Still other illustrators, such as Etienne Hajdu, Jacques Hérold, and even more radically, Paolo Boni (Figure 10), have given a third dimension to the page by embossing it (R. R. Hubert, "Four-Dimensional Book"). Ania Staritsky goes even further, for her embossed illustrations transgress the limitations of the page by spreading, so to speak, from one to the other, as evidenced in her interpretation of Guillevic's *La Prairie* (Figure 11). It goes without saying that within her various illustrations inner framing predominates in such a way that it transgresses the packaging of traditional illustrated books.

Whether verbal or visual or, as in drama, partaking of both, framing devices provide an essential means for the subordination of content to medium. In most instances, they perform a non-mimetic function by enabling perceptual activity to prevail over and sometimes take possession, innocently or even diabolically, of the objects supposedly represented. Framing pertains to, and may even represent, focusing, usually at the expense of the outside world. By compounding and intensifying scrutiny, framing may very well have liberated art from its purportedly religious matrix which paradoxically may have generated the initiating enclosure. Nowadays, museums tend to replace churches. At first, any palace or mansion could serve to secure works of art and show them as disadvantageously as possible. Spurred no doubt by curators, architects then designed buildings for the sole purpose of displaying masterpieces. The new museum of contemporary art in Frankfurt, with its dazzling angles and vistas, transcends and might even dispense with the works, good, bad, or indifferent, it exposes and protects: like the Tiers-Etat in the French Revolution, the heretofore marginalized enclosure has empowered itself.

The frame, however, functions as a supplement for it owes its existence not to nature as such but to adaptation. Thus, its aesthetic function appears strictly derivative insofar as framing provides us primarily with a means to react to and dominate our environment. Unlike the occasionally synonymous closure, it pertains to and expresses action. Closure, however, poses far greater problems than framing, whose somewhat limited functions nobody would deny for the simple reason that they hardly involve universal or definitive formulations. So as not to consider human existence absurd, we attempt to impose upon it various meanings mainly through rituals. Marriages and funerals do their utmost to impose a semblance of closure on what pertains to law — a Procrustean framing system — and biology, where beginnnings and endings appear more problematic. And way back in antiquity, tombs already provided suitable frames, if not closures, for the dear departed. Likewise, a text may lack a definitive closure, but it can succeed in framing itself to the satisfaction of discriminating readers. Indeed, framing has far less to do with truth than with packaging, an aesthetic as well as economic necessity, particularly today. Closure seeks to attain truth but discovers mainly its own limited operations and thus must fall back on framing in order to meet the audience's expectations.

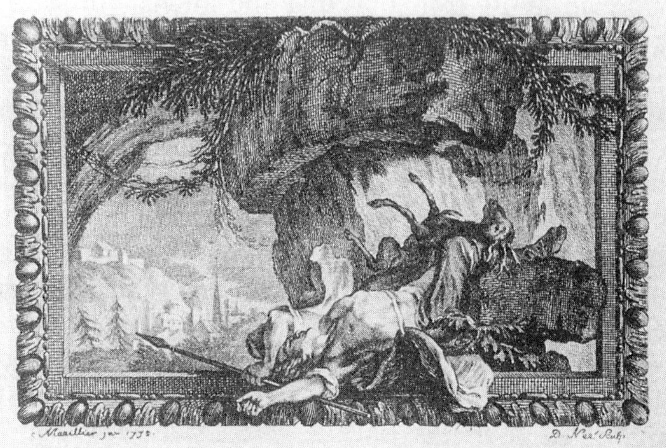

FABLE XX.

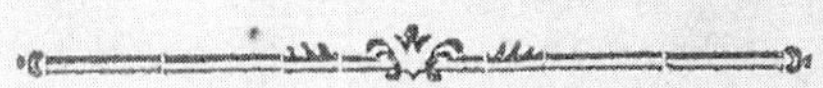

LE CHASSEUR

ET

LE CHEVREUIL.

Tout Chasseur, dit-on, est avide :
Celui-ci, dans un défilé
Relançoit un Chevreuil timide.
Las, haletant & désolé,

Figure 8. Pierre-Clément Marillier. Illustration for Claude-Joseph Dorat's *Fables nouvelles*. La Haye and Paris: Delalain, 1773. 2 vols.

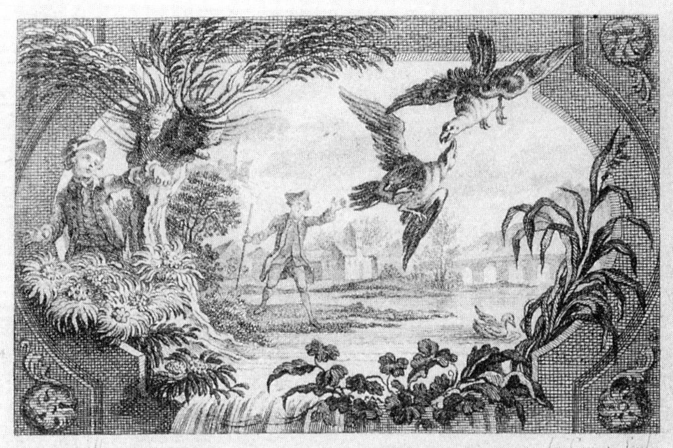

FABLE XV.

LES DEUX FAUCONS.

Deux chasseurs cotoïoient les bords d'un marécage,
Suivis de leurs Faucons, Corsaires des étangs,
Et qui sembloient impatiens
De rester oisifs au rivage.
L'un des deux lâche son oiseau,
Sur un Canard, qui, sauvé par la ruse,
Se plonge, glisse au fond de l'eau,
Et croit avoir vaincu l'ennemi qu'il abuse :
Mais celui-ci, fidèle à marquer ses détours,

Figure 9. Pierre-Clément Marillier. Illustration for Claude-Joseph Dorat's
Fables nouvelles. La Haye and Paris: Delalain, 1773. 2 vols.

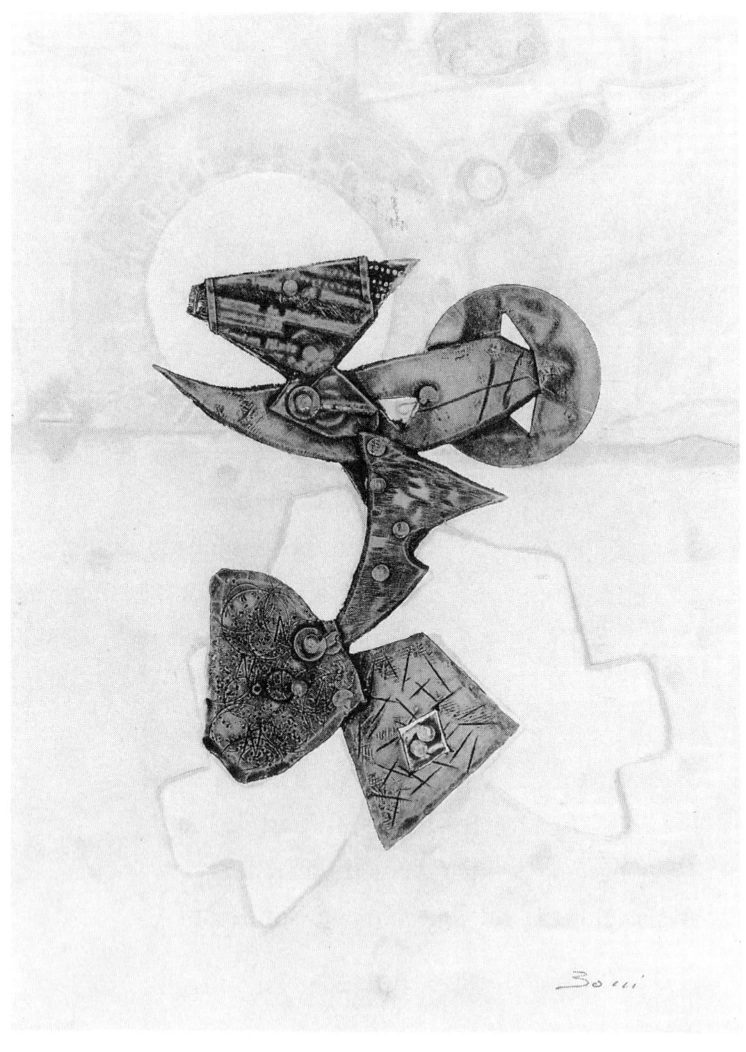

Figure 10. Paolo Boni. Colored "graphisculpture" for Michel Butor's *Chronique des astéroïdes*. Paris: Jacqueline de Champvallins, 1981. Reproduced with permission.

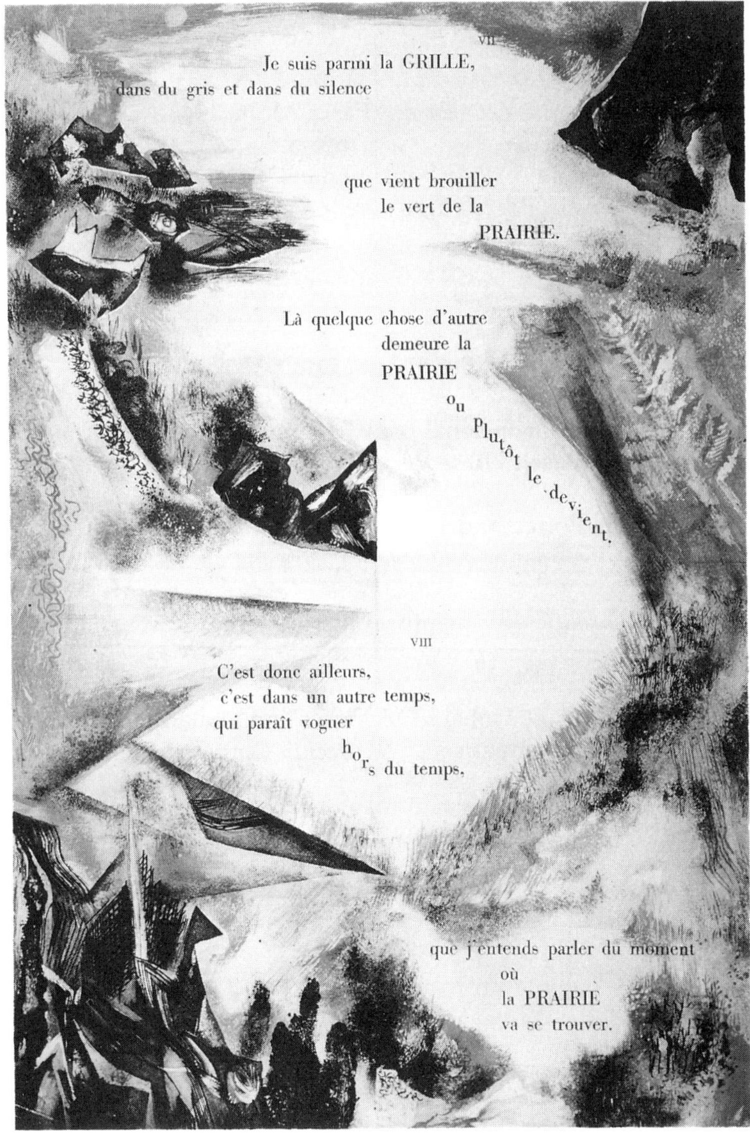

Figure 11. Ania Staritsky. Colored engraving for Guillevic's *La Prairie* (Paris: Jean Petithory, 1970).

Notes

[1]Notably in the ruins of Yazilikaya, Turkey.

[2]All translations are mine.

[3]For a commentary on the rest of the poem, see J. D. Hubert, "Jeux."

Works Cited

Bergson, Henri. *Matière et mémoire.* Paris: Alcan, 1946.

Hubert, J. D. "Les Jeux de la bordure dans 'Enfance.'" *Minute d'éveil: Rimbaud maintenant.* Ed. Martine Bercot. Paris: SEDES, 1984. 131-36.

______. *Metatheater: The Example of Shakespeare.* Lincoln: U of Nebraska P, 1991.

Hubert, R. R. *Le Berceau d'Eve.* Paris: Minuit, 1957.

______. "The Four-Dimensional Book." *Word and Image Interactions.* Ed. Martin Heusser. Basel: Wiese Verlag, 1993. 89-95.

______. "Francis Ponge and Postmodern Illustration." *Criticism* 30.3 (1988): 375-99. [Special issue: *Modern Poetry and the Visual Arts*]

______. "La Technique de la peinture dans le poème en prose." *C.A.I.E.F.* 18 (1966): 169-78.

Hubert, R. R. and J. D. Hubert. "Masson's and Mallarmé's *Un Coup de dés:* An Aesthetic Comparison." *Nineteenth Century French Studies* 18 (1990): 508-24.

Laver, James, ed. *Flowers of Evil.* London: Fanfare Press for Limited Editions Club, 1940.

Torn Pages of Deconstruction:
The Palimpsests of
Mireille W. Descombes

Claude Gandelman

"Tearing!," she said.

"Tearing paper, tearing shredded forms out of torn words printed on paper, that is for me the first step in my deconstructive procedure. . . . For me, tearing the shapes I have just created, lacerating the sentences I have just written means the destruction of all possible 'aesthetic' tendencies in me, for the destruction of Aesthetics is primarily what I am after. . . ."

"For me, to tear and wear the so-called 'aesthetic object,' or 'aesthetic product'; this, for me, is tantamount to living through this 'tearing and wearing,' experiencing it in my own flesh. . . ."

Violence	Random violence
en désordre, je saccage, cruel sacrifice à la peur qui attend	at random, I destroy, cruel sacrifice to fear that lies in wait
Don't let go Don't let me go . . .	Don't let go Don't let me go . . .

She also says:

"Tous ces mots déchirés, c'est des cris jetés. . . ." 'All these torn words are like so many forlorn cries. . . .'

Violence as Art

These quotations are by an important artist of our time, Mireille W. Descombes, whose work is currently being exhibited by the *Musée de la Poste* in Paris. Before examining her work in more detail, I will try to place the preceding statements by the artist in their art-historical context.

There are many ways of "doing violence" to one's medium. Michelangelo, for instance, was acutely aware of the fact that he was "doing violence" to the stone, to the block of marble he was working on. Extracting a form was like a "flaying" for him, and he has actually described his own artistic act as an act of "self-flaying." Moreover, it is well known that he represented himself as a "flayed skin" in his Last Judgment fresco in the Sistine Chapel and that several times in his *Sonnets* he described art as a "self-flaying" process. Here the ancient Greek myth of Marsyas (the Artist) flayed by Apollo (Art himself) received a new interpretation (Wind 188).

Yet the first modern artist who was not a sculptor but who nevertheless treated his canvas as though it were a skin to be flagellated or flayed is the Norwegian Edvard Munch. The terrible nightly scene in which he hurled himself on the portrait of his younger sister who had just died of consumption, scratching and tearing away at the canvas, almost gouging the eyes in the portrait, has been described by some of his biographers. The portrait survived with the tearing and the scratches. In Munch's case, this violent access was certainly a sort of statement concerning the insufficience of Art confronted by Death, concerning its incapacity to save a young life—but it also meant the beginning of a new aesthetic procedure for painters based on violence and destruction, a "deconstruction" before the concept was invented.

Since Munch, the history of modern art has included a long line of violent modern painters until "deconstruction," with the work of Derrida, reached its final philosophical formulation.

For instance, an artist of violent artistic temper concerning his treatment of his medium was undoubtedly Francis Bacon. He, too, used scratches and splashes. In one of his interviews with Peter Beard, Bacon even went as far as to say that he "did not like to practice the injury" (on his canvas) in the presence of his model. With him "practicing the injury" was tantamount to "painting" (Bacon 14-15).

Last in this line of violent painters is probably the Italian Fontana who slits his canvas open with a razor blade. Needless to say, Fontana knew the universally famous "slitting of a human eye with a razor" by Buñuel and Dali in their film *Un Chien Andalou*. Is not Fontana's slitting his canvas with a razor a sort of repetition of this scene: the creating of a symbolically empty orbit in the middle of the work of art?

Here, violence is done through the medium of words, which destroys the picture, and through the medium of the "pictural," which destroys words. It is a deconstructionistic violence.

Applied Deconstructionism

Now and then, I have used the word "Deconstructionism" in a rather loose way. I will now investigate why Mireille W. Descombes belongs to this current of ideas, and why the shadow of Jacques Derrida looms so large behind her work.

First of all, Deconstruction is the actuation of a paradox: a creation through destruction. The work of art comes into being through a destroying activity — one, even, of self-destroying. Deconstruction seen as a process of creation — and not simply as a methodology for textual analysis — can be a very violent affair!

But Deconstruction is not always done with a razor and a slit eyeball, as practiced by Buñuel and Dali in *Un Chien Andalou*. It is often a violence done with words and *to* words, with a razor actually applied to the slitting of words. Here, Mireille W. Descombes is probably closer to the tradition that begins with the *parole in libertà* of the Futurists. Indeed, Ballà, Carrà, and above all Marinetti were probably the first artists to destroy words in order to create an aesthetic totality. However, in Descombes' work there is an element that was never present in the Futurist movement, and seldom in Surrealism: an element of feminism. She herself says that "it is also a way to express the condition of woman. By exposing men's violence on my sheets of paper, I try to appropriate, integrate masculine violence itself."

Another "deconstructive" element is the inherent ambiguity in which the artist moves, an ambiguity echoed in the hesitation that affects the viewer of her work. What are, indeed, her exhibits: texts or pictures? Descombes moves unceasingly between these two poles, the verbal and the visual. And we, spectators, echo her permanent oscillating between these two antithetical possibilities. If her pictures are "visual" are we to read the texts? And if her pictures are texts are we to look at them as one looks at a merely aesthetic object or a landscape?

Permanent "differment" (differAnce) is the key word here. This is certainly not "kinetic" in the usual sense of the word because the pieces of paper are not actually mobile, but the "kinetics" are in our heads, in our permanent hesitation and differing.

But let us turn, first, to the verbal pole of the work. The work of Mireille W. Descombes, because her medium is mainly words on paper, words torn and scratched on paper, and because her violence is done almost always on paper, takes on a somewhat "antiquated" shape, a "medieval" "torn and scratched" manuscript form: that of the *palimpsest*.

Palimpsest as "Deconstruct"

From the Greek *psestos*, which designates a text inscribed on a surface through incising or scratching, which is sometimes synonymous with the word "graffiti" (provided said graffiti are made on parchment), *palimpsest* was also named *pergamentus rescriptus* or even *codex rescriptus* by the Latin—then by the Medieval—scholars. *Codex rescriptus*, of course, referred to a book that was written on top of another book. In the case of these scholars, the reason for such a procedure was not at all a "spirit of deconstruction" in the modern sense of the term. What happened is that pergament, parchment, was a rare commodity, a veritable luxury product, so that it was a spirit of thrift that dictated the re-utilization of manuscripts as "supports" for other, newer ones. Thus, not only were there "*codices rescripti*" but also "*codices bis rescripti*" or "*ter rescripti*," when the written "skin" was recovered twice or three times by new handwriting.

Therefore, today, composing an "artist book" or simply a picture by using "palimpsestic" methods is first and foremost (before being an act of violence or deconstruction) a *simulacrum* of something that is long past, a *simulacrum* of a product that was created by the Medieval scribes and that died with them and with the period that produced the *palimpsest*. And this palimpsestic form is a product that died with the "Gutenberg Galaxy" — to borrow the famous phrase coined by Marshall MacLuhan.

But what Mireille W. Descombes does is turn the antique form into a space for deconstruction. She herself writes: "Palimpsest for me is a space, a locus, where time becomes blurred then disappears in order to be substituted by another sort of time — instantaneous time which is a trace, a written trace of the instant of creation, a memory of the enunciative 'I.'" Thus the term "palimpsest" will, more and more, come to divest itself of its usual connotation referring to "memory" in order to designate exclusively layers of creative impulses superimposed each over the other so that the ultimate meaning is for ever "differed."

Palimpsest as "Trace"

It is one of Derrida's central ideas that there is a philosophical and aesthetic primacy of the "trace" over all other aesthetic signs. Through the "primacy of the trace," it is the Heideggerian concept of "Spur" that comes to the fore for Derrida. Heidegger, quoted by Derrida in his *Margins of Philosophy*, speaks of "*das Sein des Seienden, (dass) sich in eine Spur prägt* . . . " ("the Being of existing entities (which) marks its imprint through a trace . . . "). Similarly, there is no doubt whatever that the work Mireille W. Descombes celebrates this primacy of the trace as the primacy of "ex-(i)stance" or *ek-stance,* as the revelation of Being.

In the eyes of Descombes, there should never be a positively *definitive* act of creation. She tells me: "The definite and positive choice of one specific trace prevailing over all others but the blurring of traces is done through their superseding one another constantly and at an ever increasing speed which accelerates so that the trace becomes, ultimately, a stream of fragmentary word-impressions. This fragmentary stream of quasi-words becomes the only graspable 'tracing.' . . . Eventually I seem to collapse into the dense 'mass' of Memory, a 'mass' of such enormous density that one word only — or one cluster of words — can come to the fore. . . . "

Elsewhere, Mireille Wieland-Descombes — referring to the "necessarily inaccessible character of all founding events in the process of creation" — declares that during the act of creation "it is, nevertheless, the duty of a genuine artist to try and obtain access into the source, the (inaccessible) founding event" — even though this event recedes more and more into the distance as one comes closer and closer (or thinks one does). For her, renouncing this impossible search at the outset would be tantamount to an unforgivable vagary and "errance."

Palimpsest as Text

Yet even before Derrida another French theoretician invented techniques for dealing with palimpsestic "traces." I am speaking here of Gérard Genette. His methodology is the only existing one for the precise quantifications of layers upon layers of texts and traces. His notions of pre-text, para-text, hypo-text and hypertext enable an exact description of complex works such as those of Mireille W. Descombes.

For Genette, the "palimpsest" is first and foremost a phenomenon of intertextuality, in the now canonical definition given to this word by Julia Kristeva, as the implicit presence of a text that is not *actually* present on the page (if it were so it would have to be called a quotation).

One of Genette's categories is called the *paratext*, which is the "presentation apparatus" of a literary text, the title and subtitle, the forewords and postfaces. All of this, in the world of Mireille W. Decombes, is obliterated. There is no indication as to what part of the image is a title. There is no "reading contract" betwen her and the "reader" or "spectator." Nevertheless, there is in all of her pictures a word or a phrase that serves as a title or as a "key word" for the whole picture.

Even more important is the layer of "metatextuality," the "metatexte" (in Genette's terminology). Many of the deciphered sentences or words concern reflections on the production of the text/picture itself.

When speaking of the "picture" as *picture* perhaps the concept of the "transtextual" should be used. The palimpsests we see here are "transtextual" creations in which the "visible" turns permanently toward the "readable," in which lisibility is permanently engaged in a "death game" with visibility.

Thus the drawing entitled *Parole de . . .* (Figure 1) is organized thus:

je dansais
> MEPHISTO
>> (je?) riais

parole de
ou chansons
> je dérive
>> like a Vessel

Yet pasted underneath this metatextual poem one reads:

MEPHISTO
(Un mur s'est) jeté sur moi
(Un mur) n'a pas voulu de moi

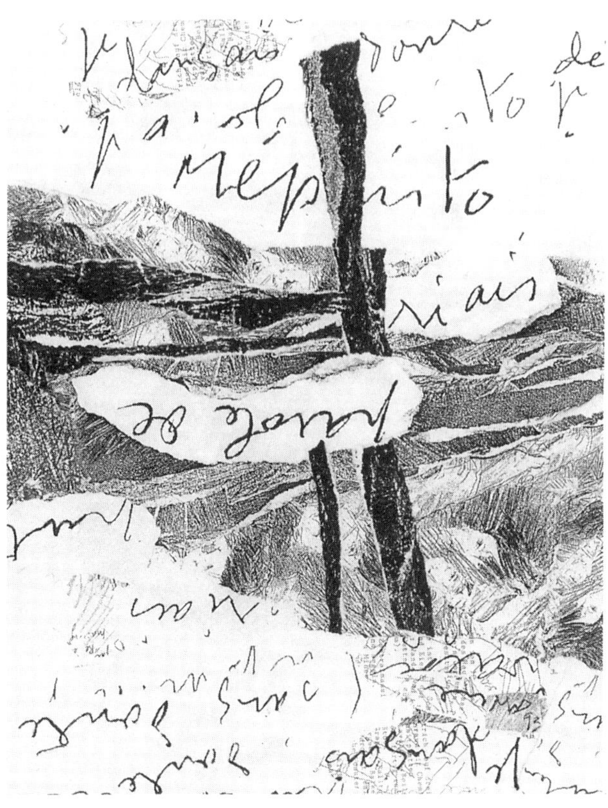

Figure 1. Mireille W. Descombes, *Parole de . . .* , 1993. 83 x 62 cm. Oil pastel, ink, pencil on paper, and transparent paper. Reproduced with the permission of the artist.

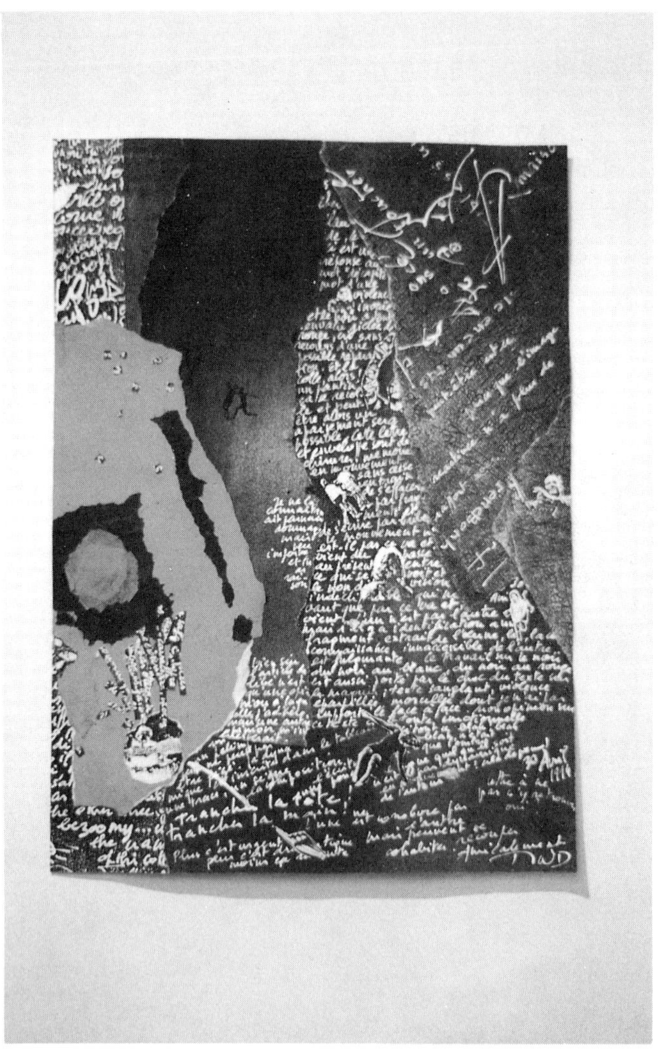

Figure 2. Mireille W. Descombes, *Cri-a!* Diptych (left), 21 x 15 cm each. Silk paper, transparent paper, ink, marker. Reproduced with the permission of the artist.

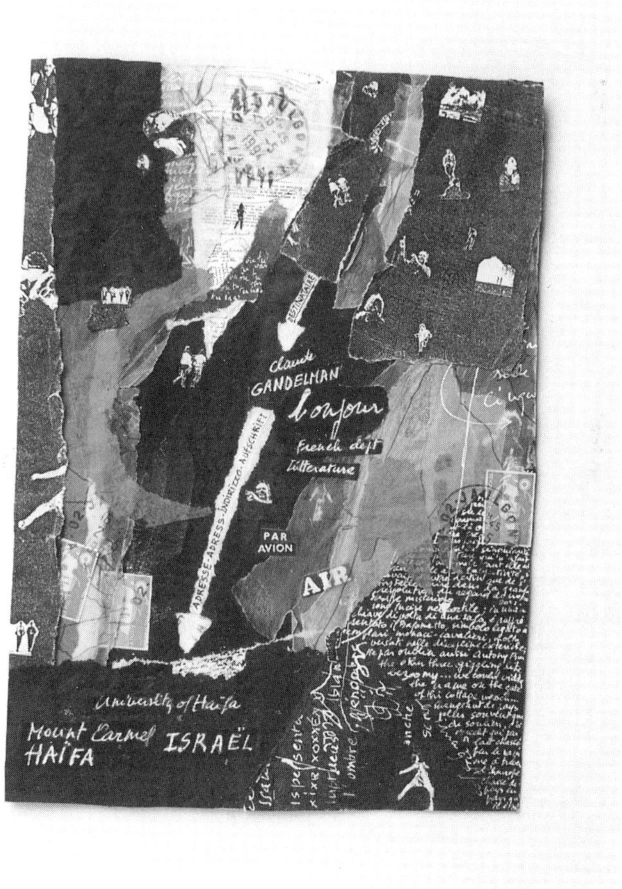

Figure 2. Mireille W. Descombes, *Cri-a!* Diptych (right), 21 x 15 cm each. Silk paper, transparent paper, ink, marker. Reproduced with the permission of the artist.

And underneath the handwriting, a German text, which becomes readable if one opens the pasted page, opens the vertically arranged strips:

```
Z  u  M
e  n  i
n  d  n
t     e
r  s  n
a  e  .
l  g  .
m  e  .
a  l
s  n
s
```

and below:

```
Raum . . .
mit Chem . . .
W.C. Boil . . .
fertig . . .
Falt . . .
Balk . . .
```

Here, one must certainly look for a "Faustian" theme, the more so as an autoportrait of the artist is visible above "parole de." But who is Faust, who is Mephisto?

The second picture I introduce here is an exhibit at the Postal Museum, a diptych entitled *Cri — a! (Shout — ed!)* (Figure 2). Here the metatextual part of the picture is certainly a reflection on violence as a means of creation, as one discerns the words *"Trancher la tête," "Trancher la main"* 'Cut off the head,' 'Cut off the hand.' The French text echoes the quotations I introduced at the beginning of this study.

Another picture, another piece of "Mail art" (Figure 3) is entitled *Agnès.* The title itself is the central inscription on the paper, a postal envelope, in white over red, black, white, and red letters. One discerns a text right in the middle, "ecr anger," obviously a warning on the "danger" in "writing," an allusion to the "dangerous verbality" that threatens the artist. Then next to it over a black surface:

Esquisse, femme s'effiloche
déraisons
voilent, qui se fragmentent de
clairs et d'ombre

Then, below:

> *"melod*
>   *comm*
>   *un peu fou*
>   *mettre*
>   *dessous"*

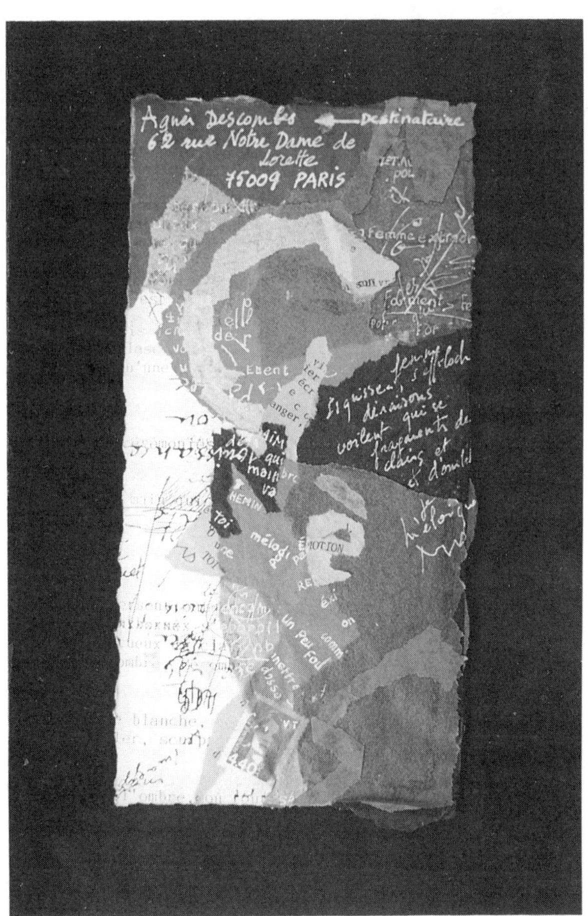

Figure 3. Mireille W. Descombes, *Agnès*, 1994. 21 x 15 cm. Pasted xerox
paper, ink, silk paper. Reproduced with the permission of the artist.

I also introduce a *Man Ray* picture (Figure 4), obviously an homage to Man Ray and perhaps an allusion to one of the sources of inspiration of the artist. Man Ray, too, used the "palimpsestic" procedure, not in his paintings, perhaps, but in his photographs and photograms, and still more in his films in which he made abundant use of the "superimposition" technique that allows pictures to appear over words (or vice versa). Was not the cinema, in its beginning stages, essentially a palimpsestic form?

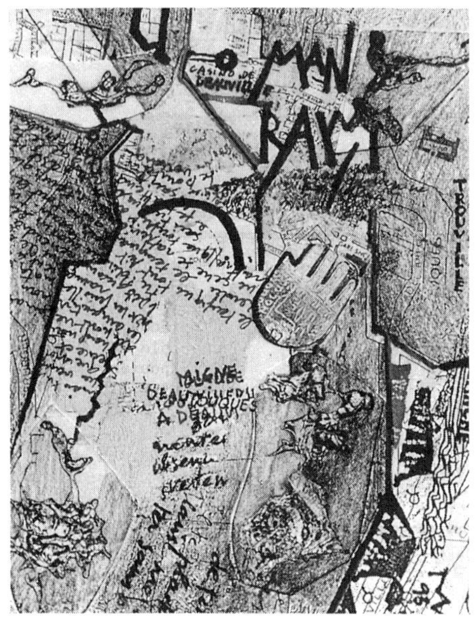

Figure 4. Mireille W. Descombes, *Man Ray*, 1993. 37 x 29 cm. Silk paper, marker, pencil. Reproduced with the permission of the artist.

Conclusion

The palimpsestic aesthetics of Mireille W. Descombes rests on a Derridian oscillating "differance" that swings between the two antithetical poles of verbality and visuality — and makes the viewer "swing" between this polarity. On one hand, the works are pictures created through the destruction of texts and of words. Yet on the other they are also permanent invitations for the spectator to "hermeneuticize" the picture, to peel and peel again the layers upon layers of meaning pasted on top of each other or, more often, juxtaposed beside one another, to "extract" meaning (thereby destroying the picture as a totality). One may claim that this had already been done by the Cubists with their *papiers collés*, by the Italian Futurists with their *parole in libertà*. Yet with these artists, the destruction and polarity was incidental. To my mind, Mireille W. Descombes is the first artist who practices the oscillation between these contradictory poles systematically and with reference to one of the dominant philosophical currents of our time, Deconstruction.

Works Cited

Francis Bacon: Recent Paintings: 1968-1974. Catalogue. New York: Metropolitan Museum of Art, 1975.

Wind, Edgar. *Pagan Mysteries in the Renaissance.* New York: Norton, 1968.

Excess, Transgression, and the Subversion of Form: Lautréamont and Dali

Laurie Edson

In her *Surrealism and the Book*, Renée Riese Hubert studies several of Salvador Dali's illustrations for Lautréamont's *Les Chants de Maldoror*, noting that most of them do not seem to refer to Lautréamont's text (205-19). She suggests that rather than attempting to provide a convincing visual translation of the text, Dali was more interested in pursuing his own "delirious activity"; thus he did not allow Lautréamont's text to "filter" his own activity. Nevertheless, according to Hubert, the painter felt a deep affinity for the poet, and "certain not always easily perceptible analogies exist between the poem and the illustrations" (218).

In this essay, I would like to follow Renée Riese Hubert's lead and pursue her suggestion about analogies existing between verbal and visual material, with specific reference to Lautréamont and Dali. Instead of studying Dali's illustrations for Lautréamont's text, however, I propose rereading Lautréamont's *Les Chants de Maldoror* through the lens of one of Dali's paintings in order to highlight the analogous textual dynamics at work in the verbal and visual material. In particular, I will be looking at syntactical, stylistic, and formal features characterizing the work of these two men: meandering formal qualities; an excess of activity and minute detail; boldness, precision, and intensity of expression; and continual fluctuation and transgression.

This focus on the dynamics of Lautréamont's text differs substantially from the many classic critical studies that have highlighted thematic and psychological aspects of the text or studied sources.[1] The thematic similarities between Lautréamont and Dali cannot be ignored: both Lautréamont and Dali create images of terrifying fantasy and violent instinct, transposing elements from the dark, repressed unconscious onto page and canvas with shocking precision and an intensity of expression. It is for this reason, of course, that the Surrealists claimed Lautréamont as a precursor and that Dali rose to such prominence in the Surrealist movement. Beyond the thematic similarities, though, rereading Lautréamont through the lens of Dali's painting allows the often neglected dynamic features of Lautréamont's text to come into sharper focus.

Dali thematizes sex and violence in his 1936-37 painting, *Autumn Cannibalism*, as two characters attempt to devour each other, literally, with knives, forks, and spoons (see Figure 1). Passion is translated into appetite, with the culinary metaphor sustained by all the food products strewn around: an apple, bread, and soft pieces of meat hanging over objects like melting camembert. The sharp knives, forks, and spoons are rendered all the more frightening because Dali has positioned them

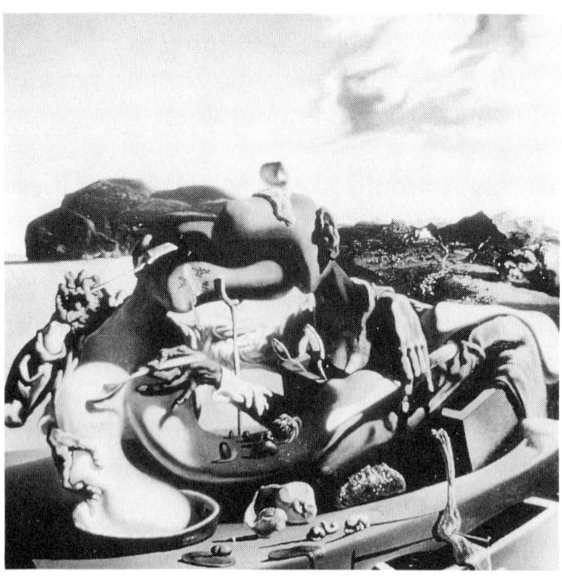

Figure 1. Salvador Dali, *Autumn Cannibalism*, 1936-37. © 1996 Demart Pro Arte (R), Geneva/Artists Rights Society (ARS), New York.

strategically so that they shine in the brilliant light coming from some mysterious source. Dali's paintings often contain such instruments of mutilation and create uncomfortable tensions of nightmarish intensity.

In this painting, each blob of the couple sucks, chews, cuts, eats, and squeezes the other. Partners in crime and passion, who is doing what to whom? The dialectics of victim and aggressor that critics have celebrated in Lautréamont is perhaps nowhere more graphically represented than here. If the figure of the left can be said to be female, we follow her arm as it encircles her lover's neck in what initially appears as an embrace, until we notice the knife in her hand that cuts into his flesh . . . or, at least, we suppose that this is his flesh because of its location in the area under his neck . . . until we realize that no, it is the prolongation of her own breast, which has meandered over to his side of the picture and extends even further to hang over what looks like his left shoulder. What at first appears sadistic turns out to be masochistic—a familiar dialectic highlighted in *Les Chants de Maldoror* as well; instead of slicing a juicy morsel of her lover, this woman is about to consume herself. In order to see all of that, though, we have to read the painting by following the meandering forms.[2]

The meandering that characterizes Dali's style here and in many of his paintings pervades Lautréamont's prose. As a point of entry, I quote from the second canto of *Les Chants de Maldoror*, the scene during which a stranger approaches an innocent child sitting on a bench in the Tuileries and sits down beside him. In a theatrical aside, Lautréamont ironically reveals to the reader what the reader already knows: that this shady figure is none other than Maldoror, about to assault innocence once again: "How sweet is that child sitting on a bench in the Tuileries Garden! A man, moved by a secret design, sits down beside him on the same bench with a questionable air. Who is he? I need not tell you, for you will recognize him by his tortuous conversation" (Lautréamont 65). By his use of the word "tortuous," Lautréamont refers ironically to the content of *Les Chants de Maldoror*, that is, all the torture, violent aggression, and sado-masochism that fills its pages. More importantly for our purposes, however, he draws attention to the way his language has been operating "tortuously," in a meandering way. Indeed, this "tortuous conversation" is the very mark that characterizes not only Maldoror's language, but also Lautréamont's.

The word "tortuous" has a certain perspective already built into it, for we say that something is tortuous if we wish to speak pejoratively of it. A tortuous discourse, then, is one that is painfully meandering or convoluted; the implied norm here would be non-meandering, direct speech, or saying what is meant without artful intricacies and elaboration. By his ironic reference to his own "tortuous discourse," Lautréamont consciously rejects direct language with its claims for a one-to-one fit between language and reality, and offers instead a deliberately provocative, complex, opaque discourse that calls attention to its own fabric.

This meandering quality manifests itself in various ways in *Les Chants*. Probably the most obvious example is found in those very long sentences in which Lautréamont keeps inserting sub-clauses, modifiers, prepositional phrases, qualifiers, and other grammatical structures within subject-verb-object sequences. Obviously, the reader cannot hope to assimilate such an excess of accumulated information, but what we do notice and remember is the very fact that this language could meander indefinitely. A relatively simple sentence from the beginning of the first canto serves as an example. Here, it is the accumulation of prepositional phrases beginning with the word "at" that propels the sentence forward:

> The dogs howl at the northern stars, at the eastern stars, at the southern stars, at the western stars; at the moon; at the mountains which at a distance resemble giant rocks reclining in the shadows; at the keen air they breathe in deep lungfuls, burning and reddening their nostrils; at the silence of the night; at an owl, whose slanting flight brushes the dogs' muzzles as it wings swiftly on its way carrying a rat or a frog in its beak, living food, sweet morsel for the fledglings. . . . (13; I have included only one-third of this sentence)

By saturating his text with long, winding sentences in which traditional subject-verb-object sequences are bombarded with constant accumulations of clauses, Lautréamont plays with our desire to arrive at the end of sentences and find closure. This technique intensifies considerably in the fourth canto, where abstract expression replaces concrete examples of Maldoror's exploits as the dominant mode. In the fourth canto, Lautréamont's sentences become even more complex as he elongates them with parenthetical clauses and other meandering strategies. After locating the subject, we unconsciously read more rapidly in an effort to locate the verb, and then speed through the sentence to find the object, as if we expect to find meaning in the traditional subject-verb-object sequence. Lautréamont occasionally includes some reference to our own frenzied activity of reading within his meandering discourse, as he does in the following example when he encourages us to relax and drink a glass of water after we have plowed through an unusually long, tortuous sentence whose "message" is no more than "it is good . . . to return . . . to the . . . subject:"

> To close this little incident, which itself is deprived of its matrix by a flippancy as irremediably deplorable as it is inevitably full of interest (which no one will have failed to verify, on condition he has sounded his most recent memories), *it is good*, if one has one's faculties in perfect equilibrium, or better still, if the balance of idiocy does not outweigh too much the scale in which repose the noble and magnificent qualities of reason, that is to say, in order to make things clearer (for until now I have been nothing if not concise, a fact that many will not admit because of my prolixity which is only imaginary since it achieves its goal of hunting down with the scalpel of analysis the fugitive appearances of truth to their ultimate entrenchments), if the intelligence predominates sufficiently over deficiencies under the weight of which it has been partially smothered by habit, nature and education, it is good, I repeat for the second and last time, for, by dint of repetition we shall finish, and this is true more often than not, by misunderstanding one another, *to return* with my tail between my legs (if it be even true that I have a tail) *to the* dramatic *subject* embedded in this stanza.
>
> It is useful to drink a glass of water before undertaking the continuation of my work. (177-78, my emphasis)

The short, succinct sentence following the exceedingly long one draws attention precisely because of its difference in length. Here, Lautréamont explicitly acknowledges the possibility that readers might want to pause and drink some water before continuing the harried activity of trying to follow his sentences. But Lautréamont's irony, if that is what it can be called, does not end there. He immediately compares the drinking of water (i.e., the temporary "pause" in the frenzy which his short sentence has allowed us) to a halt in the pursuit of a runaway slave, noting that the halt lasts only a few seconds before "the pursuit is taken up again with fury . . ." (178). The image of a runaway slave seems to refer to Lautréamont's own language that has found freedom from conventional constraints of representation. Paradoxically, it is the reader pursuing meaning who seems much more of a "slave." After this brief comparison, Lautréamont is off and running once again with the reader, having been given a "resting period" in the space of a few short sentences, in hot pursuit of the subject-verb-object units of meaning. Even in the most seemingly chaotic and meandering of Lautréamont's sentences, one can, indeed, always locate the subject, verb, and object; within the apparent confusion there is always an order and a logical structure.

A related type of meandering occurs whenever Lautréamont uses the word "like" (*comme*), the very word that opens up unlimited possibilities. Again, our attention focuses not so much on what is being said, but on Lautréamont's ability to write whatever he pleases, since he is obviously not limited by semantic constraints or the necessity of unity or coherence. Thus, the dogs howl "like a child crying from hunger, or like a cat wounded in the stomach up on the roof, or like a woman about to be delivered of a child, or like a plague victim dying in the hospital, or like a young girl singing a divine melody" (13). Nothing could be simpler than accumulating similes as a strategy for dispersing meaning. Marcelin Pleynet has singled out the importance of the adverb *comme* in *Les Chants* because it focuses on the arbitrary nature of all fiction (Pleynet 114); Lautréamont himself notes metaphor's ability to transcend specificity when he calls metaphor "this rhetorical figure [that] renders much more service to human aspirations towards the infinite . . ." (Lautréamont 198-99).

The bewildering proliferation of minute details characterizing both Dali's painting and Lautréamont's text might be called an aesthetic, if not an erotics, of excess. In Dali's work the beads in the silver handle of the knife, the reflection on the back of the spoon's smooth surface, the folds and shadows in the cloth of his shirt — all portrayed in the sort of hyper-realism for which Dali is famous — are among the many exact, little details that make the painting appear busy and excessive. The more we look, the more we see; and the more we see, the more we look for more in our desire to consume this painting. Lautréamont's prose, too, with its constant obsession for minute description and its careful attention to seemingly insignificant details, appears just as baroque and excessive. The sheer quantity of adjectives, metaphors, accumulated modifiers, and other syntactic devices makes Lautréamont's descriptive segments seem cluttered with an abundance of words, as if his language had become intoxicated or were taking pleasure in its own proliferation. In the prose as in the painting, lots of things are being done in lots of ways simultaneously.

In her study on Lautréamont, Ora Avni has examined the ways in which such excess and proliferation actually neutralizes rather than contributes to our understanding by causing the reader to forget the "message": "Under the pretext of saying *everything,* [Lautréamont's rhetorical techniques] overtax the monologic, coherent, and linear assertions, obliterating them in the end because of their sheer excess" (Avni 154, my translation). Although Lautréamont claims to want to instruct his readers, the effect he creates through his erotics of excess is to overwhelm them. Already in the opening section to the first canto, Lautréamont warns the reader to turn away from the approaching storm, that is, to avoid the onslaught of language that threatens to "imbibe his soul as sugar absorbs water" unless he is prepared to become as ferocious as what he reads (*féroce comme ce qu'il lit*). If readers insist on penetrating the text and do not want to be transformed by it, they must, according to Lautréamont, bring to their reading "a rigorous logic and a spiritual tension":

> So, timid soul, before penetrating further into such uncharted lands, set your feet the other way. Listen well to what I tell you: set your feet the other way like the eyes of a son who lowers his gaze respectfully before the august countenance of his mother; or rather, like a wedge of flying, cold-trembling cranes which in the winter time, with much meditation, fly powerfully through the silence, full sail, towards a predetermined point in the horizon from which of a sudden springs a strange, strong wind. . . . (1-2)

It is impossible for readers to "listen well to what I tell you" when the telling is so overburdened with excessive detail.[3]

A preoccupation with continual transformation of substance is yet another characteristic informing the work of both Lautréamont and Dali. In Dali, such transformation is most visible in the context of the dialectics of hard and soft that runs through his works. We are all familiar with his recurring "soft" motifs such as the famous melting watches, the limp body parts and objects held up on crutches, even runny eggs and cheeses. These "soft" motifs usually suggest an overriding of the boundaries between forms as one substance melts to merge into another. In keeping with Dali's obsession with primitive impulses and libidinal flows, such a lack of boundaries recalls what Freud has described as the infant's "oceanic self," or what Lacan calls *l'hommelette*, a human omlette that spreads out in all directions. In *Autumn Cannibalism*, for instance, the two "soft" desiring figures who ravage each other spread out and melt into one another, recalling what Deleuze has termed "desiring-machines" propelled by "schizzes-flows," or limitless exchanges and "nomadic conjunctions":

> machines in the strict sense, because they proceed by breaks and flows, associated waves and particles, associative flows and partial objects, inducing—always at a distance—transverse connections, inclusive disjunctions, and polyvocal conjunctions, thereby producing selections, detachments, and remainders, with a transference of individuality, in a generalized schizogenesis whose elements are the schizzes-flows. (Deleuze 287)

Dali's "soft" motifs can thus be located within a schizophrenic, libidinal economy that works against form and regulation, beyond what Deleuze calls "the anthropomorphic representation that society imposes on [the] subject" (296).

At the other extreme from schizophrenia is paranoia, which translates in Dali's work as ossification: bones protruding through human flesh, bones of meat sticking into the air, and sets of drawers which, in certain paintings, can suggest the ossification of knowledge into strict and rigid compartmentalization. In the world of irrationality, thought Dali, no such ossification exists: structures dictated by time and space melt and transform even before they have time to be settled. Dali's ambition was to take images from what he called "concrete irrationality" and render them just as solid, just as pursuasively thick and communicable as those images of the exterior world:

> My entire ambition in the pictorial domain consists in materializing
> the images of concrete irrationality with the most imperialistic rage
> of precision. The imaginative world of concrete irrationality must
> be of the same objective evidence, the same consistency, the same
> hardness, the same persuasive thickness, knowable and
> communicable, as that of the external world of phenomenal reality.
> (Dali 12-13; my translation)

Dali defined images from "concrete irrationality" as "images that
provisionally are neither able to be explained nor reduced by
systems of intuitive logic or by rational mechanisms" (17). Of
course, it is possible to understand Dali's obsession with painting
these images from "concrete irrationality," many of which are
often sexual or scatological in content, as a desire to master them
through representation in order to render them unthreatening.
Visual representation serves as a mediation, a buffer zone that
would keep Dali safe from the anxiety that an immediate,
unmediated encounter would produce. By representing sexuality
in painting it is kept under control, mastered and contained on
canvas.

On the pictorial level, Dali not only renders these irrational
images "solid," he also stages the opposite and represents "hard"
forms from external reality liquifying and deforming themselves,
a continual transformation and transmutation of substance
according to the dictates of his inventive imagination. Sometimes
even the image we believe to be "hard" and stable tricks us and
changes into a different image before our eyes, as in the well-
known double image of *Slave Market with Disappearing Bust of
Voltaire* (1940), where, depending on how we look, we see either
a pair of figures or Voltaire's head occupying the same space.[4]

The continual transformation of substance that informs Dali's
paintings also manifests itself in Lautréamont's text on several
levels. Thematically, we find examples like the lamp that changes
into an angel against which Maldoror struggles, or Maldoror
transforming himself into an immense eagle to fight a dragon,
or even transformations taking place as aggressor and victim
change places. Syntactically, of course, there are numerous
examples of transformations and metamorphoses made possible
through the use of metaphor. Transformation occurs, too, on a
narrative level as Maldoror and the narrator seem to exchange
identities, and on an intertextual level whenever Lautréamont

parodies the *roman noir*, the *roman populaire*, Romanticism, or any of his predecessors, since parody always involves absorbing and changing the original in some way.[5] Finally, as we have already seen, Lautréamont believed that his text would be capable of transforming unsuspecting readers and converting them to evil: "[T]he deadly emanations of this book will imbibe [the reader's] soul as sugar absorbs water," unless the reader brings a certain "hardness" to reading, what Lautréamont called a "rigorous logic and a spiritual tension . . ." (1).

As part of his poetics valorizing transformation, Lautréamont creates many examples in which people in the text are "changed" as a result of their own encounter with language. The person who discovers the madwoman's manuscript in the third canto, for instance, is so affected by the horrendous content of that manuscript and the sheer power of the language that he faints. The reader of the inscription on the bridge, also in the third canto, finds himself seduced by the inscription warning against venturing further and yields to temptation. The many representations of readers in the text undergoing change are meant, of course, to implicate the readers of the text as well. Echoing Baudelaire's call to a *Hypocrite lecteur, – mon semblable, – mon frère!*, Lautréamont would like his readers to recognize their own murderous impulses and not cling hypocritically to a belief in their own purity.

It is not only the readers within Lautréamont's text who undergo transformation, but the innocent characters as well. Virtue is transformed into vice as Maldoror poisons naive, unsuspecting minds and corrupts youth for his own ends:

> From the dawn of time [man] had modestly believed that he was filled with goodness mingled with only a minute quantity of evil. By dragging out his heart and his life-thread into the light of day I taught him the rude lesson that, on the contrary, he is made up of evil mingled with only a minute quantity of good. . . . (49-50)

Thus we watch as Maldoror easily seduces Mervyn in the sixth canto, despite the efforts of the boy's parents to protect him.

If all these kinds of transformations in Lautréamont can be considered analogous to Dali's soft, malleable substances that readily change form, then the opposite would be some constant, unchanging form equivalent to Dali's bones. For Lautréamont, that unchanging, "hard" form is represented by mathematics.

In his well-known invocation to mathematics in the second canto, he hails mathematics with its "tenacious propositions," "iron-bound laws," and "eternal axioms," and celebrates its capacity to endure long after things of the world disappear:

> But you are unchanging. No change, no envenomed wind, touches the steep rocks and wide valleys of your identity. Your modest pyramids will endure longer than the pyramids of Egypt, those ant-hills erected by stupidity and slavery. The end of all the centuries will yet see, standing upon the ruins of time, your cabalistic ciphers, your terse equations, and your sculptural lines. ... (89)

One finds in Lautréamont's writing an uncanny combination of mathematical rigor on the one hand and frenzied thematic and stylistic activity on the other, especially in the final episode in which Mervyn's body is flung through the air tracing various geometric forms according to very precisely elaborated laws of physics. This same uncanny combination of scientific precision and outrageous content characterizes Dali's work as well.

The Subversion of Form

The meandering, excessive, intense, and fluctuating features characterizing the work of Lautréamont and Dali all participate in a larger paradigm of subversion and function to unsettle codified form as well as conventional reading. Lautréamont's text participates in the counter-hegemonic discourse of nineteenth-century France that Richard Terdiman has analyzed in his *Discourse/Counter-Discourse*; Dali's paintings put the same counter-hegemonic tendencies into play in the 1930s. Considering *Les Chants* in its social and political context, Aimé Césaire has seen in Lautréamont's text "an implacable denunciation of a very precise form of society," referring to the rigid control practiced under the Second Empire (1852-1870) (Césaire 45).

The structures of conflict and the subversion that operates within Lautréamont's language have been described by Julia Kristeva in her *Révolution du langage poétique* as the dialectic between what she has termed the *semiotic* and the *symbolic*, two inseparable components of the signifying process. The semiotic, for Kristeva, refers to the pulsational energy contained in language, as well as its destructuring and explosive qualities, while the symbolic refers to codified discourse and the mechanisms of language that serve to constrain, regulate, and normalize, such as grammar and semantics. Both the semiotic and the symbolic occur simultaneously in language, with the result that the normalizing, regulating functions of grammar are constantly being undermined by the pulsations of the semiotic in various degrees, depending on the type of language under consideration. Scientific discourse, for example, attempts to filter out the semiotic in its desire to achieve clear, concise communication. Poetic discourse, infants' speech, or psychotic speech, on the other hand, are examples in which the semiotic erupts more forcefully through the rigid laws that seek to contain it. The semiotic can be thought of in terms of drives or quantities of energy like "charges and stases" that are essentially mobile, kinetically rythmic, and that undergo constant assimilation and destruction. Kristeva is attracted to Lautréamont precisely because of his use of a language that disrupts, explodes, and de-structures as it articulates. Like Lautréamont, Dali's paintings work to unsettle the symbolic order and to destroy reified form, either by rendering "hard" objects from the world soft or by rendering delusional images solid and thereby calling into question the fixed boundaries separating delusion and reality. Both Lautréamont and Dali produce works in which excess spills over and cannot be contained; both produce works that stage the transgression and subversion of logical and social codes. The ideology informing their work, then, is one in which dominant value systems are opposed.

The excessive exuberance and the resulting subversion of form enacted in Lautréamont's and Dali's works can be thought of in terms of what Georges Bataille theorized as an inevitable expenditure of energy operating in the world. The excess of energy represented here in terms of eating (consumption), sexual appetite, or killing relates closely to Bataille's theories of expenditure (*la dépense*), the idea that as excess accumulates and develops into superabundance, it must be spent "gloriously or catastrophically" as waste (Bataille 21):

> I insist on the fact that there is generally no growth but only a luxurious squandering of energy in every form! The history of life on earth is mainly the effect of a wild exuberance; the dominant event is the development of luxury. . . . (33)

Luxury, for Bataille, refers to the lavish expenditure (without return) of wealth or energy. Surely Lautréamont and Dali, with all their attention to violence, eating, and sexual activity, provide vivid examples of the excesses of energy that preoccupied Bataille.

While the semiotic as Kristeva theorizes it is not, strictly speaking, equivalent to the unconscious, her positing of the semiotic is inseparable from a theory of the subject that takes into account the unconscious. In *Desire in Language* she associates the logic of poetic language with dream logic, or the kind of logic that Bakhtin studied in carnival and called "dialogic" (70). This logic proceeds by analogy instead of causality and is diametrically opposed to the "monologism" of the Realist novel and Realist description:

> Literary semiotics can accept the word "dialogism"; the logic of *distance* and *relationship* between the different units of a sentence or narrative structure, indicating a *becoming* — in opposition to the level of continuity and substance, both of which obey the logic of being and are thus monological. Secondly, it is a logic of *analogy* and *nonexclusive opposition*, opposed to monological levels of causality and identifying determination. (Kristeva, *Desire* 71)

The work of Lautréamont and Dali exhibits the kind of transrational dream logic that Kristeva evokes here, with its obsessive exploration of the internal world of unconscious desires and repressed instincts. Disturbing, irrational images fill the pages of *Les Chants de Maldoror*, where they accumulate in rapid succession as if according to impulse and free association. Similarly, the frightening dream-like visions and deformed parts of human anatomy that appear in Dali's paintings are juxtaposed on canvas with no regard for conventional logic. That absence of conventional logic has even lead Robert Hughes to describe Dali's canvas as "the flat, desert-like plane, Lautréamont's operating table, on which strange objects meet . . ." (Hughes 238).[6] Eroticism and death are thematized in expansive, atmospheric landscapes with de Chirico-like deep perspectives and anti-naturalistic lighting, creating a frightening combination of realistic figures on hallucinatory ground. Like Dali's paintings, Lautréamont's text probes the inner workings of the mind. Like Dali, Lautréamont's obsessive attention to minute detail serves to highlight and keep attention focused on the uncanny activities of that mind, with all its unimaginable, repressed content.

Notes

[1]Gaston Bachelard, for instance, has studied what he calls Lautréamont's "phenomenology of aggression," citing the wealth of aggressive animal imagery in *Les Chants* as the mark of sadistic and brutal impulses. Like Bachelard, Paul Zweig has studied the violence of *Les Chants*, but instead of insisting on the dynamic impulses informing the component of aggression, Zweig sees violence as a strategy for ultimately achieving resemblance and a sort of equality. Similarly, in his study on Lautréamont and Sade, Maurice Blanchot talks about Lautréamont's obsession with his fellow-creatures and the need to establish communion.

[2]James Thrall Soby has perceptively suggested a connection between this wandering of form in Dali's painting and the influence of *art nouveau* (what Dali called the "undulant-convulsive" style), especially given the fact that this style characterized the architecture of Antoni Gaudì that surrounded Dali in Catalan Spain.

[3]In a perceptive analysis in her *Reading in Detail: Aesthetics and the Feminine*, Naomi Schor suggests that the current privileging of the detail be seen as part of the dismantling of Idealist aesthetics.

[4]Dali cultivated such images as part of what he called his "paranoiac-critical" method, which means looking at one thing and seeing another. As critics have already pointed out, Dali's methods really had nothing to do with paranoia, although Surrealists were quite interested in Lacan's *De la paranoïa dans ses rapports avec la personnalité* (1932), published just three years before Dali's own formulation of his "paranoiac-critical" method.

[5]For an account of this kind of intertextuality, see Jenny.

[6]Hughes is referring, of course, to the often-quoted passage from *Les Chants de Maldoror* about "the fortuitous encounter upon a dissecting-table of a sewing-machine and an umbrella" (Lautréamont 263).

Works Cited

Avni, Ora. *Tics, Tics, et Tics: Figures, Syllogismes, Récit dans Les Chants de Maldoror*. Lexington: French Forum, 1984.

Bachelard, Gaston. *Lautréamont*. Paris: Corti, 1939.

Bataille, Georges. *The Accursed Share: An Essay on General Economy*. Vol 1. Trans. Robert Hurley. New York: Zone, 1988.

Blanchot, Maurice. *Lautréamont et Sade*. Paris: Minuit, 1949.

Césaire, Aimé. *Discours sur le colonialisme*. Paris: Présence Africaine, 1955.

Dali, Salvador. *La Conquête de l'irrationnel*. Paris: Editions Surréalistes, 1935.

Deleuze, Gilles and Félix Guattari. *Anti-Oedipus: Capitalism and Schizophrenia*. Trans. Robert Hurley et al. Minneapolis: U of Minnesota P, 1983.

Hubert, Renée Riese. *Surrealism and the Book*. Berkeley: U of California P, 1988.

Hughes, Robert. *The Shock of the New*. New York: Knopf, 1981.

Jenny, Laurent. "La Stratégie de la forme." *Poétique* 27 (1976): 257-81.

Kristeva, Julia. *Desire in Language: A Semiotic Approach to Literature and Art*. Ed. Leon Roudiez. Trans. Tom Gora et al. New York: Columbia UP, 1980.

______. *La Révolution du langage poétique: L'Avant-garde à la fin du XIXe siècle: Lautréamont et Mallarmé*. Paris: Seuil, 1974.

Lautréamont, Comte de [Isidore Ducasse]. *Les Chants de Maldoror*. Trans. Guy Wernham. New York: New Directions, 1946.

Pleynet, Marcelin. *Lautréamont par lui-même*. Paris: Seuil, 1967.

Schor, Naomi. *Reading in Detail: Aesthetics and the Feminine*. New York: Methuen, 1987.

Soby, James Thrall. *Salvador Dali*. [Catalogue of the exhibition at the Museum of Modern Art.] New York: Museum of Modern Art, 1946.

Terdiman, Richard. *Discourse/Counter-Discourse: The Theory and Practice of Symbolic Resistance in Nineteenth-Century France*. Ithaca: Cornell UP, 1985.

Zweig, Paul. *Lautréamont, ou les violences du Narcisse*. Paris: Minard, 1967.

"Writing Through" Wittgenstein: Joseph Kosuth's *Abridged in Ghent*

Marjorie Perloff

The artist's book, traditionally the intersection of text and visual image (painted, drawn, engraved, graphic), has in recent years explored new possibilities. Photography, for example: Sophie Calle, Laurie Anderson, John Baldessari are just a few of the artists who have used photography to ironize verbal representations, or vice-versa. Again, the photographic image, inserted into an already existing verbal space, can provide the reader-viewer with new ways of theorizing the text in question.

For the Centennial of Wittgenstein's birth (1989), the conceptual artist Joseph Kosuth mounted a large art exhibition at the Secession museum in Vienna. Called *The Play of the Unsayable*, Kosuth's show brought together avant-gardists of the early century—Marcel Duchamp, Giacomo Balla, El Lissitzky, Kasimir Malevich, René Magritte, François Picabia, and Man Ray—with such postmodernists as John Baldessari, Marcel Broodthaers, Gunther Förg, Jenny Holzer, Jasper Johns, Sherrie Levine, Bruce Nauman, Robert Rauschenberg, Gerhard Richter, Cindy Sherman, Robert Smithson, and Cy Twombly. In the preface to the catalogue, Kosuth observed:

> The work of art is essentially a *play* with the meaning system of art; it is *formed* as that *play* and cannot be separated from it—this also means, however, that a change in its formation / representation is meaningful only insofar as it effects its *play*. My point is that primary theory is *part* of that play, the two are inseparably linked. This is not a claim that the commentary of secondary theory can

> make. *Talking about art* is a parallel activity to making art, but without *feet* — it is providing meaning without an *event context* that socially commits subjective responsibility for consciousness produced (making a world). . . .
>
> One of the lessons for art which we can derive from the *Philosophical Investigations* is that I believe the later Wittgenstein attempted with his parables and language-games to construct theoretical *object-texts* which could make recognizable (*show*) aspects of language that, philosophically, he could not assert explicitly. This aspect of philosophy, *as a process to be shown*, resists the reification of the direct philosophical assertion. (Kosuth, "Play" 249)

Here Kosuth probably has in mind the reference Wittgenstein makes in *Culture and Value* to "the queer resemblance between a philosophical investigation . . . and an aesthetic one (25). Or again, "Philosophy ought really be written only as a *form of poetry*" (24). But no longer a form of poetry or art as expressive model. For Wittgenstein, as Kosuth puts it earlier in the preface, "The *self* is grammatical — it punctuates. Thus it cannot be named because every attempt to do that would presume it. It can be shown, and, as art, it represents the limits of the world (culture, history) as a manifestation of it" (Kosuth, "Play" 247).

A few years after producing this Wittgensteinian manifesto, Kosuth himself published a remarkable "artist's book" that illustrates some of these points. The book, called *Letters from Wittgenstein, Abridged in Ghent*, takes the bilingual edition of Paul Engelmann's *Letters from Ludwig Wittgenstein, with a Memoir* (1967) and superimposes on the text, at twelve-page intervals and placed on facing pages (German on the left, English on the right), thirteen pairs of black and white 5" x 7" photographs of urban street scenes and building sites. The pages themselves have a parchment-like thickness, but the print has been made so faint one must strain to read what is otherwise an exact replica of the original Blackwell edition.[1] The glossy photographs are tipped in at their top horizontal margins and can be lifted up like flaps, so that one can read almost all of the text underneath. Each pair has identical captions, but the one on the right adds a date, 1992, which is uniform throughout. In the center of the book's gray matte front cover (a cover quite unprepossessing like that of a manual, with the name of the author and work barely visible in lighter gray letters) is a small photograph of an old building covered by scaffolding, evidently in the process of being renovated.

What possible purpose can there be in thus "treating" an edition of letters? Why Ghent rather than Wittgenstein's Vienna, and why these dreary, nondescript images of warehouses and apartment buildings, of old bridges and parking lots? Here we must reconsider the relationship between Wittgenstein and Paul Engelmann, especially with respect to the house on Kundmanngasse that Engelmann was commissioned to build for Wittgenstein's sister Margarete ("Gretl") Stonborough—a house whose design and building Wittgenstein was to complete.

In 1916 Wittgenstein, on leave from his regiment, was attending artillery school in Olmütz, an old cathedral city in what was then Moravia. He had an introduction to Paul Engelmann, whose family lived in Olmütz, from the eminent Viennese architect Adolf Loos, whom, along with Karl Krauss, he had come to know before the war through Ludwig Von Ficker (the editor of *Der Brenner*). Engelmann, who had studied architecture with Loos, had been drafted soon after the outbreak of the war, but was discharged from the army due to illness. The Engelmanns were a cultured family and Wittgenstein became a frequent visitor to their house, discussing literature, philosophy, and especially religion with Paul and his friends.[2] The letters Wittgenstein wrote to Engelmann from the front and, after the war, from Vienna and then Otterthal, where he was teaching primary school in the early twenties, give us some of the most intimate glimpses we have of Wittgenstein's mental state in these years. The memoir that follows fills in some of the blanks in these letters, although Engelmann admits he never really understood the *Tractatus* and found Wittgenstein's views on religion and mysticism puzzling.

The letters, in any case, break off late in 1925; only a single subsequent letter (dated 21.6.37) is included (Engelmann 58-59).[3] "From the autumn of 1926," writes Engelmann in the memoir, "Wittgenstein was in Vienna engaged on the building of the house in the Kundmanngasse for his sister, Mrs. Margaret Stonborough" (Engelmann 147). He makes no allusion here to what actually transpired between himself and Wittgenstein, and even Ray Monk has assumed that the execution of the Kundmanngasse project was a real partnership (Monk 235-38).[4]

But as Paul Wijdeveld's recent *Ludwig Wittgenstein, Architect* reveals, Wittgenstein, who was a severe critic of even his closest friends and who was, at best, unsuited for the role of collaborator, had been less than enthusiastic about Engelmann's earlier commissions for the Wittgenstein family (Wijdeveld 51-55).[5] Then, too, Wittgenstein had become antagonistic toward Engelmann's mentor, Loos. In a postwar pamphlet called *Directions for a Ministry of Art* (*Richtlinien für ein Kunstamt*) Loos declared that in the new Austrian Republic, there must be government support for the arts, that "[i]t was through the artist that Providence—the 'Holy Ghost'—realized civilization as a cultural flowering in man" (Wijdeveld 35). Wittgenstein wrote to Engelmann:

> A few days ago I looked up Loos. I was horrified and nauseated. He has become infected with the most virulent bogus intellectualism [*bis zur Unmöglichkeit verschmockt*]! He gave me a pamphlet about a proposed "fine arts office," in which he speaks about a sin against the Holy Ghost. This surely is the limit! I was already a bit depressed when I went to Loos, but that was the last straw (ctd. in Wijdeveld 24).[6]

Not surprisingly, then, as Engelmann was to put it in a 1953 letter to Friedrich von Hayek, from the moment that Wittgenstein signed on, "he was the actual architect, not I, and though the plans were ready when he joined the undertaking, I regard the result as his achievement, not mine" (Wijdeveld 54). This is politely put (to Hayek, who was Wittgenstein's second cousin), but Engelmann must have been quite disappointed. Indeed, although, as Wijdeveld tells us, Wittgenstein "did not change the overall conception of the ground floor plan and cubic arrangement of the building," and although he adhered to the "general asymmetric layout which seems partly descended from Loos's modernist programme" (159), he immediately set about "purifying" Engelmann's design. The house was stripped of all ornament and "reduced to an austere composition of lines, planes, and volumes" (Wijdeveld 104). If we compare one of the drawings in Engelmann's sketchbook (reproduced in Wijdeveld's book; see Figure 1) to the final appearance of the Kundmanngasse (see Figures 2 and 3), the difference is striking. For Wittgenstein, the key to architecture (as in the case of his evolving philosophy in these years) was the motto *Simplex sigillum veri* ("Simplicity is the hallmark of truth"). As Wijdeveld explains:

> In contrast to Engelmann's design, wall-planes take priority over window-planes: the distance between the windows is consistently smaller than the distance between the windows and the edges of a wall plane, while the parapets of the roof terraces are extensions of the outer elevations — all this contributes to the impression of resolve. The windows are longer than they are wide, with vertical divisions only, and they diminish in height on successive levels to suggest height. The upward thrust which is thus implied is in turn tempered by the equally severe horizontals which mark the top of the wall planes; there are no roof gutters and the roof-edge has been pared down to the absolute minimum. (106)

Such "classical" modernism, Wijdeveld further explains, "is of a completely different order from Loos's" (165), whose 1927 counterpart to Kundmangasse is the Villa Moller (see Figure 4). Here the street facade abandons the geometric purity favored by Wittgenstein in the interest of the residents' privacy and seclusion; the proportion of small window openings to large bare wall planes, an example of what Engelmann called "ornamenting with unornamented planes" (Wijdeveld 165), lacks what Wittgenstein considered essential qualities in architecture: logic and clarity.[7]

In planning the interior, Wittgenstein's concern for detail was to become legendary. His sister Hermine has remarked on his obsession with such secondary items as window-locks and radiators; she recalls that during discussions with the engineering firm responsible for the high glass doors that Wittgenstein had designed, the engineer handling the negotations broke down in tears, despairing of ever meeting Wittgenstein's standards. "The strongest proof of Ludwig's relentless-ness," writes Hermine, "when it came to getting proportions exactly right is perhaps the fact that he had the ceiling of a large room [the *Saal*] raised by three centimetres, just when it was almost time to start cleaning the completed house."[8]

It is this obsession with *getting it right*, this painful process of composition and revision, that may well have fascinated Kosuth, especially in light of the tension, everywhere visible in Wittgenstein's work, between the demand for beauty, perfection, and purification on the one hand, and, on the other, the

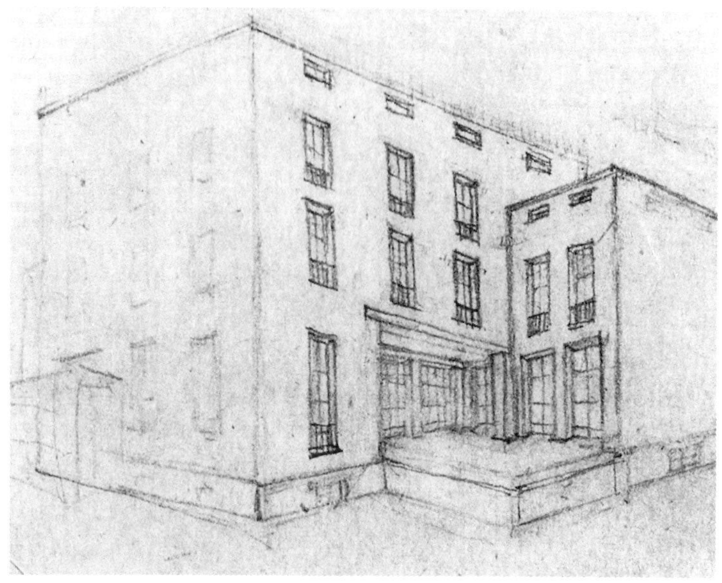

Figure 1. Paul Englemann, design for the Palais Stonborough, phase 10, southeast perspective (GC 78, 123 x 129 mm). Paul Engelmann, unpublished sketchbook (Courtesy Resource Collection of the Getty Center for the History of Art and the Humanities, Santa Monica, CA). Reproduced in Wijdeveld 93.

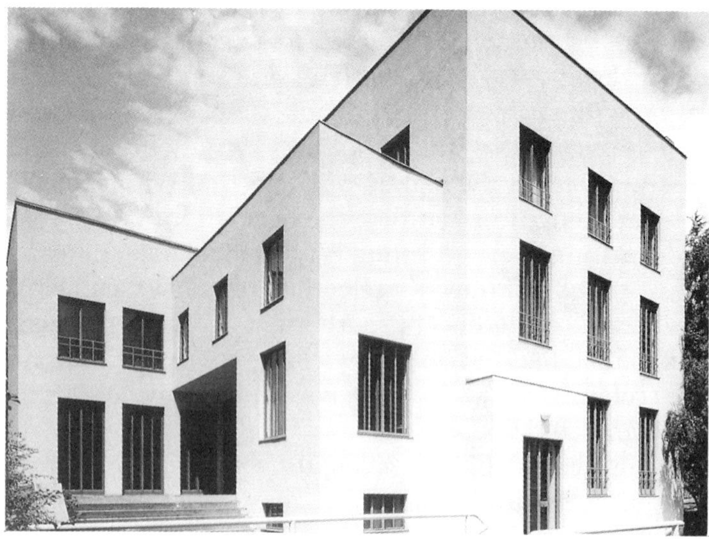

Figure 2. Ludwig Wittgenstein, *The Kundmanngasse*, Spring 1929 (Photograph Moritz Nähr, courtesy Michael Nedo, Cambridge). Reproduced in Wijdeveld 15.

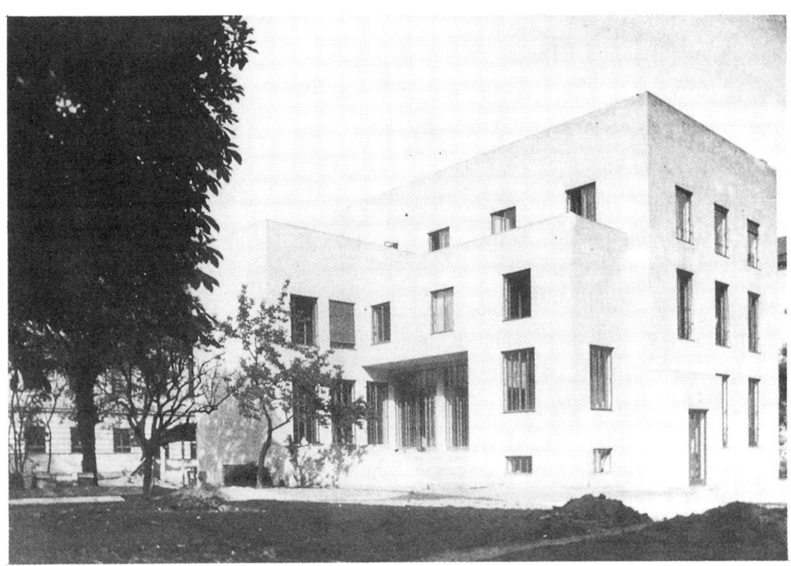

Figure 3. Ludwig Wittgenstein, *The Kundmanngasse*, south perspective, present situation (Photograph Marghareta Krischanitz Spillutini). Reproduced in Wijdeveld 107.

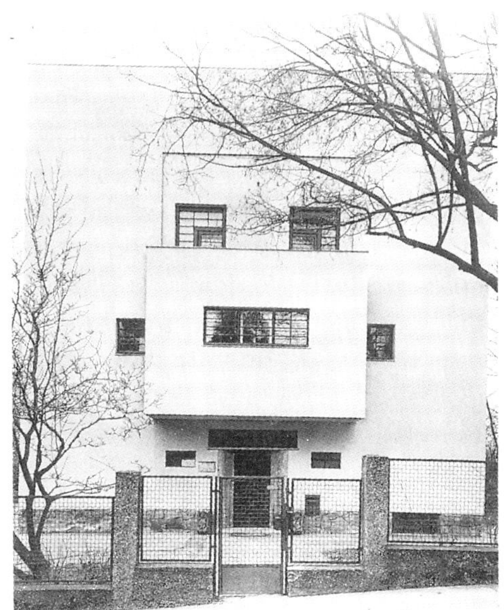

Figure 4. Alfred Loos, Villa Moller, 1927-28. Street elevation (ALA 2445). Courtesy Graphische Sammlung Albertina, Vienna. © 1996 Artists Rights Society (ARS) and Alfred Loos, Verwertungsgesellschaft bildender Künstler, Vienna. Reproduced in Wijdeveld 165.

recognition that the "Holy Ghost" of art can never be defined or even described. Indeed, from the perspective of a post-World War II conceptualist like Kosuth, the uncompromisingness and severity of the Kundmanngasse design, as of the *Tractatus*, must be understood in light of the "corrections" and revisions made in the *Philosophical Investigations* and related writings, corrections that moved the later Wittgenstein to the recognition that, after all, "Ordinary language is all right" (*Blue* 28). Hence, *Letters from Wittgenstein, Abridged in Ghent* may be looked at as a "play with the meaning system" (Kosuth's phrase) of Wittgenstein's own art. For Wittgenstein's erection of a beautiful, "perfect" house, Kosuth substitutes a series of demolition jobs. For the modernist "uniqueness" of the Kundmanngasse design, he substitutes a set of bland, impersonal photographs, chosen (but significantly not taken) by the artist to document the changing face of the contemporary city.[9]

In *Letters from Wittgenstein, Abridged in Ghent*, the "Kaiserliches und Königliches" Wien of Wittgenstein's youth gives way to the Ghent of the 1990s—Ghent, once the great medieval art city of Flanders (one thinks immediately of Van Eyck's famous *Ghent Altarpiece*), now curiously refigured as just another site of urban sprawl and wrecking crews. Just as the Engelmann and Wittgenstein designs for Kundmanngasse can be paired as "before" and "after" views, just as the "English" translation on the right side of the page comes "after" the German original on the left, so Kosuth presents "views" of the same site—sometimes with something from the old site remaining, sometimes not— and forces us to contemplate the relation of the two. But "past" and "present" are complicated because, as in so many of the examples from the *Philosophical Investigations*, no context for the images we see has been provided. We don't even know how "past" the past is, only that the present is 1992. We can surmise, of course, the date a particular photograph was taken from the cars in front of a building or the graffiti on its walls, but such estimates can only be rough. At the same time, within the confines of the individual photograph, items are contextualized by their surroundings, just as, in a given Wittgenstein proposition, the meaning of words like "blue" and "pain" are specifiable only within a given context.

"(The temptation to say 'I see it like *this*,'" we read in Part II of the *Investigations* in the section on the "duck vs. rabbit" conundrum, "pointing to the same thing for 'it' and 'this.') Always get rid of the idea of the private object in this way; assume that it constantly changes, but that you do not notice the change because your memory constantly deceives you" (*Philosophical* 207). The conundrum of *seeing as* that Wittgenstein now goes on to describe is subtly refigured in Kosuth's photographs. The first set (see Figures 5 and 6), for example, are pasted into a page where Wittgenstein expresses his impatience at two novels the *Fackel* writer Albert Ehrenstein, whom he had once helped financially, had sent him at the front ("Ein Hundedreck; wenn ich mich nicht irre" 'a pile of dogshit if I'm not mistaken') and begs Engelmann to send him a copy of Goethe's poems instead.[10]

The photographs are labelled "Fortlaan," evidently a street in Ghent. On the left, we see an ugly striped pseudo-Venetian Renaissance building bearing a sign that says "Residence Ulysse, Te Koop Luxe Appartementen." Underneath this sign, someone has written "Schande" 'shame,' 'disgrace', and on the left of the doorway a graffitus reads "Help," to the right of a sign for "Scaldimo" 'heated' apartments, the "l" being changed to "n" below to produce "Scandino" (either the noun for hot-water bottle or participle for "scanned" which is nonsensical here). On the right-hand page is an aerial close-up of a modern luxury building, perhaps the new Residence Ulysse, that has replaced the old structure. But it may also be a building next door and it remains unclear what the "Schande" is: that the old house is to be torn down, that someone still lives in it, that it itself has been converted into luxury co-op apartments, that it is perhaps a flop house? The pictures remain equivocal: why, for that matter, are the graffiti and signs in different languages—English, German, French, Italian, Flemish? And since the car parked in front of the old building is of fairly recent vintage—a Renault sedan perhaps—the time sequence of A to B is unclear.

The dreary scenes are, in any case, a far cry from the Loos-Engelmann—Wittgenstein demand for a modernist architecture based on geometric balance and harmony, an architecture of purity and transcendence. But then Wittgenstein himself was highly ambivalent about these notions: indeed, a few pages before the photographs in question are tipped into the text, he makes the scathing commentary on Ehrenstein, "Nur kein transzendentales Geschwätz" 'Only let's cut out the transcendental

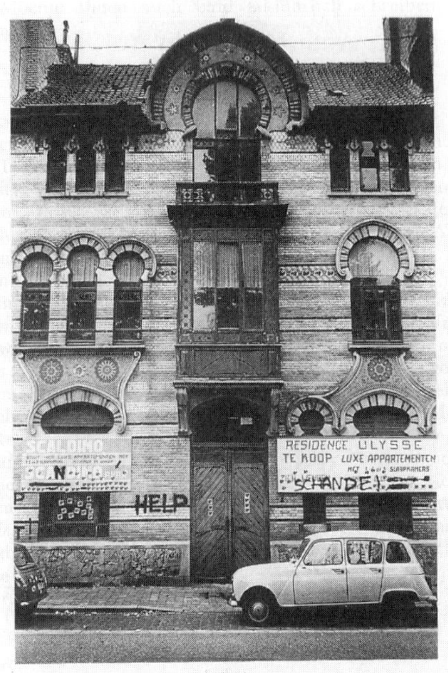

Figure 5. Michiel Hendryckx, Fortlaan (Kosuth 4). Reproduced with the permission of Joseph Kosuth.

bullshit' (Engelmann 10). And the very next set of photographs (Figures 7 and 8) are pasted into the pages where Wittgenstein complains about Loos's pamphlet, in which the architect reveals himself to be "bis zur Unmöglichkeit verschmockt!"

The photo on the left shows the corner of a room that seems to be in the process of demolition. The walls are covered with nondescript inlaid tile, the floor covered with rubble. The edge of an old fireplace is distinguishable on the far right, a double doorway (or is it a mirror in which the doorway on the other side is reflected?) on the left. Is this the interior of the old building in the previous left-page photograph, the building that made way for the Residence Ulysse? The caption says, again, Fortlaan. On the right-hand page, we see what may well be the same space,

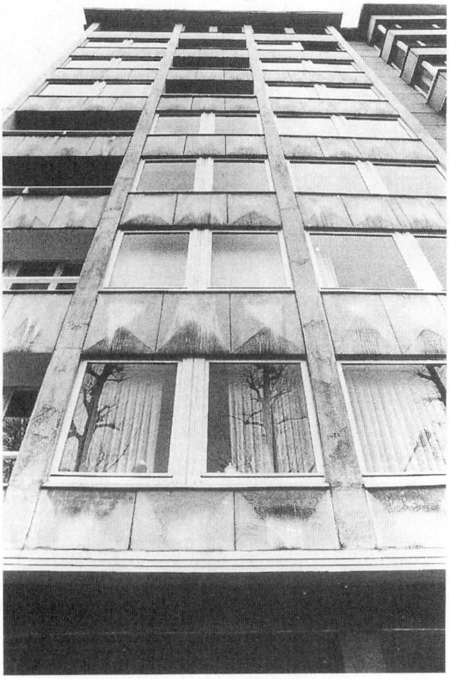

Figure 6. Wouter Rawoens, Fortlaan, 1992 (Kosuth 5). Reproduced with the permission of Joseph Kosuth.

now streamlined and modernized. There is a set of forbiddingly stark steel lockers, safes, or file cabinets on the left, each bearing a number. Bare walls, bare floors, a glass door with the names of its personnel beyond the steel cabinets. Is the "after" image worse than the "before?" It all depends, as Wittgenstein would say, on what you want to do with them. To the lay viewer, neither is especially appealing, but then it might be possible to conceive of a situation in which, say, the photo on the left would be meaningful, a reminder, perhaps, of one's childhood home. But if I were a business executive, I might well prefer the "after" picture, a publicity photograph, perhaps, which might help persuade clients that, in these steel lockers, at any rate, their files would be safe.

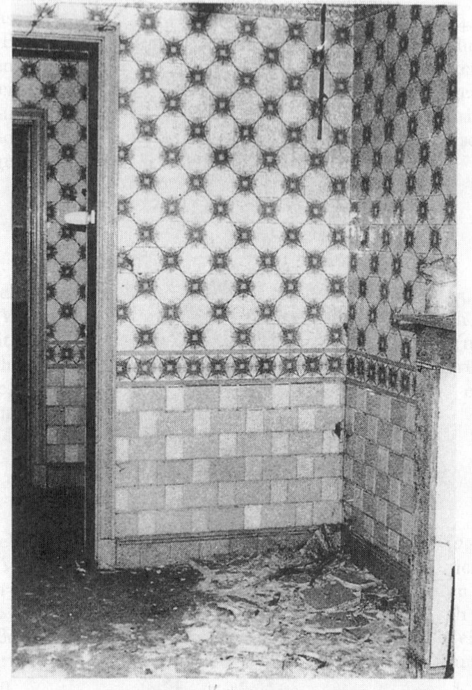

Figure 7. Michiel Hendryckx, Fortlaan (Kosuth 16). Reproduced with the permission of Joseph Kosuth.

Nor does Kosuth stick to a consistent "before-after" sequence. The third set of photos (see Figures 9 and 10) present us with two views of Koepoortkaai. On the left, we see a rather elegant old building with balustrades and pilasters, stone moldings and entablatures, which seems to be vacant. The undraped windows are charred, and a fireman is hosing out the downstairs interior, which may well have been gutted. The house is on a cobbled street. In the right-hand photograph, the old building has disappeared, but other similar houses (including what seems to be the adjoining one) may be seen at the left rear, while those on the right look like slum tenements. These buildings, in any case, now form a kind of back wall to a parking lot, to be entered from the front as the arrows indicate. Tickets are taken at the left. A sign on the right says in both Flemish and French, "Attention" and "Pay at the exit." A stop sign is at the end of the

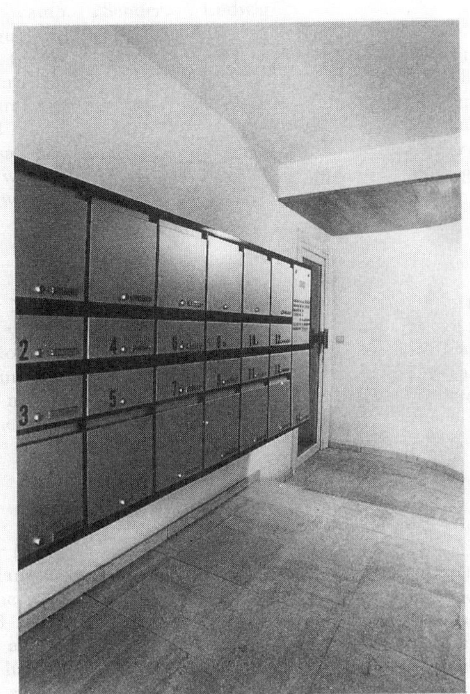

Figure 8. Wouter Rawoens, Fortlaan, 1992 (Kosuth 17). Reproduced with the permission of Joseph Kosuth.

roadway, and beyond it, the asphalt and rubble look incredibly dreary.

We can read this particular set of photos in a variety of ways. Wittgenstein, we know, wanted to get rid of all architectural ornament, but here we surely prefer the ornament on the left to the signs and arrows and the hideous asphalt roadway on the right. Indeed, even in the left-hand photograph, the "modern" fire-hoses brandished by present-day firemen seem to intrude upon the charm of what we call a "nice old building." And on the right, the large vertical arrow, silhouetted against the black background, has the *trompe l'oeil* effect of being a vertical sign, even as the striped tubular gate bearing the sign "Parking Inrit" looks like an entrance to a jail. Yet as different as this entrance is from the elegant arched doorway in the left-hand photograph, it itself has a curiously pictorial function, providing a frame for

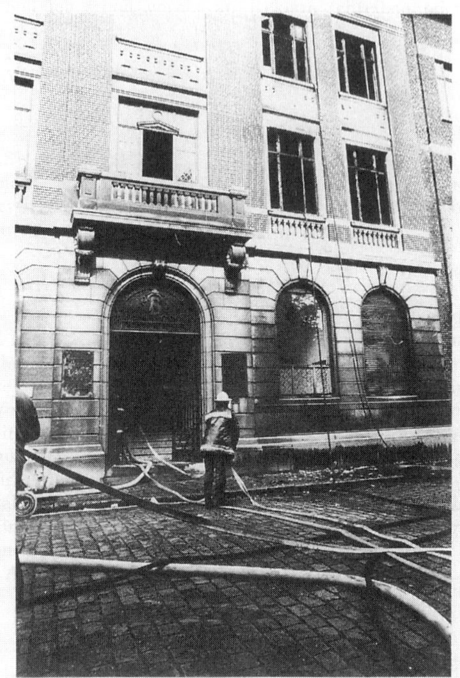

Figure 9. De Wulf, Koepoortkaai (Kosuth 28). Reproduced with the permission of Joseph Kosuth.

the "vertical" arrow, whose head is squarely in the center of the composition. The rules for "seeing" objects "as" X or Y are suspended and the fascination of the photographs' visual language is that, like the grammar of the *Investigations*, it denies the possibility of assigning a fixed meaning. Wreckage, rubble, houses and bridges torn down, parking lots and new bridges, derricks, scaffolding—and everywhere cars—how are we to read this series of images?

On the Veldstraat (see Figures 11 and 12), the old Majestic theatre, where *Chariots of Fire* is playing, is replaced by a new, upscale movie house—or is it a department store or office?— seen from slightly further away. In the text, on the page in question, Engelmann is expatiating on Loos's view that "truly modern form [must] emerge *spontaneously*," that "The path is this: God created the artist, the artist creates his age, the age creates

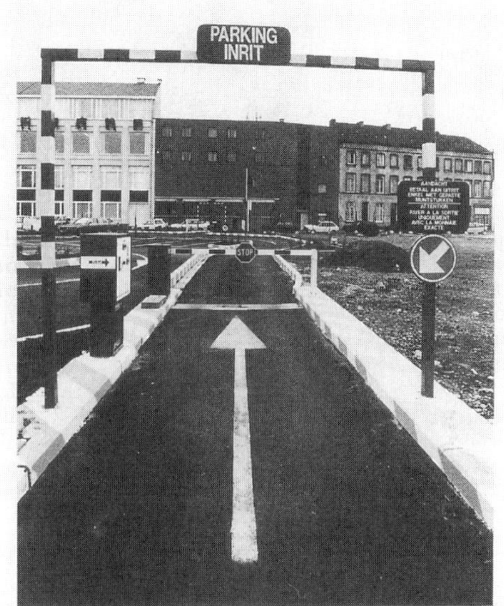

Figure 10. Wouter Rawoens, Koepoortkaai, 1992 (Kosuth 29). Reproduced with the permission of Joseph Kosuth.

the artisan, the artisan creates the button." "This," Engelmann explains, "is Loos's basic insight into the connection between the crafts and art" (Engelmann 127). For the postmodern artist, Kosuth suggests, such "modernist" theorems have become merely absurd. Ghent now displays no more than a contrast (or comparison?) between the ugly and the uglier, between crumbling facades of nineteenth-century design and modernist — deprecatingly called "modren" — kitsch. But whose eyes see things this way? The paired pictures, as I noted above, are, after all, not taken by the same photographer. What would happen if their shots were reversed? Would the "new" buildings be bathed in a more romantic glow? Couldn't their representations — witness the framing device of the Koepoortkaai image in Figure 10 — be given a special aura? And how do we locate the sites photographed vis-à-vis the tourist Ghent of churches, museums, and old squares?

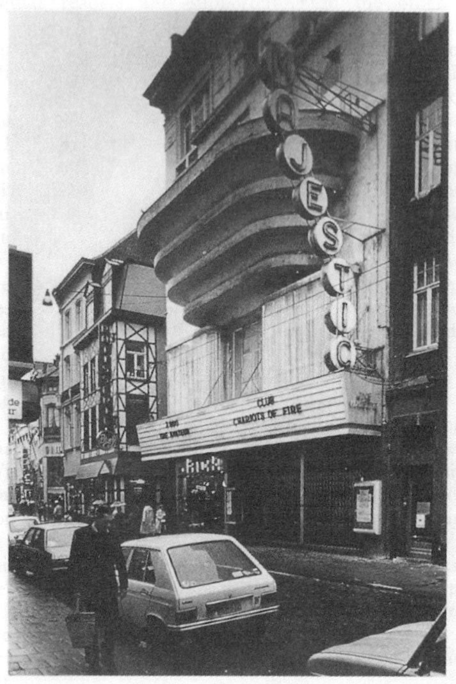

Figure 11. Michiel Hendryckx, Veldstraat (Kosuth 124). Reproduced with the permission of Joseph Kosuth.

These are questions, Wittgenstein himself would say, that cannot be answered satisfactorily. The name *Ghent* has no fixed value. Rather, Kosuth suggests, street names like Veldstraat and Fortlaan cast an ironic light on Wittgenstein's own Kundmanngasse; they frame Wittgenstein's beautiful architectural design by confronting that design, and the verbal texts that surround it, with the "ordinary language" Wittgenstein himself came to find so worthy of study. In "The Play of the Unsayable," Kosuth talks of the "indirect double reflection on the nature of language, through art, to culture itself" (247). It is just such "indirect double reflection" that characterizes *Abridged in Ghent*. For the pleasure of Kosuth's art text is that it shows (without ever making a point about it), that the visual equivalent of Wittgenstein's vehement rejection of the "transcendental bullshit" of intellectual / artistic life, as he knew it in Vienna and Cambridge, could only be the

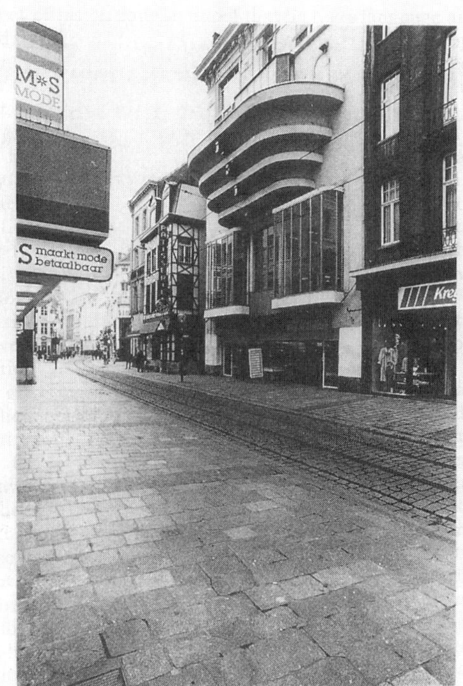

Figure 12. Wouter Rawoens, Veldstraat, 1992 (Kosuth 125). Reproduced with the permission of Joseph Kosuth.

"ugly" ordinariness of everyday life depicted in the photographs of Ghent that "overlay" the verbal text. And there is the further "double reflection" that Wittgenstein himself would have scoffed at such a notion, that he probably would have dismissed Kosuth's "abridgement" of his letters as so much "Hundedreck."

In a notebook entry for *Zettel*, Wittgenstein ponders the role of memory:

Memory: "I see us still, sitting at that table." — But have I really the same visual image — or one of those that I had then? Do I also certainly see the table and my friend from the same point of view as then, and so not see myself? — My memory-image is not evidence for that past situation, like a photograph which was taken then and convinces me now that this was how things were then. The memory-image and the memory-words stand on the *same* level. (Proposition #650)

But then of course the photograph, as Kosuth's "abridgement" suggests, is not reliable either: no more than the "memory-image" can it "convince" us that "this was how things were then." Memory "does *not* show us the past. Any more than our senses show us the present." But the language-game initiated by a sentence like "I see us still, sitting at that table," is charged with possibilities — possibilities for "philosophy" as a "form of poetic composition." Why does the person speaking remember just that particular table? Where was it located? Who are the "us" still seen in the mind's eye? The plot thickens. . . .

Footnotes

[1]In his *Letters from Wittgenstein, Abridged in Ghent*, Kosuth reproduces *Letters from Ludwig Wittgenstein with a Memoir by Paul Engelmann*. The page numbers in the two are identical.

[2]In the later twenties, Engelmann became a Zionist; he emigrated to Tel Aviv in 1934 and remained there until his death in 1963; see Monk 228-29 and Joseph Schächter's preface in Englemann ix-x.

[3]This letter concerns the mysterious "Confession" Wittgenstein had drafted at Cambridge in 1936 and distributed to some of his friends, including Engelmann (Monk 367-68).

[4]"[Wittgenstein's] role in the design of the house," writes Monk, "was concerned chiefly with the design of the windows, doors, window-locks and radiators" (236). But the Engelmann and Wittgenstein sketchbooks (see below) indicate that this was not the case.

[5]When, for example, Engelmann, who had become Loos's first assistant after the war, renovated the interior of Neuwaldegg, the Wittgenstein family's house in the Viennese suburb by that name, Wittgenstein's oral criticisms prompted Engelmann to reply, "I regret very much that you do not like my work for Neuwaldegg, as appears from the letter of your *Fraülein* sister; although I did the best I could and though nothing false can be found in the plans, I am not sure whether I succeeded" (20 December 1917, cited in Wijdeveld 51).

[6]The German phrase "bis zur Unmöglichkeit verschmockt" is more properly translated as "impossibly kitchified" or "hopelessly phony." In his memoir, Engelmann has a chapter called "Kraus, Loos, and Wittgenstein," which argues for the close conjunction of the three, glossing over what are very real differences (Engelmann 122-32).

[7]Indeed, whereas Wittgenstein's facade cannot be "read" as anything else, Loos's window and plane arrangement looks like a human face with two "eyes" above the "mouth" area.

[8]See H. Wittgenstein; and citation in Wijdeveld 168-69.

[9]According to the photo credits on the book's final page, Kosuth found these pictures in the Photoarchive De Gentenaar. Almost all the pictures on the left-hand page are taken by Michiel Hendryckx, the ones on the right by Wouter Rawoens.

[10]Kosuth 5. L. Furtmüller translates "Hundedreck" as "just muck," which is hardly accurate.

Works Cited

Engelmann, Paul. *Letters from Ludwig Wittgenstein, with a Memoir by Paul Engelmann.* Ed. B. F. McGuinness. Trans. L. Furtmüller. Oxford: Basil Blackwell, 1967.

Kosuth, Joseph. *Letters from Wittgensein, Abridged in Ghent.* Uitgevers: Imschoot, 1992.

_____. "The Play of the Unsayable: A Preface and Ten Remarks on Art and Wittgenstein." *Art After Philosophy and After: Collected Writings, 1966-1990.* Ed. Gabriele Guercio. Cambridge and London: MIT Press, 1991. [First published as the preface to the catalogue *Das Spiel des Unsagbaren: Ludwig Wittgenstein und die Kunst des 20. Jahrhunderts.* Vienna: Wiener Secession, 1989].

Monk, Ray. *Ludwig Wittgenstein, The Duty of Genius.* New York: Free Press, 1990.

Wijdeveld, Paul. *Ludwig Wittgenstein, Architect.* Cambridge, MA: MIT Press, 1994.

Wittgenstein, Hermine. "My Brother Ludwig." *Recollections of Wittgenstein.* Ed. Rush Rhees. Oxford: Basil Blackwell, 1984. 6-8.

Wittgenstein, Ludwig. *The Blue and Brown Books, Preliminary Studies for the 'Philosophical Investigations.'* 2nd ed. New York: Harper & Row, 1960.
_____. *Culture and Value.* Ed. G. H. Von Wright, in collaboration with Heikki Nyman. Trans. Peter Winch. Chicago: U of Chicago P, 1980.

_____. *Philosophical Investigations*. 3rd ed. Trans. G. E. M. Anscombe. New York: Macmillan, 1968.

_____. *Zettel*. Ed. G. E. M. Anscombe and G. H. Wright. Trans. G. E. M. Anscombe. Berkeley: U of California P, 1967.

Two Poems

Roger Shattuck

(for Renée)

ARS POETICA

I.

Only condense.
To run on
risks incriminating connections
with everything else.
Stop now
or forever . . .

II.

A poem
must both mean
and sound
like itself —
the voice
mixed and filtered
through tangled patchcords from
reality, producing
the audible shapes
of its moods.

Make no mistake.
When Emily wrote a friend
"A Pen has so many inflections
and a Voice but one"
she was complaining
about the seven types of slippage
in written messages
and choosing the forthrightness
the precise shadings
of live speech.

Prose too —
no dispensations —
must mouth its meanings
unabashed
thunderous when aroused
sometimes silent
as a free balloon.

Take Gulliver.
In Book Four he tells us
himself
how he sounds:
"In speaking
I am apt to fall into the voice
and manner of the Houyhnhnms . . . "

If you can snort
and whinny whole passages
like that one weird word
H-h-o-u-y-y-h-h-n-n-h-h-m-m-s
(in 1700 there were as many horses
in Britain as able-bodied men—
think about the prevailing sounds;
Swift did)
then and only then
you've caught his tone
and timing.

III.

Lay it out
so sheer shape
nudges the lazy voice
into every corner of the script
the way you butter toast
to have palatable
mouthfuls.

MACARONICS FOR MALLARMÉ

(To be recited with a faulty French accent.)

I.

Degas: Mallarmé, *cher maître*
please help me do better.
Ideas fill my bonnet
yet I find no sonnet.

Mallarmé: *Pauvre* Degas,
ideas—ha! ha!
A sonnet grows
only from *mots*.

II.

Poets deplore
the dark of *jour*
and mock the sweet
lightness of *nuit*.

III.

Poor Mallarmé
had lots to say.
He never quite
left the page white.

The Role of Language
in Seeing an Image

Georges Roque

> One of the functions of language (among others) is to name the unities that sight delineates (but also to help it delineate them), and one of the functions of sight (among others) is to inspire the configurations of language (but also to be inspired by them).
>
> —Christian Metz

Among the multiple ways of approaching the relation between the verbal and the visual, a question to which Renée Riese Hubert has dedicated so much of her work particularly with regard to the Surrealists whose practice has profoundly revitalized this relationship, I will focus on one precise point: the importance of verbal language for the visual image. The general context in which I will place my argument can be described as follows: It seems to me that the compartmentalization of academic disciplines and the organization of the university system (into Departments of Letters, Art History, Experimental Psychology, etc. . . .) has led to a separation between studies on the verbal and the visual. This explains the present tendency to resist such excessive specialization by those who search for the links that join the two domains, links that the study of the work of art brings to light. This also explains the proliferation, evident for some years now, of meetings and collective publications that have focused on the relation between the verbal and the visual.[1] But this tendency, as legitimate and necessary as it is, continues to presuppose, with a few rare exceptions, a *radical difference between the visual image and language*. When the attempt is made to join these two realms, it is only on the basis of the implicit or explicit assumption of their heterogeneity. Yet it seems to me, and to others, that there are important junctions where these two "universes" intersect, and not only because language is necessary for us to speak of the image, for even this claim, which has become commonplace, also expels the visual from language.

It is undoubtedly this notion of the *image* that poses problems inasmuch as its scope (*champ d'extension*) has narrowed little by little as the disciplines have become more specialized — to the point where it signifies, in the minds of art historians, nothing more than the visual image. The reality, however, is more complex. It is a question, in this case, of calling attention to the important role that verbal language plays not only in the interpretation of the image, but also in the mechanisms involved in the perception of the image, whether dealing with form or color.

My remarks here are not of a purely theoretical nature, for others have already demonstrated, and brilliantly — I'm thinking here of Mitchell's book *Iconology* — that the visual and the verbal are intimately linked; they are methodological just as much as they are epistemological. The question that concerns me is really that of trying to understand what occurs when we look at an image, when we see it, when we try to determine its meaning. My interest in this question stems from the desire, shared by other art historians, to determine the specificity of the visual and to examine the reasons for the relative failure of this attempt. I was a student at the time when the linguistically oriented, semiological vogue was at its height and, quite naturally, I rebelled against the excessive imperialism of linguistics and its tendency to dominate all else — to the point of giving a certain nobility to the visual image by showing that it was also derived from language. "There is a rhetoric of the image," we were told, "as rich as verbal rhetoric and which possesses the same tropes." Curiously enough, it is the search for a specificity of the visual image, for the characteristics that are peculiar to it, that led me to realize the importance of verbal mechanisms in both the perception and the reading of the image (Roque, "Comment"). Perhaps the time has come to find a synthesis between the opposing but nevertheless not irreconcilable positions, between: a) the idea of purely visual mechanisms, intrinsically independent of the order of language, and its corollary: the irreducibility of the visual image, as such, to the order of discourse (a romantic but very tenacious *topos*), and b) the opposite, logocentric notion which claims that the visual image is also a language possessing rules and laws that are derived in a similar manner from language.

Without forcing things too much, it is indeed possible to bring these two positions back to the same age-old debate with regard to the nature of the visual sign, a debate that can be provisionally and schematically summarized as follows: Does the image have value in and of itself, in which case it would not be a sign, or does it refer to something else, in which case it would have a representative value? In the first instance, we would be in a specifically visual realm, irreducible to all reference, in a contemplation whose meaning would be stricly confined to the enjoyment (*jouissance*) it might provide (and that only other artists, poets, for example, would be able to understand by giving the *equivalent* for it, the translation in poetic language). According to the other hypothesis, from the moment that the sign starts to refer to that for which it is a sign or to what it "expresses," we would immediately be in a representative structure that is therefore more easily susceptible to being transposed by verbal mechanisms.

We, of course, understand that each of these two hypotheses is true, and that there are grounds not to oppose but to reunite them. It must be strongly and firmly maintained, against a certain modernist and formalist tradition, that the visual image is at the same time transparent and opaque, that it makes us see and think simultaneously. Without it being either necessary or even possible to separate these two functions, the visual image involves seeing (*voir*) and knowing (*sa-voir*), whether it be on the general level of an aesthetic or philosophical comprehension or on the particular level of the supposed successive order of these phenomena in the reading of the image: perception and then interpretation.

We have believed for a long time, indeed until the 1970s, that vision proceeded, on the cortical level, from two distinct phenomena, one involving passive reception by the primary cortex, with visual impressions being formed on the retina and allowing the individual to "see," and the other consisting in the association of this vision with other anterior and similar impressions, thus permitting the individual to "understand" what he or she sees.[2] It is interesting to note that such a representation is altogether similar to the same dualism, seen this time no longer from the perspective of what occurs "behind" the eye but in front of it: the opposition between the perception of the image and interpretation.

This representation, however, has ceased to be current now that recent work has brought to our attention a functional specialization of the visual cortex. In this case, the different components of the visual image (form, movement, color) are constructed separately by different, specialized areas of the cortex, then assembled to produce the unique impression that we experience. This is not the place to enter into the details of these discoveries but rather to note, for our own discussion, some of the consequences. For not only is it no longer possible to oppose passive perception and active interpretation, it also seems that in humans there is no superior cortical zone responsible for "synthesizing" the fragmented information (color, form, movement) emerging from the specialized cortical areas. There is, as a matter of fact, an interactive system through which the specialized areas send signals back to the source of information.

> It is probable . . . that such retroactive projections allow for the reassembling of the signals coming from different, specialized visual areas. But they could also play an important role in permitting interior signals, produced at the very center of different visual areas, to be introduced into the cortex as if they came from the environment. This phenomenon is produced in dreams and hallucinations as well as during visual imagery. (Zeki 721)

A recognition of this phenomenon is, it seems to me, absolutely essential for us to understand that information from the "interior" comes to interfere, from the beginning of the phenomenon of perception, with that of the "exterior." In an analogous manner, the verbal appears to intervene very early in the visual mechanism and not only on the level of interpretation, assuming that one can even isolate this level.

In a general sense, we are indeed well aware of the importance of language and culture in the comprehension of the meaning of an image. Much of Gombrich's work was devoted to exposing these factors.[3] As soon as semantic mechanisms intervene, language is present and indispensible in the conferring of meaning. In a practice like that of parody, it is evident that knowledge of the object of the parody is indispensible if the image is to make sense.[4] But if it is true that there are no longer any grounds for separating perception and comprehension in the mechanism involved in our vision of the image, [5] there is certainly no reason to set a purely *formal* approach against another requiring *linguistic* and *cultural* knowledge.

From the point of view of a formal analysis, Arnheim made a major contribution by arguing for visual thinking, but his position led him to underestimate, as an indirect consequence, the importance of the phenomenon of language, which had the unfortunate effect of diverting the attention of many art historians away from the connections between the verbal and the visual. As Arnheim emphasizes in the preface to *Visual Thinking*,[6] his work takes as one of its principal points of departure his article on the "myth of the bleating lamb," which he outlines as follows: "The notion that the visual characteristics of an object are incapable of being distinguished and remembered unless they are associated with sound and thus related to language, I propose to call the myth of the bleating lamb" (Arnheim, "Myth" 141). Arnheim takes this question up again in the chapter of *Visual Thinking* devoted to words, a chapter that consists above all in demonstrating that we think more with images than with words: "Language, then, is not indispensable to thought, but it helps" (229). To say that there is a form of visual thought that is not expressed first in words is one thing (and there is considerable evidence for this [Fernandez 197 ff]); another is to admit that the distinguishing feature of the lamb's recognition can be more verbal than visual.

But this is what Arnheim cannot acknowledge. Essentially, he uses this "myth" to criticize Sapir and Whorf whom he cites infrequently, preferring to refer to more distant sources (Herder and Humboldt) whose occasionally excessive claims can more readily be called into question. Arnheim does not, however, actually discuss the anthropologico-linguistic hypothesis, given that his goal is above all that of revalorizing the role of the image as a form of thought. Indeed, in his effort to show that the verbal enjoys no prerogative, he explains that it is in principle no different from the visual:

> Since any verbal concept is committed to one of its particular aspects by the proposition, definition, or other context in which it is used, its visual nature is not different in principle from pictorial representation in drawing and painting. (Arnheim, *Visual* 253)

But instead of drawing the conclusion that the two aspects are indissociable, Arnheim clings to the traditional conception of the iconic sign as more "natural" than the verbal sign, which would establish the difference between the two while, at the same time, assuring the superiority of the visual.[7]

It is this well-founded desire to revalorize the visual as opposed to the verbal that prevents Arnheim from seeing that it is actually impossible to separate the lamb's visual image from the verbal signified "lamb." This is what Eco so ably argued with regard not to the lamb, but to the dog:

> The semantic analysis of a given expression can and must also contain nonverbal markers such as directions, spatial coordinates, relationships of order and so on. The content "dog" must also consist of images of the dog, just as the content of the graphic representation of a dog also consists of the concept of the dog and the word that corresponds to it. (Eco, "Pour" 166, n. 1)

If we examine the problem from a perspective that is no longer formal but iconological, we can easily arrive at the same conclusions. This is how Panofsky's famous schema of the three levels of iconological analysis came to be criticized (see Klein 353 ff; Hasenmüller 289 ff); his description of the first pre-iconographic level, which is a universe of pure forms identified as charged with "natural" meaning, already implies the intervention of language. Panofsky had, for that matter, recognized this; he knew that in order to identify a pre-iconographic motif, it is already necessary to know:

> A pre-iconographical description of Roger van der Weyden's Three Magi in the Museum of Berlin would, of course, have to avoid

such terms as "Magi," "Infant Jesus," etc. But it would have to mention that the apparition of a small child is seen in the sky. How do we know that this child is meant to be an apparition? (9)

To this question, Panofsky replies by correctly pointing out:

> While we believe ourselves to identify the motifs on the basis of our practical experience pure and simple, we really read "what we see" according to the manner in which objects and events were expressed by *forms under varying historical conditions.* (11)

Moreover, the correct identification of the apparition of a small child appeals directly to verbal language and its categories. For this reason, Panofsky's critique of Wölfflin—"a formal analysis in the strict sense of the word would even have to avoid such expressions as 'man,' 'horse,' or 'column'" (6-7)—can be turned against him. Indeed, there is no first level outside language because the identification of the object (the visual signified) is inseparable from the order of the linguistic signified. As Christian Metz has shown, there is a link between the visual and the verbal, an "inter-codal transit" which is always established by means of the signified insofar as the codes distinguish themselves through their signifiers (visual, auditory) and not through the signified that is common "to all codes and that is always the 'meaning,' the semantic material: this meaning constitutes the universal inter-codal link" (Metz 362).

It should be noted, however, that recognizing the role of the signified does not signify a hegemony that would level all meanings. Every mode of expression, every code keeps its own characteristics which are those of its signifier. But it is by means of what Metz calls a "transcodage" that an "inter-codal transit" operates, for the most part, in an almost instantaneous way, thus allowing one to pass from the perceptual code to the linguistic code, from the visual signified (a recognizable object) to the linguistic signified (the sememe designating the object). Following this conception, the issue is therefore not one of trying to privilege the linguistic signified, but of understanding how the process of naming a perceived object or of visualizing a named object functions. It is rather that, as Louis Marin has also noted, "[t]he images of things (in painting) are already the names of things (in language)" (Marin 27).

Indeed, the fact that this mechanism of intercodal transit intervenes through the signified opens the door to the intervention, in the comprehension of the image, of the tropological mechanisms peculiar to verbal language. The latter in fact possesses a characteristic that allows the same signifier to refer to two or several signifieds, whereas when it is considered in isolation, the image has in principle only one so-called "proper" meaning. The image of a pear shows only a pear. This does not mean that the image has no connotations; on the contrary, the graphic signifier allows many nuances to be introduced — which makes for the "richness" of the image — into the way of representing the "same" object. In this regard, the distinction proposed by the µ Group between the plastic and the iconic sign is of very great methodological importance,[8] but, once again, it seems to me that the legitimate desire to extricate the visual field from the grip of the linguistic leads one to underestimate the importance of the latter realm. In my view, one should add to the interferences between the plastic and the iconic those of the linguistic, for in many instances the verbal — that is to say, in this case, the linguistic — which has no doubt not yet been accorded enough importance, takes precedence over the visual. Thus, one can assign to a pear, iconically recognizable as such, the plastic qualities of aerodynamism as occurred in the advertising campaign in France where the Renault 14 was associated with a pear. But taking these icono-plastic relations into account is not always enough. That campaign was, as a matter of fact, a commercial failure. The reason offered in an effort to explain the failure was that the polysemic nature of the image makes it difficult to master its connotations. Now, the image showed only a pear. And yet it was the connotation of the word "pear" [which suggests in French the word "sucker" — tr.] that predominated. As a result, potential buyers refused to be "taken for pears" [i.e., to be "taken for suckers"], thus demonstrating quite clearly through this intercodal link how a linguistic signified comes to be added to the visual signified. In this case, the figurative expression "to be a pear" ["to be a sucker"] oriented the entire reading of this advertising image.

The possibility of such a slippage from the properties of language to the properties of the image adequately testifies to the proximity of the mechanisms in question. I call attention to it not to demand a reading of the image free from the shift of meaning toward the linguistic but to underscore, once again, the interweaving of the visual and the verbal. Consequently, the phenomenon generally recognized since Barthes that the text plays a restraining role (*rôle d'ancrage*) when faced with the polysemy of the image should be contrasted with those instances when it is the monosemy of the image that constitutes a visual intrigue that one tries to resolve by utilizing all the possibilities (*ressorts*) of verbal polysemy (Roque, "Mots" 255).

It is amazing to see the extent to which we constantly utilize, without always realizing it, tropes or verbal figures to understand images. By analyzing, for example, the posters for the French presidential campaign of 1981, Fresnault-Deruelle sees in those that show Mitterand walking in the countryside the metaphor for "political progression" that is even present on the level of the enunciation (*Images* 164).[9] Similarly, in an advertisement by Savignac for the lotto showing a man seated behind the wheel of his car, we are given to understand that "all the cleverness resides in the homophony between lotto and auto" (Scaccianoce n12-n14). Examples of this kind are legion, and my own texts are far from constituting an exception. (From another point of view, but which is akin to the one developed here, A. Danto has shown that it is through a process of metaphorization that works of art are given an artistic meaning.)[10]

It would nevertheless be incorrect to consider this phenomenon only on the level of the reception of the image when it is also valid on the level of production. The extent to which the utilization of linguistic metaphors is necessary to the representation of an abstract idea such as liberty is indeed well known. Daumier, for example, takes as his starting point the metaphor "the eclipse of liberty" in order to illustrate, for *Charivari*, the French defeat by Prussia in 1871. Here, a gigantic Prussian helmet comes to eclipse liberty which is associated with the sun (Figure 1). And in an effort to protect the loss of liberty at the time of the Olympic games of 1968 in Mexico City, Adolfo Mexiac, a Mexican graphic designer, again used the expression "liberty has been put in chains" in order to represent it literally (Figure 2). Let me add that in most cases it is not because one has represented a verbal metaphor that the image produced would also be a metaphor. Strictly speaking, there are no doubt

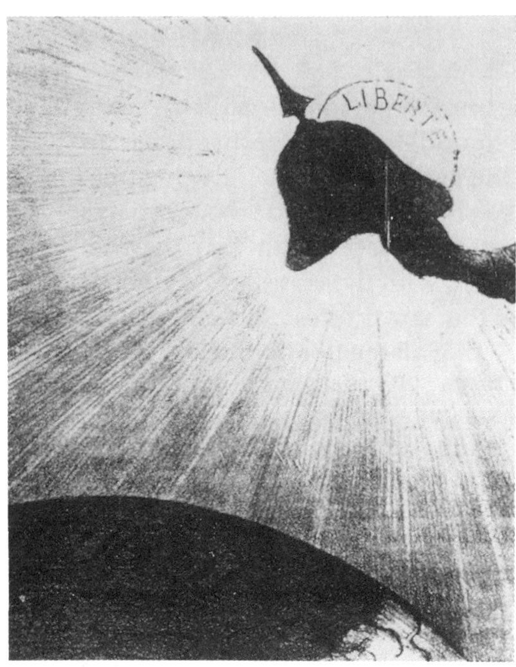

Figure 1. Honoré Daumier, *The Eclipse of Liberty*. Illustration for *Charivari*, March 17, 1871.

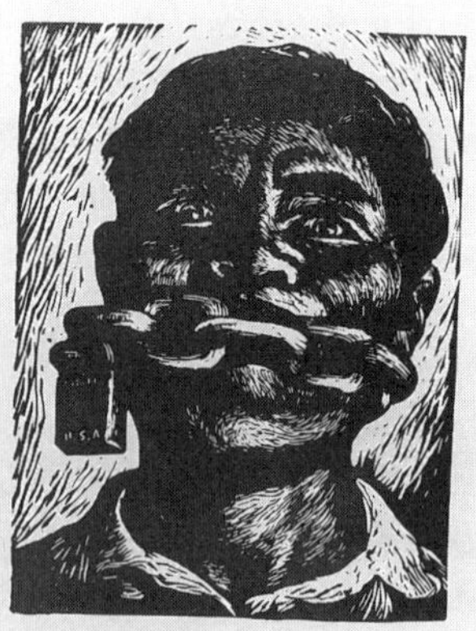

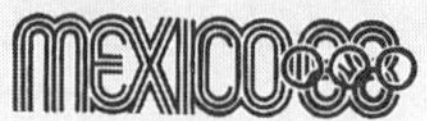

Figure 2. Adolfo Mexiac, *¡Libertad de expresión!* Poster, 47 x 30 cm., 1954. Mexico. Reproduced with the permission of the artist.

very few iconic metaphors.[11] Most of them play upon linguistic signifieds. Similarly, it is possible to show without too much difficulty that most "formal" analyses cannot do without metaphors or verbal tropes when they attempt to understand the meaning of the image. It is indeed impossible to separate the visual image from the totality of the signifieds and linguistic metaphors for which it serves as a vehicle, and which are at times, consciously or not, at the origin of images. These images always call up words in the mind of the spectator.[12] An extreme example of this very common phenomenon is the well-known poster by graphic artist Julian Key illustrating a brand of Belgian coffee. This is an extremely rare example of an advertising poster in which the name of the product does not appear. The name was supposed to spring up in the mind of the spectator of the poster which, because of the association of a cat and a coffee pot, suggested "Black Cat," the name of the brand of coffee (Figure 3).[13]

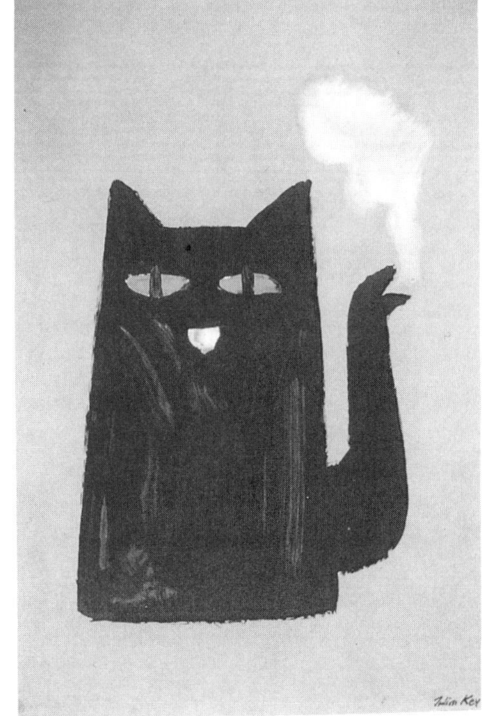

Figure 3. Julian Key, *Chat noir*. Poster, 115 x 115 cm., 1966. Brussels. Reproduced with the permission of the artist.

An important part of the contemporary image functions in this manner. Freed from the obligation to imitate, the motif often finds its meaning in the play of words or language. This is especially evident in the work of the Surrealists, for whom the discovery of the unconscious and thus the association of ideas and words assumed a particular importance. A certain number of works in the realm of the plastic arts have meaning only when the expressions represented are taken literally. Man Ray conceived a large number of his objects in this way: a featherweight boxer, for example, becomes a strange scale that is used to weigh feathers (Figure 4). Similarly, Marcel Duchamp had a door constructed in his studio on Larrey Street that closed one room while at the same time opening another (Figure 5). This made sense only in its contradiction of the locution: "A door must be either open or closed." But what is valid for contemporary art is equally valid for the entire universe of the *figure* in Western Christian art. The figure's very name straddles the rhetorical universe of language and the universe of the image, particularly the figures of Christian art which conjoin sight and the Verb. Saint Augustin called it *videre verbi*, the seeing of the verb (Didi-Huberman 608 ff).

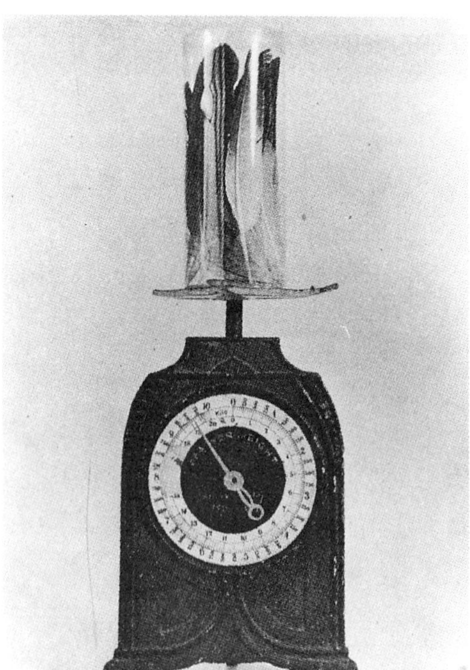

Figure 4. Man Ray, *Feather Weight II.* Object, 1964. Priv. coll., Antwerp. Courtesy Sylvio Perlstein.

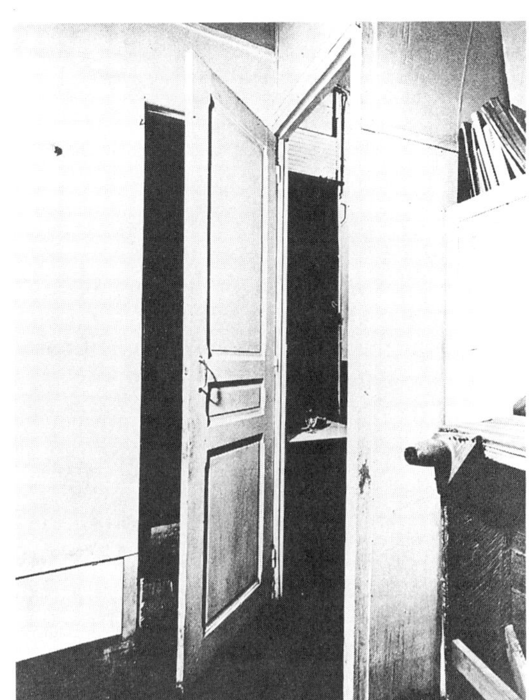

Figure 5. Marcel Duchamp, *Door, 11 rue Larrey.* Wooden door made to Duchamp's specifications, 86 5/8 x 24 11/16 in., 1927. Priv. coll. Courtesy Fabio Sargentini.

It is possible to think that the iconic constitutes a privileged realm for the study of these phenomena and of the predominant action of the verbal. But it should be remembered, subsequently, that it is the same for plastic elements, that what is, in effect, true for the figure is equally true for color.

If there is indeed one constant in a certain discourse on art, it is the consideration of colors as pure sensation, and it is precisely for this reason that they seem to escape the order of discourse or language. This idea has become so widely accepted that color has been linked, in its debate with drawing, to the feminine pole of art as sensation, emotion, sentiment (Roque, "Portrait"). Such a vision sustains, as we know, the numerous discourses on the impossibility of speaking of color (another *topos*) while deliberately accentuating an imaginary gap between color and language. If numerous works in the plastic arts leave us without a voice, it is not because they would be irreducible to language—one can have the same experience with a poem, a short story or a novel—but because there is often, on the semantic level, a visual enigma.

And as far as sensation is concerned, it cannot be naively relegated to the realm of physiology, inasmuch as it also brings in numerous conceptual and cognitive elements. Cézanne, who became the champion of "sensation," is also the one who declared that "the eye is not enough; one must also think" (Doran 89). Or again:

> In the painter, there are two things: the eye and the brain, they must both help one another; one must work on their mutual development, on the eye through the vision of nature, on the brain through the logic of organized sensations which provides the means of expression. (Qtd in Doran 36)[14]

The painters that are the most conscious of this tried not so much to imitate on the canvas "natural" colors, but to construct a "chromatic system" allowing them to obtain a more faithful reconstruction of nature than the simple "reproduction" of "what we see." This is evident in Cézanne, and before him, Delacroix in particular.[15]

If seeing is to understand and understanding is to grasp relationships (Barlow 5 ff), the importance of the interrelationship between the seeing and naming of colors is conceived through the intervention of the same differential function of discrimination at work in these two processes, and which, like language, differs according to culture.

Numerous studies have, in fact, been dedicated to the relationship between perception and the designation of colors. Based on the culturalist perspective expressed by Whorf, they insist on the importance of culture and language in the very perception of color. While its positions have been relativized and nuanced, the culturalist trend that developed these views continues to be a particularly lively and fertile field of study in the realm of perception and the denomination of colors.[16] The importance of language in the perception of colors was clearly demonstrated by Lenneberg in the beginning of the 1950s. During his investigations he raised the following question: "Do English speakers recognize colors that are easy to enumerate (that are, in other words, highly codifiable) more readily than the colors they name with greater difficulty?" On the basis of a positive response to questions of this nature, Lenneberg elaborated a useful notion of the "language of experience" to signify words that refer to the most elementary forms of experience, such as the sensation of temperature, humidity, light, and, of course, color (Lenneberg and

Roberts). It suggests that the experience that we have is inseparable from the language we use to name it.

This is where one often encounters great resistance due to the persistent idea that colors might exist ready-made in "reality" with words serving simply to describe them by assigning them a name. But the names of colors are *classifications*, a way of delineating not in reality—which is culturally fashioned—but in the continuum of the world, which comes to constitute "reality." And such delineations differ precisely according to culture.[17]

To give an example that is, in my view, very convincing, Danièle Dehouve, in the course of an ethnological mission in 1974 in the Tlapa region of Mexico (in the state of Guererro) was able to show the difference that appears in the delineation of the real to which the terms of color refer both in the indigenous languages spoken throughout Tlapa (Mixteque, Tlapaneque, Nahuatl) and in Spanish (Dehouve 285 ff). From this came an understanding of the problem that arose with the imposition of Spanish. Dehouve concluded from her study of bilingual subjects (who assimilated Spanish in addition to their native language) that the utilization of Spanish terms of color brought about a displacement of the semantic extension of indigenous terms in order to avoid certain contradictions that the passage from one language to the other could have produced.

Another direction of research, just as fruitful, is that of E. Heider who expands upon the reflections of Lenneberg and others in order to show that the verbal coding of colors acts upon our imaginary in such a way that "the 'structure' of colors in the memory comes to resemble the 'structure' of the names of colors in the given language" (qtd. in Tornay xxxv). That being the case, it is not surprising that colors interact with the perception or interpretation of colors,[18] as Barthes pointed out in a fragment significantly titled "Word-Color":

> When I buy colors, it is solely on the basis of their name. The name of the color (Indian yellow, Persian red, celadon green) traces a kind of generic region within which the exact, special effect of the color is unpredictable; the name then is the promise of pleasure, the program of my operation. (Barthes 133)

The painter Dubuffet makes the same argument:

> I also have the idea that colors gain something by being utilized not because of their vividness or the symphonies that their relations engender, but because they play upon their power of suggestion due to the immediate evocations they provoke. And it pleases me more to find in a painting colors that can be named: sand, alluvial mastic, twine, rather than chrome yellow, Prussian blue or Veronese green. (Dubuffet)

We understand, consequently, that the name of the color and the language that we use can have an effect on the way we analyze a color. I offer one last example. In her monograph on Manet, Gisela Hopp maintains that the emerald green used by Manet is oppressive — so much so that she proposed identifying the green bottle appearing to the right of the counter in the *Bar aux Folies-Bergères* as a bottle of absinth in order to make it contrast with the "hot orange" located next to it. This would have resulted in the creation of a tension and an irritation in the painting when in fact it has been established that this bottle was merely a bottle of crème de menthe. John Gage, who offers this example, suggests that Hopp's interpretation derives from the German term used to name this green, "green poison" (Giftgrün) thus leading one to wonder, he adds, whether a symbolic interpretation does not simply end up verbalizing a visual attribute (Gage, "Color" 522).

I will say, in conclusion, that in order to measure the importance of verbal phenomena to the apprehension of the image, its appears urgent to me to modify the very notion of the image by giving it a wider role than it had before, particularly during the last century.[19] It seems important to me to rehabilitate the notion of the mental image, in spite of the opinion of the specialists who tell us that it does not exist.[20] It is only by using a broader notion of the image, beyond the different specialized approaches and precisely in light of a future reunification, that we will be able to find the best opportunities for understanding this interweaving of the verbal and the visual that characterizes the global image, what P. Virilio calls the "block-image" (189 ff). Let us uphold, therefore, the idea of the global image, even though we do not yet know what it is, nor how it functions, and let it remain for the moment an enigma (*et qu'elle reste pour l'instant comme une boîte noire*).

—Translated by Joan Brandt[21]

Notes

[1] See in particular *Word & Image*; Clerc; *M/I/S. Mots/Images/Sons*; Gandelman; Montandon et al.; Reid.

[2] I am paraphrasing here the summary that Zeki offers in an article from which I draw the information that follows. See Zeki; see also Nathans.

[3] See in particular "Visual" 137 ff.

[4] This was demonstrated by several of the collaborators who assembled the volume *Dire la parodie*. See Thomson and Pagès.

[5] Except perhaps in the sense of the time of decoding, as R. Gregory suggests by distinguishing "perceptual and conceptual meaning": "Perception serves to ensure survival into the next few seconds; but conceptual understanding works over a far longer time-scale. We perceive objects in a fraction of a second, which is essential for moment-to-moment survival; but it takes a long time, even many years, to generalise experience and organise ideas for planning and for expression in words" (Gregory 330).

[6] "A few earlier essays, recently collected in *Toward a Psychology of Art*, laid some of the groundwork for the present book, notably those on perceptual abstraction, on abstract language, symbols of interaction, and 'The Myth of the Bleating Lamb'" (Arnheim, *Visual* vii).

[7] "True, the part of the concept which the eyes can see directly is limited in verbal representation to an almost totally arbitrary sign or complex of signs, whereas the visible picture contains more elements of portrayal" (*Visual* 253). For a critique of this conception see Mitchell, particularly chapters 2 and 3 on Nelson Goodman and Ernst Gombrich.

[8] On this distinction see Group μ, "Iconique" 190. These notions were reformulated as the distinction between the plastic and iconic sign in Group μ, *Traité* 113 ff, which was published after the writing of this article.

[9] The last book by Fresnault-Deruelle, *L'éloquence des images*, contains numerous examples of this type. See Roque, "Analyse."

[10]See Danto, *Transfiguration*, especially chapter 7 "Metaphor, expression, style."

[11]See particularly Kerbrat-Orecchioni 193 ff. and Le Guern-Forel 213 ff.

[12]From a similar point of view, H. Rosenberg has shown in a provocative manner how necessary language is to the acceptance of new artistic practices ("Art and Words").

[13]With regard to this poster, see Group μ, "Chafetière" 37 ff., which also contains an analysis of the notion of the iconic metaphor.

[14]It has been suggested that Cézanne, judging from his language, was familiar with contemporary theories of perception, particularly with those of Helmholtz, popularized in France by Taine. See Gage, "Constancy" 33.

[15]I began to deal with this question in Roque, *Expérience* 20-22.

[16]S. Tornay has written an excellent introduction to this problematic in the volume he edited. He examines these questions from the point of view of the physiology of vision, linguistics, and ethnology. The information that follows derives from this volume.

[17]This is the clearly affirmed basis of M. Sahlins' critique of Berlin and Kay's controversial thesis that claims that there appears to be a correlation between the number of terms for color that a culture has at its disposal and the cultural and technological "evolution" of societies. Sahlins 1 ff. See also Eco, "How" 157-175.

[18]Other authors who have drawn upon Berlin and Kay's thesis have insisted on the interrelationship between perception and the denomination of colors whose consequences for the history of art are what interest us here. See Conklin 931 ff; Ratliff 311 ff; Zollinger 1 ff.

[19]Thus, for example, in its voluminous *Traité du signe visuel*, the μ Group tries to construct a rhetoric of the image that would not be subordinated to linguistics, thus underscoring the manifest wariness with regard to the concept of the image. But doesn't confining oneself solely to the "visual image" (17), however great the merit might be of freeing and constituting a plastic sign apart from the iconic sign, presuppose the fiction of a reading freed from the linguistic?

[20]On this point see N. Goodman's polemical article (358 ff).

[21]My thanks to Judd Hubert for his advice on certain aspects of this translation - JB.

Works Cited

Arnheim, R. "The Myth of the Bleating Lamb." *Toward a Psychology of Art: Collected Essays.* Berkeley: U of California P, 1966. 136-50.

______. *Visual Thinking.* Berkeley: U of California P, 1969.

Barlow, H. "What Does the Brain See? How Does it Understand?" Barlow et al. 5-25.

______, C. Blakemore, M. Weston-Smith, eds. *Images and Understanding.* Cambridge: Cambridge UP, 1990.

Barthes, R. *Roland Barthes par Roland Barthes.* Paris: Seuil, 1975.

Clerc, J.-M. *Le Verbal et ses rapports avec le non-verbal dans la culture contemporaine.* Montpellier: Université Paul Valéry, 1989.

Conklin, H. C. "Color Categorization." *American Anthropologist* 75 (1973): 931-42.

Danto, A. *The Transfiguration of the Commonplace.* Cambridge: Harvard UP, 1981.

Dehouve, D. "Transformation de la dénomination des couleurs dans les langues dominées: Un cas mexicain." Tornay 285-304.

Didi-Huberman, G. "Puissances de la figure. Exégèse et visualité dans l'art chrétien." *Encyclopaedia Universalis; Les Enjeux.* Vol. 1. Paris: Encyclopaedia Universalis France, 1990. 608-21.

Doran, P. M., ed. *Conversations avec Cézanne.* Paris: Macula, 1978.

Dubuffet, J. *Prospectus aux amateurs de tout genre.* Paris: Gallimard, 1946.

Eco, U. "How Culture Conditions the Colours We See." *On Signs.* Ed. M. Blonsky. Baltimore: Johns Hopkins UP, 1985. 157-75.

______. "Pour une reformulation du concept de signe iconique." *Communications* 29 (1978): 141-91. [Reprinted as *La Production des signes.* Paris: Livre de poche, 1992.]

Fernandez, B. "Image et création en physique." *Comment vivre avec l'image.* Ed. M. Mourier. Paris: Presses Universitaires de France, 1989. 197-219.

Fresnault-Deruelle, P. *L'Eloquence des images.* Paris: P.U.F., 1993.

______. *Les Images prises au mot.* Paris: Edilig, 1989.

Gage, J. "Color in Western Art: An Issue?" *Art Bulletin* 72.4 (1990): 518-41.

______. "Constancy and Change in Late Nineteenth Century French Painting." *Appearance, Opinion, Change: Evaluating the Look of Paintings.* London: U. K. Institute of Conservation, 1990. 32-35.

Gandelman, Claude, ed. *Inscriptions in Painting. Visible Language* 23.2/3 (1989). Special issue.

Gombrich, E. H. "The Visual Image: Its Place in Communication." *The Image and the Eye: Further Studies in the Psychology of Pictorial Representation.* Oxford: Phaidon, 1986. 137-61.

Goodman, N. "Pictures in the Mind?" Barlow et al. 358-64.

Gregory, R. "How Do We Interpret Images?" Barlow et al. 310-30.

Group μ [Mu]. "La Chafetière est sur la table." *Communications et langages* 29 (1976): 37-49.

______. "Iconique et plastique, sur un fondement de la rhétorique visuelle." *Rhétoriques, Sémiotiques. Revue d'esthétique* 1-2 (1979): 173-92. Special issue.

______. *Traité du signe visuel: Pour une rhétorique de l'image.* Paris: Seuil, 1992.

Hasenmüller, Ch. "Panofsky, Iconography, and Semiotics." *Journal of Aesthetics and Art Criticism* 36 (1978): 289-301.

Kerbrat-Orecchioni, C. "L'Image dans l'image." *Rhétoriques, Sémiotiques. Revue d'esthétique* 1-2 (1979): 193-233. Special issue.

Klein, R. "Considérations sur les fondements de l'iconographie." *La Forme et l'intelligible.* Paris: Gallimard, 1970. 353-74.

Le Guern-Forel, O. "Peut-on parler de métaphore iconique." *Parcours sémantiques et sémiotiques*. St-Etienne: U de St-Etienne, 1981. 213-26.

Lenneberg, E. and J. Roberts. *The Language of Experience: A Study in Methodology*. Supplement to *The International Journal of American Linguistics* 22.2 (1956).

M/I/S. Mots/Images/Sons. Colloque International de Rouen, March 14-17, 1989, Rouen/Paris, Centre International de Recherches en Esthétique Musicale/Collège International de Philosophie [1990].

Marin, L. "Mimesis et description." *Word & Image* 4.1 (1988): 23-35.

Metz, Ch. "Le Perçu et le nommé." *Vers une esthétique sans entraves: Mélanges Mikel Dufrenne*. Paris: U.G.E. [10/18], 1975. 345-77.

Mitchell, W. J. T. *Iconology: Image, Text, Ideology*. Chicago: U of Chicago P, 1986.

Montandon, A. *Iconotextes*. Clermont-Ferrand: C.R.C.D.; Gap: Ophyrs, 1990.

Nathans, J. "The Genes for Color Vision." *Scientific American* 260 (1989): 42-49.

Panofsky, E. *Studies in Iconology*. New York: Icon, 1972.

Ratliff, F. "On the Psychophysiological Bases of Universal Color Terms." *Proceedings of the American Philosophical Society* 120.5 (1976): 311-30.

Reid, M., ed. *Boundaries: Writing and Drawing. Yale French Studies* 84 (1994). Special issue.

Roque, Georges. "Comment figurer la domination." *L'Affiche urbaine. Degrés* 60-61 (1989-90): m1-m10. Special issue.

_____, ed. *L'expérience de la couleur. Verba volant* 3 (1992). Special issue.

_____. "Les Mots au milieu de la figure." *M.I.S. Mots/Images/Sons*. 255-68.

_____. "Portrait de la couleur en femme fatale." *Art & Fact* 10 (1991): 4-11.

_____. "Une Analyse attentive des images." *Critique* 564 (1994): 393-400.

Rosenberg, H. "Art and Words." *The De-Definition of Art.* New York: Collier, 1973. 55-68.

Sahlins, M. "Colors and Cultures." *Semiotica* 16.1 (1976): 1-22.

Scaccianoce, L. "L'Image du manque avoir (le rêve affiche)." *L'Affiche urbaine. Degrés* 60-61 (1989-90): n1-n18. Special issue.

Texte/Image. Bild/text. Berlin: Technische Universität Berlin, 1991.

Thomson, C. and Pagès, A., eds. *Dire la parodie. Colloque de Cerisy.* New York: Lang, 1989.

Tornay, S., ed. *Voir et nommer les couleurs.* Nanterre: Laboratoire d'Ethnologie et de Sociologie comparative, 1978.

Virilio, P. "Le Bloc-image." *Faire l'image. Les Cahiers de Paris VIII.* St-Denis: Presses Universitaires de Vincennes, 1989. 188-203. [Interview]

Word & Image 4.1 (1988).

Zeki, S. "La Construction des images par le cerveau." *La Recherche* 222 (1990): 712-21.

Zollinger, H. "Correlations Between the Neurobiology of Colour Vision and the Psycholinguistics of Colour Naming." *Experientia* 35.1 (1979): 1-8.

Seeing and Knowing
in Francis Ponge

Sydney Lévy

"I shall say nothing till I have seen the body."

—Robert Louis Stevenson, *The Strange
Case of Dr. Jekyll and Mr. Hyde*

"A picture is worth a thousand words." Or so the saying
goes. And as a saying, it undoubtedly doesn't say much. Still,
assuming that it is about the amount of knowledge gained from
looking at a picture, it refers first to the information gathered by
an observer—what we say the picture depicts: a sunny or cloudy
day, a sky, a mountain or river, a woman, a man or a child, and
if an abstract painting, shapes and colors, not to mention the
various combinations, positions, and relationships of all identifiable elements. This kind of knowledge-as-information can be
very simple or extremely complex. It is in any case sayable. If
we want to be mathematical about it, we can say that it is equivalent to an observer's discourse on that picture—his or her description. Of course, the words used to describe the picture will
be more numerous than the picture itself, and in that sense "a
picture is worth a thousand words."

But a picture is worth more than words in a different sense.
Impressions, visual experiences impart also a knowledge not
easily quantifiable, because it is a knowledge *qualitatively* different from the kind we call "information" or "content." My task
here is to describe some of the characteristics of that knowledge

as Francis Ponge has intuited and posited them. The understanding of that knowledge will help us, perhaps, understand a little better the relationship of the visual and literary experiences, a field to which Renée Riese Hubert has devoted a good part of her career.

That other kind of knowledge is somewhat more difficult to express because it is precisely what is not sayable about the picture.[1] Not only is it "more" than what could be said about the picture, it is incommensurable with anything we can say about the picture's content; it cannot be measured against the words or the number of words about the picture. A discourse that attempts to express that knowledge often finds itself describing its effects—mental, corporal, and emotive—on the observer rather than its precise content. One of the most gripping expressions of this effect of the visual experience is found in an essay Francis Ponge wrote on Georges Braque. After a visit with Braque in his studio, Ponge is taken into the dining room where he sees one of Braque's paintings hanging on the wall:

> Comme nous descendions de l'atelier, Braque, sur la demande de Paulhan, nous ouvrit, au rez-de-chaussée, la porte de sa salle à manger. Cette pièce s'ouvre elle-même sur une autre, le salon, d'à peu près les mêmes dimensions. Sur le pan de mur qui les sépare, à droite, dans la salle à manger et donc, dès la porte ouverte, en face de moi, qui y pénétrai, je ne vis que ceci : un assez grand tableau, plus haut que large, barré, dans le sens de la hauteur, d'une assez large bande noire, le tuyau d'un petit poêle de fonte, avec un plat de poissons, où il y a plusieurs touches de couleurs vives, dont les rouges. A peine cette toile m'eut-elle sauté aux yeux, je ressentis ce que j'ai nommé, ailleurs, le sanglot esthétique (cet "esthétique" ne me plaît pas trop), enfin, une sorte de spasme entre le pharynx et l'oesophage, et mes yeux s'embuèrent. Sans doute (Paulhan du moins) s'aperçut-on de mon état. Nous prîmes immédiatement congé (*Atelier* 300).

As we were coming down from the studio, Braque, at Paulhan's request, opened the dining-room door on the ground floor. The room itself opens onto the living room, so that from the open door, opposite me as I stepped inside, I saw only this: a rather large painting, higher than it was wide, striped vertically by a rather broad black band, the pipe of a little cast-iron stove above a plate of fish, painted with several touches of bright colors, including some reds.

No sooner had this canvas leaped to my eyes than I experienced what I have called elsewhere the aesthetic sob (that "aesthetic" doesn't exactly please me now), well, call it a kind of spasm between the pharynx and the esophagus, and my eyes filled with tears. Doubtless they—Paulhan, at least—realized my condition. We immediately said goodbye. ("Braque" 53) [2]

The passage clearly summarizes the two kinds of knowledge afforded by the visual experience. Ponge starts the description with a narrative, the everyday circumstances that lead to the sighting of the painting: going down a staircase, entering a room . . . ; he then gives a description of the painting, its content, or what I called above its knowledge-as-information: a vertical black band, a stove pipe, a dish containing fish with splashes of red; and when he attempts to express that other kind of knowledge, he can only describe the physical effect it has on his body: a spasm between the pharynx and the esophagus, and tears. We can also infer from the passage the incommensurability between the two kinds of knowledge. If one compares the description of the content of the painting and the effect it has on Ponge it is quite impossible to find a causal relationship, or even a homologous one, between the two: there is nothing in the painting as described that seems to warrant the physical reaction. The two are incommensurable, and it would be quite absurd to measure one against the other.

There is a similar passage in *La Fabrique du pré* (*The Making of the Pré*) that shows explicitly the incommensurability of the description to the experience. It follows the same pattern as the one quoted above, going from narrative to description, then to an effect, this time emotive:

Nous étions Odette et moi arrivés en auto, par une route qui domine un site nommé Chategrenouille. Nous avions laissé là notre voiture et avions pénétré dans un bois de pins en contrebas duquel se voyait le pré longeant la petite rivière, le petit torrent assagi de montagne que l'on appelle le *Lignon*. Etait-ce dimanche? Des promeneurs par groupe, groupe d'amis, de familles, avançaient sur ce pré. Ce pré connaissait une population (au sens actif). Voilà, ce fut tout. Rien que cela. Je n'en puis dire plus. Je fus, je ne sais pourquoi, saisi d'une sorte d'enthousiasme secret, calme (tranquille); pur, tranquille. Je sus immédiatement que cette vision demeurait telle quelle, intact dans ma mémoire. Et donc qu'il me faudrait essayer

> de la dire. Pour la comprendre? comprendre n'est pas le mot. Pour essayer d'en conserver la jouissance présomptive et de la pénétrer, de la communiquer. Pourquoi? (*Fabrique* 244)

> We had come by car, Odette and I, via a road that overlooks a spot called Chantegrenouille. We had left our car there and had entered a pine woods below which could be seen the *pré* lying beside the little river, the little torrent named by mountains that is called the *Lignon*. Was it Sunday? Strollers by groups, groups of friends, families, were moving across the *pré*. This *pré* knew a population (in the active sense). There, that was all. Nothing but that. I can say no more about it. I was, I don't know why, gripped by a sort of secret enthusiasm, calm (tranquil), pure, still. Immediately I knew that this vision would remain just as it was, intact in my memory. And that therefore I would have to try to tell it. In order to understand it? Understand is not the word. To try to retain its promised joy and to perpetuate it, communicate it. Why? (*Making* 139)

The "sayable" description, the knowledge-as-information acquired upon seeing the meadow, is minimal: "ce fut tout. Rien que cela. Je n'en puis dire plus" 'that was all. Nothing but that. I can say no more about it,' while the effect it has on him is lasting. That effect is immediately framed within cognitive parameters ("essayer de la dire. Pour la comprendre?" 'I would have to try to tell it. In order to understand it?') but the kind of understanding it requires is of a different kind than what we usually mean by understanding: "comprendre n'est pas le mot" 'understand is not the word.' As to the "Pourquoi?" 'Why?,' why try to "understand" the experience, Ponge had answered the question early in his career, as we shall see shortly.

If the reaction—physical in the essay on Braque or emotive in *La Fabrique*—is unsayable, it is perhaps because the knowledge it contains is a knowledge for and of the body, or what we may call embodied knowledge. If there is communication between the painting and the observer, or between the meadow and Ponge, it is a communication addressed to the body, resulting in a constriction of the pharynx and esophagus or resulting in an emotion, which has also a physical equivalent.[3] That knowledge, moreover, belongs only to the body, in the same way we speak of "the body's wisdom" when we get sick and our body, in spite of ourselves, seeks rest. Any attempt to externalize this embodied knowledge in words, texts, or thoughts is to simplify it, to denaturalize it or, to use Ponge's neologism, to "abstrahir" it (*Lyres* 61), to betray it by making abstract something that is concrete and visual. What indeed can we say of Ponge's physical reaction to Braque's painting? Have we represented it, described it, or explained it if we say that "Ponge reacted to the painting's beauty?" Ponge resists such explanations when he says, "cet esthétique ne me plaît pas trop" 'that aesthetic doesn't exactly please me.' In fact, atrocity and horror also can result in a physical reaction. In a 1948 article on the painter Pierre Charbonnier, Ponge discusses the reaction painters have to things, objects, the world:

> Que le monde, que chaque motif, chaque objet soit "ravissant" ou au contraire "atroce": c'est bien possible [. . .]
> En face de cela que font les *artistes*? La plupart font des grimaces. De ravissement ou d'horreur, au choix. Certains vont jusqu'aux yeux blancs ou à l'épilepsie (plus ou moins simulée). (*Lyres* 60-61)

> That the world, every motif, every object be "ravishing" or to the contrary "atrocious," that is quite possible [. . .]
> What do *artists* do in front of that? Most of them make grimaces. Of ravishment or horror, the choice is yours. Some go as far as white eyes or epilepsy (more or less simulated.)

It is as though the grimace is the way the body acknowledges reception of the visual message before it registers and stocks it. Obviously the grimace is not the sole domain of the artist, nor is it limited to a reaction to the world. For the "visual" poet that Ponge is, it also plays an important role, though inverse to what he describes for the artist. In a wonderful text of 1941 entitled "La Pensée comme grimace" ("Thought as Grimace") (*Nouveau* 41-45) thinking has physical equivalents. Besides his "roupillons" (short naps) and "fringales" (momentary boulimia) there are, again, the grimaces:

> Il faudra bien que je m'applique un jour à décrire mon comportement *physique* en présence des idées, lorsque je pense. . . . Ma grimace de tension d'esprit, si accentuée qu'on me prendrait pour un fou, sans doute, si l'on me dévisageait en ces instants. [. . .]

> LA GRIMACE: lèvres fortement pincées, mâchoires serrées, narines et oreilles grandes ouvertes (bien que le bruit me gêne alors extrêmement), sourcils froncés, front plissé; l'expression des yeux beaucoup plus difficile à saisir: quelque chose comme décidés et lointains. . . . (*Nouveau* 41-42)

> I must some day make an effort to describe my *physical* behavior in the presence of ideas, when I'm thinking. . . . My grimace of mind tension, so accentuated that one could take me for mad, perhaps, if seen at these moments. [. . .]
> THE GRIMACE: lips strongly pinched, jaws tight, nostrils and ears wide open (and noise bothers me extremely then), eyebrows knit, forehead creased; the expression of the eyes much harder to grasp: something like decided and distant.

Could it be that Ponge's "thoughts" are visual? The description of his grimaces are in any case extremely so. It is as though he is in the presence of his thoughts, looking at them and grimacing. Or as though his thoughts had something physical to them, that he can describe in minute detail. Here again it is not the content of his thoughts that is expressed but an effect, almost like a reflex.

Anticipating recent thinking on the matter,[4] Ponge saw quite early in his career the cognitive value of emotions. In a programmatic text of 1928, entitled "Introduction au parti pris des choses" (literally "Introduction to Siding With Things"), we find a close linkage of the visual experience and the production of knowledge:

> Les qualités que l'on découvre aux choses deviennent rapidement des arguments pour les sentiments de l'homme. Or nombreux sont les sentiments qui n'existent pas (socialement) faute d'arguments.
>
> D'où je raisonne que l'on pourrait faire une révolution dans les sentiments de l'homme rien qu'en s'appliquant aux choses, qui diraient aussitôt beaucoup plus que ce que les hommes ont accoutumé de leur faire signifier.
>
> Ce serait là la source d'un grand nombre de sentiments inconnus encore. [. . .]
>
> Telles sont les ressources morales (aussi bien qu'esthétiques) du visible. (*Pratiques* 81)

The qualities we discover for things become quickly arguments for the feelings of man. Yet, numerous are the feelings that do not exist (socially) for lack of arguments.

I therefore reason that we can make a revolution in the feelings of man if only we applied ourselves to things. They would say immediately much more than what men have taken the habit of having them signify.

That would be a great source of still unknown feelings. [. . .]

Such are the moral (as well as aesthetic) resources of the visible.

To know the visible is to learn about emotions, or, more precisely, to discover new emotions. Thirteen years after he wrote the above text, at about the same time as the publication of his *Parti Pris* and a good thirty years before his essay on Braque, the physical reactions resulting from seeing a painting or a landscape become clearly the marks of a type of knowledge yet to be formalized. In a text of *La Rage d'expression* (1952) entitled "La Mounine ou note après coup sur un ciel de Provence" ("La Mounine or a Note After the Fact on a Provence Sky") he relates an experience similar to the one provoked by the Braque painting, this time triggered by a blue sky on a winter morning. He then proposes to use the experience to establish knowledge:

> . . . Donc, à l'origine, un sanglot, une émotion sans cause apparente (le sentiment du *beau* ne suffit pas à l'expliquer. Pourquoi ce sentiment? *Beau* est un mot qui en remplace un autre).
>
> Il s'agit d'éclaircir cela, d'y mettre de la lumière, de dégager les raisons (de mon émotion) et de la loi (de ce paysage), de faire *servir* ce paysage à quelque chose d'autre qu'un sanglot esthétique, de le faire devenir un outil moral, logique, de faire à son propos, faire un pas à l'esprit.
>
> Toute ma position philosophique et poétique est dans ce problème. (*Tome Premier* 404)

> . . . At the beginning, then, a sob, an emotion without an apparent cause (the feeling of *beauty* is not enough to explain it. Why this feeling? *Beauty* is a word that replaces another).
>
> The question is to clarify this, to put some light to it, to extract the reasons (of my emotion) and the law (of this landscape), to put this landscape to a *use* other than an aesthetic sob, to make it become a moral, logical tool, to have the mind take a step forward concerning it.
>
> My entire philosophical and poetic position is in this problem.

A couple of pages later, Ponge goes as far as dreaming of a science of visual impressions:

> Oui, je me veux moins poète que "savant." — Je désire moins aboutir à un poème qu'à une formule, qu'à un éclaircissement d'impressions. S'il est possible de fonder une science dont la matière serait les impressions esthétiques, je veux être l'homme de cette science. (*Tome Premier* 406)

> Yes, I want to be less a poet than a "scientist." — I wish to arrive less at a poem than at a formula, a clarification of impressions. If it is possible to found a science whose object is aesthetic impressions, I want to be the man of this science.

If we understand by science an area of knowledge and an accompanying set of tools for studying that area, Ponge has perhaps come close to it. The word "science" used in such a context merits comment however. If traditional science has neglected the study of the visual experience, it is perhaps because its very tools have blinded it from seeing visual impressions as phenomena to be investigated. In fact, Ponge's so-called "science of impressions" would be considered an oxymoron within the traditional scientific paradigm. Yet there is knowledge in the visual experience, but perhaps knowledge that entails different means. One of the bases of the scientific method is precisely the clear separation between the object of knowledge and the means of knowledge, the *what* and the *how*. The two are in fact not really so distinguishable since, as it has been demonstrated a number of times in the sciences *and* in the arts, an entire new world appears when the *how* changes. In other words, changing the instruments of perception and those of knowledge alters, sometimes radically, the *object* of knowledge and perception. In the arts, we only have to think of the introduction of perspective or, a few centuries later, of the introduction of new color techniques by the impressionists to realize how much the art world changed with these new instruments. And in the sciences, we know what new worlds were created by Newtonian physics or again three centuries later by quantum mechanics. The same could be said of Francis Ponge's work. It has often been called unique; never before have we had "a poetry of things." Could it be that Ponge took the side of *things* in poetry because his means of seeing and apprehending the world had changed, or, inversely, could it be that he had to construct, over almost his entire career, a new means of knowledge in order to take *things* into account in poetry? It is not so important to establish ascendancy between the *means* and the *object* of knowledge, because they are generated together, in a kind of recursive loop where the objects instruct the means that instruct the objects. This recursive loop is evident in a great number of Ponge's texts published after *Le Parti pris des choses*, when he made a conscious decision[5] to publish not only the finished product, but also the elaboration, the means of arriving at the final product. He does so not out of some exhibitionist impulse, but from a fundamental necessity: the elaboration of the text and of the means of knowing the object constitute the object.[6] The act of knowing is at the same time the result of that act. Ponge had said as much in a text written long before his decision to publish the genesis of his texts along with the result. In the significantly titled "De la modification des choses par la parole" ("Of the Modification of Things by the Word") that appears in *Proêmes* (1929), we find this argument, put once more in the context of visual perception:

> Le froid, tel qu'on le nomme après l'avoir reconnu à d'autres effets alentour, entre à l'onde, à quoi la glace se subroge.
> De même les yeux, d'un seul coup, s'accommodent à une nouvelle étendue: par un mouvement d'ensemble nommé attention, par quoi un nouvel objet est fixé, se prend.
> Cela est le résultat d'une attente, du calme: un résultat en même temps qu'un acte: en un mot une modification. (*Tome Premier* 139)

> Cold, as we name it after having recognized it because of other surrounding effects, enters the waters, to which ice is subrogated.
> Likewise, the eyes, all at once, accommodate to a new expanse: by a general movement called attention, with which a new object is fixed, is taken.
> This is the result of an expectation, of calmness: a result and at the same time an act: in a word, a modification.

"Modification" occurs when the act of knowing is confounded with its result. Francisco Varela, a biologist and cognitivist who, interestingly enough, has devoted a good part of his career to studying the biology of color perception, has coined a word for this kind of knowledge, where the product and the means of knowledge co-influence each other, where act and result "emerge" simultaneously. He calls it "enaction" (199-200, 234-35 *et passim*)[7] because, as in Ponge's case, the results of the cognitive process are the processes themselves, and therefore the observer does not *represent* the world but *enacts* it, through these very processes.

There are no words for what happens between a painting and the emotions it imparts upon us, between the visual apprehension and the constriction of the esophagus Ponge speaks of upon seeing Braque's painting. There are only metaphors, and among them are the texts themselves, not exactly in what they say but, since we are attempting to define a cognitive *process*, in the way they proceed. Indeed, Ponge's descriptions of things, oysters, oranges, meadows, or mud are also descriptions of his means of knowledge. They are like holograms from which we can retrieve a means of description and as such, they are descriptions of description as well as of things. The texts act, in other words, as cognitive operators (*cogitons? cogitemes?*) that give an indication of the cognitive process of the visual experience. We have seen so far that the visual experience imparts a knowledge other than its value as information, that it is inscribed on the body (embodied knowledge), and that it marshals a different means of knowledge which, among other things, does not distinguish between object and means (enacted knowledge). The remainder of this essay will attempt to isolate two more of its characteristics, its generative and distributive nature.

I have said that there is no word for what happens between the painting and the observer. I should have said that there is no common word, since Ponge does invent a neologism to name that experience. Among the very last books he published figures one bearing the enigmatic title of *Nioque de l'avant-printemps* ("*Nioque of Pre-Spring*"). "Nioque," he explains in the preface, is a twice-reworked neologism:

> NIOQUE est l'écriture phonétique (comme on pourrait dire *iniorant*) de GNOQUE, mot forgé par moi à partir de la racine grecque signifiant *connaissance,* et pour ne pas reprendre le GNOSSIENNE de Satie ni le CONNAISSANCE (de l'Est) de Claudel. (7)

> NIOQUE is the phonetic writing (as one could say *iniorant*) of
> GNOQUE, a word I made up from the Greek root meaning *knowl-
> edge*, and in order not to repeat Satie's GNOSIENNE or Claudel's
> CONNAISSANCE (de l'Est.)

Ponge did not coin the word out of simple wordplay or to exercise gratuitous poetic license. Transforming the word a second
time and giving it a phonetic spelling in order to "naturalize it,"
so to speak, grows undoubtedly out of a concern to facilitate its
entry into common parlance.[8] The writing of the text included
under that title dates from 1950 and was first published in two
parts in 1967 (under the title "L'avant-printemps") and in 1968
under the title "Nioque de l'avant-printemps."[9] Coming in 1983
at the end of his career, the little book with the now explicit title
and associated concept acts perhaps as a retrospective beacon
on his work as whole. Just as there is an "avant-printemps" before the declaration of Spring, for a long time there has been an
"avant-nioque," a "pre-nioque" doing its work silently in Ponge's
preceding books, before materializing and becoming explicit in
a word and title.

Only one other title with the same structure appears in
Ponge's works: *La Fabrique du pré*, for which we can immediately recognize two meanings, "the making of the meadow," the
fabrication by an agent of the meadow, and "the meadow's factory," the factory found in the meadow which, as it turns out,
manufactures the meadow. If we were to insist on the self-reference of the second meaning, we could translate that title with
"The Self-Fabrication of the Meadow" or "The Self-Creation of
the Meadow" — an expression Ponge himself uses in English in
La Fabrique du pré (26) — or even "The Self-Made Meadow." Similarly, we can understand "Nioque de l'avant printemps" as that
yet undefined way of knowing ("nioque") the pre-Spring by an
agent as well as the knowledge found in the pre-Spring — its own
knowledge, its self-knowledge. Both titles indicate at one and
the same time an agent of the making or of the knowing *and* a
state of affairs without an outside agent, where the object contains its own agent: the meadow makes itself (self-making) and
the pre-Spring acquires knowledge about itself (self-knowing).
If the Spring or the meadow were persons, we could have easily
said that their knowing or their making was enacted. Here, too,
there is a lack of distinction between the agent and the object
and between the process and the object.

Two other elements bring those texts together. "La fabrique du pré," Ponge explains, is also the making of the prefix "pré-" as a sign and as a logical category found in the words "préfixe," "préparer," and "présent" or in the word, we might add, we have adopted in English for "l'avant-printemps," "the pre-Spring":

> Le pré gisant ici comme participe passé par excellence
> S'y révère aussi bien comme notre préfixe des préfixes
> Préfixe déjà dans préfixe, présent déjà dans présent (*Fabrique* 191)

> The *pré*, here lying as the preeminent French past participle
> Revered also as our prefix of prefixes,
> Prefix, already, in prefix, present indeed in present. (*Making* 227)

The other element is that both texts contain their own genesis. They contain various drafts, tentatives, notes, lexical and etymological studies and, most importantly, reflections on the apprehension of the objects and on the writing of the object. In other words, both texts are largely constituted of their "avant-texte" or pre-text, the material necessary to generate a text, which is sometimes ultimately written and published, such as "Le Pré." At one point in his elaboration, Ponge considers giving as a title for his text "La Gnature du pré." "Gnature," he explains, is yet another neologism made out of the Latin "ginere" —"pour mieux souligner le caractère naissant — ou renaissant — du pré" 'to emphasize better the nascent — or renascent — character of the meadow' (*Fabrique* 237):

> La Nature, selon l'étymologie de Littré, est, comme je le pensais, du même radical que naître, naissance: le sanscrit *jan*, qui a donné *na* (pour *gna*; 23 juin 1964: je pourrais donc titrer mon texte: "*De la gnature des prés*," latin *ginere*, grec . . . avec le suffixe *turus, tri, tor* qui fait des noms d'agents; *natura* signifie donc l'engendrante, la force qui engendre). (*Fabrique* 236-37)

> *Nature*, according to the etymology of Littré, is, as I thought, from the same radical as *naître* "to be born," *naissance* "birth": the Sanskrit *jan*, which gave *na* (for *gna*— "23 June 1964: so I could title my text: 'Of the gnature of the *prés*'"—Latin *gignere*, Greek . . .), with the suffix *turus, tri, tor* that denotes agency; *natura*, then, signifies the engenderer, the force that engenders. (*Making* 121)

Ten pages later he actually uses the word in a tentative title for
one of his drafts for what will become "Le Pré": *Petite prose de la
gnature des prés (Fabrique* 247.) The resemblance of "gnature" and
"GNOQUE," the non-phonetic spelling of "nioque," is indeed
striking. The Littré also tells us that while the *na* of "nature"
goes back to the Sanskrit *jan*, meaning to engender and generate, the *gna* of "gnoses" and many other words of the same family (including, in English, *cognition* and *knowledge*) goes back,
instead, to *jna*. Thus, in spite of the often made association between "naissance" and "co-naissance," (and Ponge, along with
Claudel, is among those who have made it) it is clear that they
do not share the same etymology. Ponge, however, is certainly
suggesting that in the kind of knowledge he calls "nioque" there
is something of genesis and engendering. Looking again at the
two titles, we notice that the meaning of the *gen* root of genesis
and generation is repeated throughout them. "Nioque de l'avant-
printemps" could be read as "Knowledge (yet to be defined) of
pre- (what precedes and generates) Spring" and "La Fabrique
du pré" could be translated as "the genesis of the meadow" or,
if "pré" is taken as a prefix, as what precedes and engenders, as
"the genesis of genesis," "le pré du pré," "the pre- of pre-," or
again, in Ponge's own words, the *pré* is:

> Le lieu aussi de la résurrection de la vie universelle sous sa forme
> la plus élémentaire, le lieu de la renaissance de l'avenir, lieu préparé
> pour cela. Donc préfixe à tout, préfixe à tous les verbes, à toutes les
> actions, à toutes les propices résurrections. A la fois participe passé
> (paratus, paratum) et préfixe des préfixes, préfixe universel. Il
> fleurit. Il florit. (*Fabrique* 234-35)

> Also the place of the resurrection of universal life in the most el-
> ementary form, the place of the future's renascence, the place pre-
> pared for that. Hence prefix to everything, prefix to all the verbs,
> to all the actions, to all the propitious resurrections. At the same
> time past participle (*paratus, paratum*) and prefix of prefixes, uni-
> versal prefix. It flowers. It flourishes. (*Making* 115)

But isn't writing and knowing another pre-, another genesis
of the genesis of the meadow generating itself? If the meadow
fabricates itself, it is important not to forget that there is also an
agent fabricating the meadow fabricating itself. We touch here

at another self-reference, this one between the text and the poet. If the meadow, by its very nature, makes itself, the poet, by making the meadow that is making itself, is also making, forming, himself:

> [. . .] L'amour des mots est le
> chemin à la création littéraire, poétique
> c.a.d aussi bien, le chemin à la self-création. (*Fabrique* 17)

> [. . .] The love of words is the road to literary, poetic creation, that is, the road as well to self-creation.

or:

> Il ne fait, pour mon expérience, aucun doute que l'amour des mots . . . soit le chemin à la création (je veux dire par l'expression . . . l'autocréation de l'individu lui-même dans sa ressemblance et sa différence à ceux qu'on appelle ses semblables). (*Fabrique* 18)

> There is no doubt, in my experience, that the love of words . . . is the road to creation (I mean by that . . . the self-creation of the individual in his resemblance to and his difference from those we call his fellow men).

The same could be said of knowledge: if the poet is in the process of knowing the Spring knowing itself, he is also acquiring knowledge about himself.

La Fabrique du pré (the text by that name) will therefore have to take into account its own self-reflexive position as well. What could it be if not a preparation for the preparation of the writing of "Le pré?":

> En somme je me livre ici à la préparation de la préparation du pré ou encore à la préparation de la parution en préoriginale du pré. Parant au plus urgent, allant au plus pressé, je présenterai ici une première petite prose de la gnature des prés, écrite en préparation de la parution en préoriginale du pré. (260)

> In short, here I give myself over to the preparation of the preparation of the *pré* or else to the preparation of the preoriginal publication of the *pré*. Pre-paring for the most urgent, tending to the most pressing, I will present here a first little prose on the gnature of the *prés*, written in preparation for the preoriginal publication of the *pré*. (*Making* 187, with slight changes)

There is for Ponge an avant-pré as there is an avant-printemps. One helps us understand the other. It is perhaps clearer why a different kind of knowledge is necessary for the object "pre-Spring." To know what precedes Spring, to know what comes before Spring is acknowledged, before it is fixed — while it is still "*pre*-fixed" — in our minds and outside, to know, in other words, what happens before the knowledge of Spring is actualized, Ponge has to make up tools not of knowledge, but of pre-knowledge. He has to construct a pre-gnosis which would allow him to know, to "nioque" rather, the *pre* of knowledge, its genesis, as well as the genesis of Spring. When Spring arrives, we are in the world of knowledge-as-information, the equivalent of the description of Braque's painting (a black band, a stove pipe, etc.), but before it is here, we are still in the world of "nioque," an embodied pre-gnosis but a gnosis nevertheless which, in the case of the painting, constricts the esophagus and the pharynx and which, in *Nioque,* has a different effect: "mucosités," "catarrhes," and a migraine, dissipated by an aspirin just as the sun "a joué les comprimés d'aspirines pour le ciel, pour la nature" 'just as the sun played the role of an aspirin for the sky, for nature' (17-18). The writing of *Nioque* is itself a pre-writing, an approximate text of tentative descriptions, always necessarily imperfect, unfinished and unaccomplished as though writing (and knowing) perfectly a text about the pre-Spring is incompatible with the subject. A fully accomplished text would be coherent only with a fully declared (and acknowledged) phenomenon such as Spring. Ponge is aware of this imperfection of his text:

> (Ceci est très imparfait, à reprendre.)
> Je ne suis traversé, n'ai *d'idées* qu'incomplètes (incomplètement formulées) et ne tiens pas tellement à elles, que je m'efforce de les compléter. (35)

> (This is quite imperfect, to be reworked.)
> I am traversed, have only incomplete *ideas* (incompletely formulated), and I do not care much for them, that I make every effort to complete.

For an incompletely declared Spring there are only incomplete ideas and incomplete formulations. Should the temperature go up slightly ("Noter qu'il ne manque que quelques degrés de chaleur" 'Note that only a few degrees of heat are missing' [20]), Spring is declared and acknowledged and writing could be complete:

> La perfection peut brusquement venir à de tels objets — imprévisiblement — par l'insertion, le surgissement tout à coup d'une qualité supplémentaire, inouïe, nouvelle, qui s'induit tout à coup dans cette page, cette trame de maladresses (prudentes) et l'illumine, lui confère la vie. Alors l'eau vient de tous les côtés. Cela commence à vivre, à battre (comme quand l'amibe se désenkyste), à palpiter. (41)

> Perfection could come to such objects — unexpectedly — with the insertion, the sudden appearance of yet another quality, unheard of, new, that induces itself suddenly in this page, this texture of (prudent) clumsiness and illuminates it, gives it life. Water comes then from all sides. Things start to live, to beat (like when the amoeba desencysts itself), to palpitate.

It is clear that Ponge is talking here about both his writing and the weather. Should the completion of the Spring's arrival occur, "nioque," the process of knowledge of pre-Spring, would dissipate. Strictly speaking, Ponge does not first see the incompleteness of Spring's arrival and then write an incomplete text. Rather, the incompleteness of Spring produces an incomplete text, which in turn conceives, informs an incomplete Spring. The text again is not a representation of the object but its "enaction." There is a very explicit example of this enaction in "L'Oeillet," contained in *La Rage de l'expression*. Talking about its root, Ponge writes:

> C'est quelque chose qui ressemble fort à la phrase par laquelle j'essaie "actuellement" de l'exprimer, quelque chose qui se déroule moins qu'elle ne s'arrache, qui tient au sol par mille radicules adventices — et dont il est probable qu'elle cassera net (sous mon effort) avant que j'aie pu en extraire le principe. (*Tome Premier* 303)

> It is something that resembles very much the sentence with which I am "actually" trying to express it, something that unfolds less than it is uprooted, that holds on to the ground with thousands of self-propagating radicules — and that will probably break suddenly (with my effort) before I could extract its principle.

I started this essay by saying that the other kind of knowledge afforded by pictures (we now have a name for it) was unsayable. It is clear now that saying it would be precisely *not saying it*, since to say "nioque" is to move it to the realm of declared phenomenon, of acknowledgement, of complete writing, of knowledge-as-information. "Nioque," in other words, can only take place in time, the time of the *pré*, of the pre-, of the pre-perfect and pre-complete, the time of engendering and making (Ponge calls his meadow "un chapitre du *Temps Retrouvé*" 'a chapter from *Time Regained*' [243]). Once that time elapses, once Spring arrives or the meadow is complete, we leave time and enter space, the space of an intelligible picture, of a meadow or of Spring, and with it the space of definitions, of difference, and of naming.

In that flow — and because it is a flow, a movement — knowledge cannot be precisely localized, localization being a function of static space. Which brings us to the last characteristic of "nioque" that will help us understand why "nioque" is unsayable. After a long and surprisingly correct explanation of the latest scientific theories of his time concerning the gaseous, liquid, and solid states, Ponge makes in *La Seine* (1947) an analogy that is at once striking and bizarre concerning the relationship of language, thought, and objects. He explains that solids and liquids are different from gases in the distance between molecules. That distance is very small in solids, slightly larger in liquids, but not as large as in gases. Liquids, in other words, are almost solids. Density and the state of matter are almost the same in liquids and solids. It is important to understand that the distance between molecules is a statistical average: in the constant movement of molecules, some are close together in gases, but on the average they are few and sparsely distributed, while in liquids and solids they are much more numerous and can, therefore, form clusters that allow us to recognize them as solids or liquids. Ponge is very much aware of the different distribution of compact and loose molecules and says as much: "Dans un liquide, le nombre des proches voisins est aussi bien déterminé, mais en moyenne seulement, car ces voisins sont mobiles par rapport à la molecule centrale" 'In a liquid, the number of close neighbors is also well determined, but on the average only, because these neighbors are mobile in relation to the central molecule' (*Tome Premier* 536).

Pondering the phenomenon that certain thoughts are easily expressed while others are not, Ponge advances that the state of inexpressible thoughts is very much like the state of a gas that is clearly above its critical temperature: "un état *de la pensée* à la fois trop agitée, trop distendue, trop ambitieuse et trop isotrope" 'a state *of thought* at the same time too agitated, too distended, too ambitious and too isotropic' (*Tome Premier* 537). A gas in that state cannot be converted to liquid spontaneously. To bring it back below its critical point, there must be a lowering of the temperature and an increase in the pressure. At that point, according to Ponge, language appears. At a certain point a surface of separation appears where thought (gas) and liquid (writing, the text) co-exist and where the text has characteristics very close to the object, where "l'*écrit* présente des caractères qui le rendent *très proche de la chose signifiée*, c'est-à-dire des objets du monde extérieur, tout comme le liquide est très proche du solide" 'the *written* presents characteristics that make it *very close to the thing signified*, in other words, to the objects of the world, just as liquid is close to solid' (538).

One of the signs of the arrival of Spring, as we have seen, is the flow of water: "Alors l'eau vient de tous les côtés. Cela commence à vivre, à battre (comme quand l'amibe se désenkyse), à palpiter" 'Water comes then from all sides. Things start to live, to beat (like when the amoeba desencysts itself), to palpitate' (*Nioque* 41). The "avant-printemps" for Ponge is therefore the time when water has not yet appeared, when we say "Spring is in the air," when we cannot yet perceive any signs of its arrival, such as the flow of water and a higher temperature, but where it is generally felt in our bodies. By "generally" I mean there are no precisely localizable, concrete or compact signs of Spring, only sparsely distributed "infrasignifications" — to use Ponge's word (*Fabrique* 263) — which, taken all together, physically affect us. The process of knowledge called "nioque" is also the distributed apprehension of what is, itself, distributed. Its result is a text, also called "nioque." Like "proêmes," "sapates" and "randons," Ponge has either deviated words from their original meaning or coined words to avoid the word "poem" and to name appropriately his production:

Je *RELIS* (et titre) *LE PAYSAGE D'AVANT-PRINTEMPS* et j'écris ce qui suit, comme préface-réflexion:

"Je ne puis rien dire, écrire (ni penser) d'autre que ce que la saison m'inspire."

(Ces jours-ci: *paysages, nioques, proêmes, notes de l'avant-printemps*). (*Nioque* 18-20)

I reread (and give it as title) *THE LANDSCAPE OF PRE-SPRING* and I write the following, as preface-reflection:

"I cannot say, write (or think) anything but the season that inspires me."

(These days: *landscapes, nioques, proems, notes of pre-Spring*).

What he can write, inspired by the season, can only be tentative: notes, *proêmes* (which are, among other meanings, "pre-poems") concerning landscapes. The word "nioque," to designate the text he is writing, includes the meanings of all the other words in the series, and adds to them distributed knowledge. The little book, *Nioque*, is indeed parsed with infrasignifications. To show or quote one or two of them in support of my argument is useless: I would be transforming them into significations and as significations they mean, by themselves, nothing; taken separately, they cannot verify my contention. It is only in their statistical cumulation, their assembly and connectedness, actualized by the entire text, that a verification could occur. Short of that, we can still quote Ponge in *Nioque* when he takes a step back and comments on his actualization. The comment could be considered an infrasignification when connected or compacted with the rest of the text. The quote has the further merit of supporting my own contention that quoting a fragment is meaningless:

Cette infirmité reconnue de mes pensées est une des raisons de mon parti pris (des choses). Car, me proposant un objet défini, existant, durant en dehors de ma conscience, je puis bien souffrir de n'en recevoir, chaque fois que je m'y applique, qu'une idée incomplète, une brève lueur, puisque *lui* en effet, lui cependant, dure et persiste (à la différence d'un état d'âme, d'un sentiment, d'une passion), et que les idées incomplètes qui me viendront par la suite, se rapportant toujours à *lui*, seront de nouveau partiellement valables et qu'enfin la somme, l'addition de ces lueurs ou touches incomplètes pourra donner une approximation suffisamment volumineuse (solide) du dit objet, pourra enfin s'y *vérifier*. (*Nioque* 37-38)

This recognized infirmity of my thoughts is one of the reasons for my taking a side (of things). Because, considering a definite object, existing, lasting outside my conscience, I can well tolerate receiving from it, every time I apply myself to it, only an incomplete idea, a brief glimmer, since *it* in effect, it however, lasts and persists (unlike a state of mind, a feeling or a passion), and since the incomplete ideas that will come to me afterwards, having always to do with *it,* will be again partially valid and since, finally, the sum, the addition of these incomplete glimmers or touches will be able to give a sufficiently voluminous (solid) approximation of the said object, will be able, lastly, to *verify* itself in it.

From the visual experience of the object to a text that attempts to render the object there are partial impressions, incomplete ideas, "lueurs" 'glimmers' and "touches" 'touches' that are widely distributed, like molecules in the gaseous state. When these infrasignifications are added, connected, and compacted, they will give an approximation of the object as a solid.[10]

In Ponge's description of Braque's painting quoted at the beginning of the essay there is a small indication (a "glimmer?" a "touch?") of the distributed infrasignifications: the painting had "plusieurs touches de couleurs vives, dont les rouges" 'several touches of bright colors, including some reds' (300). His physical reaction upon seeing the painting seems to come from these little "touches," taken at their pre-significative stage, at the stage when their compactedness is not yet actualized, when from being meaningless they are becoming meaningful, when from pre-verbal they are becoming verbal. Ponge has quite obviously deeply felt this becoming. His strong emotion, afforded by the visual experience, is due to a very brief and quite rare moment of apprehension of the pure flow of time.

Pre-Spring and Spring 1995

Notes

[1] I have here, of course, a *parti pris* in one of the oldest debates on knowledge. On the one hand, there are those who maintain there is knowledge (and reality) only when that knowledge is expressed; on the other hand are those who postulate knowledge (and reality) outside of language. Semiotics is the latest movement based on the former position. Ponge, in spite of the numerous semiotic analyses made of his work in the 1970s, is of the latter persuasion. In my defense, I will only invoke the distinction Gregory Bateson makes between map and territory. It seems to me that semiotics, with its *parti pris* that a painting is a signi-

fying system, confuses the map with the territory. As a signifying system, a picture does "speak" a thousand words, and the semiotician's job is to translate the picture's native speech into words. But "to speak" here is metaphorical. A picture says strictly nothing; it is the semiotician who makes it speak, who draws a signifying map of the territory that is the picture. My *parti pris* is that after or alongside all the words a picture "speaks" (the knowledge-as-information), there is still a communication which is unsayable.

[2] All translations are mine, unless, as this one, otherwise noted.

[3] We need not here go into the commonly accepted fact that emotions are physically expressed. Let us just remember that this expression is the very basis of lie-detector tests.

[4] The bibliography on the cognitive value of emotions is increasingly large. Suffice it to refer to a recent book by the neuroscientist Antonio R. Damasio, who gives several good experimental arguments to that effect, and to quote the American philosopher Nelson Goodman:

> Emotions and feelings are, I agree, required for aesthetic experience; but they are not separable from or in addition to the cognitive aspect of the experience. They are among the primary means of making the discriminations and the connections that enter into the understanding of art. Emotions and feelings, I must repeat once more, function cognitively in aesthetic and in much other experience. We do not discern stylistic affinities and differences, for example, by "rational analysis," but by sensations, perceptions, feelings, emotions, sharpened in practice like the eye of the gemologist or the fingers of an inspector of machine parts. Far from wanting to desensitize aesthetic experience, I want to sensitize experience. In art—and I think in science too—emotion and cognition are interdependent: feeling without understanding is blind, and understanding without feeling is empty. (8)

[5] In an unsent letter to Jean Paulhan, Ponge goes as far as claiming a new genre for that kind of writing which includes the genesis of his text: "Je ne crois pas vraiment que ce soient des brouillons. Mais le poème en prose ne me suffit plus, et comme Joyce ou Proust je cherche ma forme" 'I really don't think they are drafts. But the prose poem doesn't suffice me any longer, and like Joyce or Proust I am looking for my form' (Paulhan and Ponge 302).

[6] For a more ample discussion of this phenomenon in Ponge see Lévy.

[7] "Un système possédant une clôture opérationelle est précisément un système dont les résultats des processus sont ces processus eux-mêmes. ... Le point crucial est que ces systèmes n'opèrent pas par représentation: au lieu de *représenter* un monde indépendant, ils *enactent* un monde comme domaine de distinction inséparable des structures incarnées dans le système cognitif" 'A system possesing an operational closure is precisely a system where the results of the processes are the processes themselves. ... The crucial point is that these systems do not operate as representation: rather than *representing* an independent world, they *enact* a world as a domain of distinction, inseparable from the embodied structures in the cognitive system' (Varela 199-200).

[8] The word "nioque" has begun that entry. There is a literary magazine by that name published in Aix-en-Provence by Jean-Marie Gleize, himself a poet and Ponge scholar.

[9] In *L'Ephémère* 2 (1967): 49-59 and in *Tel Quel* 33 (1968): 3-17.

[10] Curiously, David Ruelle, a physicist, has made the same analogy as Ponge concerning paintings:

> Given a snapshot of the configuration of atoms of helium at 20 degrees C, you should be able to distinguish it from a snapshot corresponding to another temperature or another substance, in the same way as you distinguish a Van Gogh from a Gauguin at a glance. The "cluster of probabilistic features" changes with temperature, and the change is usually gradual. In the same way, the style of a painter might gradually change as the artist gets older. And then the unexpected occurs. At a certain temperature, instead of gradual change you have a sudden jump—from gas helium to liquid helium, or from water to water vapor or to ice. (123)

Works Cited

Bateson, Gregory. *Steps to an Ecology of Mind*. New York: Ballantine, 1972.

Damasio, Antonio R. *Descartes' Error: Emotion, Reason, and the Brain*. New York: Putnam, 1994.

Goodman, Nelson. *Of Mind and Other Matters*. Cambridge: Harvard UP, 1984.

Lévy, Sydney. "De l'Infini à l'abîme . . . à pas de tortue." *Théorie, Littérature, Enseignement* 12 (1994).

Paulhan, Jean and Francis Ponge. *Correspondance.* Vol. 1. Ed. Claire Boaretto. Paris: Gallimard, 1986.

Ponge, Francis. *L'Atelier contemporain.* Paris: Gallimard, 1977.

______. "Braque, or the Meditation of the Work." Francis Ponge, Pierre Descargues and André Malraux, *G. Braque.* Trans. Richard Howard. New York: Harry N. Abrams, 1971.

______. *La Fabrique du pré.* Geneva: Skira, 1990 [1st ed. 1971].

______. *The Making of the Pré.* Trans. Lee Fahnestock. Columbia, MO: U of Missouri P, 1979.

______. *Lyres.* Paris: Gallimard, 1961.

______. *Nouveau Receuil.* Paris: Gallimard, 1967.

______. *Pratiques d'écriture ou l'inachèvement perpétuel avec des dessins de François Rouau.* Paris: Hermann, 1984.

______. *Nioque de l'avant-printemps.* Paris: Gallimard, 1983.

______. *Tome Premier.* Paris: Gallimard, 1965.

Ruelle, David. *Chance and Chaos.* Princeton: Princeton UP, 1991.

Stevenson, R. L. *Dr Jekyll and Mr. Hyde.* New York: Bantam, 1981 [1st ed. 1886].

Varela, Francisco, Evan Thompson and Eleanor Rosch. *L'Inscription corporelle de l'esprit; Sciences cognitives et expérience humaine.* Paris: Seuil, 1993.

Narration and Visual Thought: Philippe Clerc's *Revues-Images*

Anne-Marie Christin

Used to examine mixed-media creations produced in abundance since the end of the nineteenth century, the formula "text and image" is ambiguous, particularly in that its application to the whole of historical production potentially belonging to this category has increased in scope. In effect, this formula makes a pretense of considering as unfounded or unresolved the competition between the two arts; such was the reading current in the fifteenth-eighteenth centuries of the phrase borrowed from Horace, "Ut pictura poesis," which had led to the establishment of an excessively detailed hierarchization of the two arts favoring sometimes the one, sometimes the other, depending on the time period (Lee). With Manet in the mid-nineteenth century, the emergence of a conception of painting that privileges its medium over its subject—in 1890, Maurice Denis said of paintings that they are "above all a flat surface covered with colors, assembled in a particular order"—by making the material substrate appear as a sort of neutral ground where painting and literature are present in equal measure, must undoubtedly have encouraged the arts of the image and the written to be presented as parallel modes of production.

But an argument based on material concerns is not an argument, and that is all the more true in this case. Indeed, the choice of material substrate does more than valorize an element common to text and image: this choice means also that the information contained in the image is privileged over that of the text because it eliminates from the very start all expressive specificity linked to orality without excluding, however, the possibility that it might subsequently be reestablished in some indirect or analogical manner. And such is the real interest in a choice of this type, and what constitutes its novelty as well. But, curiously enough, it is rather from the opposite perspective that the formula "text and image" needs to be generally understood. In a more or less ostensible and explicit fashion, we resort to verbal values, or the theories that are derived thereof (linguistic, semiotic, psychoanalytic). The contradiction is obvious, but we don't recognize it: a civilization of words (or, more precisely, of *discourse*) is not capable of theorizing visual thought, even though an autonomy of the image powerful enough to modify, even dominate, verbal arts requires us to assume its existence. The scepticism arising from such manner of thought is sustained by the conviction that visual thinking is not capable of producing concepts, in that its motivation supposedly depends on affective intuition alone. Since the invention of astronomy and geometry, the history of science has proved sufficiently just how erroneous this assumption is. But the problem lies not so much in the capacity for invention that visual thought might have as in the principles upon which it rests. If we define this type of thinking as a creative capability based on sight, we rightly have to admit that, on the one hand, such thought doesn't have to be verbalized and that it is fully expressed through the subject's mental receptivity, and on the other, that this receptivity operates in a field (the postulate of which constitutes, moreover, its first act of abstraction) that is itself quite distinct, that of a surface conceived as continuous, a screen arbitrarily removed from heterogenous reality, an *appearance* wherein figures perceived do not refer to external objects but maintain with respect to each other relations of signs forming a system among themselves. Now, in speech-based civilizations, the definition of the subject can only be supported by the verbal activity of the speaker, and appearance can never be more than the strict surface, always judged to be more or less deceptive, of the objects designated or named by this subject.

It is at moments in its history when painting undertook most forcefully to be an art of appearance that theory in the Western world articulated most clearly its refusal to take into account this visual thinking or to speculate on it. When the invention of single-point perspective offered humanity an intellectually homogeneous space for the first time, a space utilizable in all its dimensions and where the painted surface could finally appear as the sensitized plate of the imaginary, Alberti remained prisoner, in his treatise *De pictura*, to fragmentary conception of the image whose model resides as much in discursive articulations as it does in the principle of identifying discrete objects that had dominated analysis of perception since antiquity. His definition of painting as a "open window through which I see what I want to paint" (Alberti 56) implies the preliminary delimitation of an (en)closure, the *a priori* inscription of a sort of *topical object* in the continuity of a surface considered otherwise as transparent, that is, non-existent. "What else can you call painting but a similar embracing with art of what is presented on the surface of the water in the fountain," said Alberti, interpreting the Narcissus myth in his own fashion (64). But, according to Alberti, painting within the "window" consists of "cirsumscribing surfaces" mentally cut out from objects as if it had been a matter of so many mosaic pieces, of "arranging" them, putting them in their "assigned positions," so that the image of bodies similar to sculpture can emerge. The interspaces appearing between these figures, which he calls their "solitude," can only be justified by the "story" [*istoria*]: since ancient poets had taken care to write their fables "with as few characters as possible" in view of making these fables readily understandable and to confer on them greater "dignity," the modern painter must follow suit (76). Three centuries later, Lessing sought to put an end to bombastic or anecdotal compositions, a rather literary interpretation of which had in the end become its pretext; when he undertook to define *the boundaries between painting and poetry* in the *Laocoön* and to oppose the art of space to the art of time, contrary to what one might have expected he was not any more able to defend the specificity of pictorial space (Lessing). In that his reasoning, as was Alberti's, was founded on the discontinuous conception of the forms of perception and of language—the former being simultaneous and the others sequential—he simply substitutes for the conclusions of *De pictura*, namely that "the greatest work of the painter is not a colossus but an *istoria*" (Alberti 72), his own conclusion: the "colossus" must alone constitute the whole painting. What would be the interest in keeping interspaces on the canvas if there is no longer any narration to translate? Ideal art could be no other than that represented in sculpture, closed and opaque, considering extraneous to itself any problem of spatial setting. And it is certainly no coincidence that the title of Lessing's book is borrowed from the statuary of classical antiquity.

It would be pointless to oppose these texts to all the paintings, from Botticelli's *Springtime* or Giorgione's *Tempest* to the melancholy *piazze* by De Chirico, in which European painters, having been able to reveal in the interspace a suggestive force that could make its inscription in the rational light of perspectival space all the more disquieting, have assigned a preponderant role to this apparently neutral and useless component. One might add that landscape painting was born in the empty spaces between figures. For Jean Dubuffet, the very origin of painting itself is located in the interspace. He expounds upon this idea in *Bâtons rompus*, showing also, through questions he attributes to a fictive interlocutor, just how foreign this idea is to our usual way of thinking:

> R: It is not the objects whose figuration seems to me to be fertile, but it is what lies between the objects, what cultural conditioning prompts us to regard as empty space. It seems to me that it is precisely these spaces that need to be filled. The continuum of things has been cut up by culture into twenty thousand notions, an inventory of which would correspond to twenty thousand words in the dictionary.... It's the painter's mission to displace this navigation signal system so as to reinstitute the continuum, and in surveying it from above, introduce constantly changing indices or *points d'appui*, which create for the mind all sorts of new trajectories.
>
> Q.: I don't grasp the form in which the painter will be able to fill the empty spaces separating the objects.
>
> R.: You don't understand it because you are not freed from the conditioning dictated by vocabulary and cannot conceive of the possibility that there might be more than nothingness in the space where it hasn't put any name. Now, sight doesn't have interspaces, nor does thought, which fills everything with its projections. It is these projections that are interesting to concretize, and which the work of art should represent. (Dubuffet 26-27)

It is neither the outlines that matter especially in painting nor these sorts of visual names that they enable us to give to things, but the space in which they appear. Civilizations in which words do not play the foundational role that they have come to have in our culture have made painting their primary artform precisely insofar as art born of appearance made it possible to explain the positive values of empty space better than any other art, and much more persuasively than verbal language. "The delight of plenary space is only revealed by empty space," wrote the Chinese painter Chiang Ho. "Three-tenths of the painting's quality resides in the appropriate disposition of the Sky and the Earth, and seven-tenths in the discontinuous presence of mist and vapors" (Cheng 122; also Jullien, *Procès*; Jullien, *Propension*).

Emptiness is the presence of the invisible, but even more, it is the space of investigation. Consequently, it does not give rise to signs of the same nature as linguistic signs. And it is at this point not only that the arts of language and images meet but also that the spatial domination of the latter, in formulae presenting them both equally, derives its meaning, for writing is the product of the image. To state it even more precisely, writing grows out of the interspaces where the spectator's thought is formed, like that of the diviner seeking to understand the messages that the gods would send to humans by examining the sky or the surface of tortoise shells—in short, a *reader's* thought.

Thus we may explain how the *ideogram* may not be an unambiguous sign, nor even only univocal; the ideogram appeared when the system of divination seemed able to adapt to the principles of human language, in Mesopotamia, Egypt, and China, the three civilizations in which it was invented at about the same time, and perhaps simultaneously. A representation of verbal meaning, the ideogram is still in effect virtually also one of its homophonic properties—a *phonogram*—or even its own signifier, but a silent one—a *determinative*, a *key* in Chinese. There is no paradox, no mystery in these potential variants. The medium is at once their originating point and their support, having provided a system based on a visual model (that is, one whose properties remain fundamentally undecidable) but giving all the indicators that might make these properties distinguishable: a calibration enabling the separation of the sign from its realist references and encouraging the association of the sign (in order to make it complete and to shed light on it) with neighboring signs and the underlying material whose substance and form should orient reading towards a particular semantic field — a stone with a sacral function, in the case of hieroglyphs; Mesopotamian clay tablets, rectangular in shape for texts on household expenses, round for a literary text. . . .

The speaking subject is not at all absent in ideogram-based writing. But he shows up in the past, having had to put his mark within a space instead of having constructed a discourse, such that one might see with one's eyes exactly what he meant to say. Thus we get this "telegram" form that all the specialists have noted in the first written texts: sequences retaining from the spoken utterance only selected words essential for meaning, and leaving it to the reader to reconstitute a sentence from what has been read. The reader is not really master of the meaning but only of a form; but as inspired interpreter, the reader is its creator.[1]

Peirce is, to my knowledge, the only theoretician who has given the ideogram a sufficiently accurate definition, speaking of it as a "non-logical icon" (Peirce, *Ecrits* 150).[2] But this definition remains unsatisfactory. Indeed, it does not reveal anything about the imperative determining the sign's visual motivation, in that Peirce seems to consider that any perceptual effect emanates necessarily from a single "dynamoid" source, which is global and homogeneous. On the other hand, if the semiotician classifies this sign among icons, it is because he sees in it a meaningful "image." Now, this definition is false on two counts: firstly, insofar as it is partial, and owing to its verbal value, the ideogram as such depends on the "legisign" as much as on the "qualisign"; secondly, because the ideogram, wherever it has appeared, has never been conceived as that sign "with a well determined identity" constituted in principle by the "legisign." Its originality comes, rather, from its being a *floating* sign, or, to be more precise, an *alternate* sign. Such is the dynamism of the icon-ideogram, and Peirce must have been delighted to see that the innovative force with which he had endowed the first level of his system, by purely logical calculation, was confirmed in the least debatable manner, since it did not result from the material properties of the object but from the reader-subject's initiative. But in Peirce's system, the sign does not float.

The reason for this misapprehension stems from the fact that Peirce, like all theoreticians of the sign, belongs to a civilization of the alphabet. Adhering to the word as if it only projected the phonetic divisions directly before the eyes, this type of writing has comforted us in the idea that its material substrate was only an accessory fact, without repercussions for the elaboration of meaning. Besides, is the alphabetical system not the latest form of writing invented, which would undoubtedly mean that it is the most perfect of all writing forms? But what is their purpose? It will have taken two thousand years for the Western world to admit that hieroglyphs were also phonetic signs; the Egyptians' indifference toward their alphabet of consonants still seems more or less suspect or shocking to Westerners. Our Asian neighbors are also astounded, unable to comprehend on their side what our stakes are in this question: isn't the ideogram better adapted to the volatile juggling tricks of the computer screen than this pitiful letter by letter accounting, this pretense of toting up meanings, that constitutes the alphabet?

We must recognize this fact: at the origin of the written is the surface on which it is inscribed through the empty spaces legitimized by the surface, but which also attest to this mysterious evidence of the *continuous*, which enables it to be interrupted without, however, being broken up into pieces. From this point of view, whether writing is ideographic or alphabetical is of no consequence: the alphabet, to be *readable*, must effectively reconquer by other indirect means — spelling, typography — those elements of the functional indecidability, provided by its visual substrate, that its phoneticization caused it to lose. Whatever the system might be, in writing it is the *medium which is the sign*, to borrow MacLuhan's formula, but to a quite different effect.

It is impossible, however, to stop here. The particular telegraphic form that the verbal message has taken when it is written is the reflection of the ideogram as much as it is its product. Along with its conclusive linearity, this message has lost its voice. But can we say that it has been betrayed? In modeling its principles on those of the image, could we not say that writing, empowered by the laws of appearance, has created in discourse a mutation just as rich as that known to the verbal sign? Lessing was right: narration is foreign to the image, as it is not essential to its semantic specificity. And writing confirms this for us: myth and epic were not present in ancient Chinese civilization at the time that ideograms were invented. Narration is exclusively a matter of orality and speech [*langue*]. But—and in this Lessing was wrong—it will not be by eliminating or neglecting its empty places and interspaces that we will restore to the image its true function and creative power. It will be, rather, by taking them into account above all else. Thus, the first hypothesis to which the appearance of writing at the intersection of word and image leads us—*the medium is the sign*—must be complemented by a second, which is its corollary: *the sign is the message.*

Only those limit cases of the image in which the image chooses to approach closely the written, in the name of its specific difference, and to give it more prominence, can allow us to verify this double hypothesis. For this purpose, I will take as my example *Riga*, the first of the "revues-images" produced by Philippe Clerc by xerography, and which was an offshoot of his "polygrams." This example should be significant, as I have shown elsewhere (Christin, *L'Image*), insofar as the "polygrams" produced by the artist during the 1980s transpose, on the level of individual creation and without premeditation (the term "polygram" was invented after the fact), the original principles of writing: heterogeneity of iconic sources; creation conceived as a reading and not as an act of affirmation; staging of images on the printed page, grouped in scenettes, where their association with white or black modules invites us to consider them as signs linked together by some sort of syntax—a purely fictive rationality that makes the sequential logic of these images as enigmatic as the images themselves are. Such an unusual enterprise can be explained by the nature of the technique chosen. We have gotten to know xerography through "copy art," but the use Philippe Clerc makes of it is different. What he has retained from the process is the possibility that it offers to the image to *come into existence in print*, to be the double of an other image from the very start and capable of being multicopied in turn, identically or in variants, which, when obtained mecanically, will preserve the same objective character. Parodic sign, code without norm because it can be reinvented *ad infinitum*, the xerographic image has all of the powers belonging to the ideogram without having to respect the main constraint, that of having to remain faithful to a discourse: it banks absolutely on the visual event, that is, on a revelation.

In 1990 Philippe Clerc had the idea of using this technique to create a magazine, *Riga*. This first magazine was soon followed by a second, *Akte*. A third, *Ox*, which is still being published, was their successor in 1991. A fourth, *Cobalt*, barely got off the ground in 1992 and had to be abandoned a year later.[3]

The number of different titles, the small print runs of each one of their issues (a maximum of about thirty copies), and the fact that each image is developed xerographically and thus constitutes in reality an original work — all of these indicate that the designation "magazine" should not be understood in the literal sense of the word. This expression is only a lure.

The magazine concept has its origins in *L'Immédiate*, a magazine of which Philippe Clerc had been one of the co-authors. *L'Immédiate* grew out of the desire to challenge structuralist theories of the time by showing in seemingly the only possible and most adequate way, that is visually, what these theories — from my standpoint — fail to take into account: the heterogeneity of creations combining text and image; the cultural diversity of writing systems and their applications. Taking the effect of surprise as the most effective argument, I have conceived of this magazine as a series of double pages in systematic rupture the one with the other (Christin, "Towards").

Through his experience with *L'Immédiate*, Philippe Clerc discovered that despite the booklike connotations that such a presentation implies, image sequences presented successively, rather than assembled on the same printed page, did not change in nature. But his approach would be of a different order in the magazines that he would create ten years later. As is customary, a printer unassociated with the project was responsible for the actual production of *L'Immédiate*. The substitution of the term "magazine" for "polygrams" has significance only insofar as xerography is used as a technique of simultaneous creation and printing. Moreover, the care taken by the artist to keep his copies visibly and solidly sewn or stapled together (although they are not devoid of a certain ludic quality, given the extreme unpretentiousness of these publications) makes it also apparent that the "magazine" springs more from the book tradition than it does from the magazine as such, which constitutes the real horizon with respect to which it can be situated. Producing books that would not, however, be books; using an unfolding of the pages in a unitary perspective that would, however, escape from the absolute control of an "author" — that is what Clerc has ventured to do here. In other words, it is a matter of exploring the iconic capabilities of fragmentation and succession while keeping in the background any possible discursive recuperation, whether the latter takes the indirect route through textual linearity or is embodied in an enunciation. Moreover, this refusal of enunciation is all the more remarkable in that, setting aside the several issues entrusted on occasion to partners (in *Akte* or in *Cobalt* especially, magazines whose publication were rather quickly suspended), Philippe Clerc is the only master of his works. Whether the images he treats come from others or from his own photographic production, what matters is that he alone selects them, decides what will be their final form and sequential order. To place oneself in conditions that engender the narrative in the most irresistible manner (such as those into which cartoon strips and photo-novels rush headlong), but in such a way that all narration might still be impossible and so that the game remains purely visual — that is the challenge that the experience of the "magazine" was to put to the reader.

This project was not absurd. It was, however, founded on the conversion of the notion of interspace, in the spatial sense to which I have just alluded, to another, very different sense, where it has the status of asyndeton, that is, of a rupture that is not only logical but temporal as well. But was the image lost in all this? This could not be the case in principle since the book — or *codex* — if it was invented as a material substrate of the written, can be distinguished from the scroll that preceded it, the *volumen*, by its capacity to break the linear order of the written surface, so that it can be looked at from every direction as if it were an object, and no longer read as one would read discursively. We know that it took centuries for our Western world, blindly faithful to the fluidity of speech, to make use of this function. But, as a matter of fact, temporal discontinuity and spatial continuity are in no way antinomies: on the contrary, they complement each other neatly. If the spacing, the empty space, does not produce a hiatus effect in the continuous cloth of appearence, it is because the hypothesis, preliminary to any visual thought, of a screen seemingly erected before that thought liberates for this very reason the gaze from the constraint of having constantly to adhere to it.

The absence of a "blind spot" in the scenes we observe, even when a blind spot is inevitable given the structure of our retina, is ample proof that we are dealing with a mental operation, a sort of instinctive convention of visual perception. Given this screen, and especially because it is a given, the gaze skips around. Until Descartes, the western optical tradition refused to accept this, seeking unceasingly to link people to objects by means of "rays," just as they are connected to other people by voice. Another illustration of this naively logocentrist appropriation of the visible can be found in medieval treatises on the art of memory where, so that the logical sequence of several "places" might be remembered, a precondition is assumed that the paths leading from one place to the other will be meticulously foreseen, as if one had to be physically assured of their nearness.[4] It is the inverse in the Orient, and precisely because the word has no value there: it is in this very act of liberating the gaze, concretely signified and exalted by the misty and cloud-like expanses set between the mountain and the water at the heart of its landscape paintings, that Chinese thought has expressed its intuitive sense of an Emptiness that could be at once the latency of things and human creative energy. Two certainties really determine sighted thought: first, the certainty that appearence is continuous and that by virtue of its continuity it authorizes any erratic displacement; and second, contrary to the speaker, who always fears — or hopes — that the *Self* might be *Another*, the certainty that the looker is always the self regardless of what it looks at. Our dreams are only incoherent when viewed through discursive logic. The dream screen guarantees the continuity of the visions it offers us, just as our gaze guarantees our identity, going from one vision to the other.

The narrative pretext is thus not at all necessary for spatial continuity, encompassing a discontinuous experience of time, to induce thought in other ways than does pictorial space. It suffices to modify its material substrate so that the "visual leap" is freed from any material alibi — just as the clouds in a Chinese landscape are — or so that, one might say, the blind spot, made real by an actual break in vision, is also part of the message, undermining the evidence of the appearance, not by passing through it as would the clinical gaze analyzed by Michel Foucault, but by alerting spectators to the pure act of their contemplation. The binding of Philippe Clerc's magazines has the same cathartic function as does anamorphosis in a painting designed with frontal perspective: it reveals an act of thought at the very core of the illusion.

The first issue of *Riga* is entitled *L'Obscurcissement de l'Arsenal de Metz* (*The Obscuration of the Metz Arsenal*). It is this formula that gave rise to the artist's desire to create a book—or magazine—"effect," and through a sequence of images, first cut up and then bound together, to translate a word that indicated just the opposite: a continuous and progressive movement. He wished to substitute one type of death for another, but also to make of it a show that negated death since it would have this marvelous quality of a book filled with images that delight children, just as they are delighted by such odd words as "obscuration."

But just what does this "obscuration" mean? The ambiguity of the term is masked by the precise indication of the place in question. Is it a metaphor referring to a construction site, with this building the object constructed? Or does it concern this blackness onto which the thin booklet opens, replacing with an abstract flat tint—another form of metaphor—what should have been a wall (Figure 1)? The author kept the key to the enigma to himself: by means of a title as definitive—or so it would seem—as it is problematic, he redirects to the objects' exterior, and beyond the title itself, any answer to questions "readers" might pose to make sense of what they are given to see. Only the paper commands attention, in the thick royal blue pasteboard that serves as case and binding, and its paper whose vaguely ocher coloring and low-grade material make it appear already old and worn, a sort of physical incarnation of a memory. When at least the black enclosure doesn't impose the impartial geometry of the polygram, the module of which is maintained throughout this issue of the magazine, it seems as though the images are flush with the surface of the paper, as if they were its product. This is the effect rendered by xerography, and what distinguishes it from other printing processes: not only is there no obvious manual intervention, but also—in that a ruled half-tone screen is not necessary to bring out the gray—white can be suggested directly by the shade of the paper itself.

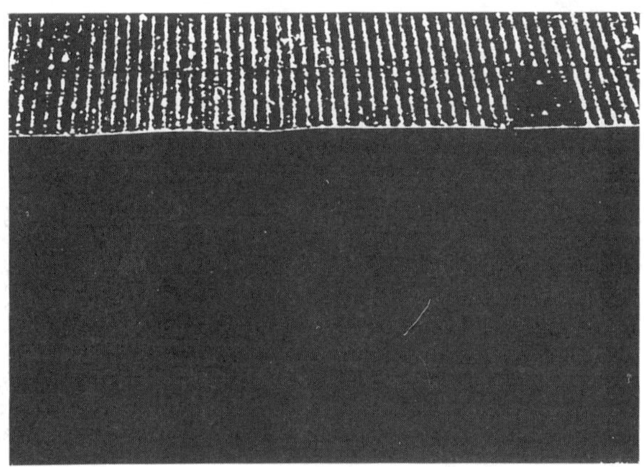

Figure 1. Philippe Clerc, "*revue-image*" produced by xerograpy, *Riga* n° 1 (January 1990) [*L'obscurcissement de L'Arsenal de Metz*]. Reproduced with the permission of the artist.

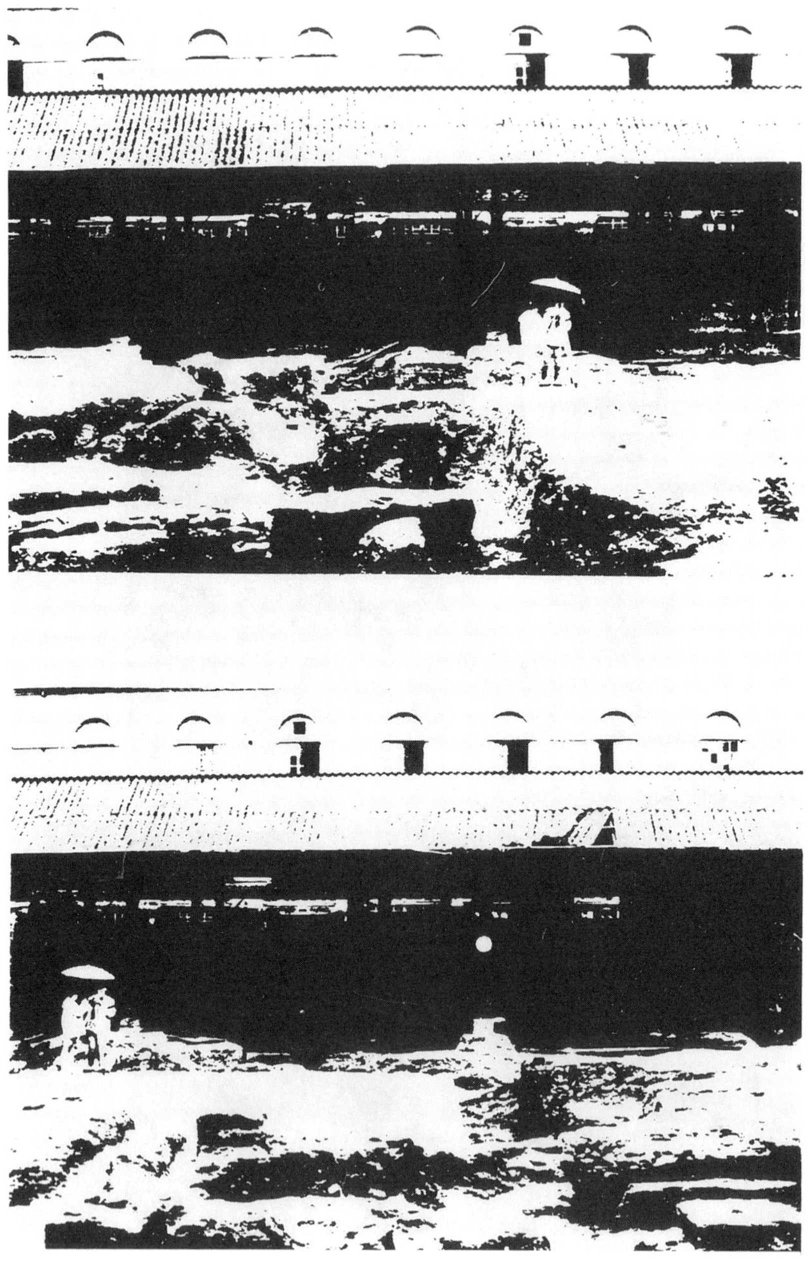

Figure 2. Philippe Clerc, "*revue-image*" produced by xerograpy, *Riga* n° 1 (January 1990) [*L'obscurcissement de L'Arsenal de Metz*]. Reproduced with the permission of the artist.

A single series of photographs shot face on and panorami-
cally is used to advantage in the greater part of the pictures
making up *L'Obscurcissement de l'Arsenal de Metz*: they show a
uniformly shaped, low facade, open at ground-level, and with
ample and regularly-spaced bay windows; the lines of the facade are cut at mid-point by the grooves of a tiled roof extending along its entire length (Figure 2). In the foreground, chaotic
excavations, a monstrous sprouting of chthonian architecture,
stand in contrast to the facade's linearity. The gaze hesitates, or,
rather, since the images are presented vertically and, on almost
every page, two at a time (on the right side only, the back side
always remaining blank), the unity discovered or constructed
by the gaze, by associating these superposed visions, is put into
question by the following sequence, where once again two different propositions come into view as a pair. Details reappear,
however, from one page to the next, identical or framed in a
slightly different way, to highlight an irregularity in the roof or
two surveyors under an umbrella. Or, again, they focus on aspects of the building that had previously been "obscured": the
French windows, for example, which are not visible in the first
pages (Figure 3). But might they not be present, rather, as a *mise-*

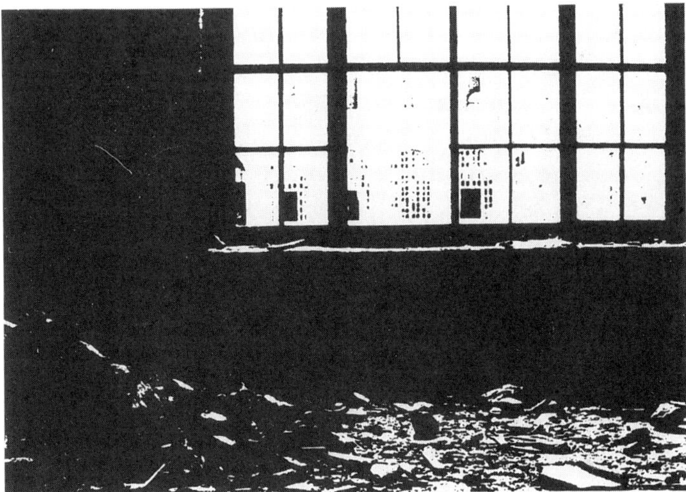

Figure 3. Philippe Clerc, "*revue-image*" produced by xerograpy, *Riga* n° 1
(January 1990) [*L'obscurcissement de L'Arsenal de Metz*]. Reproduced
with the permission of the artist.

en-abîme in the real of the perpendicular module that governs polygrams? And this oblique white line in a black splotch, how can we *recognize* the enlargement of this simple wire which, in a previous picture, lay about in piles of debris? And this flat, white shape that closes the issue, is it once again an enlarged detail of an image seen earlier, or a conclusion, an *end*, like that of a novel or a short story?

The metamorphoses undergone by the representations of the Metz Arsenal from one page to the next bar us from seeing in this sequence of images the equivalent of a *description*, as one would normally expect. But for all that, they do not warrant our finding therein any narrative intention or structure. The entirely accessory role that the surveyor figures play is, moreover, proof of this. A time scheme is inscribed within the space scheme through fantasized travel through a place. However, narration comes into play only as a fleeting and illusory convention, endowed with much less structuring power than the two other literary indices constituted by the binding of these images into a book and their title. Taken together, they really signify that this booklet was conceived both as a *closed work* and, in an apparently contradictory manner, as a *message*. But in truth the contradiction doesn't exist since this message could never be a form of discourse. The ambiguity gap that separates the booklet's title from its printed illustrations is not really a simple denial of enunciation; it is also, and above all, a mark of visibility, as is the title of a painting. It indicates that these images are readable in a sphere other than that of linguistic exchange, where the author of the message is credible only on condition that he stays at a distance. This separation/displacement should not be surprising. Unlike language, a product which is internal to, and reserved exclusively for, the group, visual communication constitutes in all societies a link with the outside world; it is the gods who transmit their dreams to humans, leaving traces on these magical screens where soothsayers attempt to decode them. This is why there is no *origin* here that can claim to be read, be it the origin of a "story" or of the author's personal life; there is no genesis whose visual message would be the interpreter or the mime. *L'Obscurcissement de l'Arsenal de Metz* is a *mutus liber*, a *mute book*, the pretext of which is the metamorphosis of a place revisited by a certain gaze, a place that will be transformed into a message by the double alchemy of a technique of direct impregnation of the images and of the discovery of the other. For, and this allows us to understand in still another way how the message could never be a discourse here (and to an even lesser degree, of course, a narration), there is no way to dissociate the message from its material substrate in this compilation: it is in the experience of the latter, and only of the latter, that the reader-spectator will find the message revealed.

As a consequence, the message is fundamentally uncertain. But in this light, in what way would it be different from any other message—oral, perhaps—once it is subject—as such is its mission—to an other's whims? We could suppose, moreover, that it is precisely insofar as it reckons with uncertainty, with the whim of the other, that the gaze is not only our most sure form of identity but also the form that we can best share. Merleau-Ponty has posited in principle that it is impossible to *see as the other sees*. But this principle has no meaning, here again, unless we construct the gaze according to the model of the utterance. It is, rather, on the evidence that any gaze is uncertain—namely, that it neither ever affirms nor denies—that the silent communication essential to Chinese philosophy is based.

It is only with reference to the model of the ideogram that the *message without content* present in *L'Obscurcissement de l'Arsenal de Metz* can be understood. Viewed as an "icon," according to Peirce's terminology, the figure of the ideogram is already more of an act than a representation. Apart from the fact that from the very start it fulfills several functions at once, in our interpretation the ideogram is a verbal node at the same time that it is a figure. Its dynamism resides in a disengagement from the real that it is able to capture and systematize. Just as the ideogram, what the *revue-image* establishes with respect to its realist pretext is not the idea that "there is nothing more," but that there is undeniably much more here, since there is the both personal and plastic appropriation by a creator, similar in all respects to that of a language [*langue*] that adapts the ideogram to its needs. There is nonetheless "nothing else," nothing other than what is present on or between these pages made of poor-quality paper, and which doesn't have any content because what is occurring here is a transformation of visual thought into spectacle. In ideographic writing, the sign is the message. Here, we find just the opposite: *the message is the sign*. Duration does not change anything in the enigma of the images except that the gaze can, this time, take stock of itself in the blind displacement of its leaps and thus contemplate its thought.

The fourth issue of *Riga*, the title of which is *Baigneur en 1988* (*Bather in 1988*), is the only issue to feature on its cover the author's name: Philippe Clerc. Its 80 pages—eight fewer than in the first issue—are made from a paper of the same grey-ocher tones but much heavier, and its rough texture gives it a more immediate and dense feel. The issue is built around a single image, that of the black and roughly reproduced silhouette—in the style of expressionist linocuts—of a man preparing to wade out the sea (Figure 4). In any case, that is what is suggested in the bust shown from the waist up, leaning forward, and emerging from the undulations formed by short little marks resembling the shadowy movement of the last waves running along the shore's edge. As if he wore a cowl, the features of his face, rounded and black, are not visible. His right arm has just been drawn out of the water, as if to assist the upper body in its effort. Nonetheless, the drops still flowing from his hand, captured so sharply as they are in the picture, give the strange impression that the figure is still connected by them to the sea.

The decisive instant of a narration (if this is one), is when the hero is surprised the moment that he is about to cross one symbolic threshhold among many. It is Birth, the Beginning: "Once upon a time. . . . " But this birth will remain irrevocably suspended, and the hero will not be freed from the briny prison he wishes to flee to enter into a story. His story stops here. The story is entirely in this moment, in this *congealed image* that traps him, because we will not see him elsewhere in any other pose than this vain attempt, his first gesture towards freedom.

The passing of time, however, plays a role here to be sure, as it does in the first issue of the magazine: the fact that its title is dated is the proof. But what sort of duration is it? A pretense is made of announcing an event in ourselves by citing the year, as if we were to be assured of the truth of this event and of its importance. But the time gap appearing between this information and the image it introduces (this man emerging from the water as he must have done a thousand times) completely alters the effect: what is the point of telling us that we are being shown

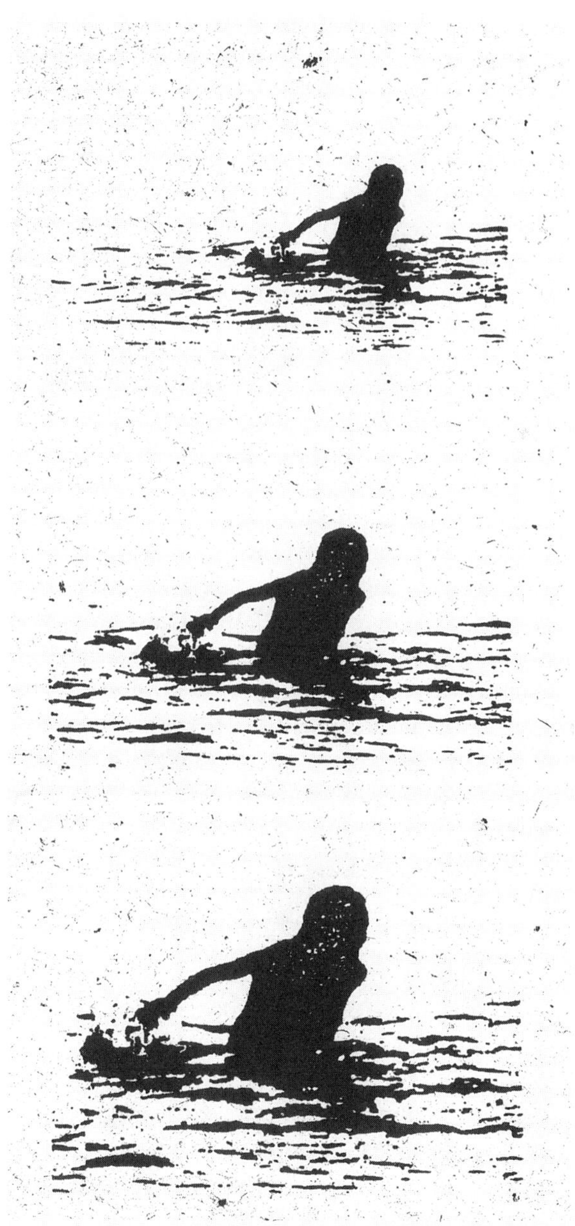

Figure 4. Philippe Clerc, *"revue-image"* produced by xerograpy, *Riga* nº 4 (July 1990) [*Baigneur en 1988*]. Reproduced with the permission of the artist.

this man at that particular time, and why do it two years later (issue number 4 of *Riga* came out in July 1990)? We know nothing about this man with the invisible face, nothing about his life before or after his swim. We don't even know if the photograph upon which the image is based might not have been lost in the meantime, or even if it wasn't really the date of the photographic act that the author wished to remember. This is the portrait of an instant, an *image-sign*. Duration is at play in its movement, but its hero is only the pretext, the schematic reference.

The message constructed from this sign is founded, like that of the first issue of *Riga*, in the reader's experience during the time it takes to skim through the book. The process, nevertheless, is different. *L'Obscurcissement de l'Arsenal de Metz* provides interpretive variants for consideration to which the panoramic view of a building could be subjected. Here, the time of commentary is borrowed from the time of the image itself, which will develop from within, keeping to this double and throbbing urgency for movement and paralysis, for birth and death at the same time, to which it is condemned by its singularity. As the author-manipulator is bent on emphasizing—since he signed it— the message is obviously personal, but it can only be formulated within the space of the other's gaze. At times the figure is magnified by fits and starts as if he were coming to breathe progressively closer to shore, and at other times he is face to face with his shadow, his own skull obstructing the foreground of the image like a fat, black sponge (Figures 5-7). The figure, reproduced systematically three times on each page, is subjected to processes that end up making it unrecognizable, either because the swimmer's arm becomes emaciated to the bone through an optical trick, or because its porous skull is inflated like a cloud and fills out the entire polygram, or still yet because the water splashes that bind him to the sea become a bouquet of blackness. Its most frightful metamorphosis was created by a technical accident during the enlargement of the image, slicing the figure's head into two unequal parts; the image is thus presented to us, a divinity in pieces, geometric Janus, since, the game still continuing, we discover it entirely recomposed, starting from pieces taken by chance from his sad kingdom.

But this final transformation is also the signal that if Philippe Clerc's purpose is to give visual definition to the theme of an

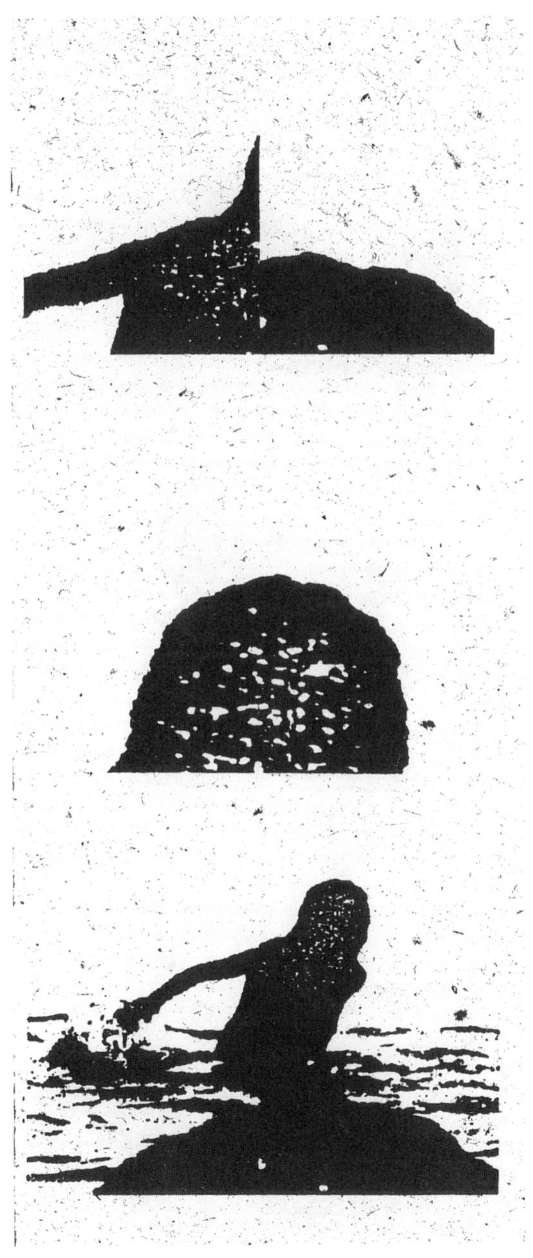

Figure 5. Philippe Clerc, *"revue-image"* produced by xerograpy, *Riga* n° 4 (July 1990) [*Baigneur en 1988*]. Reproduced with the permission of the artist.

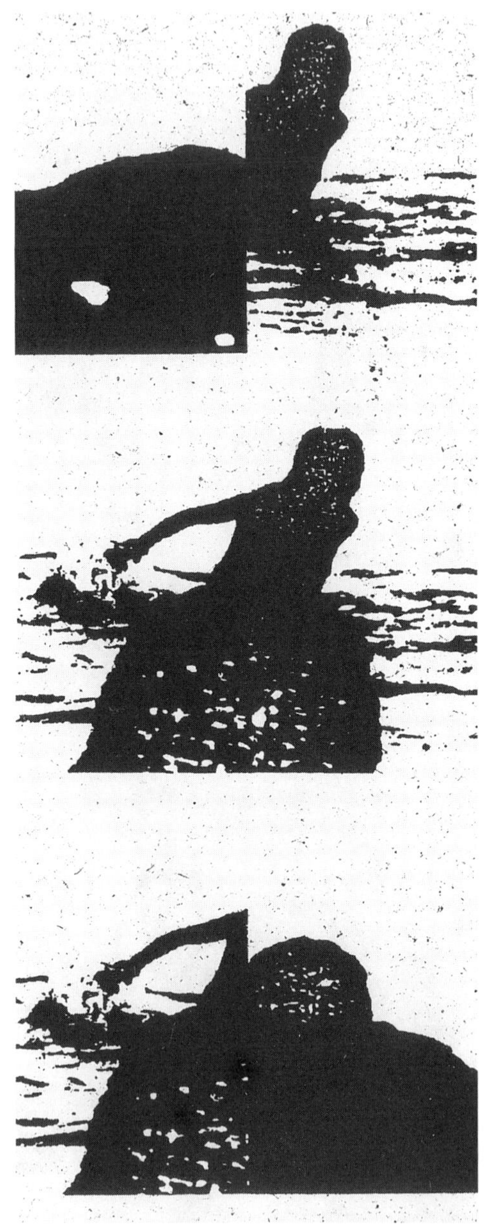

Figure 6. Philippe Clerc, "*revue-image*" produced by xerograpy, *Riga* n° 4 (July 1990) [*Baigneur en 1988*]. Reproduced with the permission of the artist.

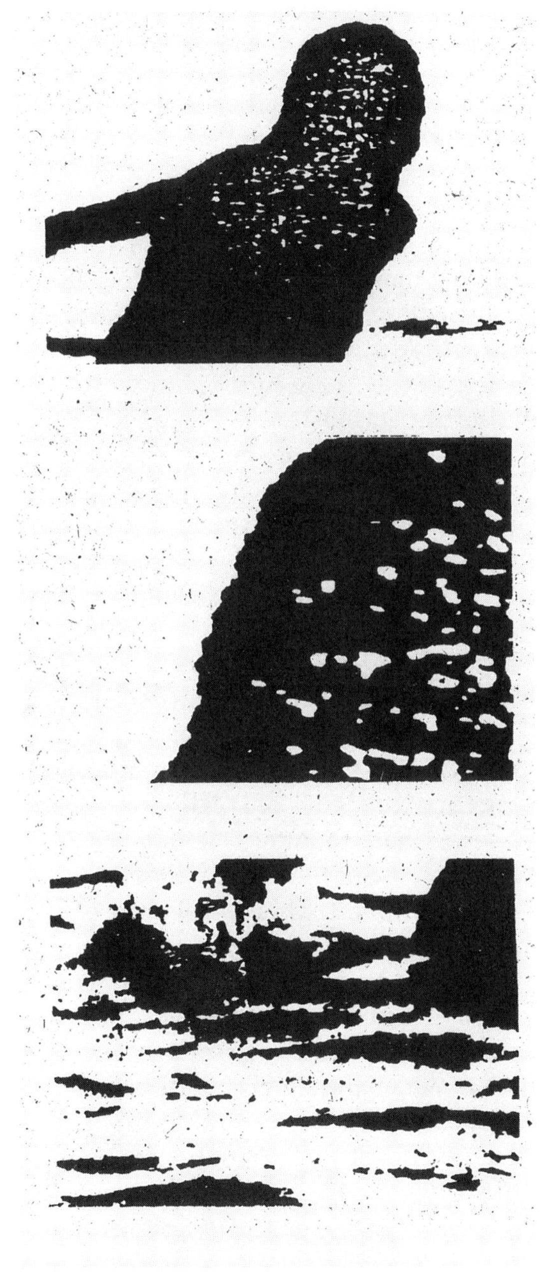

Figure 7. Philippe Clerc, "*revue-image*" produced by xerograpy, *Riga* n° 4 (July 1990) [*Baigneur en 1988*]. Reproduced with the permission of the artist.

impossible birth, it is the play with form created by this definition as such and the images made visible by xerography (in this
instance before his very eyes) that matter to Clerc, more than the
content of these images. As controlled as it might be, repeated
on each page, in three stages, with no respite and with the per-
sistency of litany, the use of distant space that is brought nearer
or of forms that change into others quite different from the first
ones once they have been too enlarged, while simultaneously
forcing an oppressive reading rhythm (analogous to the
swimmer's futile attempts to leave the water) on the gaze, leads
to the end-point where the only true or possible birth can take
place: the artwork. Abstraction is the product that saves the dis-
integrated image of the living figure, but with it a creation also
takes form, asserting its existence.

In this issue of *Riga*, the message is summed up once again
in its *sign*, but in a manner more intense and more paradoxical
than in the preceding case. It does not hang on the fact that a
single image is treated, or that this image could be interpreted
as a "portrait" of the author. We can easily see that what makes
this swimmer unreplaceable is precisely his anonymity, and that
rather than his face hidden by shadows, what is most moving in
the figure is his half-raised arm and the fistful of water attached
to it. What distinguishes this type of message from the preceding are the characteristics of the sign that are developed therein.
In its characteristics, the sign is not really comparable to the ideogram, in the sense that the latter operates by transmutation of
the real, as was the case of the Metz arsenal pictures, but by the
arbitrary decision implied. This message is contingent on the
conventional image of the subject, of the "I," just as the "I" is
itself a convention of language *[langue]* and constitutes a pro-
nominal index of the subject utilizable by any speaker. This characteristic corresponds to the ideogram's second function, that of
"phonogram," in which the sign is not directly semantic but signifies through derivation. It is clear that this derivation cannot
have been obtained here by means of homophony since we have
not left the field of the visible, but it proceeds similarly, by a
shift in register—in other words, if I am permitted this neologism, by *homogeny*.[5]

In writing systems that use this sign type, the third characteristic of the ideogram is that of the "determinative," of the

"key," that is, of the sign that does not need to be pronounced to keep its original meaning and which is put alongside another sign in order to orient reading in a purely visual manner. The third issue of *Riga*, dedicated to the city of Riga itself, offers an illustration of the city that also constitutes (could this be by chance?) the third process in image-writing that can be identified in this magazine. From an iconographic point of view, this issue is rather close to the issue focusing on the Metz Arsenal in its organizing principle. Indeed, it presents a series of panoramic views of Riga taken from along the river Daugava in the early morning: silhouettes of belltowers, roofs, or streetlamps above the motionless water, and deserted bridges where one catches sight of only one or two cars. The intent behind this series is different, however. In this issue, each photograph is reproduced in full-page format, the magazine having been bound horizontally like an artist's sketchbook. But what is quite new and enters into the message of this issue in an essential manner, playing immediately upon the spectator's gaze, is the material substrate that was chosen: tracing paper. Uniting in the same shadow the horizons of water and land, causing the silhouettes to fade into the blurry depths of an imaginary city, our eyes effect their sweep across these mysterious and falsely ephemeral scenes in a time frame partaking at once of that of the image and that of the book. Penetrating the inner space of the empty places standing out among the as yet semi-nocturnal silhouettes of the port, the gaze enters directly into the vacant spaces of the pages that follow. Time is immobilized: nothing moves, from one image to the next one caught in the same structure; but time is kept alive by the irregular yet sustained surprise of the eyes, by this examining gaze transpiercing appearances, which resembles memory's quest.

In the ideographic writing system, the "key" represents its highest degree of visual sophistication. Separating from the sign's verbal value its one and exclusive *color*, if I may put it this way, the key attests in the most essential way to the image's capacity to appropriate discourse in terms of its own laws, which are on the order of the *proximity effect* and not of narrative elaboration. If it can be illumined through this attribute of the ideographic sign, the set of tracing-paper scenes of Riga also enables us to understand the mechanisms that control it. Immaterial, the medium on which the signs appear gives access to the mirage; the medium does not disappear into transparency, as Alberti thought, but guides the gaze towards its memory.

—Translated by Judith E. Preckshot

Notes

[1]A precise demonstration of all of this can be found in Christin, *L'Image*. See also Christin, "Déraison."

[2]The reader is also referred to Peirce, *Papers*; for a discussion of Peirce's theory of the sign see Spinks.

[3]*Riga*, published 1990-91 (12 issues), with a 14 x 20 cm format; *Akte*, published 1990-92 (8 issues), with a 14.8 x 37 cm format; *Cobalt*, published 1992-93 (4 issues), with a 10.5 x 15 cm format; and *Ox*, published 1991-present (37 issues as of September 1994), with a 21 x 29.7 cm format.

[4]See Yates. Quintilian was both more bold and more subtle, and he didn't bother about the order of lines on the wax tablet that served as his mnemonic model (see Christin, "Mémoire").

[5]Translator's note: Although *homogeny* is a true neologism in French, *homogeny* already exists in English as a term used in biology.

Works Cited

Alberti, Leon Battista. *On Painting [De pictura]* (1435). Trans. John R. Spencer. Rev. ed. New Haven: Yale UP, 1966.

Cheng, François. *Souffle-esprit*. Paris: Seuil, 1989.

Christin, Anne-Marie. "La Déraison graphique." *Textuel* (Université de Paris VII) 17 (1985): 5-12.

______. *L'Image écrit*. Paris: Flammarion, 1995.

______. "La Mémoire blanche." *Rhétorique et image; Textes en hommage à A. Kibédi Varga*. Eds. Leo H. Hoek and Kees Meerhoff. Amsterdam: Rodopi, 1995. 83-98.

_____. "Towards a Theory of Mixe(d) Messages: The Experience of *L'Immédiate.*" *Word & Image* 3.4 (1987): 292-304.

Dubuffet, Jean. *Bâtons rompus.* Paris: Minuit, 1986.

Jullien, François. *Procès ou création, Une introduction à la pensée des lettrés chinois; Essai de problématique interculturelle.* Paris: Seuil, 1989.

_____. *La Propension des choses. Pour une histoire de l'efficacité en Chine.* Paris: Seuil, 1992.

Lee, Rensselaer W. *Ut pictura poesis: The Humanistic Theory of Painting.* New York: Norton, 1967.

Lessing, Gotthold Ephraim. *Laokoön* (1776). Ed. Dorothy Reich. London: Oxford UP, 1965.

Peirce, Charles S. *Collected Papers.* 8 vols. Cambridge: Harvard UP, 1931-66.

_____. *Ecrits sur le signe.* Trans. G. Deledalle. Paris: Seuil, 1978.

Spinks, C. W. *Peirce and Triadomania; A Walk in the Semiotic Wilderness.* Berlin/New York: Mouton de Gruyter, 1991.

Yates, Frances A. *The Art of Memory.* Chicago: U of Chicago P, 1966.

Two Poems

Richard Vernier

(for Renée)

L'Ecole Buissonnière

Il commençait à faire nuit sur les crêtes. Le guide se tenait sur la gauche, soigneusement éloigné du précipice. Certainement, on n'arriverait jamais au sommet. Dans le pré spongieux, au bord du chemin embourbé, des bêtes se coulaient entre les nuages. Quelqu'un portait dans ses bras un faon rétif: c'était pour son bien. A contre-coeur, nous avons fait demi-tour dans l'ombre pluvieuse.

Mais en bas, il faisait grand jour. Dans la belle maison, les autres faisaient comme s'ils n'avaient pas même remarqué notre absence. A notre tour, nous avons fait semblant de comprendre, et repris avec eux la visite organisée.

C'est du fond d'un autre salon que la musique est venue, on eût dit des graines portées par le vent. Je crus reconnaître le piano du Maître, celui dont on dit qu'il jouait à l'heure de sa mort. "Mais non, voyons," dit la présidente, "qu'est-ce que vous allez chercher? C'est celui qu'on a déménagé de la ferme modèle . . ."

Ces dames en ont ri, en ont ri aux larmes!

L'Arbre qui Chante

Vous entendez parfois peut-être de ces voix, moins
lointaines que difficiles à placer, à reconnaître même. D'où
vient ce chant, dites-vous, est-ce une femme, et quelle est cette
langue inconnue?

Vous approchez à pas couverts l'orée du bois d'où
semblait sortir une voix entre toutes, mais bien vite elle
s'efface, elle s'enfonce dans le bruissement des feuilles,

car l'arbre qui chante se confond à ses mille complices,
tous les autres murmures de la forêt changeante, et votre recherche s'épuise, elle se perd dans des futaies soudain rendues
au silence, et c'est bientôt la nuit où votre patience est enfin
récompensée, car entre les halliers, à travers les ronces, vous
avez si bien avancé à pas de loup, sans donner l'éveil à la forêt
soupçonneuse, que vous vous retrouvez au seuil inattendu de
cette clairière, et l'arbre qui chante ne peut plus vous éluder,
vous allez enfin le toucher, c'est l'instant suspendu entre ciel et
terre, juste

avant le cri de douleur dans lequel se déchire la voix de
l'arbre qui chante, qui chantait . . .

The Secret Life of the Book:
The *Livre d'artiste* and
the Act of Reading

Breon Mitchell

In the spring of 1992, I was invited along with several other scholars, artists, and book-makers to a conference sponsored by the J. Paul Getty Foundation in Santa Monica. The general topic on this occasion was "Reading and the Arts of the Book." My own task was to summarize the origin and development of the *livre d'artiste* from 1875 to 1960 for a public audience, not all of whom would be familiar with the history of the illustrated book. Although my presentation consisted in the main of a historical overview of the subject, with standard slides of several of the greatest of these books, I was tempted by the stimulating company of so many colleagues in the field to advance a thesis I thought might strike them as original and worthy of discussion. To my dismay, however, I angered many of them instead — for I suggested that, in a literal sense, most of the great *livres d'artiste* had never been read.

Thinking back on that occasion, I should have realized that these would be fighting words to those intimately involved in creating such books. My remarks could too easily be seen as a criticism of the genre itself, a sort of sweeping indictment suggesting that the readership for such books is extremely limited and elitist by nature. If, as I suggested, no one reads such books, why should anyone produce them? Many of those in the audience felt, to the contrary, that these books were open to all, not of necessity expensive or limited by nature, and should attract a wide audience. In fact, I agreed with this position. I simply had a different notion of what it means to "read" a *livre d'artiste*.

In this essay I would like to enlarge upon the all-too-brief remarks I made then. In doing so I hope to show that far from impugning the genre by suggesting how seldom such books are read, I mean to point toward their special nature. For I believe that the *livre d'artiste* is one of the most fascinating forms of modern art in our century, and that reading such books, in the sense I discuss below, offers a special, perhaps even unique, aesthetic experience, an experience open to all.

An apt metaphor for the type of reading engendered by the very nature of the *livre d'artiste* presented itself to me not long ago in the reading room of the Lilly Library at Indiana University. Renée Riese Hubert, a Ball Brothers Fellow that year, was hard at work on the archives of a fascinating book-artist from Paris, Ania Staritsky. Staritsky offered a rich field for Renée's special talents. In the book that lay before her, the texture and color of the paper, the interpenetrating spaces achieved by intentional openings of various shapes through the pages themselves, the changing visual impression as the pages were turned, and a hand-calligraphed text illustrated with original collages combined to produce a stunning effect.

Renée, as always, was deeply absorbed in her reading. As she slowly turned the pages, the visual, tactile, and intellectual pleasures of the book were clearly reflected in her whole demeanor. Hers was a "reading" that went far beyond our normal use of the word. What was involved was clearly an aesthetic experience *actualized* by "reading"—something far different from our conventional notions of reading a book.

The metaphor that occurred to me was one of performance. To me, Renée seemed to be "performing" the book, her role an active and participatory one, not simply that of a passive recipient. The physical object lay before her like a musical score that she was transforming into its true essence by the very act of reading. Here was something that lay outside standard reader-response theory. Renée was not simply filling in the gaps in Wolfgang Iser's sense, nor was her role merely that of a member of a scholarly community constituting the meaning of the literary text, as Stanley Fish might have suggested. She was in fact "playing" the book, actualizing the elements Staritsky had so carefully built into it, including size, texture, color, calligraphy, word, image, and yes, even fragrance. (And when on one occasion her husband Judd sat beside her and they turned the pages of the book together, it seemed as if a duet were in progress, four hands on the instrument that lay before them.)

How might one describe such an experience? What is the source of its pleasure? And just how rare is it? These are the questions that had occurred to me at the Getty Conference, and that I had addressed there so briefly and inconclusively. As I watched Renée pour over the Staritsky book I thought how fortunate the Parisian artist was, how pleased she would be were she still alive to know that she had found this reader. For Renée was not only the "implied" reader of the book, she came very close to being the "ideal" reader as well. And when I asked myself how often that particular book had received its "reading" in this sense, I doubted that it had happened more than a handful of times over the intervening years. Indeed it seemed to me possible that in the truest sense it was being read here for the first time.

By now it should be clear that I do not mean that no one had ever looked at the Staritsky book before, nor even that it lacked readers who had turned its pages consecutively and read the text. But I think it is a fair question to ask how many readers "performed" the potential work before them as Staritsky might have wished.

This was the question I posed at the Getty Conference. I had just emerged from an in-depth exploration of one of the great monuments of the nineteenth-century book: the collaboration of Stéphane Mallarmé and Edouard Manet on Poe's *The Raven*. Published in Paris in 1875 in a bilingual edition with Mallarmé's French version and four full-page original lithographs by Manet, the book was a commercial failure. Although nothing like it was attempted again for almost twenty-five years, it remained one of the great forerunners of the modern *livre d'artiste*, opening the door into the twentieth century.

I had originally been drawn to the book by a strange fact. Although it was supposedly published in a single edition of 240 copies, numbered and signed by the author and artist, a close comparison of two copies at the Lilly Library revealed that one of them had been completely reset, and thus constituted a different edition. In collaboration with Juliet Wilson-Bareau, whose work on Manet's graphic art is unparalleled, the complicated printing history of the book was gradually unravelled, including the identification of a new and hitherto totally unknown state of the most famous of the lithographs. A census of all known copies indicated that probably no more than 150 copies were ever actually distributed.

Tracking down the rare and elusive copies of this book first raised in my mind the question of its readership. Mallarmé and Manet had poured their creativity into this joint venture. It had attained the status of a revered monument of the illustrated book. Yet how many people had actually read it? Not, "had seen the illustrations" (often reproduced), or "had read Mallarmé's French translation," or "had sat down with a greatly reduced and photographically reproduced 'facsimile'" (equivalent perhaps to seeing a slide of a painting), but had actually held the original book itself, turned its pages, and read the text (in which Poe's English alternates with Mallarmé's prose), absorbing the full effect of Manet's carefully-placed original illustrations. Finally, how many had been able to experience the wrappers or portfolio so carefully chosen by Mallarmé to house the loose folios? (These were often missing in the copies we examined, many of which were rebound.)

Did the few contemporary reviewers who received the book (Mallarmé's first, when he was far from well known) actually take the time to read it? Did *anyone* among those who received the approximately 150 copies actually read it all the way through? We have no way of knowing, but there can be no question that the contemporary readership, by any standards, must have been extremely small.

And how many subsequent readers has the book found in the course of the last century? Unless you are one of the fortunate few in a financial position to own the original edition (a copy was offered in the fall of 1994 for $45,000), you will have to visit a major museum or rare book library even to see a copy. How often has this happened over the years? And how often have those consulting the work done just that—examined the illustrations, leafed through the text—rather than actually engage in the sort of actualization of the book clearly envisioned by Mallarmé? How many scholars have written about the book, at least in passing, without ever having seen an actual copy?

My own estimate would be that in the full sense described above, fewer than twenty-five individuals have read *Le Corbeau* — one of the greatest monuments of the nineteenth-century book, with one of the shortest texts. The number of those who have shared Renée's experience with the particular book by Ania Staritsky is no doubt even smaller. The book she was reading was printed in an edition of only twenty copies, the artist is far less well known, and the number of institutions outside France that even possess the work can be counted on one hand. Nevertheless, it is not simply scarcity that limits the readership of a *livre d'artiste.* Even works far more readily available in this genre, if my argument is correct, often remain unread in a deeper sense.

What I had wanted to do at the Getty Conference was establish this point in order to suggest, with some sense of excitement, that a world of undiscovered and rich aesthetic experience lay ahead of us, particularly with regard to the past. This is what I meant by the secret life of the book: the living potential of hundreds of major *livres d'artiste* that still slumber in our rare book libraries and museums.

Assume for a moment that an important, unknown work by Beethoven existed as a musical score, but had only been performed before an audience on a handful of occasions. Such a situation would strike us as ludicrous. Yet the parallel to many of the great *livres d'artiste* in our own century is not that farfetched. For what is true of the Mallarmé/Manet *Corbeau* is no doubt equally true of Kandinsky's *Klänge*, Matisse's *Jazz*, and, more recently, the Jasper Johns/Beckett *Fizzles*.

I suggest above that the *livre d'artiste* offers a unique aesthetic experience, one that has never been fully acknowledged. What is the nature of this experience? The nineteenth-century Wagnerian ideal of the *Gesamtkunstwerk* has a long and rich history, and lies in part behind Mallarmé's project of The Book as well. In our own century, multi-media approaches to the arts and a blurring of traditional genres have become commonplace. The rise of cinema, with its powerful visual images, its simulation of the movement of life, together with life's words and sounds and music, has offered a further impetus to art forms that strive toward totality, assaulting all our senses simultaneously. The proliferation of rock and rap videos in the MTV generation, interactive video games, electronic texts, and excursions in virtual reality are all a part of a future permeated by the aesthetics of the *Gesamtkunstwerk*. Yet a great deal of multi-media art remains aimed at passive consumption in which the viewer, the listener, the reader plays no real role.

In the *livre d'artiste*, a much more intimate relationship exists between the reader and the book. Unlike such multi-media genres as opera or film, the aesthetic experience of a *livre d'artiste* is simply missed unless the reader is directly and *physically* involved. What other art form in our century requires such total, lived interaction with an aesthetic object? What other art form so engages our intellect and our senses? In quite different ways, the dancer and the musician simultaneously produce and consume their aesthetic product, but they are themselves instruments for yet a further audience. The reader of the *livre d'artiste*, on the other hand, is both performer and audience.

Like any aesthetic object, the *livre d'artiste* offers constraints to our reading, but opens itself to almost infinite possibilities in its actualization. Novelists are well aware that readers may turn to the end of the story to "how it comes out" before they have actually reached the last page. Similarly those involved in the creation of a *livre d'artiste* will realize that a sensitive reader may still depart from the program or "score" the physical object initially suggests. In the case of the Mallarmé/Manet Poe, for example, the reader may well choose to "perform" the book by reading the entire poem first in English, then a second time in French, vis-à-vis the Manet lithographs, rather than following the given sequence that alternates between the two languages. Like any aesthetic experience, a multitude of factors will affect the manner in which the work is realized. Nevertheless, one can hardly claim to have "read" a *livre d'artiste* without having fulfilled certain minimum conditions.

I take the "performance" or reading of a carefully conceived *livre d'artiste* to include at least the following elements: a close attention to the format and shape of the book, as well as its cover and binding, as they affect the physical act of reading, an intellectual and sensual interaction with the book in full awareness of its overall graphic design and typography, a close reading of the text and images in the order in which they appear, turning the pages with a sense for the effect produced by that process, an intellectual awareness of the way in which words and images interrelate in the book as a whole, and a sensitivity to the physical qualities of the materials. If the book includes a musical score, or a recording, "reading" the book clearly involves "hearing" the music within the constraints offered or implied. The box, container, or slipcase of a *livre d'artiste* should form an element in the reading process.

In a recent issue of *Bookways*, Barbara Tetenbaum's column "Book Spy" offers a fine contemporary example of such readings. Her review of four "visual books" not only tells us what we need to know as a potential audience for the books, it conveys as well a strong sense of her own "performances" and encourages us by example. There are, of course, many such sensitive and intelligent readers in the present world of book art, readers for whom the remarks I've offered here are hardly necessary. But even for those most deeply involved in the field, it may be worth remembering how much of the rich past of the *livre d'artiste* remains, in a profoundly literal sense, unexplored territory.

Works Cited

Tetenbaum, Barbara. "Book Spy." *Bookways: A Quarterly for the Book Arts* 13-14 (1994-95): 83-86.

Ethical Loops
in Eluard

Steven Winspur

When viewed in its more outlandish modes, surrealism might well appear to be the very opposite of an ethical endeavor. For how could any theory of social life possibly be inferred from precepts such as André Breton's suggestion to run into the street with a revolver and shoot indiscriminately at the crowd?[1] Yet in his very next sentence Breton stresses that such a "simple act," motivated by a very real despair with bourgeois morality, has been envisaged by countless people, surrealists and non-surrealists alike.[2] A distinction must be made, then, between such desperate attacks against bourgeois *moralism*, on the one hand, and the positive *ethical* thrust of many surrealist claims, on the other.

This thrust is evident in the opening statement of the first *Manifeste du surréalisme*, in which it is precisely a detachment from life that signals the bankruptcy of traditional beliefs and goals: "Tant va la croyance à la vie, à ce que la vie a de plus précaire, la vie *réelle* s'entend, qu'à la fin cette croyance se perd" 'So far goes the belief in life, in what is most precarious about life, *real* life that is, that at last this belief is lost' (Breton 11). Once lost, Breton goes on to argue, a belief in life is restored only after we free our imagination and have the courage to act out the consequences of this liberation (12-14). Reuniting persons with their own lives or potential is a common thread running throughout all writings on ethics, and it is the reason why such texts give priority to human acts instead of elaborating general theories of truth or knowledge. The underlying model behind the sentence quoted above illustrates this preeminence of living over knowing. For by transforming the saying "Tant va la cruche à l'eau qu'à la fin elle se cache" 'The pitcher goes so often to the well that at last it breaks,' Breton's sentence establishes a pairing of means (*la cruche, la croyance*) and ends (*l'eau, la vie*), whereby the former are subordinated to the latter.[3] In addition, "The pitcher goes so often to the well" means figuratively in French that exposing oneself to a danger—which Breton identifies with life's most risky and emotional moments—will eventually make one succumb. No belief or knowledge can protect us from the sometimes harsh, yet occasionally intoxicating, realities of existence. Indeed, it is only by undermining pretensions to knowing what life is all about and by replacing them with a new style of thought-in-action that life can be restored to beleaguered humankind. "Le surréalisme," writes Breton in his initial definition of the term, "tend à ruiner définitivement tous les autres méchanismes psychiques et à se substituer à eux dans la résolution des principaux problèmes de la vie" 'tends to definitively ruin all the other psychological mechanisms and to take their place during the resolution of life's main problems' (Breton 37-38).[4]

Yet no surrealist poem was ever able to reconnect its readers to life by simply showing them the power of another person's imagination. Startling representations or "images" could not in themselves accomplish human restoration. Instead certain poems tried to engage the reader in an ongoing creation of form that he or she would carry over into everyday actions. One of the ways in which Paul Eluard achieved this goal was to write into his poems strange loops that pull the reader within the confines of the text, thus abolishing the boundary between a poem's verbal performance and its re-enactment by the reader.

I have borrowed the name "strange loop" from Douglas Hofstadter, who uses it to label the strangely recursive structure that one finds in many musical compositions by Bach and also in M. C. Escher's wood-cuts and lithographs. Hofstadter defines a loop as any hierarchical system of commands or rules that is laid out in one direction (Hofstadter 8, 17). An example of this would be a musical canon (or the introduction of a theme that is then played out against itself, as in "Three Blind Mice"). Certain mathematical equations that include repeatable operations in their formulation are another illustration. *Strange* loops, however, occur when the sequence of rules keeps going in one direction and yet suddenly brings its user back to the start. Hofstadter gives Bach's "Canon per Tonos" in the *Musical Offering* as an example of this (10), and also Escher's "Head with Reflecting Globe" (13). This lithograph is composed exclusively of a bare hand rising up from the bottom edge of the picture and holding a glass ball. Inside the ball we see the curved reflection of a bearded man looking towards us as he sits in a living-room, surrounded by bookshelves and armchairs. The picture forms a strange loop once we realize that the image in the globe, which we began to scrutinize as any old interior with a man, is in fact a reflection of the person whose hand holds the globe. It is a reflection of the artist and, more importantly, of ourselves inasmuch as we occupy the viewing position to which the globe points. Deciphering the lithograph's lines and shadings has eventually brought us back to our own gaze.

Poems constitute loops insofar as they are sets of rules that guide their readers in their interpretation and gradually point them in one direction to an overall understanding of the text. However, some of Eluard's poems are strange loops since at one moment or another their readers understand that they are not only decoding signs of literary meaning but also signs of their own activity. In the following opening stanza the reader is instructed to take over the position of a portraitist, as in Escher's lithograph:

Oeil de sourd

Faites mon portrait.
Il se modifiera pour remplir tous les vides
Faites mon portrait sans bruit, seul le silence
A moins que — s'il — sauf — excepté
Je ne vous entends pas.
(Eluard, *Oeuvres* 119)

Eye of a Deaf Person

Make my portrait.
It will adapt itself to fill up all the holes
Make my portrait without a sound, alone the silence
Unless — if it — except — save for —
I don't hear you.

The "eye of a deaf person" named in the title would appear to be a metonymy for the poet who asks us to compose his picture: he cannot hear the words as they are pronounced by the reader. Consequently, the reader is put into the position of poet since it is the former who becomes the creator of the art-work in question. Hence the poem's closing lines: "Sans fatigue, têtes nouées [namely the poet's and the readers'] / Aux mains de mon activité [the author's tracing of words upon the page]" 'Without tiredness, heads joined / To the hands of my activity.' This switching of roles between writer and reader is quite common in Eluard's early poetry, and it turns the reader into the true locus of poetic activity—as in "Le Jeu de construction" ("The Building Game") whose title tells us that we are to unscramble the poem's disorderly fragments of narrative and build them into our own poem (*Oeuvres* 142-43), or in "L'Invention" ("Invention") where we read that "Toutes les transformations sont possibles" 'All transformations are possible' and that our creativity can be enacted in a multiplicity of spheres such as "L'Art d'aimer" ("The Art of Love,") or "l'art incohérent, l'art de fumer, l'art de jouir" 'incoherent art, the art of smoking, the art of pleasure' (*Oeuvres* 104-05).

In all of these texts the reader is invited to carry on creating meaning at exactly the point where the writer stops. A short poem from *Répétitions* (*Rote-Learning*) makes the point clearly:

Sans musique

Les muets sont des menteurs, parle.
Je suis vraiment en colère de parler seul
Et ma parole
Eveille des erreurs

Mon petit coeur.

(Eluard, *Répétitions* 35)

Without Music

Dumb people are liars, speak.
I am really angry about speaking on my own
And my speech wakes up errors

My little heart.

As a periphrasis for lyric poetry, the title "Without Music" calls for a new type of lyricism in which readers would no longer remain mute in their silent decipherings of another person's poem. In this new lyricism the poet would no longer have the frustration of speaking alone about the errors of his "small heart," but would instead be joined by readers speaking their *own* poetry. Indeed the main impetus of the collection *Répétitions* (from which this poem and two of the ones discussed earlier are taken) is to make fun of the model of rote-learning that the traditional poet (or metaphorical *répétiteur* [tutor]) inculcates.[5] In the poem just quoted, for instance, the first stanza apes the instructions of a teacher faced with recalcitrant pupils who will not recite their work ("If you remain silent you are lying about your assignment, so speak up!"). However, only when readers are freed from the repetition of words made for them can they come to speak poetically.[6]

Even if these poems have the effect of putting their readers in a poet's shoes, their strange loops do not, however, seem to go much further than that. In Eluard's 1937 collection *Les Mains libres* (*Free Hands*—which is described on its cover page as a series of Man Ray drawings "illustrated" by poems) there is nevertheless one text whose recursive structure gives each of its readers a model for living. Here is the poem along with the drawing that appears on the left-hand facing page (Figure 1):

> Où se fabriquent les crayons
>
> La dernière hirondelle
> A tresser une corbeille
> Pour retenir la lumière
> La dernière à dessiner
> Cet oeil déserté
>
> Dans la paume du village
> Le soir vient manger les graines
> Du sommeil animal
>
> Bonne nuit à la pensée
>
> Et j'appelle le silence
> Par son plus petit nom. (*Oeuvres* 663)

Where Pencils Are Made

The last swallow
To weave a basket
In order to hold in the light
The last one to draw
This deserted eye

In the village's palm
The evening comes up to eat the seeds
Of the animal sleep

Good night to thought

And I am calling forth silence
With its smallest possible name.

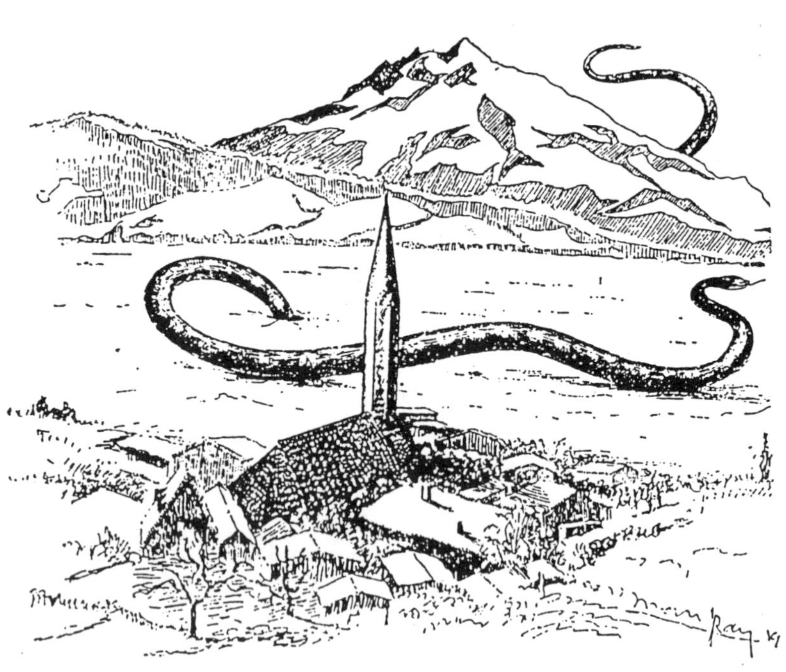

Figure 1. Drawing by Man Ray from Paul Eluard, *Les Mains libres*, 1937. © 1994 Artists Rights Society (ARS), New York / ADAGP / Man Ray Trust, Paris and Editions Gallimard for the poem.

On first reading the title would appear to designate a workshop or factory where pencils are made, but this interpretation is soon dispelled by the rest of the poem which describes the very opposite of a manufacturing scene. For there we find a rural landscape before the onset of night, in which the compound metaphor of stanza two identifies the village with a person, and the evening light with an animal that eats out of the person's hand. This rural setting is confirmed by a glance at Man Ray's accompanying drawing where we find long shadows in the village square, located next to the church, that indicate the late hour of the day. Indeed, each stanza in the poem is a development of words associated with nightfall. The opening line, which reverses a standard metonymy for the start of spring (and hence new beginnings), "the first swallow," goes on to emphasize the disappearance of daylight: the swallow's flight traces out a metaphorical basket to preserve the little light that remains. In stanza two, if we follow through the logic of its extended metaphor, the nourishment that the personified (or animalized) night receives will give sustenance to night-time's activity. That this activity is not rational thinking is underscored by the next stanza, and yet the poem's last two lines, in their call for silence, do not give us many clues as to what the activity might be. All the enigmatic metaphors of the previous lines seem to be anchored in the grammatically straightforward statement of the last stanza, which is both a performative utterance *addressed to* a particular realm of silence, and a description of the form this utterance takes: "I am calling forth silence with its smallest possible name." What this name is is not clear, but the smallest possible typographical mark does come right after it—namely, the period that closes the poem. In many ways it seems that the entire text eventually shuts itself down and collapses into a black point.

When examined more closely, however, this gradual progression throughout the poem towards the silence of night clearly embodies other figurative meanings. First, the narrator's call to silence in the final stanza also addresses the smallest point in the drawing—namely, the pencil tip that is located just above the center of the painting, occupying the place of the church steeple (Figure 2). I shall return to the significance of the pencil shortly, but for now I want to consider the other entity (besides silence) to which the poem is addressed: "Cet oeil déserté" (line

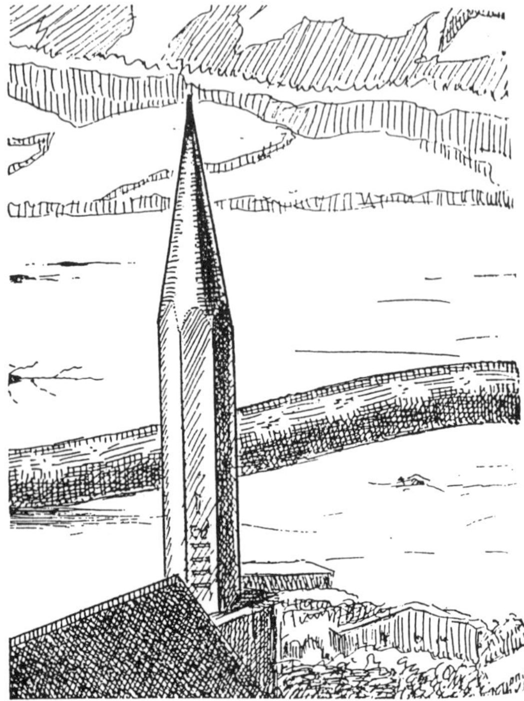

Figure 2. Drawing by Man Ray from Paul Eluard, *Les Mains libres*, 1937 (detail). © 1994 Artists Rights Society (ARS), New York / ADAGP / Man Ray Trust, Paris.

5). The eye is "abandoned" because it simply is not in the drawing. Nor can it be since it is not an object that the viewer is able to see, but rather the latter's very act of looking. I shall demonstrate in a moment that this act of looking retraces a movement mapped out by both the snake's body and the pencil in Man Ray's picture. Consequently, what Eluard's first stanza describes is this creative movement as seen in turn by the draughtsman, the poet, and the reader.[7] In the opening stanza a swallow's flight and basket-weaving are used to metaphorize this motion that sustains the drawing. The verb *trisser* 'to twitter' is the standard technical term for a swallow's cry, which, as we know, announces a new event (namely, spring). But here the swallow's call has one of its letters changed (to *tresser* 'to weave'), and so becomes the figure for a much broader event described both as weaving a basket of light and as drawing the picture's missing eye — that of its viewer. The poem is claiming that Man Ray's drawing depicts our own capacity to see art by using our imagination to recreate the movement behind a drawing. The gradual movement towards darkness that we noticed earlier in each stanza is significant, then, precisely because it is at night when creative seeing (or dreaming) takes over and the viewer becomes a poet. Eluard stresses this active collaboration of the spectator in the preface to *Les Mains libres*, where he discusses the "sleepless night" of a dreamer in front of a page: "Le papier, nuit blanche. Et les plages désertes des yeux du rêveur" 'The paper, sleepless night. And the deserted beaches of the dreamer's eyes' (557).

Put simply, the key references made by Eluard's poem to objects in the rural scene that Man Ray depicts are not so much names for objects *within* Man Ray's landscape as pointers towards the very activity of drawing the picture, an activity that we are invited to continue. Such is the loop traced out by Eluard's accompaniment to his friend's work. Words that we initially thought were describing a scene depicted in a drawing now appear to describe a curious picture that draws itself.

The strange loop in these two paired art-works goes even further, however, since it clarifies disruptions of meaning in the picture as well as the poem. To begin with the latter's title, this is not a periphrasis for a pencil-factory but an ellipsis for "Où se fabriquent les dessins faits au crayon" 'Where pencilled drawings are made,' so that the poem is actually an investigation into how drawings (as well as pencilled poems) come into being. This in turn clarifies the most disturbing aspect of Man Ray's picture: namely, the serpent and pencil point that together occupy the center of the composition. It is a strange serpent for several reasons. First of all its head, which appears on the right hand side of the picture, would seem to be too small or narrow to match the thick body of the snake that emerges from the drawing's center. This anomaly prods the viewer into looking for another head to the serpent, and in fact if we let our fingers follow the sinuosities of the reptile's body, we discover that this head cannot be located where the tail appears on the horizon but must instead occupy the space taken over by the pencil point that re-emerges from the earth in place of the church steeple. The moving serpent does not, then, have a referential function within the rural landscape code (this much, at least, is obvious), but plays another role. It would seem that it has the same figurative value as the swallow's flight in Eluard's poem—namely, to metaphorize the acts of drawing and looking that produce the landscape.

Understood in this way, Man Ray's serpent sheds light on two other obscure elements in the picture. First, the pencil point in the middle of Man Ray's picture apparently emerges from nowhere. It seems to be none other than the actual pencil that the artist used to trace the rest of the lines in the drawing, and so, in a movement similar to that of weaving a basket (line 2 in the poem), Man Ray's pencil plays the role of a needle that threads a series of lines over the surface of the paper and then plunges behind the paper (where the snake's body burrows into the ground) only to resurface as the guiding thread for the entire construction. A second problem is also solved since now it is clear why there is no swallow in the drawing. For the bird and its flight as mentioned in the poem are not parts of the drawn landscape but instead figures for the on-going production of the art-work.

One question nevertheless remains to be answered in "Où se fabriquent les crayons." Why should the poieitic force of doing or making have as its figure the body of a snake? If we consider that the Eluard-Man Ray text is replacing an image-based model for thought with an action-based one, the answer becomes clear. For by saying, in effect, "Bonne nuit à la pensée sous forme de représentations" 'Good night to thought as it is made up of representations,' Eluard's poem puts to sleep any reader who is in search of a thought that the poem would express. However, for those readers who are attuned to Eluard's definition of thought as an activity, or as "le penser" 'thinking' rather than its by-products (or "pensées" 'thoughts'), then Man Ray's "serpent" 'snake' is especially relevant since it is a phonetic anagram of this activity.

More importantly, the peculiar contortions of Man Ray's snake, which appears to be both *in* the picture and outside of it (since it has apparently pierced the page to reappear as a pencil), function in a way similar to Paul Valéry's emblem of a snake biting its own tail. For both figures illustrate a form of thinking that bends back upon itself in order to move forward. Moreover, the snake-pencil makes sense only if the viewer incorporates its movement into his or her own three-dimensional space lying outside the confines of the emblem itself. By using the pencil point in the center of Man Ray's drawing as a call to the reader, that is itself situated on the reader's plane, Eluard makes the picture quite literally point onward and upward to its viewers' own potential actions. The answer given to the question implicit in the poem's title ("Where indeed are pencil drawings made?") is, quite simply, "In the people who look at them." We, the readers of poems and the viewers of pictures, are the centers of artistic creativity.

That such creativity is ethical (being connected as it is to our actions as well as to our thoughts), and not merely contemplative or aesthetic, is made quite plain in some of Eluard's earliest writings. "Connaissons ce dont nous sommes capables" 'Let's be aware of what we can do,' he declares in the preface to his 1920 collection *Les Animaux et leurs hommes, les hommes et leurs animaux* (*Animals and Their Men, Men and Their Animals*) (*Oeuvres* 37). The "we" here includes both author and reader, since the collective surrealist enterprise was intended precisely to abolish the separation between these. Hence Eluard's famous statement that "Le poète est celui qui inspire bien plus que celui qui est inspiré" 'The poet is the one who inspires, much more than he is the one inspired,' which he offers as a commentary on Lautréamont's "La poésie doit être faite par tous. Non par un" 'Poetry must be done by all, not by one' (Eluard, *Donner* 76-77). The preface to *Les Animaux et leurs hommes* goes on to examine the actions of which we are capable and which do not derive their value from external criteria but instead from their own internal necessity:

> Qu'une force honnête nous revienne.
> Quelques poètes, quelques constructeurs qui vécurent jeunes nous l'avaient déjà enseigné. (. . .)
> La beauté ou la laideur [i.e. external norms for judging our achievements] ne nous paraissent pas nécessaires. (. . .) La vanité qui pousse l'homme à déclarer ceci beau ou laid, et à prendre parti, est à la base de l'erreur raffinée de plusieurs époques littéraires, de leur exaltation sentimentale et du désordre qui en résulta.
> Essayons, c'est difficile, de rester absolument purs. Nous nous apercevrons alors de tout ce qui nous lie. (37)

> May an honest impetus return to us.
> Some poets, some constructors who lived young had already taught us this. (. . .)
> Beauty or ugliness do not seem to us to be necessary. (. . .) The vanity that pushes humans to declare that something is beautiful or ugly, and to take sides on the issue, is at the basis of the refined error in several literary periods, of their exalting of sentimentality, and of the disorder that results from it.

Let's try, even though it's difficult, to remain absolutely pure.
We will then become aware of everything that ties us together.

The poems introduced by the preface set up as models for this new community of action the apparently insignificant, but in fact exemplary, lives led by animals. A dog, for instance, is not torn by contradictions between its goals and acts; it lives at one with both of them:

Chien chaud,
Tout entier dans la voix, dans les gestes
De ton maître,
Prends la vie comme le vent
Avec ton nez.

Reste tranquille. (42)

Warm dog,
Entirely in the voice, and in the gestures
Of your master,
Take life like the wind
With your nose.

Stay calm.

As we discover in the opening poem of the collection "Animal rit" ("An Animal Laughs"), once this simplicity of life is attained a harmony between creatures and their environment comes about: "Le monde rit, / Le monde est heureux, content et joyeux. / La bouche s'ouvre, ouvre ses ailes et retombe" 'The world laughs, / The world is happy, content and full of joy. / Our mouth opens, opens its wings and falls back down' (39).

Throughout most of their lives, however, people are different. In order to mollify the worst things that happen to them and give direction to their days, they invent the notion of "usefulness" which explains away the misery and destruction wrought by their work on, and supposedly "for," others:

Homme utile

Tu ne peux plus travailler. Rêve,
Les yeux ouverts, les mains ouvertes

Dans le désert,
Dans le désert qui joue
Avec les animaux — les inutiles.

Après l'ombre, après le désordre,
Dans les champs plats, les forêts creuses,
Dans la mer lourde et claire,
Un animal passe — et ton rêve
Est bien le rêve du repos. (44)

Useful Man

You cannot work any more. Dream,
With your eyes open, your hands open
In the desert,
In the desert that plays
With the animals — the useless ones.

After the shadow, after the disorder,
In the flat fields, the hollowed out forests,
In the clear and heavy sea,
An animal goes by — and your dream
Is indeed the dream of sleep.

It is not that we should simply become animals, according to Eluard. However, since we have decimated the world around us (by "flattening" the fields and "hollowing" out the forests — either through labor or war [line 7]), there is no more purpose for utilitarian morality other than the continued transformation of nature into a man-made desert. In other words, sooner or later individuals will come to recognize the hollowness of their standard work-goals (namely more work), and that a use*less* life, in which one opens out on to the surrounding world (rather than controlling it), offers the dream of permanent equilibrium to which all creatures aspire. Individuals are truly useful to themselves (and others) when they are not undermining their own happiness through misplaced goals — for instance, the accumulation of wealth that bourgeois society hides under its dual facade of "utility" and "duty."

Eluard had already attacked the latter smoke screen in his previous volume of poems, *Duty and Worry* (*Le Devoir et l'inquiétude*) (1917):

> Me souciant d'un ciel dévasté,
> De la pluie qui va nous mouiller
> Je vais pensant au grand bonheur
> Qui nous saisirait si nous voulions.
>
> Le devoir et l'inquiétude
> Partagent ma vie rude
> (C'est une grande peine
> De vous l'avouer.) (*Oeuvres* 21)
>
> Worrying about a devastated sky,
> About rain that will soak us
> I go forward thinking about the great happiness
> That would come over us if only we wanted it.
>
> Duty and worry
> Share my harsh life
> (It's a great disappointment
> To admit it to you.)

The "inquiétude" 'disquiet' mentioned here must be understood in its strongest possible sense: namely, a dissolution of the logically prior state of quietude that characterizes any person at ease with their acts. For such a person exemplifies the life-without-internal-strain (or "grand bonheur") that Eluard compares, in the poem quoted earlier, to a dog's faithful acceptance of the real: "Cette fidelité précieuse / Entre toutes: l'espoir de vivre" 'This precious faithfulness / Over and above all others: the hope of living' (*Oeuvres* 19). Moreover, it is precisely the concept of "devoir" 'duty,' or of *having* to do something (rather than doing things that flow effortlessly from one's choices), that leads to the ideological disquiet that Eluard unpacks in these early works.

Returning to "Où se fabriquent les crayons," we can now understand that the sort of doing to which the poem's loop leads us is not the dutiful adherence to a course of action expected by others but rather a recreation for ourselves of the particular formal necessity inscribed within the poem and the drawing it accompanies. In other words, the formal self-sufficiency of the conjoined poem and picture (which leads us to retrace the movements of the pencil-snake and unravel the poem's metaphors) triggers an activity, or type of thinking, in the reader that is its own justification. We do it not for any particular goal but because it is itself joy-creating. This self-enclosed loop action teaches us a model of joy that replicates the movement of life: it too is followed not because it leads to fixed goals (economic gain, self advancement, or whatever), but because it is a self-sustaining happiness in and of itself. We live for life, despite the diversions that cloud this fact for us, and much surrealist poetry brings home the full force of this experience.

When readers follow the strange loop in Eluard's poem, applying the poem's rules to their own action blends together the text's formal constraints with their particular idiosyncracies of interpretation. There is an ethical counterpart to this blending of formal rules and individual choice, since the ability to extract impetus for one's own acts from constraints imposed upon them is the hallmark of living effectively. Turning the necessities of form (in poems) or of circumstance (in one's life) to one's own use is learning to live more fully.

Art-works with strange loops in them thus transform their spectators in a wide variety of ways, since these people no longer simply consume artistic commodities. Instead, through their cooperation in the work's performance, they are reconnected to a type of form-making that is at the basis of living. Indeed, it was between these two opposed definitions of art (as commodity consumption or as human transformation) that surrealism's fate was held. It is no exaggeration to say that when the movement lost the ethical thrust sustaining the latter project, it finally died.

Notes

[1]See Breton's "Second manifeste du surréalisme" (1930): "L'acte surréaliste le plus simple consiste, revolvers aux poings, à descendre dans la rue et à tirer au hasard, tant qu'on peut, dans la foule." 'The simplest surrealist act is to go down into the street, with a revolver in each hand, and shoot at random, as often as you can, into the crowd' (Breton 78). All translations are mine.

[2]"Qui n'a pas eu, au moins une fois, envie d'en finir de la sorte avec le petit système d'avilissement et de crétinisation en vigueur" 'Who has not wanted, at least once in their lives, to be finished in this way with the petty degradations and stupidities that are thrust upon us by the system in force' (Breton 78).

[3]An important discussion of the parallelism between Breton's sentence and the saying it transforms can be found in Russo 14.

[4]For the importance of ethics to the surrealist project see Chénieux-Gendron 93, 107, 115-16; and also Hubert 24-26, 52.

[5]See Ernst's collage, in the original edition of *Répétitions*, in which a teacher tells four boys at his blackboard what to write. The collage is reproduced in Hubert 56, and a discussion of the multiple meanings of "repetition" for Eluard and Ernst's collaborative work can be found in Hubert 55-58.

[6]Cf. the following commands and advice addressed to us or to the poet in *Répétitions*, with the intention of making poetry happen: "La rivière que j'ai sous la langue, / (. . .) mon petit bateau, / (. . .) parlons" 'The river that I have under my tongue, / (. . .) my little boat, / (. . .) let's speak' (*Oeuvres* 107); "Le coeur sur l'arbre, vous n'aviez qu'a le cueillir" 'The heart on the tree. / You have only to pick it off' (108); "La vie est bien aimable. / Venez vers moi, si je vais à vous c'est un jeu" 'Life is very pleasant. / Come towards me, if I go to you it's a game' (105). The poem entitled "La Parole" ("Speech") on p. 106 of the collection describes the new eloquence and accompanying joy that poetic liberation brings.

[7]The perception of form-making has close ties with Eluard's active definition of looking at art, found for instance in the epigraph to *Donner à voir* (*To Make Seen*): "Voir, c'est comprendre, juger, transformer, imaginer, oublier ou s'oublier, être ou disparaître" 'Seeing is understanding, judging, transforming, imagining, forgetting or forgetting oneself, being or disappearing' (*Oeuvres* 918). This perception of form-making has nothing passive about it, which is why so many attempts at explaining surrealism in terms of image consumption go astray. For as Eluard implies in one of his poems in *Le Devoir et l'inquiétude*, to see is to make or produce in the sense of *poiein* rather than fabricate something for its exchange value: "Je ne peux rien faire, je ne peux rien voir" 'I cannot do anything, I cannot see anything' (*Oeuvres* 22). Seeing and doing are one and the same.

Works Cited

Breton, André. *Manifestes du surréalisme*. Paris: Gallimard, 1975.

Chénieux-Gendron, Jacqueline. *Surrealism*. Trans. Vivian Folkenflik. New York: Columbia UP, 1990.

Eluard, Paul. *Donner à voir*. Paris: Gallimard ["Poésie"], 1978.

_____. *Oeuvres complètes*. Vol. 1. Eds. Marcelle Dumas and Lucien Scheler. Paris: Gallimard [Pléiade], 1968.

_____. *Répétitions. Capitale de la douleur*. Paris: Gallimard ["Poésie"], 1976.

Hofstadter, Douglas R. *Gödel, Escher, Bach: An Eternal Golden Braid*. New York: Basic, 1979.

Hubert, Renée Riese. *Surrealism and the Book*. Berkeley: U of California P, 1988.

Russo, Adelaide. "Picking Up the Pieces: Tzara's Explosive Text and the Surrealist Strategy." *Miorita* 9.1-2 (1985): 1-18.

The Hanover *Merzbau*: Tracing a Lost Masterwork

Roger Cardinal

To visit Hanover only makes sense if one
is interested in ruins.

     —Helma Schwitters, unpublished
letter of October 3, 1943

Of the various irreparable losses that modern warfare has
inflicted on works of art, that of Kurt Schwitters's first *Merzbau*
must count as one of the saddest. Begun during the earliest years
of *Merz* creativity, this legendary installation occupied the artist
for the best part of two decades and eventually took over the
whole studio in his Hanover home on the Waldhausenstrasse.
But the *Merzbau* was interrupted in its development when
Schwitters fled from Nazi Germany in late 1936, and seven years
later it was completely destroyed in an air raid.

Of course, it is well known that there were other embodi-
ments of the *Merzbau*. During his years in exile, Schwitters was
to initiate two significant supplements. The first was the *Haus
am Bakken*, a mainly wooden structure assembled at Lysaker near
Oslo, Norway, in 1937-40. The second was the *Merzbarn*, begun
in 1947 inside a barn at Elterwater near Ambleside, England,
and left unfinished when the artist died the following year. Neither of these versions could be said to rival the original construction in scale or development. Moreover, the former burned down

in 1951; and while the latter was salvaged and relocated in a gallery in Newcastle, it remains, comparatively speaking, scarcely more than a poignant fragment.[1]

There are at least two further constructions which can be cited as authentic *Merzbau* variants, and it is always possible there were other minor satellites of the Hanover original that have not been remembered.[2] Even so, given its ambitious size and complexity, the long period of its gestation, and its chronological priority over all other versions, no one would deny that it is indeed the Hanover version that constitutes the quintessential *Merzbau*. Archetype and macrocosm, it remained the prime achievement of Schwitters's entire career, as indeed the artist himself acknowledged in referring to it as "my life's work" (Schwitters, *Wir spielen* 180). Yet what traces remain today of that momentous creation? Where and how did it come into existence, and what exactly was lost when that fatal bomb fell in 1943? In this inquiry I shall review the surviving evidence of its original constitution and try to outline the range of meanings we might attribute to a work whose robust myth seems to belie its actual fate.

The obvious place to start is in Schwitters's native city. I shall begin by proposing three actual locations in today's Hanover as likely places for tracking down spatial and visual clues about the *Merzbau*. They are the Rathaus, the Waldhausenstrasse, and the basement of the Sprengel Museum. I shall also cite ancillary documentation drawn from the Schwitters Archive in the City Library.

Restored in the postwar years after extensive bomb damage, the Rathaus or City Hall (built 1901-1913) today dominates the south side of the city center. Within and to either side of its great staircase, the visitor will find four large and impressive scale models of Hanover. Three bear the dates of 1689, 1939, and 1945, while the fourth shows a thriving postwar metropolis under the caption "Hanover Today." Whereas three of the models articulate local pride in the past and present status of an attractive and prosperous city, the 1945 version speaks very differently. Here the city is depicted in utter ruin, the exactitude of detail in its flattened landmarks and broken walls conveying a sickening vision of apocalyptic destruction, most of it effected in a series of massive night bombardments carried out by British bombers during September-October 1943.[3]

One stray bomb happened to fall on an innocuous street in the suburbs. When, accompanied by his teenage son, Kurt Schwitters had departed from Hanover on Boxing Day 1936, he had left his wife Helma in charge of the group of apartment houses whose rents had traditionally consolidated the family income.[4] The bombing was a catastrophe for them both. In a harrowing letter to her Swiss friend Edith Tschichold, Helma announces the annihilation of Schwitters's studio and all its contents:

> Sadly I must tell you we have lost all four houses. Two were probably destroyed by incendiary bombs, only their outer walls have survived, and two were destroyed by an explosive bomb which struck the house next door, those were the houses on the Waldhausenstrasse. What hurts me almost more than anything is that Kurt's studio has been destroyed along with everything else, perhaps one of the most interesting things, and if you like one of the loveliest things in the whole world, and along with it a whole lot of his best pictures. . . . (Unpublished typescript letter dated October 3, 1943, Schwitters Archive item 886)

Exiled in England, Schwitters was himself to learn of the disaster only several months later. Yet as his correspondence touchingly reveals, the Hanover *Merzbau* remained uppermost in his thoughts throughout the years of exile. A letter of July 18, 1938 to Carola Giedion-Welcker mentions that she cannot visit the *Merzbau* because it is *zugebaut* — which I take to mean semi-permanently walled-in (Schwitters, *Wir spielen* 148). (Schwitters had not anticipated permanent exile when he left Hanover in December 1936, so we may surmise that he afterwards felt worried enough to send word to Helma to have the studio closed up.) Helma died of breast cancer in October 1944. Subsequent letters to his many friends indicate that for several months the artist nourished hopes of returning home and restoring the site. Still grieving for Helma, he seems entirely incapable of digesting the fact of the utter loss of his masterwork and keeps fantasizing about rescuing it from the rubble. As late as April 25, 1946 he is still writing to his Hanover friends Christof and Luise Spengemann, doing sketches of the floor-plan of the house from memory and insisting that they keep the workmen away, since he alone is entitled to undertake the salvage operation (Schwitters, *Wir spielen* 193-94). Another letter to the painter Otto Gleichmann on July 17, 1946 refers to a photograph of the bombed site that a former neighbor had sent him; it shows No. 3 to be completely flattened, while the adjacent façade of No. 5 still stands. While conceding that he is well aware that the rear of No. 5 has been destroyed, he still cannot bring himself to believe as much from the photograph and needs visible proof.

> I see it clearly now. The façade remains intact. Number 3 is completely destroyed. Also that part of my house nearest the woods, where my studio was located on the *parterre* floor. Even so, I cannot make it out precisely from the photo. I would very much like photos of the studio taken from the side of the woods, so that I can see whether there is anything that can be rescued. (Unpublished letter, Schwitters Archive item 379)

Another letter to Spengemann of November 11, 1946 finds the artist in an obdurate mood, announcing that "I'll just have to make a *new Merzbau* — out of the remnants and the dust of the old one" (Schwitters, *Wir spielen* 246). A letter of December 9, 1946 to Lotte Gleichmann expresses regret that she had been unable to sketch the ruins for him and announces his intention to visit Hanover during the coming year (Unpublished letter, Schwitters Archive item 388). A subsequent letter from Otto Gleichmann indicates that his wife did indeed later make such a sketch and send it to Schwitters in Ambleside (Unpublished letter of early 1947, Schwitters Archive item 645). Contacts with the Museum of Modern Art in New York, mediated by his friend Katherine Dreier, were to eventuate in a grant in support of a new *Merzbau* project, the Elterwater *Merzbarn*, but were for some months premised on the expectation that Schwitters would indeed get back to Hanover and work on the original site. Of course, Schwitters never did return from exile and not a single remnant of his masterwork has survived.

Today's visitor to the Waldhausenstrasse takes a fast underground train from the city center, which soon emerges above ground to follow the route of the former tram line so dear to Schwitters, southwards along the Hildersheimerstrasse until the Döhren Tower. The residential Waldhausen district was no military target, and is indeed not even in central Hanover, being a semi-rural neighborhood some four kilometers out from the old city. The extensive Engesohde cemetery (where Schwitters is now buried) and a big lake, the Maschsee, lie within walking distance. At one end of the present Waldhausenstrasse are a pharmacy and a restaurant, but otherwise the street remains devoted to respectable bourgeois houses with balconies, front gardens, and trees. Today's No. 5 — like No. 3, where the bomb fell — is a functional modern apartment house; it clashes with the taller and far more elegant building next to it, No. 5A, one of the row built here at the turn of the century.[5] An old photo of the original No. 5 shows it to have been structurally consistent with the surviving row, being a tall, rather imposing house with a cellar, a ground floor, two upper stories, and an attic.[6]

The Schwitters family moved into the newly built No. 5 in 1889 when Kurt was two, so that it literally became his childhood home. Following their marriage in 1915, Schwitters and Helma lived elsewhere, but once the war was over they moved into a four-room apartment on the second floor at the front of No. 5, sharing the house with Schwitters' parents and various lodgers. At this time Schwitters had the use of a room as his studio, in the middle of the house on the floor below. In 1921 or thereabouts, new tenancy regulations forced Schwitters's father to take in more lodgers, and Schwitters was obliged to shift his studio to the room right at the back of the house (a second adjoining room was annexed a few years later). There was also a balcony to the side, above a narrow courtyard. All the houses on the north side of the street back onto a narrow strip of garden bordered by a tiny stream, beyond which lies a section of the wooded Elfenriede park. A curtain of dense foliage some twenty feet away would thus have been Schwitters's view from his studio window. These arrangements were to continue until 1936, so that it was on the inside of an entirely conventional bourgeois house that one of our century's most remarkable works took shape.

The precise inception of the Hanover *Merzbau* is of necessity undocumented. It was of its essence to be unplanned, to derive its shape through accretion over time. While Schwitters's early *Merz* productions in the formats of the paper collage (*Merzzeichnung*) or the wood-based assemblage (*Merzbild*) were by definition transportable, certain sculptural pieces began to assume larger proportions and to acquire a permanent footing within the studio, eventually modulating into fixed architectural features thereof. It is likely that by the time Schwitters moved into his new studio in about 1921 he had completed a number of *Merz* pieces resembling architectural maquettes, and very probably had begun the free-standing piece commonly seen as the foundation of the *Merzbau* proper, the *Merzsäule*, a column of wood and plaster that underwent several revisions before completion in about 1923. The proliferation of such columns prompted the elaboration of connective struts and intermediary alcoves or grottoes, some enclosed with glass. Mirrors, framed collages, paintings, newspaper cuttings, painted objects and a profusion of miscellanea adorned the corporate structure as it gradually asserted its dominion over the studio space, which was thereby transformed from workshop into artwork.

By 1927 the installation had spilled over into the next room (once Ernst's playroom), and thence reached the balcony, which had been given a glass roof and which communicated with the first room by way of a window of blue glass. Steps inside the body of the *Merzbau* led up to a tiny alcove where Schwitters occasionally slept. Subsidiaries of the main structure spread along corridors and up and down internal staircases, as well as down a spiral staircase built in 1936 to link the balcony to a water cistern in the courtyard (Schmalenbach 142). At least two other rooms elsewhere in the house were *gemerzt*, and Schwitters employed the occasional workman for special tasks such as fixing the electrical wiring. The enterprise was grandiose, though one might query the claim Schwitters made in an emotional letter of 1946 that as many as eight rooms had received the full *Merz* treatment (Schwitters, *Wir spielen* 246). Certainly the boisterous tales told by Hans Arp and Hans Richter of the *Merzbau* bursting through ceilings and plunging down to the cellar are exaggerated; there were, after all, several families living under the same roof, and it is unlikely that Schwitters had any entitlement to invade apartments other than his own.[7] My inference is that while sections of the structure could have been seen from next door and from the back of the house, the *Merzbau* remained invisible from the street.[8]

Today's visitor to Hanover is fortunate enough to have access to a life-size likeness of the *Merzbau*. Fabricated in 1981-83 by the Swiss stage designer Peter Bissegger, a reconstruction of the main section of Schwitters's masterwork is on permanent display in the Sprengel Museum amid an array of his smaller works.[9] Centrally located in the basement of a building whose exterior design suggests a defensive compound, the replica seems almost to ask to be seen as a gesture of defiance, a symbolic rejoinder to the Rathaus model of Hanover in ruins. An unassailable enclosure where visitors circulate, touch surfaces and corners, and look out of the window onto a tinted photograph of trees, it succeeds in suggesting a space charged with meaning. Nevertheless, Bissegger's simulacrum is a little too clean, a little too circumspect to be entirely persuasive. For one thing, it is based almost exclusively on three crisp photographs taken in 1933, at the time when Schwitters's flirtation with Constructivist purism was in the ascendent. Inevitably, the replica remains mute about what lay beneath the surface in the original. Moreover, its visual information relates strictly to the rear studio room, ignoring the adjoining room, the balcony, and other extensions of the structure.

"The *Merzbau* exists most authentically through its absence," writes Uta Brandes (47). It must be emphasized that we have only the most meager visual documentation to go by: a few floor plans, a clutch of some twenty photographs taken in the 1920s and 1930s, and Bissegger's reconstruction.[10] Those who seek to grasp what the *Merzbau* was all about are accordingly obliged to rebuild it in their minds, a task that, for lack of visual prompts, depends on a deep accumulation of verbal commentaries and extrapolations — those of the artist himself, the reminiscences of contemporary visitors, those of Ernst Schwitters (who last saw the structure at the age of eighteen), and the speculations, whether scholarly or feverish, of postwar commentators who never saw the place. Naturally, it can be said that any masterpiece evolves across time as discussions and interpretations accrue around it; yet it is peculiarly true of the *Merzbau* that, curtailed in 1936, it still proliferates as a disparate amalgam of recollection, hearsay and conjecture.

One text must be the foundation of our imaginary reconstruction. It is Schwitters's own programmatic "Ich und meine Ziele," 'Myself and my Aims,' composed in December 1930 at a mature point in the *Merzbau*'s evolution.[11] Despite the occasional nonsensicality of his idiom, Schwitters offers here what is assuredly the most confident and serious statement about the *Merzbau* he ever released.

His specific comments on his methods begin with a brief account of the *Merz* process of recycling everyday rubbish to make artworks, specifically the *Merzbilder*. He then goes on to highlight what is undeniably the *Merzbau*, although he insists on referring to it by the flamboyant title *Kathedrale des erotischen Elends* (*Cathedral of Erotic Misery*) or *KdeE* for short.[12] The Cathedral, we are told, comprises some ten columns and is still growing.[13] To elucidate the way it has evolved, Schwitters compares it to a large city whose planning authorities need to ensure that each fresh building is properly integrated into the total configuration. Schwitters underlines his readiness to admit new material, even if it is at the expense of old; already many additions have stepped across the corpses of past components, so that the work contains traces of many items that have forfeited their integrity and been superseded. The Cathedral, he assures us, is a near exhaustive orchestration of all the things that had surfaced in the past seven years that were "either important or unimportant in purely formal terms," adding that "a certain literary form" has infiltrated into the structure (344). Despite this touch of mystification, the artist has emphatically foregrounded the procedures of plentiful collation and supersession.

Schwitters now goes on to list the individual grottoes that make up the Cathedral. Here it should be noted that while ordinary usage would suppose a grotto to be at least man-size, Schwitters's "grottoes" would seem to range between what might be called alcoves to smaller "Höhlen" 'hollows' and tiny niches, crevices, or hideyholes. He mentions such features as "The Nibelung Treasure Cave," "The Goethe Grotto," "The Sex Crime Cave," and "The Grotto of Love." Several details are cited, including a musical box that plays "Holy Night, Silent Night," a reproduction of the *Mona Lisa* with Raoul Hausmann's face pasted over the famous smile, a brothel inhabited by a three-legged woman made by Hannah Hoech, a child with syphilitic eyes, a figure called the "Lavatory Attendant of Life," and a vial containing a specimen of the artist's urine, in which is dipped a sprig of forget-me-nots. All these structures, he adds, were at one time wired for electric light, but technical faults have led to a more modest use of fairy-lights, giving the impression of "an unreal illuminated Christmas tree" (344).

Schwitters reinforces the precept of *supersession* when he explains how the "Luther Corner," a relic of his Dada period, has, like some archaic quarter in a modern city, subsided beneath the present surface to the point of invisibility. He observes benignly that since its inception some seven years earlier—the implied date of 1923 marks the beginning of Schwitters's *concerted* effort—the Cathedral has undergone considerable structural change. It is now integrated within "a system of cubes of strictly geometric shape" and boasts an armature of linkages or "ribs." Schwitters teasingly suggests that one might see here a hint of Cubism or even of Gothic architecture.

The text ends on a note of tomfoolery and self-aggrandizement as its author boasts that only three people in the world (namely Herwarth Walden, Sigfried Giedion and Hans Arp) are capable of grasping the point of what he has done, although he is quick to add that perfect understanding may not be all that necessary in this context. We infer that Schwitters wishes us to be intrigued by the mystery of it all, while he avoids any definitive statement about what is still a work in progress—he casually coins the momentous axiom that the work is "unfinished, on principle" (343).

The testimony of those friends, colleagues and neighbors who saw inside 5 Waldhausenstrasse during the 1920s and 1930s is an invaluable supplement to the artist's own semi-evasive account. Several reliable witnesses provide further details of what went into the *Merzbau* and convey impressions of its impact. At least two local journalists had seen the first studio in 1919; one of these, Alfred Dudelsack, likened it to a crowded carpenter's shop in which there was scarcely a place to stand for all the planks, piled newspapers, cheese boxes, cigar boxes, tram tickets, and the rest (Elger, *Der Merzbau* 23-24). Proliferation and its corollary, cramming, were functional necessities of the *Merz* approach, and are the hallmark of Schwitters's aesthetics.

Schwitters's son Ernst has recorded his imprecise yet vivid memories of the early *Merzbau*, whose birth coincided with his own, and in and around which he grew up. He recalls how, at the age of four or five, he would play in his father's studio and help hammer in some of the nails. He notes his father's habit of emphasizing connections between the works juxtaposed on the walls by joining them up with lengths of string or wire, and later with wood and plaster. "This construction grew and grew and in the end filled several rooms on different floors of our house and resembled a gigantic abstract cavern," he writes (qtd. in Büchner, *KS 1887-1948* 25).

The Dada artist Hans Richter visited Schwitters's studio in 1925 and again in 1928 and comments pertinently on the *Merzbau*'s progress. On the first visit, the *Merzsäule* was displayed as a complex assemblage of compartments devoted to such individuals as Mondrian, Arp, Gabo, Lissitzky, Richter, Helma, and Ernst. Each cavity enshrined a talismanic object, for instance a shoelace, a nail-paring, a broken pen, a half-smoked cigarette. Three years later, all these cavities had been entirely buried beneath subsequent excrescences and curvilinear shapes (Richter 152-53).

The painter Rudolf Jahns was one of a group of local abstract artists who convened at Schwitters's house on March 12, 1927. His report refers to a column "which, rather, had matured into a grotto" and notes that one entered by a narrow door and had to squeeze past various obstructions. The space seemed soundless. A visitors' book lay on a small table, inviting comments. Once he had worked his way around all the alcoves and protuberances, Jahns took a seat at the center of the installation, whereupon he was overwhelmed by "a strange sensation of rapture" (qtd. in Büchner, *KS 1887-1948* 261). A second visit soon after was to confirm that the *Merzbau* was in constant flux and the space progressively more confined.

In her memoirs Kate Steinitz, an old Hanover friend of the artist, recalls visiting the Waldhausenstrasse many times. She tells how the place gave off a smell reminiscent not of a workshop or a kitchen or a zoo, but of all of these at once (14). A rare snapshot she took in about 1929 confirms that at least one pet guinea-pig had taken up residence inside the structure. (Schwitters loved pets and once alluded to experiments with white mice running around inside *Merzbilder* [Schwitters, "Ziele" 135].) Like Richter, Steinitz observes how the overall growth steadily subsumed the many niches and hideyholes (in one of the niches Schwitters had mischievously hidden the key she was frantically looking for; in another were a prescription and box of pills issued by her physician husband). She reflects:

> The cathedral contained much more than just his erotic misery. This was perhaps rather complex, but not nearly as tragic as his struggle for pure form, which eventually won out over the chaos of the darkest erotic grottoes, over the confusions of the historical grottoes and the grottoes of friendship. (149)

Though an enthusiast of Schwitters's smaller works, Alexander Dorner, director of the influential Kestner-Gesellschaft in Hanover, is one of the rare contemporaries to have voiced unequivocal dislike of the *Merzbau*, which he evidently saw as a symptom of regression. He is cited as referring to "a sick and sickening relapse into the social irresponsibility of the infant who plays with trash and filth" (qtd. in Elderfield, *Schwitters* 162; see also Falguières 152).

Subsequent critics and theorists coming to the *Merzbau* without direct experience of the original have offered innumerable commentaries ranging from the enlightening to the preposterous. Let me review a selection of these before offering my own final speculations.

In the first monograph on Schwitters, Werner Schmalenbach mentions that the *Merzbau* reminded him of the nightmarish sets devised for the 1919 Expressionist film *The Cabinet of Dr. Caligari* (134). Following up the cue, John Elderfield points out analogies with other experimental film sets of the same period, as well as with the work of such avant-garde architects as Antoni Gaudí, Bruno Taut, and Hans Poelzig (*Schwitters* 163-65). Roman Hollenstein draws parallels with Rudolf Steiner's Goetheanum and with the visionary architecture of Taut and Erich Mendelsohn (66). Dietmar Elger points out that Schwitters did indeed enjoy a brief association with Taut's utopian architectural group, the Gläserne Kette (Glass Chain) and even wrote a piece for its publication *Frühlicht* in 1922, proposing a scheme for transforming the whole city of Berlin into a *Merz* artwork ("L'Oeuvre" 145; see also Bergius, "Aspekte" 200).

Probing further into contemporary architectural debates, Dorothea Dietrich draws attention to the prominence of the Gothic cathedral as a symbol of artistic and social harmony; the Gläserne Kette circle adopted it as their archetypal structure, while the Bauhaus Manifesto of 1919 bore on its front cover Lyonel Feininger's woodcut of a Gothic cathedral titled "The Cathedral of the Future" (Dietrich 166). (We might note in passing that in 1920 Schwitters published a textless album of eight lithographs under the title *Die Kathedrale*.) Dietrich goes on to examine the motif of the column, linking the *Merzsäule* on the one hand to Johannes Baader's 1920 Dada assemblage, *The Great Plasto-Dio-Dada-Rama: Germany's Greatness and Decline* (also a work that would be destroyed), and on the other to the classic German type of the memorial pillar (178, 182). (Dietrich fails to mention that Hanover itself boasts one prominent example, the 46 meter-high Waterloo Column of 1832.) But what was the *Merzsäule* meant to memorialize? Both Elderfield and Dietrich suggest, but then shy away from, the thesis that it commemorated Schwitters's second son, who died in infancy. (The suggestion that the "doll's head" on top of the column was in fact a plaster cast taken from the dead child originated with Ernst Schwitters; see Elderfield 159 and Dietrich 181, 221). It is noteworthy that when he describes the Cathedral in 1931, Schwitters himself states that "the name *KdeE* is only a label. It doesn't refer to the content, or hardly so" (Schwitters, "Ziele" 344).

Sensitive to the artist's often devious relation to his audience, Elderfield underlines the contrast between the work's massive scale and the "hallucinatory confusion of tiny fetish objects" buried at its heart (*Schwitters* 175). His assessment of this self-absorbed structure is that it embodies a fantasy of omnipotence (169). For his part, Werner Schmalenbach sees the *Merzbau* as an instance of rational method serving an irrational goal; he argues that the dynamic skewing of the installation is in fact at odds with the geometric-constructivist principle that many have assumed it to exemplify. Perhaps inspired by Jahns, Schmalenbach ultimately wants to see the work as more mystical than aesthetic, an expression of a yearning for infinity, an infinity secreted "within its imaginary center, at the point of intersection of its secret spatial co-ordinates where indeed he wanted to see the viewer positioned" (144).

Evoking its magical character, Brian O'Doherty salutes the *Merzbau* as "a chamber of transformation" (45), while Hanne Bergius rhapsodizes about it as "a labyrinthine alchemical grotto" for converting rubbish into gold, as well as a channel for "a simultaneous stream of consciousness manifested as an overlapping and an intermingling of impressions and reminiscences, of sediments from different layers of experience" ("Aspekte" 198, 200).

Developing the notion of the *Merzbau* as a modern embodiment of the German Romantic ideal of the *Gesamtkunstwerk*, or total artwork, a notion that had been proposed by Elderfield among others ("Merz-Gesamtwerk"), Beatrix Nobis links Schwitters's project to Friedrich Schlegel's dream of the poetic reconciliation of the finite and the infinite; at once an abandoned fragment and a lifetime's effort, the *Merzbau* registers "the ambivalence of the provisional and the definitive" and is thus a true modern expression of Romantic irony (98-99). In much the same vein, Bettina Blumenberg reminds us of the Romantic cult of ruins and praises Schwitters for his essentially modern vision of the auratic fragment, "that which is smallest betokening that which is largest, namely the reality in which we live" (49). Roman Hollenstein identifies the *Merz* project as an early manifestation of a general twentieth-century impulse toward reconciling art with everyday existence and cites such artists as Edward Kienholz, Arman, and Joseph Beuys as working in the Schwitters lineage (66).

Given that the *Merz* project is synonymous with the practice of collecting samples of contemporary litter (El-Danasouri "Sammler" and Cardinal), Dorothea Dietrich likens the *Merzbau* to "a museum of mass culture" (191); Ernst Nündel reflects on the long list of individualized compartments, commenting that whereas other people collect stamps, Schwitters "collected friendships" (59).

Yet O'Doherty feels disposed to warn us that "the *Merzbau* was a tougher, more sinister work than it appears in the photographs available to us" (44). Dietrich, among others, has drawn attention to the Sex Crime Cave and the Grotto of Love with their macabre preoccupation with mutilation and sexual violence, something found both in the popular press of Schwitters's time and in the work of artists like Otto Dix (Dietrich 193-94). Brandes broods upon a compulsive proliferation that harbors an irresoluble tension between the familiar and the uncanny as the contents of subjectivity battle with their material counterparts. From one angle, she suggests, the *Merzbau* might seem like a cozy private refuge; from another it could seem a stifling and deranged exercise in self-incarceration.

Finally, Patricia Falguières rejects as misleading the analogy with public architecture, preferring to draw parallels with the claustrophobic private museum of Sir John Soane or the annotated curiosities hoarded by the French pastor Jean-Frédéric Oberlin. She identifies a telling paradox about the *Merzbau*, namely that its expansion was always dependent on processes of burying and sedimentation. Since all trace of the teeming influx of component parts was obliterated within the greater whole, the work's real function was not just to multiply but also to eradicate all contributory meanings. "The *Merzbau* is first and foremost a machine for forgetting," she stresses, while "oblivion is invention by another name" (152, 154).

It is amusing to observe the widespread critical reflex whereby, in an attempt to clarify this vexed work, commentators go hunting for analogies across a range of familiar or more remote constructions. If unsubstantiated resemblances have any relevance, I would propose one of my own by setting Schwitters alongside certain self-taught and largely unrecognized Outsiders of this century who have produced utopian environments of singular inventiveness and size (see Seitz; Conrads; Beardsley). Most particularly I am thinking of the fantastic building at Hauterives in France made by the postman Ferdinand Cheval, who in the space of three decades singlehandedly devised his Ideal Palace with ornamented towers, shrines, and grottoes housing scale models of other exotic buildings, as well as relics like his own trusty wheelbarrow and trowel. It is thought the Palace was conceived as its maker's own mausoleum. Or again there is the visionary environment realized in the Swiss Alps by Armand Schulthess, who crammed his house with plaster casts, old newspapers, and a home-made archive on sexology, and laid out a garden whose steep paths meandered amid trees on which were nailed tin lids inscribed with arcane astrological and scientific messages in five languages. Yet again, there is the House of Mirrors in New York State, a massive seven-story structure set against a steep slope and built out of discarded timber and glass by Clarence Schmidt, who, like Schwitters, wired up his master-work with fairy-lights; the House also had a sculpture garden full of ramshackle shrines inset with masks and dolls' heads and junk assemblages wrapped in silver foil.[14] Each of these single-handed structures is the work of a lifetime, and each exhibits the same brooding engrossment, a palpable sense of self-reliance, an arrogance tempered by furtiveness. Here may be posited a link between compulsive procedures of accumulation and interpolation and an obdurate inner resolve, a link that I think sheds some light on Schwitters's creative persona.

What general import might the *Merzbau* have as an example of uncommon architecture? Although some of the *Merzbau* variants, in common with the three visionary environments just mentioned, were constructed in the open, it is perhaps significant that both the lost original and Schwitters's last desperate attempt to reconstitute it, the *Merzbarn*, were built indoors. I take this to imply not that the relevance of the *Merzbau* is restricted to the field of interior design, but that its relation to the world at large is somewhat that of an architect's small maquette to his huge actual building. This is to suggest that the *Merzbau* may be the microcosm of other spaces beyond itself. Did not Schwitters once joke about applying the *Merz* treatment to the entire city of Berlin? Perhaps the key word here is "treatment," insofar as Schwitters's curious tenderness toward urban trash carries resonances of a therapeutic or redemptive kind. Perhaps we can say that his was not so much an architectural experiment as it was an inquiry into the processes of structuring and re-structuring as they operate on both the material and the spiritual plane of metropolitan life. How should modern individuals shape the buildings and the belief-systems they need to live within? Should they make do with what is outdated, or can they modernize the world without losing touch with origins? If one can create for oneself a simultaneous mental picture of the successive historical states of Hanover as imaged in the Rathaus models, then it might be possible to envisage the *Merzbau* in like fashion as a sort of archaeological model of an ancient metropolis. It was after all a structure shaped by sedimentation, by deposits, by accretion and supersession, much as a city progresses through successive stages of collapse and reconstruction. The accumulated traces of its material history are fixed within a defined space to form a record of the passage of time—or perhaps we should visualize its past as a simultaneity of layerings manifesting a timeless continuum.

The cultural arguments fed into the *Merzbau*—all those provocative tableaux of mythical, historical, political, and sexual themes—seem so variegated that the thought of comparing the work to a museum would seem to fly in the face of curatorial discipline; this must truly be the most incongruous collection of specimens of public culture. Perhaps there is more consistency in the personal sphere. This cabinet of curiosities does have a bias toward private affinities, not least in the compartments dedicated to the artist's intimates. Furthermore, we remember that Schwitters located the *Merzbau* within the house of his childhood, that his infant son played inside the structure, and that the grown man even slept inside it, regressing as it were to the blissful intra-uterine state (while also acting the part of the Bohemian in a bourgeois household). Again, we remember that the 1923 *Merzsäule* may in part have been a tribute to his dead second son, and he referred to the *Merzbau* as the Cathedral of "Erotic Misery." In other words, the project seems to be shot through with feelings of grief and nostalgia for long-lost states of happiness, feelings that surely erupt most powerfully when, in his English exile, Schwitters suffers the double trauma of the loss of Helma and of his masterwork, feelings that still run strong as he tackles the *Merzbarn*.

We might be forgiven for suspecting that the whole history of the *Merzbau* is a Borgesian fantasy expressly devised to tease us. Its qualities are so exasperatingly ambiguous, never clearcut. We feel obliged to call it incomplete (indeed incompletable), ruinous, provisional, planless, anarchic, irrational, hermetic, imponderable, ironic. Many of the relevant documents are tinged with uncertainty, and even experienced commentators seem to panic when the time comes to interpret the work. One thing is sure: the inventions of conjecture and comparison will continue to abound. Ernst Nündel seems prepared to welcome the notion that "each person has their own (idea of the) *Merzbau*" (58). I have given some indication of how, in their eagerness to apply their own label, critics have envisaged the work as Neo-Romantic, Symbolist, Cubist, Expressionist, Dadaist, Constructivist, or Abstract-Concrete, as if its protean adaptability qualified it under every sub-heading of Modernism. Schwitters once observed that "next to experience, analogy is man's best teacher" ("Ziele" 336), and so (as in the surrealist game of "L'Un dans l'autre") we may hope to pick up something from the exhilarating play of comparisons: the *Merzbau* is like a magpie's nest, a flea-market, an Aladdin's cave, a department store, an arcade, a peepshow, a cabinet of curiosities, an archive of mass culture, a chamber of horrors, an encyclopedia, a total work of art, a monument to friendship, a visitors' book, a bulletin board, an album of memories, a playground, a children's zoo, a Christmas grotto, a winter garden, a mirror-maze, a secret hideout, a suffocating oubliette, a sepulchre, a temple, an alchemist's laboratory, an ivory tower, an ideal palace, a womb, a catacomb, Eden, Pyramid, Pompeii, Berlin, Tardis, Caligari's cabinet, Frankenstein's uncontrollable monster, a hobby-horse, a chimera, a machine for forgetting, a sewer, an orchestration of incompatibilities . . . and so on, indefinitely. Our delight in connotation encourages us to collect partial similitudes, when we may only be drawing up a star map of our own fantasies. Yet, returning to the guiding principles of accumulation and supersession, we may find the most intriguing image to be that of the archaic palimpsest whose last message buries and obliterates all previous messages. Could it be that the *Merzbau* was unconsciously designed to become inaccessible — that its destruction, however regrettable, simply gave expression to an inbuilt proclivity, like some well-organized aesthetic suicide?

However, I suggest that the ultimate paradox (which would surely have delighted its inventor) is that, despite its material obliteration, the *Merzbau* has after all failed to achieve oblivion. Half a century on, we still feel entitled to probe for meanings in the layers of association its absence secretes. Perhaps indeed the work survives because we cannot lay hold of it except within language — and, crucially, because the words we use to speak of it and to give it life are so fruitfully ambiguous. We are stimulated because we want to see both sides of the coin at the same time. We are fascinated by the fact that the work we reconstruct in our minds embodies both the sacred and the profane, the cozy and the macabre, the innovative and the regressive, the social and the private, the purposeful and the aleatory. There is something of cunning yet also of naivety on either side, as the work alternately baffles us and surrenders to us, by turns serene and delirious. It is something perfect teetering always on the brink of ruination; it is art, and it is something monstrous that damns art. To arrest the momentum of this seduction may now be impossible. Sublime and evasive, insubstantial and dynamic, the destiny of this lost masterwork is to be the everlasting talking-piece of art criticism, the aggregate of all that it is possible to say about it, whether true or false. Naturally, this attempt to trace it cannot but help extend its uncanny afterlife.

Notes

[1]The *Haus am Bakken* (House on the Slope) was built outside the small town of Lysaker during 1937-40 under conditions of secrecy, given that it went up without planning permission in direct line of sight from the local police station (Schwitters, "Ziele" 366). Curiously, no photographic documentation seems to have survived, though we know that photographs taken by Schwitters or his son Ernst did at one time exist, since in a letter from Norway on July 18, 1938, Schwitters himself offers to send his friend Carola Giedion-Welcker some good photographs of the structure he has in his possession (Schwitters, *Wir spielen* 148). Moreover, shortly after the war Ernst settled in Norway as a professional photographer and had ample opportunity to make a record before the *Haus am Bakken* was destroyed. In his monograph, John Elderfield essays a sketch of the floor-plan based on Ernst's recollections (Elderfield, *Schwitters* fig. 316). The *Merzbarn* of 1947-48 has been much more assiduously documented (Elderfield "Merzbarn;" *Kurt Schwitters Almanach* 8 [1989]).

[2]The two other recognized variants raise to five the total number of concerted attempts to realize a *Merzbau*. The first survives entirely by report. In 1926, Schwitters spent a family holiday at Kijkduin on the Dutch coast, staying with a young artist friend, Lajos d'Ebneth. Years later, the latter was to record how Schwitters erected an outdoor monument some 2 1/2 meters high out of wooden planks dragged back from the beach, adorning it with assorted flotsam, frayed ropes, a bird's nest, and so forth (Nündel 58). During the 1930s the Schwitters family spent several summers on the Norwegian island of Hjertoy in the Molde Fjord, where they had leased an ancient forge; Schwitters built up its interior with sections of plaster and wood and pasted variegated layers of printed matter over the walls (Elger, "L'Oeuvre" 144). I judge as

inconclusive Fred Ullmann's passing reference (Lemoine 311) to a wooden "grotto" made in late 1940 in the attic at 19 Hutchinson Square, Douglas, on the Isle of Man, since I take it as axiomatic that a *Merzbau* variant must at least attain a certain size and complexity. (Of course, any collage or assemblage made by Schwitters could in principle count as a *Merzbau* in embryo.)

[3]Both Elger ("Entstehung" 28) and Elderfield (*Schwitters* 157) date the *Merzbau*'s annihilation to the night of October 8-9, 1943 on the basis of a reference in a letter Schwitters wrote from Ambleside on July 16, 1946 (Schwitters, *Wir spielen* 204). Certainly that climactic night remains notorious in Hanoverian popular memory. Yet if we accept the accuracy of the date of October 3, 1943 on the crucial letter to Edith Tschichold in which Helma Schwitters reports the destruction of her house, we must suppose that the *Merzbau* was hit during an earlier bombardment, those of September 22-23 and 27-28 being the most likely possibilities.

[4]Schwitters's cousin Frau Keitel recollected in 1984 that the Schwitters owned two houses on Waldhausenstrasse itself, a third on Freytagstrasse and a fourth on Adelheidstrasse (near the city center). See "Übermalter Teppich und Normalität," *Kurt Schwitters Almanach* 3 (1984): 59. Schwitters's mother owned a fifth house at 13 Güntherstrasse.

[5]I have been unable to determine why the editors of the recent Pompidou Center catalogue (Lemoine) should have altered the address of the Schwitters house to "Waldhausenstrasse 5 bis" when the formulation "Waldhausenstrasse 5" appears consistently on all Schwitters's envelopes and documents, and even on his visiting card from the 1930s displayed in the Pompidou exhibition. Perhaps they have misread the old photo of No. 5, in which the number plate for No. 5A accidentally obtrudes.

[6]I surmize that this unique snapshot was taken by Schwitters himself. It has been variously dated as 1926 and 1920. If the child of four or five posing in a cap is indeed his son Ernst (born November 1918), the photo might be dated to about 1922-23; the younger child of no more than two holding Ernst's hand might then prove to be Schwitters's second son, who died in infancy —which death would coincide with the inception of the *Merzsäule* and thus of the *Merzbau* proper. In the photo, the top of the façade bears the device of a smiling sun, identical with one still visible on No. 7 (which bears the date 1901).

[7]Elger refutes the notion that the *Merzbau* burst through the ceiling by citing a witness, Elisabeth Maack, who until 1934 lived without interruption in the room directly over Schwitters's studio (*Der Merzbau* 15). Elderfield gives a careful summary of the way the structure ramified through the house between 1923 and 1936 (*Schwitters* 156-57).

[8]Schmalenbach reports that one column built in an attic room extended through a window and up to the roof ridge (142). However, the fact that a sunbathing platform was built next to it in 1936 suggests that these extrusions were not located on the street side.

[9]A second, more mobile replica has subsequently traveled to Edinburgh and Paris. It is interesting to note that Schwitters had intended the *Haus am Bakken* to be transportable.

[10]It is likely that textual and visual documents concerning the *Merzbau* were housed at No. 5 and disappeared along with the work itself. It is known that along with many of Schwitters's own pieces and his personal collection of paintings by Arp and others, two visitors' books were among the casualties of the bombing (Schwitters, *Wir spielen* 284). (Interestingly, Schwitters also kept up the tradition of the studio album in Lysaker, intending to collate texts sent in by friends [Schwitters, *Wir spielen* 145]). Elger's scrupulous monograph on the Hanover *Merzbau* reproduces floor plans of the house interior drawn up in 1907 and 1921, as well as the two modest plans Schwitters drew from memory in 1946. The photographs that Ernst took at his father's request of the final state of the *Merzbau* before their departure in late 1936 appear to have vanished (Elger, *Der Merzbau* 10). Most importantly, Elger reproduces all extant photographs of the structure. If one discounts four photographs of isolated sculptural components not displayed *in situ*, the number of authentic photos of the interior amounts to no more than twenty. Moreover, several of these are close-ups of details. This means that in the end there survive only thirteen or so photographs that convey any sense of a three-dimensional environment.

[11]The paragraphs specific to the *Merzbau* are given in English in the same volume containing "Ich und meine Ziele" (423-24).

[12]This contraction has been taken to be an echo of the contemporary abbreviation of the Berlin department store *Kaufhaus des Westens*, or *KaDeWe* (Bergius, "Aspects" 447). This could imply that the *Merzbau* also represents a satire on consumerism.

[13]The dimensions Schwitters cites here (3.5 x 2 x 1 meters) are far too modest to correspond even to the single studio room on which Bissegger's replica is based (the latter's measurements being 3.9m high x 5.8m wide x 4.6m deep). The implication is that the artist is still talking about a group of columns rather than a total environmental installation, which suggests that he had yet to cross the conceptual watershed between the notion of a series of independent works and that of a *Gesamtkunstwerk* synonymous with the dimensions of an architectural space (the house) pre-dating its inception.

[14]Those who savor such parallels should note that while Cheval's Ideal Palace survives as a listed monument, both Schulthess's environment and Schmidt's House of Mirrors have been destroyed (the former by bureaucratic decree, the latter by arson).

Works Cited

Arp, Hans. *Onze peintres vus par Arp*. Zurich: Die Arche, 1949.

Bailly, Jean-Christophe. *Kurt Schwitters*. Paris: Hazan, 1993.

Beardsley, John. *Gardens of Revelation. Environments by Visionary Artists*. New York : Abbeville, 1994.

Bergius, Hanna. "Kurt Schwitters: Aspects of Merz and Dada. 'In the Elysian Fields of the Inventory.'" *German Art of the Twentieth Century. Painting and Sculpture 1905-1985*. Eds. Christos M. Joachimides, Norman Rosenthal, and Wieland Schmied. London: Royal Academy Of Arts/ Weidenfeld and Nicolson, 1985. 445-49.

______. "Aspekte zum Merzbau von Kurt Schwitters." *Architektur-Experimente in Berlin und anderswo. Für Julius Posener*. Eds. Sonja Günther and Dietrich Worbs. Berlin: Sabine Konopka, 1989. 198-205.

Blumenberg, Bettina. "Schwitters ist MERZ." *Neue Zürcher Zeitung* 170 (July 25-26, 1987): 49.

Brandes, Uta. "Merzbau im Biedermeier: Die Kathedrale des erotischen Elends." *Kurt Schwitters Almanach* 1 (1982): 39-48.

Büchner, Joachim. *Kurt Schwitters*. Hanover: Thomas Schäfer, 1988.

______ and Norbert Nobis, eds. *Kurt Schwitters 1887-1948*. Exhibition catalogue. 2nd rev. ed. Hanover: Sprengel Museum/Propyläen, 1987.

Cardinal, Roger. "Collecting and Collage-Making: The Case of Kurt Schwitters." *The Cultures of Collecting*. Eds. John Elsner and Roger Cardinal. London: Reaktion, 1994. 68-96.

Conrads, Ulrich and Hans G. Sperlich. *The Architecture of Fantasy*. New York: Praeger, 1962.

Dietrich, Dorothea. *The Collages of Kurt Schwitters. Tradition and Innovation*. Cambridge: Cambridge UP, 1993.

El-Danasouri, Andrea. "Der Sammler Kurt Schwitters: 'Der Abfall der Welt dient mir zur Kunst.'" *Kurt Schwitters Almanach 7* (1988): 9-24.

______. *Kunststoff und Müll. Das Material bei Naum Gabo und Kurt Schwitters*. Munich: Scaneg, 1992.

Elderfield, John. "Kurt Schwitters' Last Merzbarn." *Artforum* 8.2 (1969): 56-65.

______. "On a Merz-Gesamtwerk." *Art International* 21.6 (1977): 19-26.

______. *Kurt Schwitters*. London: Thames and Hudson, 1985.

Elger, Dietmar. "Die Entstehung des Merzbaus." *Kurt Schwitters Almanach* 1 (1982): 28-38.

______. *Der Merzbau. Eine Werkmonographie*. Cologne: Walther König, 1984.

______. "L'oeuvre d'une vie: Les *Merzbau*." Lemoine 140-51.

Falguières, Patricia. "Désoeuvrement de Kurt Schwitters." Lemoine 152-58.

Gohr, Siegfried et al. *Kurt Schwitters. Die späten Werke*. Exhibition catalogue. Cologne: Museum Ludwig Köln, 1985.

Haldenwanger, Maria et al. *Schwitters-Archiv der Stadtbibliothek Hannover. Bestandsverzeichnis 1986*. Hanover: Stadtbibliothek Hannover, 1986.

Hausmann, Raoul. *Courrier Dada*. Paris: Terrain vague, 1958.

Hollenstein, Roman. "'Vereinigung von Kunst and Nichtkunst im Gesamtweltbilde.' Zu Kurt Schwitters' Werk und dessen Rezeption." *Neue Zürcher Zeitung* 50 (March 1/2, 1986): 66.

Jürgen-Fischer, Klaus. "Der Merzbau—Pantheon des Dadaismus." *Vernissage* 1.7 (1960): n.p.

Kurt Schwitters. Exhibition catalogue. London: Tate Gallery, 1985.

Lach, Friedhelm. *Der Merzkünstler Kurt Schwitters*. Cologne: DuMont Schauberg, 1971.

Lemoine, Serge and Didier Semin, eds. *Kurt Schwitters*. Exhibition catalogue. Paris: Centre Georges Pompidou, 1994.

Malsch, Antje. "Auf der Fährte des Merzbaus. Zum Kathedralengedanken im Werk von Kurt Schwitters." *Kurt Schwitters: "Bürger und Idiot." Beiträge zu Werk und Wirkung eines Gesamtkünstlers*. Ed. Gerhard Schaub. Berlin: Fannei und Walz, 1993. 63-71.

Nobis, Beatrix. *Kurt Schwitters und die romantische Ironie. Ein Beitrag zur Deutung des Merz-Kunstbegriffes*. Alfter: Verlag & Datenbank für Geisteswissenschaften, 1953.

Nündel, Ernst. *Schwitters*. Reinbek bei Hamburg: Rowohlt, 1981.

O'Doherty, Brian. *Inside the White Cube: The Ideology of the Gallery Space*. Santa Monica/ San Francisco: Lapis, 1986.

Richter, Hans. *Dada. Art and Anti-Art*. London: Thames and Hudson, 1965.

Schmalenbach, Werner. *Kurt Schwitters*. 2nd ed. Munich: Prestel, 1984.

Schneider, Christian. "Schwitters Kathedrale. Eine Parodie." *Kurt Schwitters Almanach* 2 (1983): 25ff.

Schwitters, Kurt. "Ich und meine Ziele" [1931]. *Das literarische Werk* 5. Cologne: DuMont, 1981. 340-48.

_____. *Wir spielen, bis uns der Tod abholt. Briefe aus fünf Jahrzehnten*. Ed. Ernst Nündel. Frankfurt/ Berlin/ Vienna: Ullstein, 1974.

Seitz, William. *The Art of Assemblage*. Exhibition catalogue. New York: Museum of Modern Art, 1961.

Stark, Franz. *Schwitters-Archiv der Stadtbibliothek Hannover. Bestandsverzeichnis. Nachtrag 1987*. Hanover: Stadtbibliothek Hannover, 1987.

Steinitz, Kate T. *Kurt Schwitters. Erinnerungen aus den Jahren 1918-1930.* Zürich: Arche, 1963.

Text und Kritik 35-36 (1972). Special issue on Kurt Schwitters.

Vordemberge-Gildewart, Fridel. "Kurt Schwitters (1887-1948)." *Die Bauwelt* 13 (1959): 404-05.

Spiritual Quest and
Scriptural Inquiry:
Pierre Jean Jouve's
Art Criticism

Robert W. Greene

Pierre Jean Jouve did not write often about the plastic arts, nor by the end of his life had he produced an enormous body of art criticism. Nevertheless, his writings in this realm are substantial, and they hold great interest for his readers, as well as for anyone curious about the significant if still largely neglected phenomenon of *poésie critique*, as the art criticism of twentieth-century French poets has been called (Apollinaire 35). Moreover, except, notably, for the pioneering study of the poet's writings on art that, in 1972, Marcel Raymond contributed to the *cahier de l'Herne* devoted to Jouve, critics have paid little attention to this aspect of his oeuvre (Raymond). The present essay may thus be viewed as a belated coda to Raymond's article.

One cannot assess Jouve's art criticism without first at least noting Baudelaire's influence on him. The choice of artists that Jouve considers at any length—Delacroix, Meryon, Courbet—seems virtually dictated by Baudelaire's interests in this area. It is therefore hardly surprising that in 1958, when Jouve reissued his essays on the aforementioned artists, he published them, as he had done before, together with his monograph on Baudelaire, but reworked and included now in a new edition of *Tombeau de Baudelaire* (Jouve, *Tombeau*). The figure of his eminent predecessor thus openly presides over Jouve's thinking about these three "beacons" of the last century.

Before examining Jouve's writings on art, however, we must also identify two other formative influences on him, two life-altering experiences: his celebrated, highly idiosyncratic religious conversion, which took place in 1924, and, at almost the same moment, his discovery of Freud. The catalytic figure in the latter event was Blanche Reverchon, psychiatrist, translator of Freud and, eventually, Jouve's second wife. These major turning points in the poet's inner life coincided with, and quite probably precipitated, his dramatic break with the past, including his repudiation of his writings and beliefs prior to 1924.[1] And so, remarriage, rebirth, vita nuova.

The foregoing equation of course simplifies what must have been an extremely complex change of direction in the poet's spiritual and artistic journey. Indeed, it would probably be truer to the actual circumstances of Jouve's development in 1924 to treat his discovery of Freud, as well as his rediscovery of religious faith (Catholicism in his case), as his twin responses to a hunger that had been gnawing at him for years. From his earliest publications, one senses his need to locate, beneath the anguish of day-to-day existence, a transcendent value justifying his (and our) anguish, but without denying either the reality of our pain or our flawed, sensuous nature.

A pivotal text along Jouve's way, one associated with the events just related, is the preface that he wrote for the 1933 edition of *Sueur de sang*. This essay, entitled "Inconscient, spiritualité et catastrophe," amounts to an eloquent statement of the convictions underlying everything the poet produced after 1924, including his writings on art. In this key piece, the poet offers a concise yet passionate synthesis of his mystical and psychological (i. e., Freudian) ideas. His sure, supple deployment of terminology that must have been pristine at the time (e.g., *inconscient, libido, sur-moi, condensation*) is nothing short of dazzling. Obviously, Jouve has digested an utterly new vocabulary and mastered the conceptual system carried by the new lexicon. In the process, he has assimilated basic Freudian notions and combined them with his deepest spiritual beliefs. He affirms: "L'homme moderne a découvert l'inconscient et sa structure; il y a vu l'impulsion de l'éros et l'impulsion de la mort, nouées ensemble, et la face du monde de la Faute, je veux dire le monde de l'homme, en est définitivement changée" 'Modern man has discovered the unconscious and its structure; in it he has seen the erotic impulse and the death impulse, tied together, and the face

of the world of Error, I mean the world of humankind, has been
forever changed by it' (*Noces* 140).[2] After invoking the name of
Freud, he speaks of the psychological phenomenon of sublimation and maintains:

> pour certains esprits (les mystiques) doit exister la possibilité de
> rapports et d'accords fondamentaux entre le sur-moi, puissance
> contraignante archaïque, et le Fond érotique plus universel qui est
> leur non-moi. . . . Ainsi il y aurait des natures pour lesquelles
> l'inconscient universel, plus lointain que l'inconscient du moi, a
> des pouvoirs secrets . . . comme certain érotisme . . . imprègne les
> actes sublimes des saints . . . et que le plus bas dans ces natures
> privilégiées rejoint instantanément le plus haut. (141-42)

> for certain minds (mystics) the possibility must exist of fundamental
> relationships and harmonies between the superego, a primeval
> force for control, and the more universal erotic Base, their counter-
> self. . . . Thus there must be human natures for which the universal
> unconscious, more remote than the individual unconscious, has
> secret powers . . . just as a degree of eroticism permeates the sub-
> lime acts of saints . . . and the lowest instantly merges with the
> highest of these privileged natures.

Elsewhere in this text Jouve places poets on a par with saints, at
least poets like Lautréamont, Rimbaud, Mallarmé, and, most of
all, Baudelaire, and asserts that the poet's (and the artist's) task
is to confront humanity's death drive and transmute it, so as to
avert the catastrophe of collective suicide.

The concluding paragraph of "Inconscient, spiritualité et
catastrophe," an extended oxymoron, reverberates like a sensual ascetic's call to arms:

> La révolution comme l'acte religieux a besoin d'amour. La poésie
> est un véhicule intérieur de l'amour. Nous devons donc, poètes,
> produire cette "sueur de sang" qu'est l'élévation à des substances
> si profondes, ou si élevées, qui dérivent de la pauvre, de la belle
> puissance érotique humaine. (144)

> Revolution, like the act of religious faith, needs love. Poetry is an
> inner vehicle of love. Poets, we must thus produce this "blood
> sweat" that is the rising up to substances so deep, or so elevated,
> which stem from the spare, beautiful power of human love.

The several psychological notions packed into the last sentences of "Inconscient, spiritualité et catastrophe," and touched on throughout the preface, are reprised and made more explicit in subsequent Jouve texts, notably in his "Commentaire à Vagadu," where he lists three basic principles:

> 1. L'inconscient existe à tout moment, de proportions beaucoup plus vastes que le conscient, et la personne y a accès par l'émotion;
> 2. L'inconscient affectif est dominé par l'énergie sexuelle ou érotique; le pôle contraire, également primitif, est l'instinct de la mort;
> 3. Le développement de la vie sexuelle inconsciente, en tout homme, s'accompagne de culpabilité, ou en d'autres termes du sentiment d'une faute profonde. (*Commentaires* 55)

> 1. The unconscious exists at every moment, on a scale much vaster than the conscious mind, and humans have access to it through emotion;
> 2. Affective unconsciousness is dominated by sexual or erotic energy; the opposite pole, equally primitive, is the death instinct;
> 3. The growth of an unconscious sexual life, in every human being, is accompanied by guilt, or in other words by the sense of a profound transgression.

Hence for Jouve, as for other twentieth-century thinkers (e.g., Lacan, Breton, Duras), desire plays a crucial role in the human drama. What sets Jouve apart in this company is that for him desire must be sublimated, purged of sin, transformed in the crucible of poetry. In *En miroir*, his most autobiographical work, for example, he avows with regard to the new direction of his writing after the mid-twenties:

> J'étais orienté vers deux objectifs fixes; d'abord obtenir une langue de poésie qui se justifiât entièrement comme chant . . . et trouver dans l'acte poétque une perspective religieuse — seule réponse au néant du temps.
> Un mouvement vers le haut, un mouvement de conscience que je propose de nommer "spirituel," se présentait à l'esprit par ces deux objectifs réunis. Ce mouvement n'a plus varié, dans tout le cours postérieur de ma vie et de mon travail. (26)

> I had two clear goals in mind; first, to achieve a poetic language entirely justified as song . . . and to find in the poetic act a religious perspective — the only response to time's void.

> An upward movement, a movement of consciousness that I would
> call "spiritual," came to mind through the linking of these two goals.
> This movement has not varied since then, in all the subsequent
> course of my life and work.

The "work" to which Jouve is referring in this passage is not just
his poetry, but includes his writings on art as well. The
"mouvement vers le haut," moreover, assumes a particular form
in his pages on Delacroix and other artists; it becomes a veritable quest, where the poet elucidates the spiritual essence of a
painting by miming its deepest attitude or stance. This gesture,
in turn, becomes an inquiry that scrutinizes detail as well as ensemble, uncovering the heart of a painting, paradoxically, by
perusing its surface texture with love, admiration, and rever-
ence. In Jouve's art criticism, a scrupulously attentive scriptural
activity thus acquires a spiritual dimension, for the poet's eye,
in rendering fully what it sees, reaches under the visible to disclose the artwork's hidden layer of meaning.

In 1972, Marcel Raymond spoke of the "grand sujet des relations de la poésie et de la peinture" 'great subject of the relations
of poetry and painting' in Jouve's writings (345), specifically of
the place of the pictorial poem in this corpus. (Raymond, for
example, studies four poems by Jouve that were directly inspired
by paintings of Claude Lorrain.) But a label other than "pictorial
poem" is available for this type of poem, namely ekphrasis, a
term that refers to the "literary imitation of a work in the plastic
arts."[3] "Ekphrasis," both the term and the concept, is pertinent
in any discussion of Jouve's writings on art, inasmuch as the
poet includes passages describing works of art, precisely yet
evocatively, not only in his poetry but also in his essays in art
criticism. In addition, what Jouve achieves in these essays illustrates the double focus of his art criticism, the spiritual quest
and the scriptural inquiry he is conducting simultaneously.

The very idea of ekphrasis tends to conflate painting and
writing, to make the acts of drawing and depicting with words
interchangeable. Significantly, twice in his study of Delacroix,
once in his essay on Courbet, and once in his text on Meryon —
and each time in relation to the artist's creative act or gesture —
Jouve uses the words "écriture" 'writing' and "écrire" 'to write'
in contexts where one would expect to find "peinture" 'painting' and "peindre" 'to paint' (*Tombeau* 77, 88, 113, 147).

To some extent, the interchangeability of painting and writing for Jouve simply reflects the subjects chosen by the artists he treats, or the narrative content (historical or mythical) of, for example, Delacroix's paintings. If, as Jouve contends, "les aventures chevaleresques du Tasse" 'the knightly adventures of Tasso' gave Delacroix many of his subjects (*Tombeau* 84), Tasso, particularly his "Jérusalem délivrée" 'Jerusalem Saved,' fascinated Jouve, as his essay "Folie et génie: Le Tasse," published posthumously, indicates.[4] And if Jouve identifies Tasso as an important source for Delacroix, the poet refers to Delacroix in his article on Tasso. An amalgam of Tasso and Delacroix seems to haunt Jouve's imagination, together with a comparable enthusiasm for the two creative spirits. In his essay on Tasso, Jouve comments on "Jérusalem délivrée" in terms that recall certain ekphrastic passages in his study of Delacroix. In both "Folie et génie: Le Tasse" and "Delacroix," the same psychological obsessions surface:

> Un thème domine cette montagne poétique [Jérusalem délivrée], c'est celui de l'Eros guerrier. Nudités féminines, vouloirs mâles et jugements sexuels se mélangent aux cuirasses, aux combats singuliers, aux ruses militaires.
> Plaisirs et batailles, luttes à mort et délices amoureuses alternent et se livrent dans les mêmes couples, toujours formés d'un chrétien et d'une païenne. . . .
> Ce désir obsédant des guerriers, cette tentation perpétuelle dans le cours du combat et la bizarre présence de femmes militaires, cette puissante défaillance aux prises avec l'honneur, voilà bien la transposition chevaleresque du vieux débat entre instincts, Eros, mort, magma de l'inconscient. ("Folie" 11-12)

> One theme dominates this poetic mountain [Jerusalem Saved], the theme of Eros as warrior. Female nakedness, male will, and sexual judgment mix with breast-plates, single combats, soldiers' dodges. Pleasure and fighting, struggles to the death and amorous delights alternate and are unleashed within the same couples, always involving a Christian and a pagan.
> This obsessive desire of the warriors, this perpetual temptation in the midst of combat and the bizarre presence of woman warriors, this powerful flinching that grapples with honor, here we have the knightly version of the old debate between instincts: Eros, death, magma of the unconscious.

Jacob, vétu d'une peau de panthère, se jette contre l'ennemi, la tête basse, aveugle; sa main droite veut lui briser le bras; sa main gauche veut l'étouffer au corps. Une jambe est comme un arc-boutant dans la terre. Mais l'autre jambe — saisie à la cuisse — est sous la main griffante de cet Ennemi qui tout entier léger et droit, comme un danseur ailé, est plus fort que la force, et contre la force continue d'avancer, concentré et mélancolique. Cet acte de mort — cet acte d'amour — devant une lance abandonnée, se passe inlassablement dans le mystique paysage. . . . (*Tombeau* 92-93)

Jacob, dressed in a leopard skin, flings himself against the enemy, head lowered, blind; with his right hand he would break his adversary's arm, while with his left he would squeeze the breath out of him. One leg resembles a flying buttress planted in the earth. But the other leg — grabbed at the thigh — is gripped by this Enemy who, completely lightfooted and straight, like a wingèd dancer, is stronger than strength itself, and against strength it continues to advance, focused and gloomy. This act of death — this act of love — before an abandoned lance, occurs effortlessly in a mystic landscape.

As we see, these extracts from Jouve's essays on Tasso and Delacroix offer the astonishing spectacle of a fight to the finish that is also an act of love. In both texts, Eros and Thanatos are literally superimposed on each other.

The final pages of Jouve's "Delacroix" concentrate on the murals the artist undertook to paint toward the end of his life in the Chapel of the Holy Angels in Saint-Sulpice Church. The poet deals primarily here with the painting entitled "Jacob et l'Ange du Seigneur" on the alcove Chapel's left wall, "le plus achevé des ouvrages solennels de Delacroix" 'the most finished of Delacroix's solemn works,' according to Jouve. The conclusion's thrust and tone, plus its terminal location within the essay, embody a trait that typifies Jouve's writings on the plastic arts, the poet's habit of climbing, so to speak, across such a study toward a summit, a peak, so as to close his scriptural meditation with an analysis of a superb specimen of the artist's mature period. Readers of Jouve's art criticism can in fact detect a rising convergence of themes structuring each one of his essays in this domain. A "mouvement vers le haut," an 'upward movement,' the end to which Jouve consciously aspires in his poetry, thus seems to organize his essays in art criticism.

This "mouvement vers le haut," the specific teleology that may be glimpsed shaping Jouve's essays on art, bespeaks one of his fundamental preoccupations, his eschatological concerns, his abiding wish to confront the great question of humankind's last end, and the poet's need always to raise this question in a spiritual if not a religious context. Of interest to the present discussion is that humanity's last end, its inexorable progress toward God (for Jouve), may be discerned in "Delacroix," near the beginning of the poet's description of "Jacob et l'Ange du Seigneur." The relevant passage is eminently ekphrastic:

> Dans le paysage immense d'une sur-Nature, on voit s'ouvrir deux routes. C'est d'un côté la route où chemine la caravane de Jacob, où il a "fait passer tout ce qui était à lui." C'est d'autre part la voie étrange et paisible, par derrière le combat, qui mène à une haute vallée de secret et d'invincible douceur—le lieu qui sera "nommé Phanuel." Séparant les routes, il a trois arbres, chataîgniers géants, dieux du sol. Le mouvement, l'inclinaison, la sève tragique de ces trois arbres, au dela desquels les deux voies finalement se rejoignent, fait songer au commandement divin surgi des choses, appuyé sur les nombres, afin que le combat ait lieu ici. (*Tombeau* 92)

> Within the immense landscape of a super-Nature, two roads are seen opening. To one side is the road on which Jacob's caravan is advancing, where he "brought along all of his belongings." To the other side is a strange and peaceful way, in back of the battle, leading to a high, secret valley of invincible gentleness—the place "named Phanual." Separating the roads are three trees, giant chestnut-trees, gods of the earth. The movement, the bending, the tragic sap of these three trees, beyond which the two roads finally meet, makes one dream of a divine commandment arising out of the things, based on numbers, so that the combat might take place here.

Thanks to this passage, we see that what first attracts the poet's gaze is neither Jacob nor the angel, but, rather, located high up in the painting, deep in the background of the scene depicted, two roads crossing. Moreover, the roads hold the poet's attention right through to the end of the paragraph, where the painting's significant detail (for Jouve) is to be found, a detail that shows the ultimate convergence of all human pathways in God: "ces trois arbres, au delà desquels les deux voies finalement se rejoignent." We are partaking here of an old dream, the hope of heaven, of ultimate union with and in God.

Yet the dream inhabits the text so discreetly that we almost miss it. Still, radiant, shining forth in a detail on high, the dream points to the last end (for Jouve) of all human beings, and it does so while in no way diminishing the merciless combat, the battle without quarter unfolding in the painting's foreground below, the eternal struggle between love and death. Toward the end of "Delacroix," significantly, Jouve speaks of Jacob's struggle as a "lutte avec Dieu pour voir Dieu" 'struggle with God to see God' (*Tombeau* 94).

The entire last part of the essay amounts to a climactic demonstration of a truth that is central to Jouve's thinking, namely, that the necessary task of the artist—whether poet or painter—comes down to ever repeated acts of sublimation, constantly renewed attempts to transform the most contrary human impulses into a painful but fruitful dialectic, an activity that results in a redemptive, even sanctifying work of art. As Jouve proclaimed in *En miroir*: "Je n'aurais jamais écrit une ligne si je n'avais pas cru au rôle sanctificateur de l'art" 'I would never have written a line if I had not believed in the sanctifying role of art' (143). A similar "mouvement vers le haut," a comparable process of sublimation, but in miniature now, informs the brief study called "Images du XIIIe" that the poet published in his 1943 collection of essays entitled *Défense et illustration*. Once again, the poet's argument culminates in a discussion of a single, supreme artistic achievement, this time the bas-relief of the Nativity at Chartres. The description, lengthy, detailed, admiring, and reverential, is a true ekphrasis, with, once more, eschatological hints underlying the text. Here is its concluding sentence:

> Avec quelle tendresse, prescience et acceptation, la mère regarde-t-elle cet enfant prédestiné, avec quelle perfection le drame humain et divin est-il tout entier présent entre eux! (*Défense* 192)

> With what tenderness, prescience and acceptance, does the mother gaze at her predestined son, with what perfection is the human and divine drama entirely present between them!

By their form, Jouve's essays on Meryon and Courbet suggest the same human entelechy, the same destiny for humanity, that is inscribed in the shape and movement of "Delacroix" and "Images du XIIIe." The poet's study of the great realist painter, entitled "Un tableau de Courbet," is divided into three sections, with the first two paving the way for the third, and with the last three pages of the final section devoted to a description of a single painting, the point of arrival announced in the essay's title. To our initial astonishment, the work of art in this case is a living tableau. In Jouve's words, it is "un Courbet véritable, un Courbet réel; le tableau que Courbet aurait voulu peindre et qu'il n'a pas peint" 'a true Courbet, a real Courbet; the painting that Courbet would have wished to paint and that he did not paint' (*Tombeau* 154). The setting is 1936, in Père-Lachaise Cemetery, at the ceremony commemorating the anniversary of the executions by firing squad that took place in May 1871 after the Commune. The essay concludes as follows:

> L'on apercevait, à différentes hauteurs et en d'innombrables endroits, des groupes de spectateurs assis sur les tombes, sur les toits des petits temples du souvenir, pour voir. Et tous ces groupes étaient des "Courbet." Dans leur candeur ils s'étaient assis sur les tombes, mais avec tout le respect possible. Ce respect familier tenait à leur attitude, à leur silence. Ils étaient fortement et amoureusement dessinés sur la verdure. Ils occupaient l'espace sans lui faire violence parce que la tranquillité infinie des morts les inspirait tous ensemble. Le lendemain, des journalistes assureraient que le Père-Lachaise avait subi une profanation; eux étaient majesteusement calmes, remplis du sentiment de l'espérance, mais non moins contenus et sobres. Et leurs traits étaient chauds et rudes comme dans les tableaux du peintre d'Ornans. (*Tombeau* 156)

One noticed, at different levels and in countless places, groups of spectators sitting on the tombs, on the roofs of the little temples of memory, in order to see. And all these groups were "Courbets." In their candor they had sat down on the tombs, but with all the repect possible. This familiar respect came from their attitude, their silence. They were boldly and lovingly drawn against the greenery. They occupied the space without doing violence to it because the infinite peace of the dead inspired them all together. On the next day, some journalists claimed that Père-Lachaise had been desecrated; they [the spectators] were majestically calm, filled with the feeling of hope, but no less restrained and sober. And their features were warm and rough as in the works of the painter from Ornans.

When placed in the context of the whole essay, this stunning terminal description acquires a special resonance, the timbre of a peak experience. The word "espérance" in the second last sentence, for example, must be read and pondered within the frame of reference established by the sentence that begins the essay's final section: "Courbet, qu'il l'ait su ou non, était homme de foi" 'Courbet, whether he knew it or not, was a man of faith' (153). This apparently peremptory remark echoes a passage from the second part of the essay, where Jouve contends that in Courbet, "sous la libre-pensée de surface, sous l'état de rébellion contre la croyance, il y avait une croyance, le fond véritable et robuste, chantant la louange par les oeuvres" 'beneath the surface of free-thinking, under the state of rebellion against belief, there was belief, a true and robust foundation, singing hymns of praise through works' (150). It is in this perspective that one must read the word "espérance," for (to gloss Jouve's implicit thesis) it is thanks to Courbet's unavowed, even unknown "faith" that the hope which he inspired with his works is transformed, changed into a noble sentiment. More precisely, by virtue of the spiritual movement of the essay as a whole, in it, as in religious tradition, the idea of hope takes on the aura of the sacred.

But something else in this conclusion deserves our attention even more than the accumulated power of the word "espérance." From the very beginning of the essay, Jouve outlines a theory of eroticism specific to Courbet, a theory postulating that "l'érotisme de Courbet est un pouvoir d'homme, une fonction génitale parvenue à son plein développement" 'Courbet's eroticism is a human power, a genital function that has reached its full development' (142). According to the poet, the painter's eroticism is "répandu à la masse humaine et sociale" 'stretched over the human and social masses' (143). He states that this "amour vraiment génital" 'truly genital love' extends to "la terre" 'the earth' and to the "créatures qu'elle porte" 'creatures it bears' (144) and that "la femme de Courbet est plutôt une géante en laquelle converge la nature et où se retrouvent les montagnes, forêts et vallons" 'Courbet's woman is rather a giant in whom nature converges and where mountains, forests and valleys meet' (147). It is in light of this theory, this way of seeing the artist and his works, that one must reread the last section of Jouve's essay, especially perhaps its very last sentence:

"Et leurs traits étaient chauds et rudes comme dans les tableaux du peintre d'Ornans" (155). The warmth of the colors, the ruggedness of the forms, their "réalité rugueuse" (in Rimbaud's memorable phrase), are thrown into climactic relief here. The eroticized collection of humans, lively and peaceful, is sitting literally on death, on the cemetery's dead. As before in Jouve, Eros reclines on Thanatos, love stretches out across death, with hope, religious virtue par excellence, transcending their union and constituting the sublimated form of Courbet's eroticism.

The procedure that Jouve utilizes in "Le quartier de Meryon" ("Meryon's Neighborhood"), the poet's essay on the mysterious, troubled engraver of the Second Empire, another contemporary of Baudelaire, follows (more or less) the one he used in his studies of Delacroix and Courbet. Here again the text's trajectory embodies a crescendo with, towards the end, a disproportionately large section devoted to the treatment of a salient achievement of the artist's maturity — this time a close examination of Meryon's "cinq pièces maîtresses, les dernières" 'five masterworks, the last ones' (*Tombeau* 113).

On the other hand, unlike the method he uses in discussing the two great painters, in his study of the engraver Jouve adopts a chronological approach, providing (in summary form) a biography of the artist, along with analyses of the artist's production. Why so much biographical information this time? Perhaps because the basic facts of Meryon's life are far less well known than comparable data concerning Delacroix and Courbet. Perhaps also because the interpenetration of artist and work is greater with this figure than it is for the other two. Whatever the reason for this difference in content and approach, in "Le quartier de Meryon," at approximately that point where in a narrative with a fictional hero one would find the climax (roughly three-quarters of the way into the text), besides giving us a strong sense of place (Paris), Jouve reaches the culminating point or summit of his essay. He presents in rapid succession his analytical descriptions of the engraver's "dernières grandes planches" 'last great woodcuts' (125) along with a discussion of "la plus grande des estampes de Meryon sur Paris" 'the greatest of Meryon's prints about Paris' (126), the engraving entitled "Collège Henri IV, ou Lycée Napoléon," which takes up more than six of the essay's total of 38 pages. The analysis in question, moreover, concludes only four pages before the end of the essay.

The Paris neighborhood represented in this engraving, and the moment in the artist's life when the work was executed, are indicated at the beginning of the analysis/description:

> La vue est prise au sommet du Panthéon; elle rassemble tout le quartier de Meryon, le lieu de toute sa vie. Elle est exécutée quatre ans avant sa mort. (*Tombeau* 127)

> The view is seen from the summit of the Pantheon; it takes in all of Meryon's neighborhood, the locale of his entire life. It was done four years before his death.

This passage, and the pages immediately following it, furnish the essay's title and focus. After the quoted passage comes a series of commentaries on the successive versions or stages of the engraving, along with extracts from Meryon's writings, cited in support of Jouve's argument. Not surprisingly, the style of the commentaries — precise, detailed, admiring — is close to ekphrasis, writing that seeks to reproduce a work of art scripturally. Here, for example, is how the poet begins his description of the scene depicted in the engraving:

> On voit principalement à gauche le vaste quadrilatère des bâtiments du Collège, avec la tour gothique émergeant entre deux cours. Au milieu les jardins, à droite les maisons serrées de la rue de l'Estrapade. La construction étendue de la Montagne-Sainte-Geneviève est présente avec un souci incroyable du détail; on éprouve la beauté des longues façades de style, on sent la vie des ombres portées. (127)

> On the left one sees the huge rectangle of the College buildings, with the Gothic tower rising between two courtyards. In the middle are the gardens, on the right the houses, close together, of rue de l'Estrapade. The extensive construction of Mount Sainte Geneviève is rendered with incredible attention to detail; one experiences the beauty of the long stylish façades, one feels the vitality of the cast shadows.

Next, Jouve explores the various states or stages of the engraving, so as to uncover its hidden meaning, its secret sense. Soon enough, via the deft intercalation of quotation (from Meryon) and commentary (by Jouve), the poet lays bare "la symbiose . . .

entre le génie et la maladie mentale" 'the symbiosis . . . of genius and mental illness' (129) that for him defines the artist at work here.

But these apparently divergent projects—examining the engraving's successive stages, uncovering a symbiosis between the engraver's genius and his madness—actually converge in these pages. By tracing the representation of the sea through the various cuts of the engraving, Jouve tracks the sea's progressive disappearance, its gradual repression and eventual transformation into "l'océan des maisons de Paris" 'the ocean of the houses of Paris' (129). In the process, the poet shows that "le drame de la carrière de Meryon . . . est . . . secrètement inscrit ici" 'the drama of Meryon's career . . . is . . . secretly inscribed here' (132), that the artist's earlier life, the time he spent as a merchant seaman during his youth, is there, just behind these roofs, these streets, these façades, behind this Paris neighborhood. Also, according to Jouve, in "Collège Henri IV, ou Lycée Napoléon," the ocean "est synonyme de montée de l'inconscient" 'is synonymous with the rise of the unconscious' and "le 'vieil Océan' de cet esprit malade équivaut au surgissement des pouvoirs psychiques véhéments et redoutables" 'the "old Ocean" of this sick spirit matches the upsurge of vehement and fearsome psychic powers' (132).

But an even greater fusion takes place here, according to Jouve: the total integration of the constituent elements of the phenomenon called "Charles Meryon." Meryon, the sea, madness, genius, love, death, Paris, the engraving—all form a perfect continuum. As Jouve observes: "Meryon prend pour ainsi dire le courage de placer sa vie à l'intérieur de son oeuvre" 'Meryon has the courage, so to speak, to place his life within his work' (130). In order to put himself, literally, into his engraving, the artist placed the letters "C.M.," his initials, in the middle of it, together with the letters "L.N.," the initials of Louise Neveu, a young woman with whom he had become hopelessly infatuated, as he confessed in a letter quoted by Jouve (131). That the initials of the young woman were also those of the building that inspired (part of) the engraving's title (Lycée Napoléon) seems but another aspect of the complete integration of widely disparate elements that Meryon has realized here. With him, one senses, all things flow together in convergent streams, but especially the artist and the work. Whence the perfect logic of the manner in which Jouve concludes his long reflection on "Collège Henri IV, ou Lycée Napoléon": "Et désormais Meryon habite sa gravure" 'And henceforth Meryon inhabits his engraving' (133).

In a sustained scriptural inquiry, Jouve peels away, one after another, the layers of the artist's life as these are inscribed in the stages of his engraving. He shows how the alienated, lonely engraver, doubtless unwittingly, right up until his death in abject poverty, unceasingly attempted to disclose the hidden beneath the visible, to reveal death crouching in everything. Meryon would thus appear to have pursued a blind spiritual quest, an entirely intuitive search for "des analogies lointaines, indicibles, à travers lesquelles le temps immédiat n'existe plus, remplacé par des temps essentiels" 'remote, inexpressible analogies, through which proximate time no longer exists, has been replaced by essential time' (137). Heretofore obscure analogies between the engraver and his city emerge, revealing their common destiny — both are lost, both are saved, redeemed. As Jouve asserts: "Dans l'oeuvre de Meryon . . . il s'agit somme toute de la ruine et de la folie de Paris, sous la forme authentique et durable de Paris" 'In Meryon's work . . . it is a matter, finally, of the ruination and madness of Paris, under the authentic, enduring form of Paris' (136).

To see everything in terms of layers, strata, and footings, with invisible substance beneath visible accident, seems a deep-rooted tendency on Jouve's part. It is detectable even in his few remarks on Balthus that appear in *En miroir* or in the review of Artaud's *Cenci* that he wrote for *La Nouvelle Revue Française* in 1935. In the latter text, he sings the painter's praises for his "symboles secrets et agissants qui vivent là juste en dessous de la réalité visible" 'secret and working symbols living just under visible reality' (*Cenci* 914), while in the former he extols the artist for having produced an "oeuvre peinte . . . où la réalité formelle la plus fortement exprimée en dessin et en couleur recouvre à peine un rêve des objets et des êtres plus considérable encore, une profondeur non dite, mais impérieuse, le monde d'une certaine confidence" 'body of painted work . . . in which formal reality most boldly expressed in form and color barely overlays a still more considerable dream of objects and beings, an unsaid but imperious depth, the world of a certain secrecy' (*En miroir* 181).

As is now perhaps clear, a series of analogous polarities obsesses the poet and governs his thinking about art. If, for example, the marriage of madness and genius in Meryon intrigues the poet, the same combination of seemingly contrary capacities draws him to Tasso and Nerval. As for Delacroix, Courbet and, again, Meryon, the synthesis of conscious will and unconscious drives in these artists may explain their attraction for the poet. It should be stressed, however, that in Jouve's art criticism, the essential dialectic remains the endless battle between Eros and Thanatos, between the ever-warring forces of love and death. And in this permanent struggle, according to Jouve, only the catharsis provided by a truly spiritual art, sublimation alone, offers solutions capable of responding to humanity's gravest concerns and resolving its deepest problems. In the meantime, it is a matter of constant effort, of perpetual trials, tribulations, and travails, of the need to *durcharbeiten*, the obligation to work through the eternal conflict of Eros and Thanatos. To use Jean Starobinski's marvelously apt title for his preface to Jouve's collection of poetry entitled *Les Noces* (7-25), this struggle is "la traversée du désir" 'the passage of desire.' Jouve's criticism, like the art it lovingly peruses and memorializes, faces up to death by moving through desire, merging a deeply spiritual quest with a meticulous scriptural inquiry.

Notes

[1]For useful discussions of some of the repercussions of Jouve's decision in 1924 to break with his past see Starobinski; Bonnefoy.

[2]*Sueur de sang* has been reprinted in Jouve, *Noces* 139-44. All translations from the French are my own.

[3]For illuminating discussions of ekphrasis see Stamelman; Krieger; Heffernan.

[4]It is worth noting that, again thanks to Claude Esteban and Daniel Leuwers, Jouve's essay, "Gérard de Nerval," was also published posthumously in *Argile*.

Works Cited

Apollinaire, Guillaume. *Méditations esthétiques: Les Peintres cubistes.* Eds. Leroy C. Breunig and Jean-Claude Chevalier. Paris: Hermann, 1965.

Bonnefoy, Yves. "Le Problème des premiers livres." Jouve, *Oeuvre* lxxxvii-xci.

Heffernan, James A. W. *Museum of Words: The Poetics of Ekphrasis from Homer to Ashbery.* Chicago: U of Chicago P, 1993.

Jouve, Pierre Jean. "Les Cenci d'Antonin Artaud." *La Nouvelle Revue Française* 44 (1935): 914.

———. *Commentaires.* Neuchâtel: A la Baconnière, 1950.

———. *Défense et illustration.* Neuchâtel: Ides et Calendes, 1943.

———. *En miroir: Journal sans date.* Paris: Mercure de France, 1972.

———. "Folie et génie: Le Tasse." *Argile* 16 (1978): 5-13.

———. "Gérard de Nerval." *Argile* 17 (1978): 25-33.

———. *Les Noces,* suivi de *Sueur de sang.* Paris: Gallimard, 1966.

———. *Oeuvre.* Vol. 1. Ed. Jean Starobinski. Paris: Mercure de France, 1987.

———. *Tombeau de Baudelaire.* Paris: Seuil, 1958.

Krieger, Murray. *Ekphrasis: The Illusion of the Natural Sign.* Baltimore: Johns Hopkins UP, 1992.

Raymond, Marcel. "Pierre Jean Jouve devant les peintres." *Pierre Jean Jouve.* Eds. Robert Kopp and Dominique de Roux. Paris: L'Herne, 1972. 345-51.

Stamelman, Richard. "Critical Reflections: Poetry and Art Criticism in Ashbery's 'Self-Portrait in a Convex Mirror.'" *New Literary History* 15 (1983-84): 607-30.

Starobinski, Jean. "Le Feu de la chair et la blancheur du ciel." Jouve, *Oeuvre* xi-lxxxvi.

Painter Beholding Poet: Recent Illustrations for Rimbaud's "Voyelles"

Eric T. Haskell

A sept ans, il faisait des romans sur la vie
Du grand désert, où luit la Liberté ravie,
Forêts, soleils, rives, savanes! — Il s'aidait
De journaux illustrés ou, rouge, il regardait
Des Espagnoles rire et des Italiennes.[1]

At the age of seven, he made up romances about life
In the great desert, where Liberty shines in joy,
Forests, suns, shores, savannahs! - He was inspired
By illustrated journals, in which, with blushing face,
He stared at smiling Spanish and Italian women.[2]

—Rimbaud, "Les Poëtes de Sept Ans"

Whether culled from "journaux illustrés" or from his own phantasmagorical imagination, visual imagery is a prominent feature of Arthur Rimbaud's poetic universe. The narrator of "Les Poëtes de Sept Ans" ("The Seven-year-old Poets") uses it to construct his "romans" much in the same way that Rimbaud calls upon it to compose his poetry. The visual influences the verbal; hallucination is concretized into text. This is the essential configuration of the Rimbaldian aesthetic. It is fitting, then, that the poet would in turn inspire painters and that his work would serve as a source for hosts of twentieth-century artists beguiled by his precocious brand of *modernité*. Fernand Léger, Sonia Delaunay, as well as Masson, Miró, and Mapplethorpe are just a few to have made pictures from Rimbaud's poems. Their work, along with that of numerous lesser-known artists, constitutes a rich chapter in the history of modern book illustration.[3]

And yet, "Voyelles," one of the most seminal of Rimbaldian texts, has been curiously neglected by illustrators. The poem is not short on visual images. In fact, their proliferation is so aggressively striking across the landscape of the text that rendering them into graphic terms seems, at first glance, simple. This perhaps accounts for the problem. It seems that artists have been attracted to the more linear narrativity of "Le Bateau Ivre," *Les Illuminations*, and *Une Saison en Enfer*. In contrast, "Voyelles" lends itself less to traditional modes of pictorial narrativity. The poem's esoteric content has no doubt exacerbated this problem and further served to distance illustrators from it. However, two contemporary artists, August Ohm and Abdallah Benanteur, have recently changed the graphic fortune of "Voyelles." What was once the most unillustrated of Rimbaud's poems has become eminently illustratable. Their work is the focus of this image-text inquiry.

In order to establish a context for their interpretations of "Voyelles," it is useful to pause for a moment and consider Hermine David's 1952 illustration of the poem (Figure 1). This image shores up traditional approaches to picturing poetry which were to be subverted a few decades later by the work of Ohm and Benanteur. David's illustration is one of twenty-eight drypoint etchings published in a limited edition by Omphale in Paris.[4] Following convention for the illustration of poetry, each text is accompanied by a single corresponding image. The one for "Voyelles" is simple to decipher. David selects specific elements from the text which she displays on the graphic plane as a landscape. In the foreground, a female portrait translates the poem's "rire des lèvres belles" 'laughter of beautiful lips' (l. 7) into visual terms. A bit higher to the right, we find the text's "tentes" 'tents' (l. 5). Then on the left, the artist proposes the "pâtis semés d'animaux" 'pastures dotted with animals' (l. 10) above which the viewer encounters an indication of the text's "mers virides" 'viridian seas' (l. 9). At the center of the composition, an angel plays a curious trumpet whose neck has been fashioned into a circle, most probably in order to form the vowel "0."

How effective is this illustration at illuminating Rimbaud's "Voyelles?" Does its conjugation of various textual details pro-

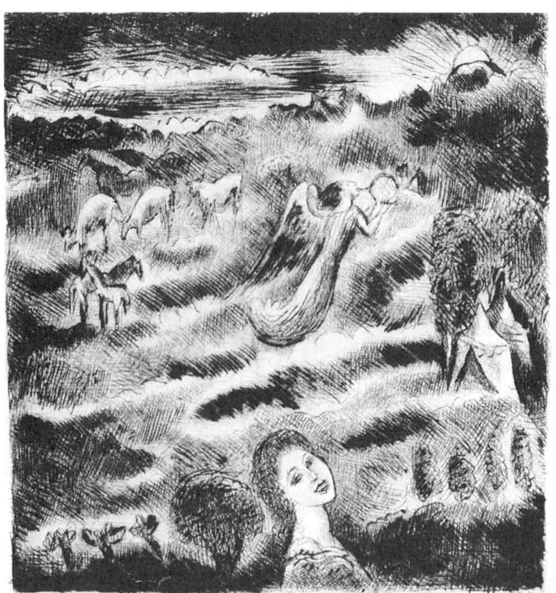

Figure 1. Hermine David, illustration for Rimbaud's "Voyelles," 1952. © 1995. Artists Rights Society, New York / A.D.A.G.P., Paris.

pose either new strategies for approaching the poem or contiguous planes of visual analogies that enrich its meanings? David's selection of elements from the text is strictly limited to transcendent imagery. Thus, the process betrays Rimbaldian poetics from the outset. Neither "mouches éclantants / Qui bombinent autour des puanteurs cruelles" 'brilliant flies / that buzz around cruel smells' (ll. 3-4) nor "sang craché" 'spat blood' (l. 7) are allowed to disrupt the lyrical contours of this aestheticized vision. Such a restrictive graphic choice proposes only a simplistic, superficial, and sentimental rendition of Rimbaud's vital textual swells. Here, Romanticism preempts revolution as David's graphics bleed the prophetic vigor right out of the poem.

Perhaps the sole point of interpretive interest in this illustration is the artist's treatment of the trumpet. The positioning of the angel at the center of the image mirrors Rimbaud's affinity for the vowel "O" which is privileged by its placement at the end of his text. The circular configuration of the trumpet does allow for the inscription of the final vowel onto the pictorial plane and thus infuses it with the symbolic essence of "l'Oméga"

(l. 14). However, the fact that the angel actually plays the trumpet constitutes yet another travesty in the artist's interpretation of the text. Rimbaud associates these two entities, but they remain clearly separated:

> O, suprême Clairon plein de strideurs étranges,
> Silences traversés des Mondes et des Anges

> O, sublime Trumpet full of strange piercing notes,
> Silences traversed by Worlds and by Angels (ll. 12-13)

The trumpet is the crucial performer in this scenario, not the angel. The instrument's silent sound inhabits the final tableau of the text and infuses it with an almost Mallarméan tonality. But such abstraction, so central to the success of "Voyelles," remains too arcane for David whose image ultimately fails to transcend mimesis.

Having David's illustration as a backdrop to our discussion of Ohm and Benanteur allows for a more comprehensive understanding of their breaks with traditional methods of picturing poetry. August Ohm's illustration for "Voyelles" appeared in a 1988 edition of Rimbaud's poetry published in Germany.[5] Bold coloration is the first thing that strikes the viewer who contemplates this image (Figure 2). For a poem whose opening verse — "A noir, E blanc, I rouge, U vert, O bleu: voyelles" — is above all colorifically obsessive, Ohm's illustration seems initially fitting. In retrospect, David's omission of color recalls the inadequacies of her graphic power over the text. In Ohm's composition, color is the singularly most readable element. In fact, the retina registers the black, white, red, green and blue with an immediacy that mirrors our assimilation of the text's first line. It is only after this initial contact that the eye returns to read the less striking aspects of this image which, although faintly traced in graphite, are actually responsible for its intellectual unity.

A head and nude torso are featured at the base of this illustration. Upon them rests a monolithic cube on which the vowels are inscribed. This illustration eschews simplistic transmission of information from the verbal onto the visual plane. Rather than lose itself in descriptive details haphazardly selected from the poem, Ohm's image functions as an icon for Rimbaud's textual totality. Language itself, pictured here in its schematized state, reposes on the reclining figure of poet/narrator. The five vowels are not presented as singular, discrete entities. Rather, each proliferates into multiple states within the context of the five distinct color planes designated by Rimbaud's poem. Some vowels are complete, others near completion and still others offer mere prototypical tracings of the letter's eventual form. In this, they cunningly emulate the syncopated patterns of language. Their visual repetitions across the monolith insinuate verbal resonances. In other terms, the illustration produces sounds graphically and thus aligns itself with the problematic of language so central to the poetic aspirations of "Voyelles."

The relationship between the figure and the vowelled cube is symbolically charged. The poet serves as a pedestal for the whole of language portrayed here by the archiTEXTual essence of the vowels. From this essence, he extracts the very verses that compose his poetic universe. His eyes are closed to the landscape yet open to the dreamscape. Rimbaldian alchemy is assured by the fine lines that link the eyes to the cube in a delicate

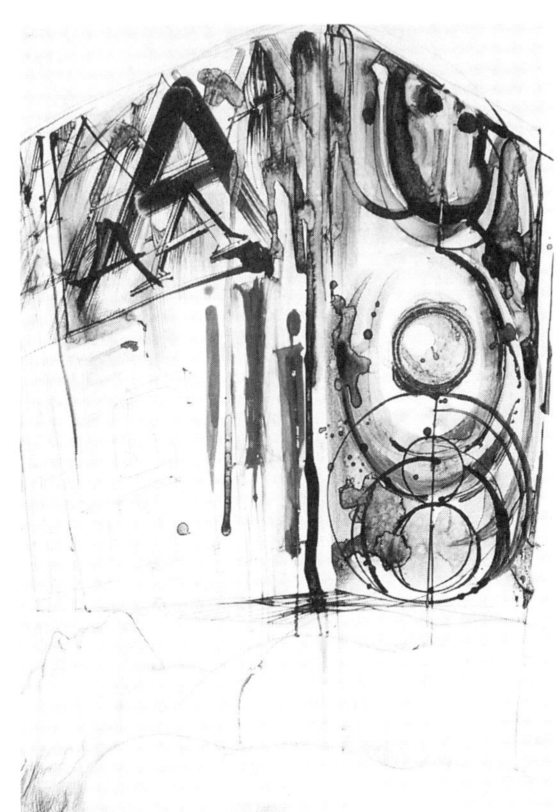

Figure 2. August Ohm, illustration for Rimbaud's "Voyelles," 1988. Reproduced with the permission of the artist.

balance that is the leitmotif of all creative gesture. But the mono-lith can also be interpreted as the weight of language that rests upon the poet like a gravestone. In this light, the "Voyelles" con-stitute Rimbaud's *ars poetica* as they are recast by Ohm on this arcane stele—a monument to the poet-preacher.

In his celebrated letter to Paul Demeny, Rimbaud states "Je dis qu'il faut être *voyant*, se faire *voyant*" 'I say that one must be a *seer*, make oneself *seer*' (Rimbaud, *Oeuvres* 270). The composi-tion of "Voyelles" is part of the process of becoming seer on the verbal plane. Ohm's illustration functions similarly on the vi-sual plane by picturing this process in a potent image whose power is suggestive, whose symbolism is expansive. The graph-ics are often sketched, seemingly unfinished, prophetically unrestrictive. Poised against a white plane, they hold the prom-ise of perfection. At any moment, the cube seems capable of ex-ploding into endless poetic configurations all dependent on the directives of the slumbering poet. This pictorial energy endows Ohm's illustration for "Voyelles" with symbolic complexities that distinguish it from the simplistic approach of David's etching and place it worlds away from traditional modes of picturing poetry. Ohm's focus is on meaning. Rather than losing himself in textual detail by mindlessly cataloguing it, he opts for a single image whose visual potential is charged in such a way that it serves as an icon for the very notion of poetic construction. His illustration thus becomes illumination.

Abdallah Benanteur shares the abstract plane on which Ohm's work resides. His illustration moves us to this plane's edge, for he approaches "Voyelles" in an essentially experimen-tal mode. Rather than limit himself to one illustration, he pro-poses seventeen. Benanteur transfigures the poem into a book. Within its covers, typographical rather than pictorial concerns prevail in a novel system whose dynamics reframe the visual constellation of "Voyelles" in new terms. Benanteur's edition of "Voyelles" was produced in 1974 for the "Collection Charef" at the Imprimerie B.A.M. in Paris.[6] The colophon states that the book was "tiré pour le plaisir" 'printed for the pleasure of it' in an edition of twenty copies each signed by the artist. In the spirit of the text at hand, he fittingly lettered, not numbered, them from A to T. This is the first and only book-length illustrated edition of "Voyelles." It is a technical achievement for the mastery of its press work, but it is also a milestone of image-text articulation.

The book's exterior prefigures its interior. The vowels, randomly placed and printed in a variety of type sizes, are blind embossed upon the cover. Their helter-skelter positioning insinuates the threat of fragmentation soon to be resolved within the covers of the book. Here, disorder seeks order or, in more appropriately Rimbaldian terms, re-order. "Voyelles" is, after all, the poet's revivification of a pre-existing linguistic system whose alphabet has become dysfunctional and devoid of poetic possibility. The blind embossing of the cover features old typographical forms cleansed and awaiting new colorific codification as well as spacial reconfiguration. Like Rimbaud's text, Benanteur's image seeks to break boundaries in search of uncharted lyric terrains. But for this to occur, the very roots of language—its vowels—must be empowered with new oneiric mobilities.

Benanteur works in arcane ways. His title page, for example, is remarkable for its simplicity. And yet, all of the vowels in the author-title sequence have been printed in blue ink. Such a detail provides a subtle premonition of this color's privileged role within the textual fabric. Indeed, Rimbaud will go so far as to rework the normal sequence of the vowels from A,E,I,O,U to A,E,I,U,O in order to end with the "O." Implicit in this reordering is, of course, the end that serves as the beginning. The "O" of the omega portends nothing less than infinity.

Benanteur displays the poem's title on the following page in a stark typographical scheme that cleanses the eye for the subtleties ahead. The text then appears (Figure 3). Printed in five colors, it responds to the tonal directives established by the first verse. Grey, used in place of blind embossing, assures readability of the E section of the poem and accords completion to the paginal dynamics at work. This single page of text acts as instigator for the next seventeen pages that combine image and typography in unexpected ways. These pages constitute what would traditionally be regarded as the illustration for the poem. And yet, the visual systems at play refuse to banish the verbal from their picture plane and instead incorporate it as a dominant feature of their graphism.

These seventeen images can be divided into two sections: one primarily typographical, the other essentially pictorial. The

A noir, E blanc, I rouge, U vert, O bleu : voyelles,
Je dirai quelque jour vos naissances latentes :
A, noir corset velu des mouches éclatantes
Qui bombinent autour des puanteurs cruelles,

Golfes d'ombre ; E, candeurs des vapeurs et des tentes,
Lances des glaciers fiers, rois blancs, frissons d'ombelles ;

I, pourpres, sang craché, rire des lèvres belles
Dans la colère ou les ivresses pénitentes ;

U, cycles, vibrements divins des mers virides,
Paix des pâtis semés d'animaux, paix des rides
Que l'alchimie imprime aux grands fronts studieux ;

O, suprême Clairon plein des strideurs étranges,
Silences traversés des Mondes et des Anges :
- O l'Oméga, rayon violet de Ses Yeux !

Figure 3. Abdallah Benanteur, text for *Voyelles*, 1974. Reproduced with the permission of the artist.

first is comprised of ten images, two for each vowel; the second proposes seven abstract lead etchings. The first section opens with a woodcut of the vowel A that is inscribed with the first words of Rimbaud's poem "A noir" (Figure 4). This image prefaces a second state of the woodcut that has been reworked on the handpress by the artist (Figure 5). From it, the text has been removed, and abstract imagery has been added to the oval cavity left blank in the initial state. The removal of the textual reference from the second state does not constitute absence of text from image because the typographical inscription still dominates the illustration and serves as both recipient and frame for the pictorial entity. Benanteur presents each of the five vowels in the same fashion. The palette changes across the suite in order to replicate Rimbaud's colorific specifications and the oval field of abstract imagery varies slightly from vowel to vowel, but the overall architecture of the scheme remains constant.

The strategies at work here are complex. By the fifth vowel's first state, Benanteur has completed the opening verse of the poem with "O bleu: voyelles." From this point on, the poem extrapolates, letter by letter, color by color, upon the potency of

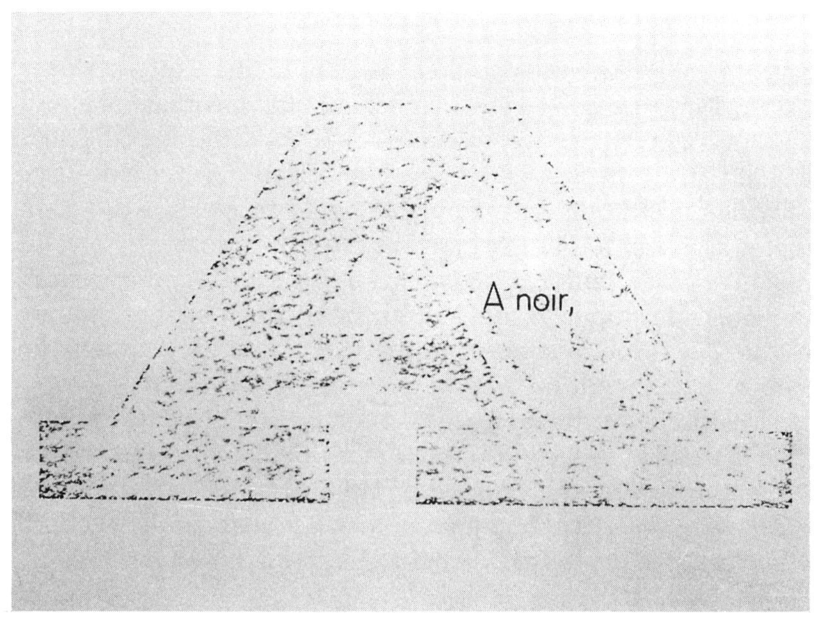

Figure 4. Abdallah Benanteur, first state of illustration for the vowel "A," *Voyelles*, 1974. Reproduced with the permission of the artist.

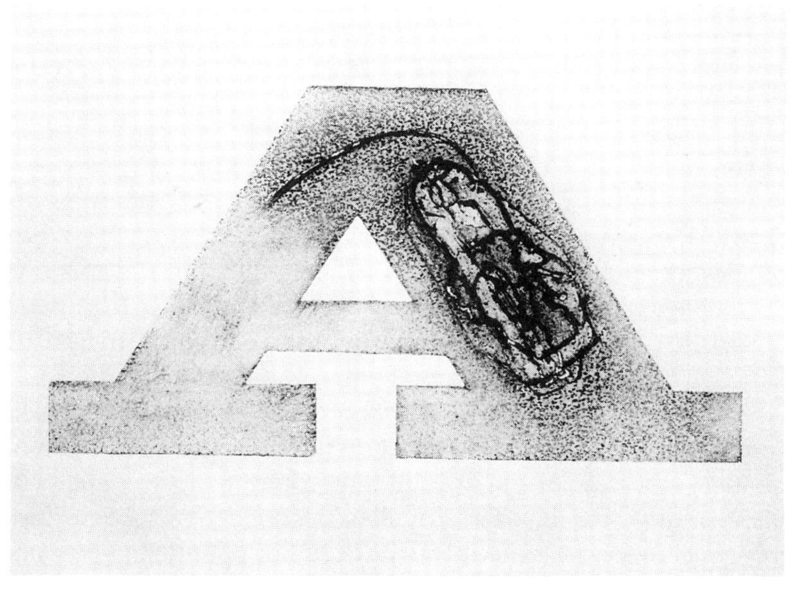

Figure 5. Abdallah Benanteur, second state of illustration for the vowel "A," *Voyelles*, 1974. Reproduced with the permission of the artist.

each vowel (Figures 6 and 7). Through their audacious juxtapositions, Rimbaud's five verbal vignettes made sure that the physiognomy of French poetry could never be the same after the publication his "Voyelles." Like Ohm, Benanteur refuses simplistic pictorial replication of these vignettes. Thus, once he has completed the first ten illustrations that set the poem's first verse firmly in place, he takes his cue from Rimbaud's poetic gesture by embarking upon a series of abstract compositions that are essentially visual responses to the verbal energy displayed in Rimbaud's vignettes.

These compositions enlarge the contexts of the pictorial fields placed within the second state of each vowel in the first section of Benanteur's suite. Here, typographical frames are removed to allow for the sort of untamed exuberance characteristic of each vowel's verbal vignette as exemplified in such a stanza as:

> U, cycles, vibrements divins des mers virides,
> Paix des pâtis semés d'animaux, paix des rides
> Que l'alchimie imprime aux grands fronts studieux
>
> U, cycles, divine resonance of viridian seas,
> The peace of pastures dotted with animals, the peace of the
>   furrows
> That alchemy embosses on grand studious foreheads (ll. 9-11)

If the first section of Benanteur's graphic vision typographically re-structured and visually re-codified the vowels in order to charge them with new energies for charting new poetics, then clearly the second section pictures the potential of these new poetics as boundless. Within them, Benanteur has, in his own graphic terms, "fix[é] les vertiges" 'defined vertigos' (Rimbaud, "Délires") and found the "incroyable Florides" 'incredible Floridas' (Rimbaud, "Bateaux") of the Rimbaldian universe.

Voltaire stated that "L'alphabet fut à l'origine de toutes les connaissances de l'homme . . . et de toutes ses sottises" 'The alphabet was at the origin of all of man's knowledge . . . and of all his stupidity.' Rimbaud's "Voyelles" inscribe themselves within this trajectory adding to it the dialectics of phantasmagory and hallucination. A, E, I, O, and U are the keys to the innumerable drawers of a *cabinet de curiosités* that is language itself. When, at

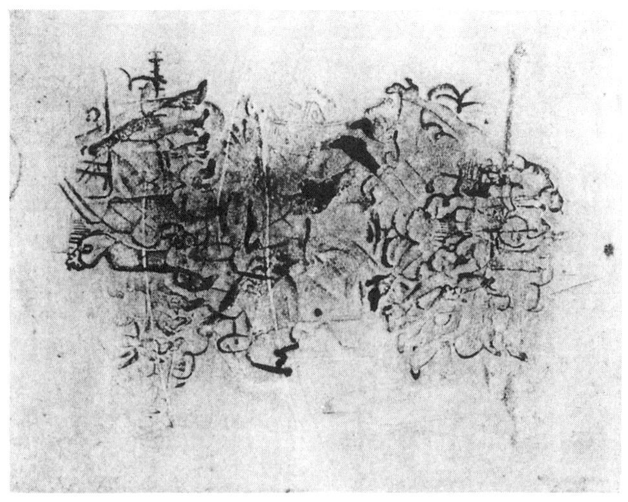

Figure 6. Abdallah Benanteur, illustration for *Voyelles,* 1974. Reproduced with the permission of the artist.

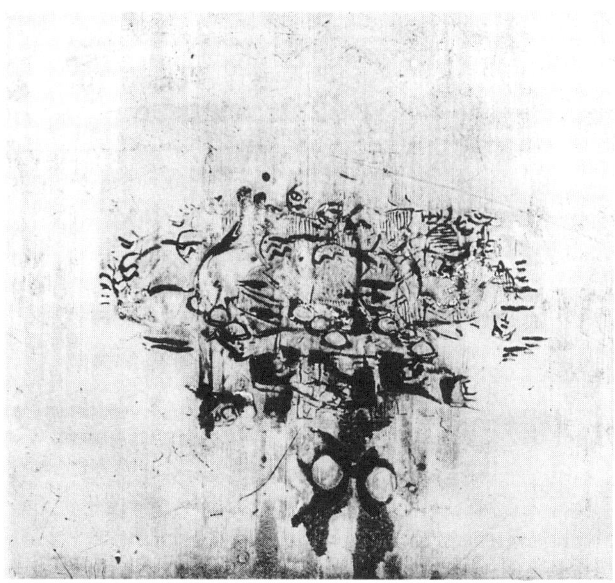

Figure 7. Abdallah Benanteur, illustration for *Voyelles,* 1974. Reproduced with the permission of the artist.

the close of "Parade," the narrator says "J'ai seul la clef de cette parade sauvage" 'I alone hold the key to this barbarous side-show' (Rimbaud, *Oeuvres* 180), he sums up the most meteoric configuration of poetic creation. Providing a pictorial equivalent of Rimbaud's poem is problematic due to the essentially visual nature of the text. Such a task calls for experimentation on the graphic plane to match Rimbaud's invention on the verbal plane. David, Ohm and Benanteur illustrate the text, but only the latter two artists illuminate it. Only they triumph over traditional modes of picturing poetry. In so doing, they point to new ways of revealing the revelation, of rationalizing the irrational and, most importantly, of viewing the invisible.

Notes

[1]For this and for all other quotations from Rimbaud's poetry, I have used the *Oeuvres complètes*.

[2]Unless otherwise noted, all translations of Rimbaud are mine.

[3]The most prolific author on the illustrators of Rimbaud is Renée Riese Hubert. See especially her *Surrealism and the Book* as well as a paper entitled "Rimbaud and the Artist Book."

[4]See Rimbaud, *Choix*. This edition was limited to 190 numbered copies.

[5]See Rimbaud, *Bilder*. This book was printed in both limited (150 signed and numbered copies) and trade editions. As the author of this volume's preface, my first comments on "Voyelles" appear there. Ohm is a German artist who lives and paints in Hamburg.

[6]See Rimbaud, *Voyelles*. This book was limited to twenty copies each signed and "lettered" by the artist, A to T. The edition is illustrated with a double suite of five vowels—one in woodcut, one re-worked on the hand press by the artist—and seven additional lead etchings. Benanteur is an Algerian artist who works and lives near Paris.

Works Cited

Hubert, Renée Riese. "Rimbaud and the Artist Book." Unpublished paper. Nineteenth-Century French Studies Colloquium, Univ. of California-Santa Barbara, October 20-23, 1994.

______. *Surrealism and the Book.* Berkeley: U of California P, 1988.

Rimbaud, Arthur. "Bateau ivre." Rimbaud, *Oeuvres* 101.

______. *Bilder und Gedichte.* Ill. August Ohm. Walsburg: Literaturkontor Alte Schmiede, 1988.

______ *Choix de poèmes.* Ill. Hermine David. Paris: Omphale, 1952.

______. "Délires II—Alchimie du verbe." Rimbaud, *Oeuvres* 233.

______. *Oeuvres complètes.* Paris: Pléiade, 1963.

______. *Voyelles.* Ill. Abdallah Benanteur. Paris: "Collection Charef" de L'Imprimerie B.A.M., n.d. [1974].

Joan Miró and Composition of the *Livre de peintre*

Harriett Watts

J'ai fait des essais qui m'ont permis de voir ce que c'était de faire un livre, non pas de l'illustrer, l'illustration est toujours une chose sécondaire. L'important est qu'un livre ait toute la dignité d'une sculpture taillée en marbre.

I've been conducting experiments that have helped me realize what it means to make a book, not just to illustrate one. Illustration is always secondary. What is of primary importance is that a book exist in all the dignity of a sculpture hewn from marble. [1]

In this letter of June 19, 1949 to his editor Gérard Cramer, Joan Miró discussed his overall concept for the *livre de peintre* with which he had been commissioned some months before. Foreseen were color woodcuts for Paul Eluard's collection of poems from the year 1930, *A toute épreuve*, and an initial contract stipulated release of the work in one year's time. As Miró maintained in a subsequent letter to Cramer, the book necessitated planning to the last minute detail so that text, typography, and graphic image would be fully coordinated. A change, even in the positioning of a comma, could necessitate a graphic revision of the entire page.[2] A book, Miró insisted, must be realized with the same degree of exactitude and precision as that employed in the construction of a clockwork,[3] and he refrained from beginning work on his woodcuts until Eluard had finalized the typographical composition of the pages. Ten years later, after 47,000 passages through a handpress in a year of uninterrupted printing by Miró's master-printer Jacques Frélaut, the edition of 130 copies was completed and the book released. *A toute épreuve,* with 79 woodcuts by Miró, received immediate critical acclaim as a unique and spectacular achievement, a milestone in 20th century book art and an homage as well to Paul Eluard, who had died six years before the book appeared. As Miró had envisioned in his initial letter to Cramer, this book now existed with "all the dignity of a sculpture hewn from marble."[4]

Miró's interpretation and realization of *A toute épreuve* was preceded by years of involvement with the poetry of his Dada and Surrealist compatriots. No painter of the "Ecole de Paris," with the exception perhaps of Max Ernst, committed himself with greater intensity or in more depth to such collaborations with poet friends. Miró's approach to their work has been eloquently characterized by Jacques Dupin in his introduction to a catalogue of Miró's graphic art:

> Il refuse toutes les contraintes et pense que c'est en allant le plus loin dans l'affirmation de soi et de sa propre écriture qu'il a la chance de rencontrer l'autre, l'écrivain venu d'ailleurs, et d'ouvrir l'unité d'un espace à leur échange et à leur accord. Pourtant il est d'abord le lecteur scrupuleux du texte. Il s'en approche longuement, non sans candeur, avec un scrupule et une ferveur minutieuse. Il s'imprègne du poème, il s'endort avec les mots, les rythmes, les senteurs qui en émanent; il les incorpore jusqu'à l'inconscience et l'aveuglement. Il laisse l'écrit se couler et fondre en lui, éveiller des échos, des images, agir sur sa propre rêverie et entraîner, en les altérant, en les contaminant, les figures, les signes, les couleurs de son langage de graveur. (Dupin, n.p.)

He ignores all constraints and proceeds from the conviction that only through the utmost affirmation of himself and his own script will he create a possibility for encountering the other—the writer coming from elsewhere—for opening a shared space in which mutual exchange can take place. At the same time he is the most scrupulous reader of the text, which he approachs gradually, with candor and fervent attention to the most minute detail. He impregnates himself with the poem, lulls himself to sleep with its words, their rhythms, their odors; he saturates himself with words to the point of unconsciousness and blindness to all else. He allows the stream of the text to carve its own path within him, to awaken echoes and images, to enter his own reveries and to sweep along in its wake the figures, the signs, the colors of his own graphic idiom, altered and contaminated by this encounter.

Miró's illustrations consistently reflected his personal engagement with the poet and texts in question, but his progress as book artist towards the mastery necessary for realization of the complete ensemble in *A toute épreuve* was gradual. This development is manifest in the illustrations produced by Miró over the span of two decades for three editions of works by another poet friend, Tristan Tzara. In 1930 Miró contributed original graphic work to a book edition for the first time: four lithographs for Tzara's *L'Arbre des voyageurs*. In 1949 Miró's initial postwar *livre de peintre*, *Le Désespéranto*, Volume III of Tzara's *L'Antitête*, was published by Bordas in Paris with eight etchings prepared by Miró in New York in 1947. On his first visit to Paris after the end of World War II, Miró accepted a commission from Aimé Maeght for an edition of Tzara's 1945 collection of poems, *Parler seul*. This commission in 1948 was accompanied by Miró's commitment the same year to Cramer for production of *A toute épreuve*. *Parler seul*, in an edition of 250 copies with 72 lithographs by Miró, appeared in 1950 and was greeted with great enthusiasm, above all by Tzara's and Miró's poet friends in Paris.

Each of the three editions preceding his work on *A toute épreuve* is the result of Miró's individual reponse at a given moment to the poetry of his friend Tzara. In his "affirmation de soi et de sa propre écriture," as Dupin expressed it, Miró the graphic artist created from the beginning a highly personal terrain for his encounter with a work from another domain. It was only after the war, however, that Miró's iconography reached its full maturity and the flexibility that enabled him to transpose the texts of his friends into books with a veritable double text of word and image, works in which the text, once one has experienced it as *livre de peintre*, is all but impossible to imagine without its graphic setting, and vice-versa.

Miró himself was well aware of the gradual development of his visual vocabulary, an evolution that, as he explained in an interview with Yvon Taillandier on February 15, 1959, had often seemed to take place beyond and even against his own volition:

> I work like a gardener or wine grower. Things develop slowly. I did not discover my form-language all at once. It developed on its own, practically against me. (Qtd. in Rowell 250)

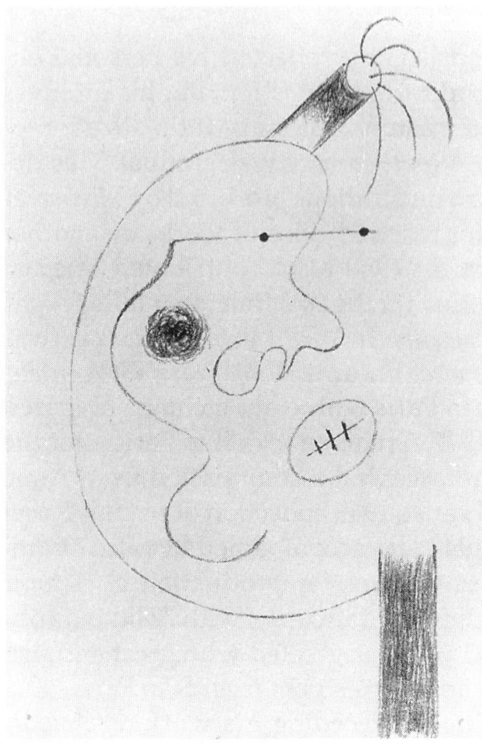

Figure 1. Joan Miró. Lithograph (1929) for Tristan Tzara, *L'Arbre des voyageurs*, 1930. Herzog August Bibliothek, Wolfenbüttel [9.4, 143 Malerbücher] © 1996 Artists Rights Society (ARS), New York/ADAGP, Paris.

This step by step evolution of Miró's form language can be followed through the three Tzara editions prior to Eluard's *A toute épreuve* as well as in the 1948-49 cycle of gouaches *Constellations*, which prompted a notable cycle of prose-poems by André Breton. What can also be observed in the three Tzara editions is how Miró's understanding of the book as a graphic genre in its own right evolved from his first "illustrated" book in 1930 to the composition of Tzara's *Parler seul*, a work that was planned and executed, like *A toute épreuve*, with all the precision and exactness of a clockwork.

The four lithographs in *L'Arbre des voyageurs* offer examples of Miró's biomorphic form-language in the late 1920s, the formal idiom that he shared with Hans Arp and surrealist painters with whom he associated in Paris. In the lithograph reproduced here (Figure 1), the head and nose are profiled in wavy contours characteristic of Miró's drawings of the late 1920s. The two points of the eyes, the laced line of the mouth, and the hairs sprouting from a tube on top of the head reappear later in Miró's reduced sign for the human head. In 1933 Miró contributed similar lithographs to an edition of Georges Hugnet's *Enfances*. In both cases, the lithographs offer a parallel in a surrealist graphic idiom to the texts they accompany, but there is no indication that Miró produced these graphic works as part of a comprehensive plan for the books in which they appeared.

Towards the end of the 1930s Miró addressed himself intensively to the acquisition of new graphic techniques, working from 1938 to 1939 on drypoint engravings and etchings in the Paris studios of Stanley William Hayter and Roger Lacourière. The graphic experiments he was pursuing in the well-equipped workshops of his friends were interrupted when Miró was forced to leave Paris at the outbreak of World War II. As he withdrew into isolation, first to Varengeville on the coast of Normandy and then to Palma de Mallorca, he also abandoned for a time his ideas for new graphic projects, including a book of his own poems. During this difficult period immediately before and during the German occupation of France, Miró initiated a series of gouaches that proved to be the point of departure for his mature iconography as a book artist. The *Constellations*, begun in January 1940 in Normandy with the work "L'Aurora" and completed 18 months later in Mallorca with "Le Trajet d'oiseau divin," comprise the most concentrated cycle of works that Miró produced. Figures in these 23 gouaches still echo the monsters of his so-called "tableaux sauvages" from the years 1934-36, works in which Miró's horror over events in Spain and the approach of World War II found expression in his sketches and paintings. The exaggeratedly grotesque figures of the "tableaux sauvages" are however now sublimated, tamed, and lyrically deployed throughout the densely populated and interwoven net of the *Constellations*, for example, the work entitled "Chant du rossignol à minuit et la pluie matinale" (Figure 2). André Breton, who introduced the *Constellations* at their initial showing in New York, commented on the creative energies summoned by Miró in his extraordinary discipline and concentration necessary for realizing this series:

Dans une heure d'extrême trouble, celle qui couvre de la première à la dernière ces *Constellations*, il semble que, par une tension réflexe au plus pur et à l'inaltérable, Miró ait voulu déployer, dans l'éventail de toutes les séductions, le plein registre de sa voix. . . .

Du "Lever du soleil" au "Passage de l'oiseau divin" s'accomplit
un cycle parfait — autant dire hermétiquement clos — comme je n'en
sais pas d'autre dans l'oeuvre de Miró. Les grands êtres de heurt
qui la traversaient avec un surcroît d'impétuosité depuis la guerre
d'Espagne se sont écartés tout à coup, à charge de revenir de la
suite. L'équilibre et l'harmonie disposent souverainement de la
scène, sur laquelle une paix singulière est descendue. (Breton 8-
10)

In a time of extreme uneasiness, extending from the first to the last
of these *Constellations*, it seems that through a reflex-tension striving for the purest and the least changeable, Miró wanted to display his voice's full register in its whole range of seductions. . . .
From "Sunrise" to "Passage of the Divine Bird" a perfect cycle is
achieved, that is to say, a cycle hermetically closed to an extent
that I have not experienced elsewhere in Miró's oeuvre. The great
creatures of collision traversing his works with ever increasing
impetuousness since the outbreak of the Spanish war were suddenly pushed aside, charged with the eventuality of a later return.
Equilibrium and harmony now determine the scene, over which a
unique peace has descended.

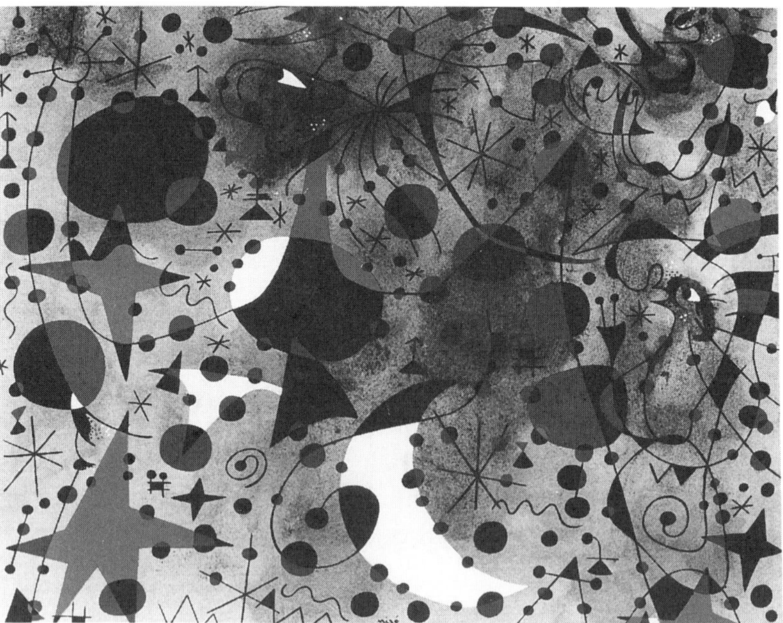

Figure 2. Joan Miró. Gouache, *"Chant du rossignol à minuit et la pluie
matinale,"* (1940) from the *Constellations*, ed. Pierre Matisse, 1959. Herzog
August Bibliothek, Wolfenbüttel [9.2, 8 Malerbücher] © 1996 Artists Rights
Society (ARS), New York/ADAGP, Paris.

The equilibrium and harmony of these works are the result not only of Miró's rigorous sublimation of the horror of the war and tensions of his own precarious situation into such a consummately realized cycle but also of his insistence upon a compositional balance for his visual elements in the creation of each work. His two primary sources of inspiration, as Miró recounted in 1948 in an interview with James Johnson Sweeney for *Partisan Review*, were music and nature:

> At Varengeville-sur-Mer, in 1939, began a new stage in my work, which had its source in music and nature. It was about the time that the war broke out. I felt a deep desire to escape. I closed myself within myself purposely. The night, music and stars began to play a major role in suggesting my paintings. Music has always appealed to me, and now music in this period began to take the role poetry had played in the early twenties—especially Bach and Mozart when I went back to Majorca upon the fall of France. . . . I began a group of gouaches which were shown here in New York at the Pierre Matisse Gallery just after the war—an entirely new conception of things. I did about five or six of them before I left Varengeville for Spain. There were twenty-two [sic] in the series. They were based on reflections in water. Not naturalistically—or objectively—to be sure. But forms suggested by such reflections. In them my main aim was to achieve a compositional balance. It was a very long and extremely arduous work. I would set out with no preconceived idea. A few forms suggested here would call for other forms elsewhere to balance them. These in turn demanded others. It seemed interminable. It took a month at least to produce each watercolor, as I would take it up day after day to paint in other tiny spots, stars, washes, infinitesimal dots of color in order finally to achieve a full and complex equilibrium. (Qtd. in Rowell 209-10)

This deepened appreciation for a complex equilibrium amongst diversified visual elements would find expression after the War in Miró's approach to an overall composition of the *livre de peintre*, in which all the various aspects of a book are taken into account.

In 1945 Pierre Matisse exhibited Miró's *Constellations* in his New York gallery. The exhibition, which showed the first works from Europe to be seen in New York after the War, was introduced by Breton. In 1959 Matisse reassembled 22 of the *Constellations* in high quality reproductions for a portfolio edition, which he accompanied with Breton's address from the exhibition opening and prose-poems composed by the poet in retrospect for each of the 22 gouaches. In these poems Breton achieves in his own medium the intensity of encounter between word and image that Dupin attributes to Miró in his collaboration with poet friends.[5] In these 22 oblique but highly charged encounters between word and image, Breton creates a new resonance for each individual gouache and for the cycle itself. Such enhancement of the visual series was made possible in this case by Breton's own "affirmation de soi et de sa propre écriture."

The *Constellations* mark a new plateau in the maturation of Miró's formal vocabulary. This iconography still bears witness, however, to initial impulses from his childhood, his first exposure to the art of prehistoric Iberian cave paintings. When asked in 1947 in a New York interview with Francis Lee which old masters or schools he preferred, Miró responded: "My favorite schools of painting are as far back as possible: the cave painters—the primitives" (qtd. in Rowell 203). In his Catalonian notebooks of 1941-1942 Miró designates hieroglyphs from Spanish prehistoric art, in particular figures from wall paintings in Las Batuecas, as models for his forms. In her discussion of the influence of prehistoric sources on Miró's stylistic development, Sidra Stich has commented on the probable relationship of Miró's iconography to the petroglyphs reproduced in Henri Breuil's four-volume catalogue, with which Miró was almost certainly familiar:

> Miró may have been referring here to the four-volume catalogue by Henri Breuil which documents schematic rock paintings in the Iberian penisula and includes an extensive section on Las Batuecas. In almost all of its numerous illustrations, it is possible to discern features which predominate in the "Constellations" compositions. The Breuil reproductions show images that are sharply defined as flat, silhouetted shapes or transparent, linearized configurations. . . . Perhaps the most evident affinity between Miró's designs and the prehistoric paintings is in the the imagery itself. In both there are radiating sun forms, stars, ladders, wheels, point and bar alignments, birds, snake-like forms, animals of unidentifiable species, figures with crescent, circular and cross form bodies, and dumbell or bi-triangular signs. Breuil viewed the latter as women, possibly representing female idols. (Stich 48)

Above all, the Iberian hieroglyphs now revealed to Miró how essential characteristics of the human figure could be presented in the most reduced manner possible. His mature vocabulary of highly reduced, multivalent, and endlessly recombinable signs constitutes an iconography particularly suited to the creation of books.[6]

A commission to paint wall murals for the Hilton Hotel of Cincinnati made it possible for Miró to leave Spain in 1947 and to spend a good part of his nine months abroad in New York, working in the studio of Stanley William Hayter. Hayter had left Europe in 1940 and his New York "Studio 17" became a meeting point for the surrealist painters in American exile. Together with Max Ernst and Yves Tanguy, Miró began work on a three-volume edition of Tristan Tzara's *L'Antitête*. Each of the three artists produced eight etchings in "Studio 17" for one volume of the set. All the plates were then printed by Roger Lacourière in Paris. The appearance of this three-volume *L'Antitête* in 1949 with illustrations by Ernst, Tanguy, and Miró signaled a new wave of book art in Paris after the war.

Miró's *eaux-fortes* etchings in *L'Antitête* were executed in the iconography to be employed in both of the major books with which he was commissioned in 1948, *Parler seul* and *A toute épreuve*. The human countenance is signaled by the presence of a straight line for the mouth and the two circles or points for the eyes, often joined to one another by the curved line of the nose. Three hairs invariably indicate the head of a human being. On occasion, arms and legs of these figures are discernable. From the entangled, labyrinthian lines of the etchings one or more human heads emerge. The red, blue, green, and yellow ovals and circles in these etchings exist as elements in their own right, to be combined at will by the artist together with his reduced signs for human beings—man and woman—and for stars and the moon (Figures 3 and 4).

The random play of lines out of which Miró's minimal figurations emerge echoes the free play of words from which Tzara's prose-poems materialize. Already in 1924 Miró acknowledged in a letter to Michel Leiris the affinity he sensed between the generation of form in his visual art and the free play of words he admired as an engendering force in the poems being written at the time by his surrealist friends:

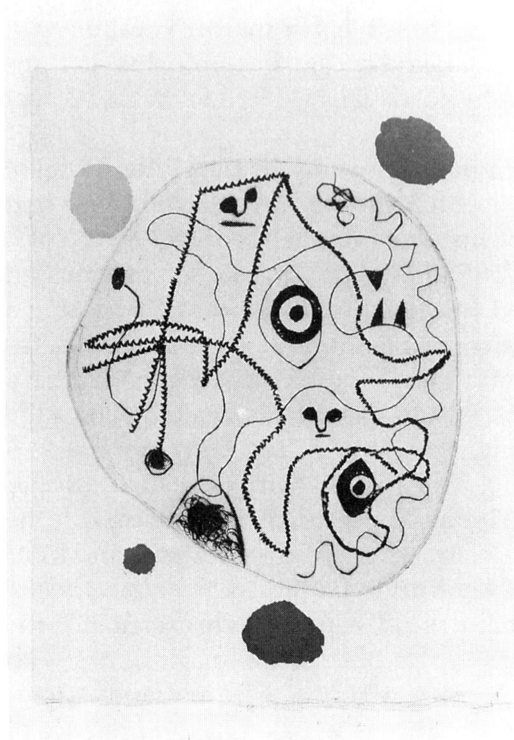

Figure 3. Joan Miró. Etching (1947) for Tristan Tzara, *L'Anti-tête*, Vol III, 1949. Herzog August Bibliothek, Wolfenbüttel [12.8, 361 Maler-bücher] © 1996 Artists Rights Society (ARS), New York/ADAGP, Paris.

> I am working furiously; you and all my other writer friends have given me much help and improved my understanding of many things. I think about our conversation, when you told me how you start with a word and watched to see where it would take you. I have done a series of small things on wood, in which I take off from some form in the wood. Using an artificial thing as a point of departure like this, I feel, is parallel to what writers can obtain by starting with an arbitrary sound; the R.R. from the song of a cricket, for example, or the isolated sound of a consonant or vowel, any sound, be it nasal or labial. This can create a surprising metaphysical state in you poets, even when you use the sound of vowels or consonants that have no meaning at all. (Qtd. in Rowell 86)

After the dormant period in his graphic production during the war, Miró's attraction to the self-generating capacity of language manifests itself again in his new initiatives as a book artist. In *Parler seul*, the seminal aspect of language in Tzara's poetry is matched page for page by the generative force of Miró's own signs. Sensitive to the typographical as well as the graphic composition of the pages on which he was to work, Miró incorporated two basic elements of typography—the line and the point—into his own alphabet. Michel Leiris focused on the generative power of these typographical signs in his enthusiastic critique of *Parler seul* upon its release in 1950:

> Parallèlement aux mots qui sont des graines ("grains et issues" a dit ailleurs Tzara) les signes typographiques, ici, se révèlent capables des germination eux aussi. Rien de plus hasardeux et, à la fois, de plus organisé que ce livre qui est naissance du livre ou création progressive dont imprimerie d'une part et vocabulaire d'autre part constituent, semble-t-il, les seules principes animateurs. Sans doubt parlent-ils seuls, ces mots qui s'enchaînent d'eux-mêmes sans loi autre que la poésie, et seuls aussi ces matériaux que Miró met en oeuvre: caractères, chiffres, quand ce n'est simples points ou traits, bref, marques apparemment quelconques sur le blanc de la page. . . . (Leiris 2)

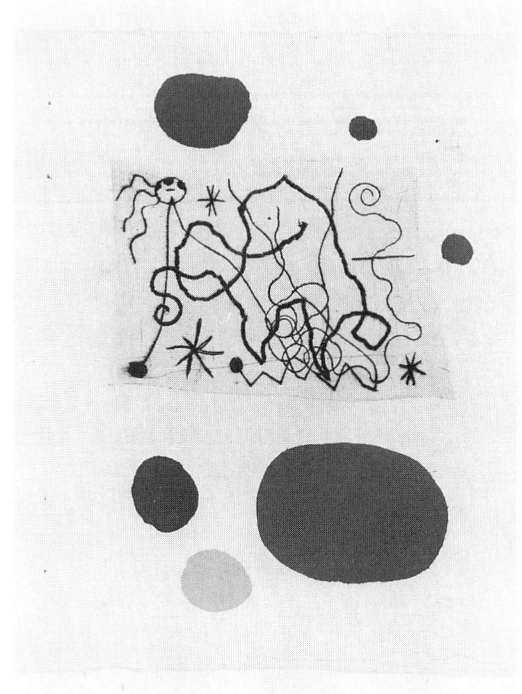

Figure 4. Joan Miró. Etching (1947) for Tristan Tzara, *L'Anti-tête*, Vol III, 1949. Herzog August Bibliothek, Wolfenbüttel [12.8, 361 Malerbücher] © 1996 Artists Rights Society (ARS), New York/ADAGP, Paris.

Parallel to words that function as seeds ("seeds and origins" Tzara said elsewere) here the typographical signs reveal themselves to be equally capable of germination. Nothing could be more accidental and at the same time more organized than this book, which in essence presents the birth of a book, the creation of an object in which the graphic elements on the one hand and words on the other are the sole generative principles involved. Without doubt they speak alone, these words, joined together purely on the basis of poetic attraction; isolated, too, are the graphic materials that Miró puts into play: letters, numbers, or even more basic points and lines, abbreviated and deployed at random, it would seem, across the white of the page.

As in Tzara's earlier poems, seed-words in *Parler seul* germinate from image to image, from line to line in a progressive generation of the poem out of its own verbal constituents. These words, as Leiris observes, converse amongst themselves, engender themselves in accordance with poetic impulses and in disregard for all rules of logical progression. Miró's seemingly spontaneous, childlike iconography is an appropriate accompaniment to the disjunctures and surprises in the language of the poem. And like Tzara's words, the typographical elements that Miró incorporates as basic visual building blocks, the point and the line, function as "principes animateurs," generative forces in the progressive creation of a double text in *Parler seul.*

Tzara wrote the poems of *Parler seul* after a two-month stay in 1945 in the psychiatric clinic of Saint-Alban at the invitation of the director. In daily contact with the mentally ill for the first time in his life, Tzara was profoundly moved by his conversations with certain of the patients whom he found to be congenial and saw frequently:

> Il y avait des hommes, des femmes et des enfants, et j'ai été extrêmement touché par ce côté de sympathie qui s'en dégageait, cette quête, cette demand constante d'humanité que j'ai trouvée chez eux. (Qtd. in Béhar 582-83)

> There were men, women, and children living there, and I was very touched by the sense of sympathy they emitted, by the quest for and constant insistence upon humanity that I experienced in their midst.

This insistence upon a shared humanity is a quality that Tzara celebrated in his collection of poems, a volume later to be considered one of his most successful post-war works.

In his conversations with the men, women, and children of Saint-Alban, Tzara experienced what he felt to be the unmediated access to human consciousness denuded of its customary layers of psychic defenses. In the poetic idiom of *Parler seul* he sought to recreate this impression. Tzara speaks in a tongue attuned to the otherwise imperceptible message of these solitary voices, to a communication that does not assume the mode of rational discourse. Words engended by childlike rhymes can provide a fleeting vision of deliverance:

> sable sable à ma façon
> table ronde table rase
> je t'ai vu à la peine
> truite de la déliverance

> sand, sand as I would have it
> round table, table swept clean
> I caught a glimpse of you
> trout of deliverance

Sustaining a momentary, alogical equilibrium based upon grammatical pairings, assonance, and repetition, words enact a balancing act on the high wire, following a thread that could lead out of the world and into the light. Tzara summons the inhabitants of Saint-Alban to witness the show, a performance with which many were intimately acquainted:

> le couteau dans la plaie
> coup de sifflet fini départ
> un autre train nous dit que dit-il
> il dit pauvres gens de-ci de-là

> somnulents ou insolents
> vifs alerts indifférents
> dépêchez-vous, dépêchez-vous
> l'acrobate sur la corde
> transpercé de part en part
> une aiguille ou bout du monde
> fait éclater la lumière

    c'est un oiseau de sel
    brisant la nuit
    et la liberté se répand
    comme du lait comme du sang.

    the knife in the wound
    whistle blow ended departure
    another train says to us what does it say
    it says unfortunate people from here from there

    sommulent and insolent
    quick alert indifferent
    hurry, hurry
    the acrobat on the wire
    pierced through and through
    a needle at the world's end
    makes the light explode

    it is the seabird
    that breaks the night
    and liberty flows forth
    like milk like blood

Although the final text in the collection recapitulates the monologue in the title of the book, "parler seul," the poet Tzara deploys words, poem for poem, in search of spontaneous openings for dialogue. The last two lines of the book promise deliverance from solitary confinement in the midst of other voices, all speaking alone:

    enfermé dans l'horizon des voix
    il n'y a pas de mur qui résiste à ta chaude mémoire
    face à la voix rompue
    les rats peuvent courir entre tes jambes
    l'herbe fine n'a pas fini d'échapper à ton appel
    avec un bruit invisible sur la bouche et les doigts
    tu est sorti vivant

    enclosed in the horizon of voices
    there is no wall that can resist your ardent memory
    faced by the broken voice
    the rats can run between your legs
    the young grass has not yet managed to escape your call
    with an invisible noise on your mouth and fingers
    you have come out alive

On completion of the volume, Tzara began preparations with Aimé Maeght for an illustrated edition of the poems. From the beginning, Tzara's assumption seems to have been that the poems would be published as a *livre de peintre*, and there was no real question as to whom he wished as his collaborator on this project:

> Alors, lorsque j'ai terminé ce poème, le problème s'est posé à moi de savoir qui pourrait l'illustrer; or, il n'y avait que mon vieil ami Miró qui était le plus près de cet esprit, à cause de la fraîcheur de ses sentiments et de l'univers dans lequel il vit, où il a mis sa peinture et tout son art. Il sent des racines très profondes qui rapprochent le plus de l'homme à l'état de nudité de la conscience. (Qtd. in Béhar 583)

> Once I had finished the poem, the problem arose of whom I should find to illustrate it. For my part there was no one other than my old friend Miró close enough to the spirit I sought, thanks to the freshness of his sentiments and of the universe in which he dwells and where he situates his painting and all his art. He has a sense of the profound roots through which man in a naked, unprotected state of human consciousness can be approached most closely.

Miró, equipped with both the sensibility and an iconography suited to convey the levels of human consciousness that Tzara had discovered himself to share with inmates in Saint-Alban, recreates Tzara's poetic world as a *livre de peintre*. He endows the collection of poems with a new resonance made possible only through the iconographical translation of Tzara's texts into his own graphic medium within the very specific context of a book. From page to page Miró's figures and graffiti-like signs enact the dialogues in which the title of the book, "Parler seul," might be transcended, if ever so provisionally, and the sense of humanity explored in the poems be communicated from one human being to another.

In the previously cited 1959 interview with Yvon Taillandier, Miró also explained the function of his reduced figures:

> Little by little, I came to use only a small number of forms and colors. . . . My figures underwent the same simplification as my colors. Simplified as they are, they are more human and alive than they would be if represented in all their details. Represented in

detail, they would lose their imaginary quality, which enhances everything. When a viewer recognizes himself in one of my figures, he does not think about what separates him from other men, he thinks about what unites him with everyone else, whether he is black or white, from the North or South, from Africa or China. (Qtd. in Rowell 250)

Such a point of departure enabled Miró to complement Tzara's approach to the patients of Saint-Alban. The poet Tzara, in search for dialogue with the inmates there, now found himself engaged in a further dialogue in this realization of his book, a dialogue sustained by Miró as graphic artist from the first to last page of *Parler seul.*

With this undertaking Miró launched his impressive postwar achievements in the realm of the *livre de peintre.* Above all, he now approached the book itself as a compositional entity. In *Parler seul* the lithographs no longer exist as an independent graphic suite or self-contained, isolated illustrations, but are wholly integrated into the book in accord with its own rhythm of organic development. Reversing Lessing's classical dichotomy between the sequential perception of the written text and the simultaneous perception of a painting, Miró appropriates the sequential nature of the book to his visual advantage by establishing progressions of visual signs and repeating and varying these series from poem to poem.[7] With fundamental elements of typography — the line and the point — with the numerical series in Arabic numbers from 1 to 4, in Roman numerals from I to XI, and with five colors — black, red, blue, yellow, and green — Miró builds up his graphic progressions. They all begin with a thematic statement of the elements involved in any one series and are then elaborated into new constellations. In every one of these progressions, Miró's sign language moves invariably towards a condensed figuration of human beings — man, woman, and child. Interspersed between the initial statement of elements and their ultimate reconstellation are text pages and pages of black, graffiti-like signs. These black graffiti evoke alternatively human figures — man, woman, and child — labyrinths, and speaking tongues, tongues that evoke the title, "Parler seul," as well as final lines of the last poem: "avec un bruit invisible sur la bouche et les doigts / tu est sorti vivant."

Miró's initial series of illustrations accompanies the first two poems of the collection, "Etrangère" and "Egarées." It is composed of two signs — lines and points — and the five basic colors of the book, which function as independent pictorial elements in their own right. The points are ovals, more dynamic in their effect than perfect circles. The upper half of the first text-page includes all these elements in a constellation of two black ovals, one red oval, and one blue, one yellow, and one green line (Figure 5). With the poem "Egarées" this initial statement of elements is reduced to an absolute minimum: one point — red, one broad line — black. Two black lines and one blue point constitute the next stage of the progression. The series develops further with three black lines and one green point, then four black lines and one yellow point. Once all four colors have appeared, the ovals as well as the lines begin to multiply, first into five black lines and two ovals, green and yellow, then six black lines and three ovals, yellow, green, and blue.

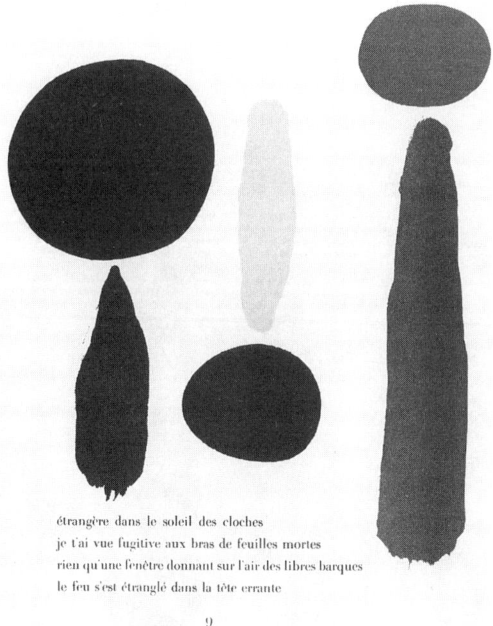

Figure 5. Joan Miró. Lithograph for Tristan Tzara, *Parler seul,* 1948-50. Herzog August Bibliothek, Wolfenbüttel [8.2, 13 Malerbücher] © 1996 Artists Rights Society (ARS), New York/ADAGP, Paris.

Throughout the development of each macro-series in its color and numerical progression, interspersed graffiti pages establish their own patterns of progression, usually in a single or double-page combination of text and black lithographic signs. On the first page printed with graffiti, one sign is immediately identifiable: Miró's star composed of four intersecting lines. It is accompanied by a crescent suggesting the quarter moon, a crescent that transforms itself into the curve of an opened mouth with an erect, speaking tongue (Figure 6). This tongue with its phallic implications is often paired with a figure created with a vertical black stroke and a black triangle, the graffiti indication of a woman with a skirt. A black line surging upward in the margin of a subsequent text page in this series is transformed into a human figure through the addition of arms and legs, indicated by two horizontal black lines. This page faces an *hors-texte* illustration in which the four figures — red, yellow, blue, and green — have been endowed with legs and feet and inquisitive heads

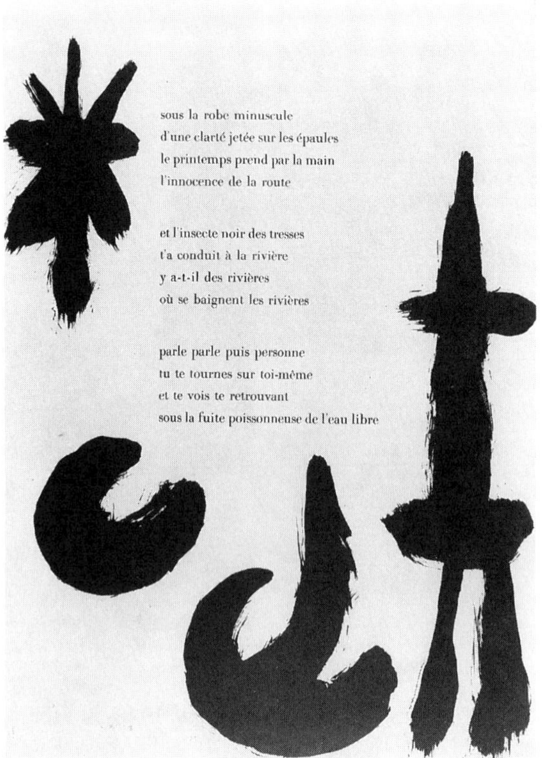

Figure 6. Joan Miró. Lithograph for Tristan Tzara, *Parler seul*, 1948-50. Herzog August Bibliothek, Wolfenbüttel [8.2, 13 Malerbücher] © 1996 Artists Rights Society (ARS), New York/ ADAGP, Paris.

(Figure 7). This inquisitive stance is characteristic of numerous graffiti-like figures in the *hors-texte* colored lithographs interspersed throughout the macro-series (Figure 8). The rudimentary human figurations are on occasion replaced by a tangle of swirling black lines, for example a labyrinthian, serpentine path that meanders beneath the final two lines of the poem it accompanies: "délivrées du retour / vous voilà sur la bonne route."

The second macro-series, "Le Rire d'eau," progresses through the Arabic numerical row 1-4. The point that accompanies the numbers consists in each case of a loosely textured, centrifugal swirl of lines, a configuration that evokes the image of a whirlpool in the first line of the poem: "arbres aux yeux innombrables tourbillons." In the second lithograph of the series, the number 1, which was accompanied by a red swirl, is converted into a male figure (Figure 9). The 2 is paired with a blue swirl and then converted into a horizontal, snail-like figure with three antennae, which can also be interpreted as the three human hairs in Miró's work. The 3, accompanied by a green swirl, is transformed

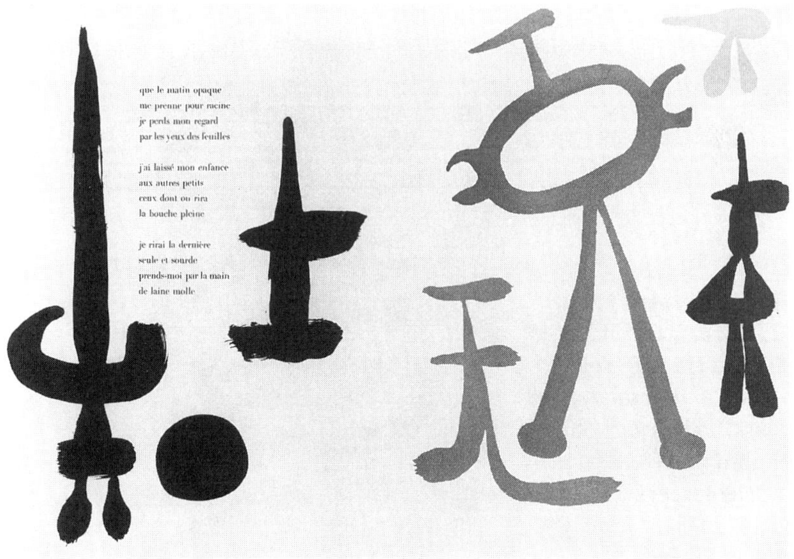

Figure 7. Joan Miró. Lithograph for Tristan Tzara, *Parler seul*, 1948-50. Herzog August Bibliothek, Wolfenbüttel [8.2, 13 Malerbücher] © 1996 Artists Rights Society (ARS), New York/ADAGP, Paris.

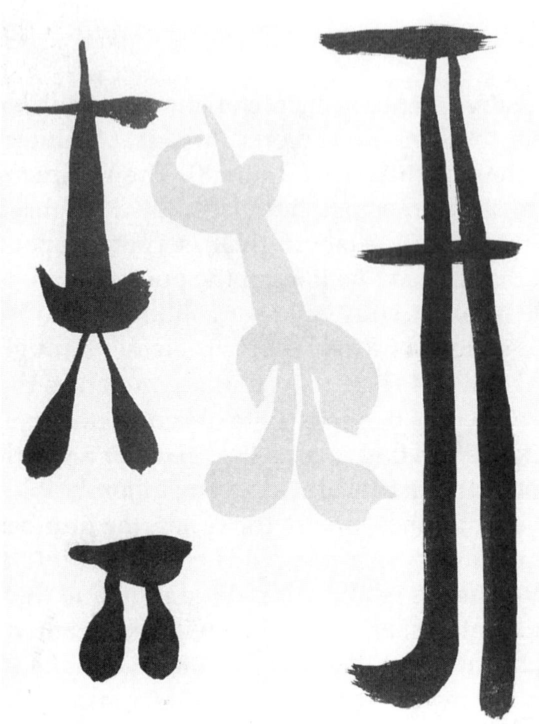

Figure 8. Joan Miró. Lithograph for Tristan Tzara, *Parler seul,* 1948-50. Herzog August Bibliothek, Wolfenbüttel [8.2, 13 Malerbücher] © 1996 Artists Rights Society (ARS), New York/ ADAGP, Paris.

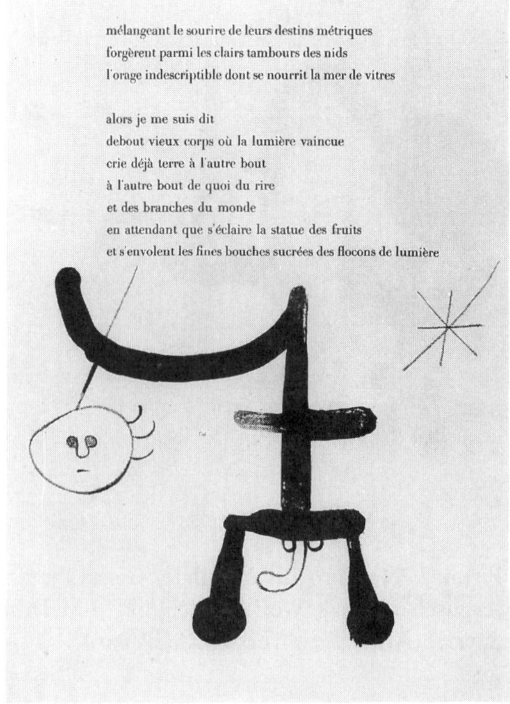

Figure 9. Joan Miró. Lithograph for Tristan Tzara, *Parler seul,* 1948-50. Herzog August Bibliothek, Wolfenbüttel [8.2, 13 Malerbücher] © 1996 Artists Rights Society (ARS), New York/ ADAGP, Paris.

into a human figure with three hairs bearing a 3 on its back (Figure 10), and with a 4, accompanied by a swirl of yellow, the Arabic countdown comes to an end.

The third macro-series "Les Mots de paille" progresses from Roman numeral I through XI. The Roman I streaks across the first text page, followed by a red point with a splattered periphery (Figure 11). The introduction to the series recalls the opening statement of elements in "Egarées" with one upward surging black line accompanied by a red point. As the macro-series in "Les Mots de paille" develops, different colored ovals accumulate one by one with each newly augmented number in the series, for example, the Roman numeral VIII (Figure 12). In the end, eleven colored points accompany the Roman numeral XI. In this series, the numerals are not produced with the solid black lines of the first macro-series but with a ragged stroke such as that produced by a Japanese reed brush. The uneven texture contributes to the dynamic sense of motion in this series, as does the unpredictable positioning of the colored points in relation to the numerals and the printed text. Each new numeral is followed

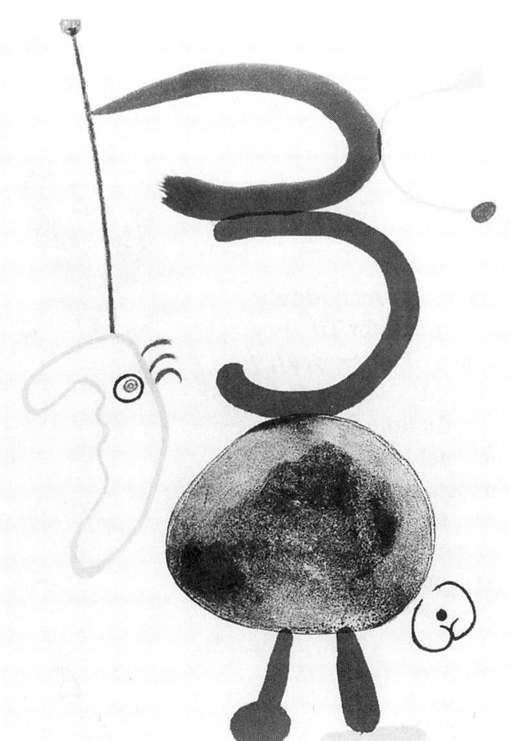

Figure 10. Joan Miró. Lithograph for Tristan Tzara, *Parler seul,* 1948-50. Herzog August Bibliothek, Wolfenbüttel [8.2, 13 Malerbücher] © 1996 Artists Rights Society (ARS), New York/ ADAGP, Paris.

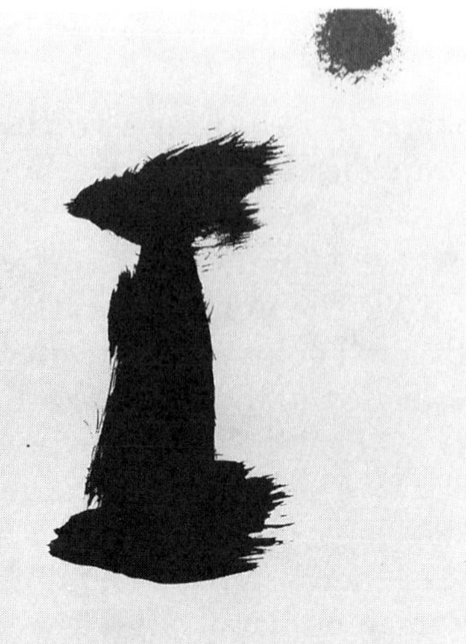

Figure 11. Joan Miró. Lithograph for Tristan Tzara, *Parler seul,* 1948-50. Herzog August Bibliothek, Wolfenbüttel [8.2, 13 Malerbücher] © 1996 Artists Rights Society (ARS), New York/ ADAGP, Paris.

Figure 12. Joan Miró. Lithograph for Tristan Tzara, *Parler seul,* 1948-50. Herzog August Bibliothek, Wolfenbüttel [8.2, 13 Malerbücher] © 1996 Artists Rights Society (ARS), New York/ ADAGP, Paris.

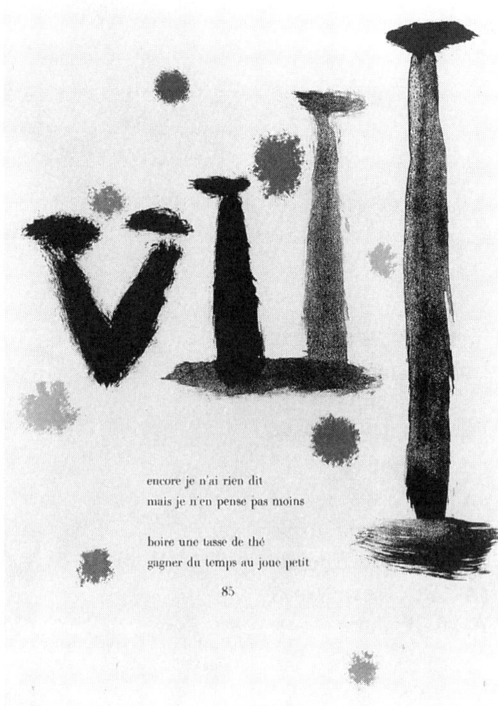

by text pages with graffiti and, on occasion, by pages in which the numeral itself is converted into one or more human figures, for example, the V (Figure 13).

The final poem "Parler seul" is introduced by a full-page, seven-colored figure that embodies within one image, now in terms of the Greek alphabet, Miró's principle of serial progression throughout the book (Figure 14). The oval 0, or Omega, laid horizontally across an upended V, creates the letter A, or Alpha. At the same time this oval Omega frames a human face with open mouth and with three hairs. Overhead, a blue star accompanies this figure, which embodies at one glance the progression from Alpha to Omega, the alphabet from beginning to end. The 0 and the upended V also constitute further variations of the two typographical elements, point and line.

This lithograph functions as a second frontispiece in the book for the poem "Parler seul," the title of which is printed alone on the facing page. The first text page of this last folio confronts an *hors-texte* lithograph in which the line manifests itself as an inpenetrable labyrinth, all but obliterating a black star. Four col-

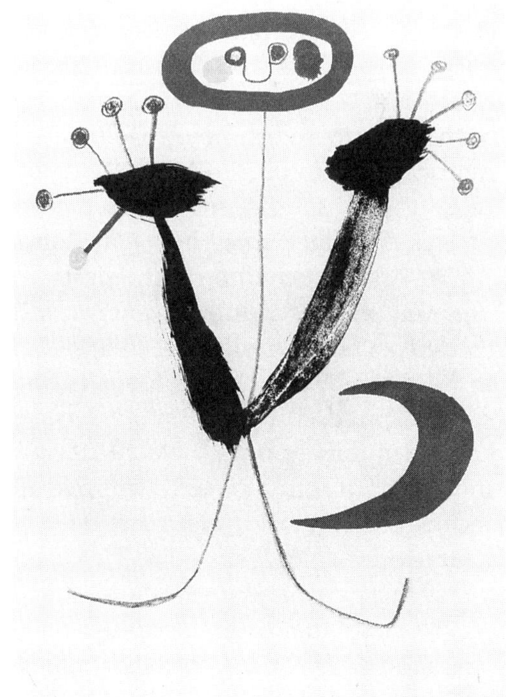

Figure 13. Joan Miró. Lithograph for Tristan Tzara, *Parler seul*, 1948-50. Herzog August Bibliothek, Wolfenbüttel [8.2, 13 Malerbücher] © 1996 Artists Rights Society (ARS), New York/ ADAGP, Paris.

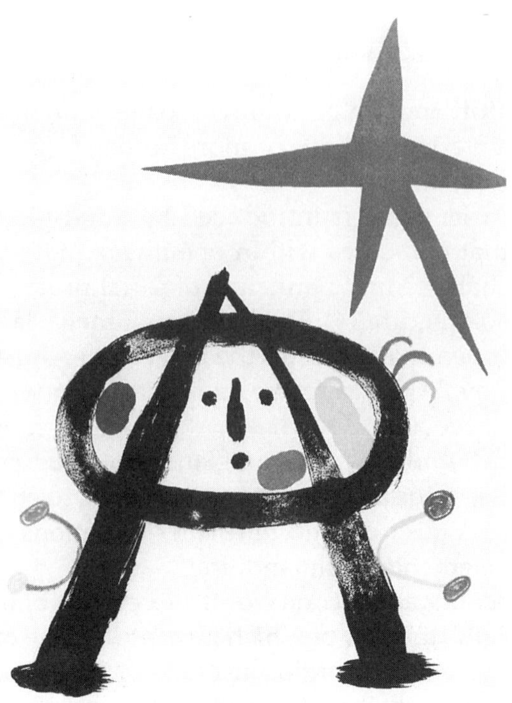

Figure 14. Joan Miró. Lithograph for Tristan Tzara, *Parler seul*, 1948-50. Herzog August Bibliothek, Wolfenbüttel [8.2, 13 Malerbücher] © 1996 Artists Rights Society (ARS), New York/ ADAGP, Paris.

ored points — red, blue, yellow, green — assert themselves against the obscure maze. The last black graffiti entry of the poem includes three variations of the erect, speaking tongue within the curve of the upturned mouth (Figure 15). In the full-page color lithograph with which this series ends, Miró introduces three human figures with heads delineated by the three plane-geometrical figures used repeatedly throughout the book: an open rectangle, a triangle, and a closed elliptical curve. Each of these figures is accompanied by a star (Figure 16).

At first glance, the rudimentary human figures of these series may appear primitive and childlike, as spontaneously recorded as the unpredictable twists of association between words in the poems. Miró has deployed his signs, however, with highly sophisticated compositional intent, endowing them with enhanced significance in the context of a progressive evolution of the book from title page to impressum. His recapitulation and reconstellation of his elements does not cease with the final illustration for the last poem. The first page of the table of contents, the two-page impressum, and a final page with a brief word of explanation concerning the origin of the poems are also inscribed with Miró's iconograpy, once again with the minimal

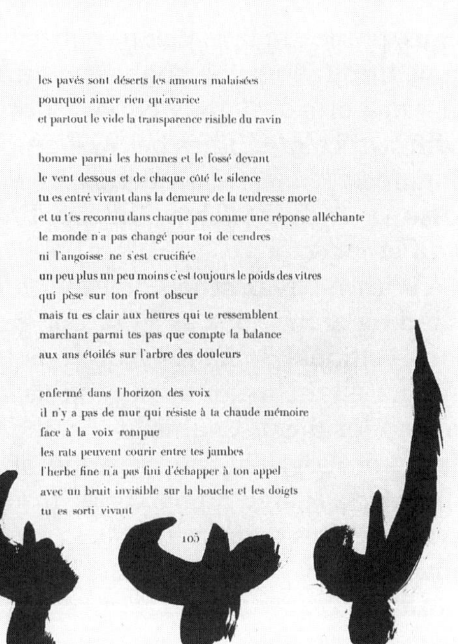

Figure 15. Joan Miró. Lithograph for Tristan Tzara, *Parler seul,* 1948-50. Herzog August Bibliothek, Wolfenbüttel [8.2, 13 Malerbücher] © 1996 Artists Rights Society (ARS), New York/ ADAGP, Paris.

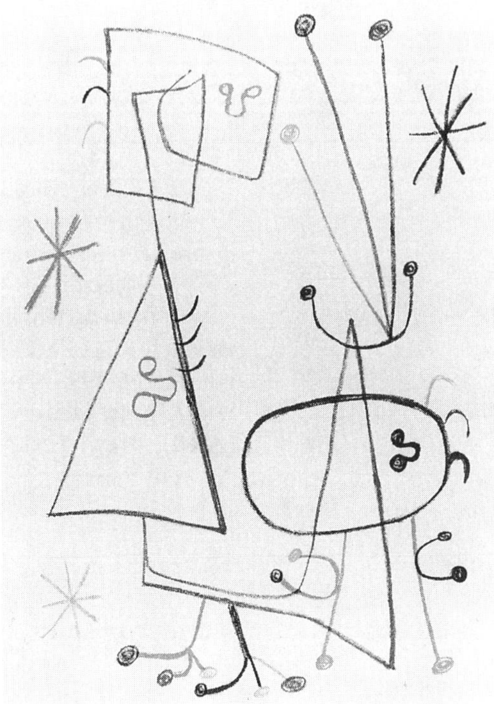

Figure 16. Joan Miró. Lithograph for Tristan Tzara, *Parler seul,* 1948-50. Herzog August Bibliothek, Wolfenbüttel [8.2, 13 Malerbücher] © 1996 Artists Rights Society (ARS), New York/ ADAGP, Paris.

signs, point and line, that have been used in ever new combinations throughout the book. The human presence is articulated first in a broad, slightly curved, horizontal black line as a torso with two colored lines below — one brown, one green — as legs (Figure 17), and subsequently in a horizontal green oval as a torso, defined as such by the four lines of arms and legs, each in a different color.

With his realization of *Parler seul*, Miró's matured understanding of the book as a graphic genre with its own particular compositional demands manifests itself as the point of departure for all the major book projects with which he was to be involved for the rest of his life. In the musical sense of a *Lied* setting, Miró's visual transposition of Tzara's poetic text and its appeal to a shared humanity is "through composed" from cover to cover. This composition is to be experienced by reading sequentially, page for page, the book's double text of image and word.

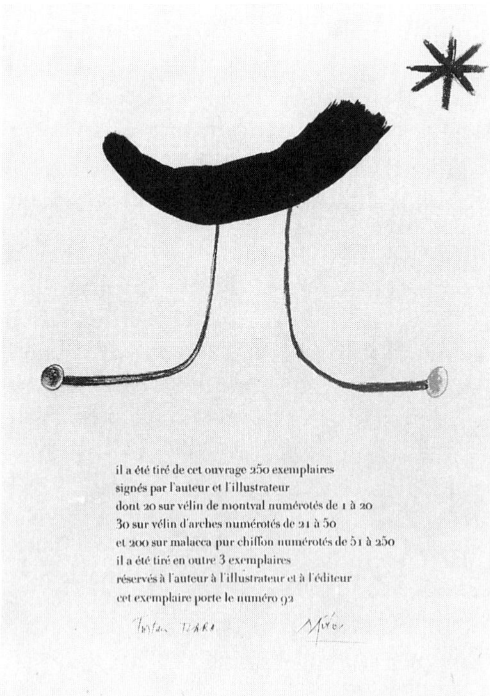

Figure 17. Joan Miró. Lithograph for Tristan Tzara, *Parler seul*, 1948-50. Herzog August Bibliothek, Wolfenbüttel [8.2, 13 Malerbücher] © 1996 Artists Rights Society (ARS), New York/ ADAGP, Paris.

Notes

[1]Joan Miró, in a letter to Gérald Cramer of June 19, 1949. Archive Gérald Cramer, Bibliothèque publique et universitaire, Geneva. All translations are mine unless otherwise noted.

[2]Joan Miró, in a letter to Gérald Cramer of June 28, 1949. Archive Gérald Cramer, Bibliothèque publique et universitaire, Geneva.

[3]Joan Miró, in a letter to Gérald Cramer of October 2, 1949. Archive Gérald Cramer, Bibliothèque publique et universitaire, Geneva.

[4]For discussions of Miró, Eluard, Cramer, and the creation of *A toute épreuve* see Greet; Ehrenström 57-81; Hubert, *Surrealism* 285, 290-97; Watts 22-47.

[5]For discussions of the *Constellations* with respect to Breton as poet and with his relation to Miró see Hubert, "Miró"; Raillard; Balakian; Edson; Bohn; Hubert, *Surrealism* 125, 130-38.

[6]In a recently published, provocative discussion of Miró's iconography in the 1920s and 30s, Hubertus Gassner situates the increased importance of Iberian hieroglyphs for Miró's work in the 1930s within the framework of the artist's efforts to create "anti-paintings," works that require a return to a collective, pre-historic iconography of primitive man. See Chapter X, "Anti-Malerei" (Gassner 238-77). Gassner discusses Miró's iconography of the 1920s in terms of its relation to astrological and alchemical iconography, comparing images in Miró's paintings to certain specific works of Paracelsus and Jacob Boehme. Unfortunately Gassner can provide no documented evidence of Miró's exposure to the actual texts and engravings in question and works only from the inference that Miró could have seen and read these works in the course of his friendship with Michel Leiris. Nevertheless, Gassner's analysis of paintings such as "The Harlequin's Carnival" (1924-25) provides convincing evidence of Miró's general acquaintance with alchemical themes and iconography, themes that can be identified already in works of the early 1920s. See in particular Chapter VII, "Alchemistische Experimente" (Gassner 145-56).

[7]See the discussion of Miró's sequential ordering of images by Harriett Watts in Haenlein 50-56.

Works Cited

Balakian, Anna. "From 'Poisson soluble' to 'Constellations.'" *Twentieth Century Literature* 21 (1975): 48-59.

Béhar, Henri. *Tristan Tzara: Oeuvres complètes.* Vol. IV. Paris: Flammarion, 1980.

Bohn, Willard. "Semiosis and Intertextuality in Breton's 'Femme et oiseau.'" *Romanic Review* 71 (1986): 415-29.

Breton, André. Introduction. *Constellations.* Joan Miró. Exhibition catalogue. New York: Pierre Mattise, 1959.

Dupin, Jacques. Introduction. *Miró graveur.* Vol. 1. Exhibition catalogue. Paris: D. Lelong, 1984.

Edson, Laurie. "Confronting the Signs: Words, Images, and the Reader-Spectator." *Dada-Surrealism* 13 (1984): 83-94.

Ehrenström, Annick. *Un éditeur genevois: Gérald Cramer.* Geneva: Bibliothèque publique et universitaire, 1988.

Gassner, Hubertus. *Joan Miró; Der magische Gärtner.* Köln: DuMont Buchverlag, 1994.

Greet, Anne Hyde. "Miró, Eluard, Cramer: *A toute épreuve.*" *Bulletin du Bibliophile* 2 (1983): 223-42 and 3 (1983): 346-68.

Haenlein, Carl, ed. *Das Buch des Künstlers.* Hanover: Kestner Gesellschaft, 1989. [Katalog 3/1989]

Hubert, Renée Riese. "Miró and Breton." *Yale French Studies* 31 (1964): 52-61.

______. *Surrealism and the Book.* Berkeley: U of California P, 1988.

Leiris, Michel. Commentary. *Derrière le miroir* 29-30 (1950) (Supplement on *Parler seul*).

Raillard, Georges. "Breton en regard de Miró: 'Constellations.'" *Littérature* 17 (1974): 3-13.

Rowell, Margit, ed. *Joan Miró; Selected Writings and Interviews.* Trans. Paul Auster. Boston: Hall, 1986.

Stich, Sidra. *Joan Miró: The Development of a Sign Language.* St. Louis: Washington University, 1980.

Watts, Harriett. "Joan Miró: Begegnungen mit der Materia." *Leuchtend klare Metamorphosen: Paul Eluard und Joan Miró, "A toute épreuve."* Eds. Sabine Solf and Harriett Watts. Wolfenbüttel: Herzog August Bibliothek, 1990. 22-47.

Juliette Roche
and the Ideoplastic Method

Willard Bohn

In addition to the Alfred Stieglitz circle, the New York avant-garde during and immediately after World War I embraced numerous individuals associated with Walter Conrad Arensberg, whose apartment at 33 West 67th Street served as their principal meeting place. Besides Francis Picabia and Man Ray, who frequented both groups, these included the composer Edgar Varèse, Marcel Duchamp, and writers such as Mina Loy and Juliette Roche. Married to the Cubist artist Albert Gleizes, who also participated in their activities, Roche chronicled her experience in a book of poems and a *roman à clef*. Published in 1920 and 1924 respectively, *Demi-Cercle* and *La Minéralisation de Dudley Craving MacAdam* were written during her stay in New York. The daughter of a former French cabinet minister, she enjoyed a certain success as a painter before the war forced her to leave her homeland and settle in America. Excluding some ten months spent in Barcelona, the Gleizes' sojourn in America lasted nearly three and a half years.[1] During this time they functioned not only as aesthetic catalysts but as important conduits between New York, Barcelona, and Paris.

Returning from Spain early in 1917, Roche threw herself into avant-garde activities with renewed vigor. Although her poetry continued to draw on Cubist aesthetics, it acquired a forcefulness and a willingness to take risks that were previously lacking. While her earlier poems were obviously experimental, their arrangement on the page was fairly traditional. By contrast, the newer works stressed the physical appearance of the printed text.

Like literary cubists elsewhere, Roche began to spatialize her poems by dividing the lines into expressive groups. On at least two occasions she felt the need to transcend this rudimentary device and to create actual visual poems. The first of these, apparently completed soon after her return, was also the first work to illustrate her new method. Since the poems in *Demi-Cercle* are arranged chronologically, it not only signals a change in her style but serves to introduce the subsequent works.

Entitled BREVOORT, the composition features a large, solid black, right triangle at its center that is juxtaposed with several circles and numerous verbal fragments (Figure 1). At first glance it recalls Apollinaire's "L'Horloge de demain" ("The Clock of Tomorrow"), which Picabia — who had followed the Gleizes to Barcelona — published in his journal *391* on March 25, 1917 (Apollinaire 682). Since the Gleizes and the Picabias were close friends, he would have sent them a copy as soon as the issue appeared. At second glance, however, one realizes that Roche took as her model not Apollinaire's poem but rather de Zayas "Mental Reactions," composed with the aid of Agnes Ernst Meyer.[2] Not only do the physical layouts have much in common, but the second composition includes two solid black right triangles. In any event, triangular forms predominate in more than one of de Zayas' works. Although the function of Roche's triangle is far from clear, its massive proportions and central position make it impossible to ignore. On the one hand, it unifies the verbal as well as the visual elements. On the other hand, it constitutes a powerful visual statement in its own right.

The text itself is initially as disconcerting as its physical appearance. How is one to interpret the enigmatic title, for instance? Does it represent an exclamation, is it an example of onomatopoeia, or does it serve as a proper noun? And how are the various linguistic fragments, many of which violate compositional norms, supposed to fit together? Contemporary readers would presumably have recognized that the poem was situated in a popular café attached to the Hotel Brevoort in New York. Henri-Pierre Roché, who also frequented the Arensberg circle, provides the following description:

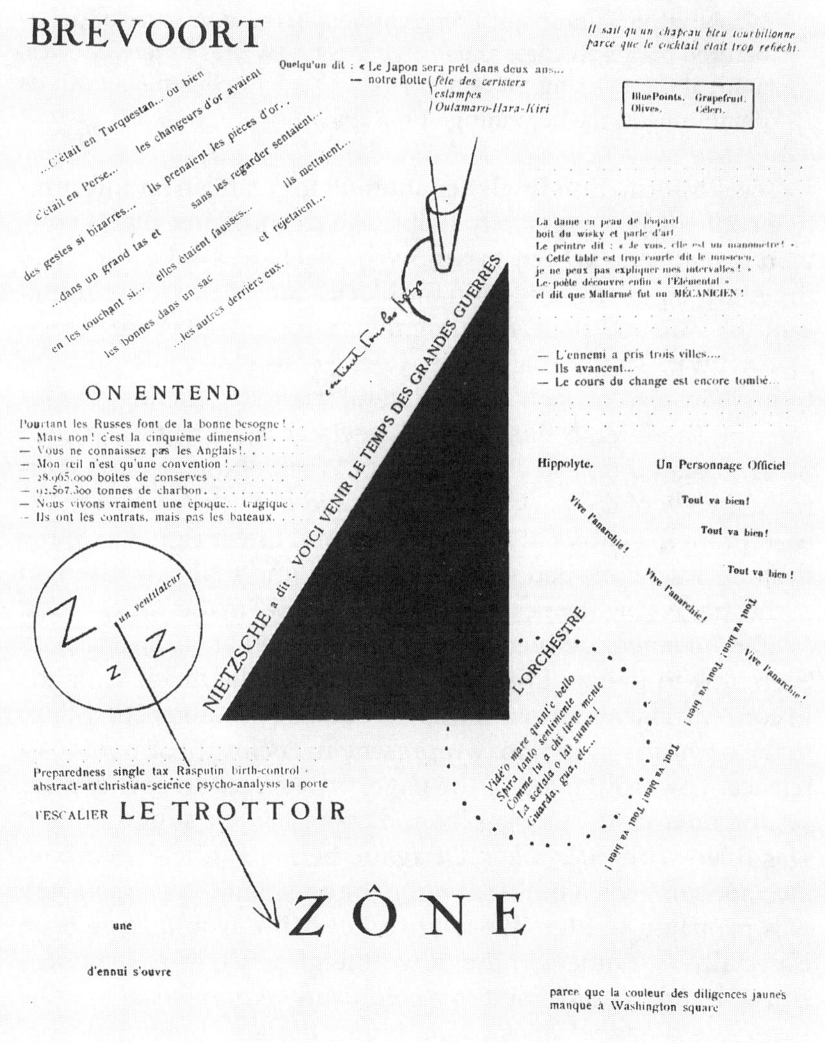

Figure 1. Juliette Roche, *BREVOORT*. Photograph from *Demi-Cercle*. Paris: Editions d'Art la "Cible," 1920.

[C'était un] grand hôtel-caravansérail dans le style haussmannien, édifié sur la 5e avenue, à un angle du Washington Square, son atmosphère "à la française," mélange de laisser-aller bon enfant et de bonne chère, et ses cafés-terrasses en firent, jusqu'à sa démolition au début des années 1950, le lieu de rendez-vous de l'intelligentsia new yorkaise. (98)

[It was a] grand hotel-caravansary in the style of the Baron Haussmann, situated at one of the corners of Fifth Avenue and Washington Square; its "French atmosphere," a mixture of good-natured permissiveness and festive cheer, as well as its terrace cafés, made it the meeting place of the New York intelligentsia until its demolition at the beginning of the 1950s.[3]

This information finally enables us to establish an interpretive context. It is especially helpful in deciphering the poem's visual features, which can now be seen to evoke the Café Brevoort. Upon investigation the black triangle proves to represent the café and the remaining images objects that are associated with it. This explains why Roche chose to employ a right triangle instead of, say, an equilateral triangle. The café was located at the intersection of two streets at right angles to each other. Situated on the upper edge of Washington Square, it offered a view of the park to the south and of Fifth Avenue to the east. From the circles at the lower left and lower right we know the café was equipped with ceiling fans and that it boasted an orchestra. As the former devices hum quietly in the background "Z Z Z," a singer delivers a moving rendition of "Come Back to Sorrento" in Italian. Like the vocal sounds, the music expands in concentric waves until it fills the room. The intersecting lines to the orchestra's right may represent an enclosure or perhaps a terrace. Toward the top of the page, one notices an empty glass resting on a saucer whose size and conical shape suggest that it was filled with *café au lait*. Or again, perhaps it held a carbonated soda or even a milkshake. On the one hand, since the poem was probably written in March, a hot drink would have been especially welcome. On the other, the glass seems to contain a straw, which would point to a cold drink. Arranged in parallel rows, the diagonal lines at the upper left are somewhat puzzling. While it is difficult to be sure, they may represent a café awning or possibly a set of venetian blinds. Enclosing several words, the rectangle at the upper right is also ambiguous. Although it resembles a section of a menu, the selection itself is problematic. If the celery, the olives, and the bluepoint oysters are common appetizers, the grapefruit would appear to belong to a different category. Was dinner preceded by citrus fruit in those days, or is there another explanation? Inevitably one is forced to conclude that the dishes represent a random assortment. This suggests that the rectangle depicts a cart or a side-table where they are momentarily assembled. The same fondness for synecdoche and metonymy can be observed at the verbal level. Like the visual images, the verbal fragments belong to a larger picture where they are subordinated to global principles. Like their visual counterparts, the phrases are related to each other through contiguity. If the design evokes the café's physical appearance, the text provides a glimpse of the people who congregate there. In addition, it permits us to witness one of their favorite activities — discussing the issues of the day. The crowd is drawn to the café not so much because of its food and drink but because of the opportunity to exchange ideas. Like Apollinaire's "Lundi rue Christine" ("Monday Christine Street") (Apollinaire 180-82), therefore, on which it is partially modeled, the work is a conversation poem. As de Zayas had previously remarked, one encounters a "polyphony of simultaneous voices which say different things."

Reflecting simultanist precepts, the text is governed almost exclusively by parataxis. Like the various sections, the phrases are arranged in no particular order. Rather they are uttered simultaneously by people sitting in different parts of the café. At most they share a unity of time and space that produces a certain harmony. Although the composition is intended to be apprehended instantaneously, the reading process is unavoidably sequential. The text must still be deciphered word by word as the reader puzzles out its meaning. In theory its simultaneity could be preserved by transforming it into an oral performance. In practice, there are simply too many competing messages for this to succeed. For one thing, at least half the remarks would be drowned out by interference. For another, a listener would still need to process them sequentially. Interestingly, it seems that true simultaneity can only be experienced after the fact, that is, intellectually. Once the various elements have all been apprehended, they coalesce to form a mental collage.

As in traditional poetry, the work appears to begin at the upper left and to conclude at the lower right. What happens in between is anybody's guess. Several possible paths lead from the poem's title to the final date and place. It cannot only be read clockwise, for example, but also counter clockwise. Or, alternatively, it can be divided into two columns and processed like a conventional text. With a little effort it is even possible to devise diagonal readings that link opposing corners. The comments that follow, therefore, are arranged in no definite order. Within the frame mentioned above, one reading seems as valid as any other. Beginning at the upper left, the reader discovers that the café has a certain exotic quality. While one patron recounts an anecdote concerning the Middle East, another analyzes Japan's military capabilities. The money changers in Turkistan or Persia, the first speaker declares, can tell a gold coin simply by touching it. According to the second, the Japanese fleet will be able to challenge the American navy in two years. This remark is juxtaposed with several block prints by Utamaro portraying the Cherry Blossom Festival. Or rather, since their status is ambiguous, it appears to be. On the one hand, the pictures may actually decorate the café's walls. On the other, they may be mental images evoked by the mention of Japan. To the triangle's left, the words "ON ENTEND" 'ONE HEARS' stress the fact that the phrases are all snatches of conversation. Indeed, at least two discussions are taking place at the same time. One of these is evidently concerned with modern art, with its attempt to transcend physical realism. Arguing that perception is learned rather than innate, one person exclaims "Mon oeil n'est qu'une convention!" 'My eye is merely a convention!' If modern artists are to revolutionize painting, they must learn to see things differently. They must learn to disregard the physical world and to cultivate the fourth dimension. As Linda Henderson has shown, the concept of an extra, non-Euclidean dimension, first developed by mathematicians, appealed to many artists who were struggling to find a new language. Unexpectedly, another speaker (or perhaps the same one) protests that even this concept is outmoded: "Mais non! C'est la cinquième dimension!" To remain on the cutting edge artists must exploit the fifth dimension. These remarks are intermingled with a second conversation about the war. We learn that, like the British soldiers, the Russian army is putting up a good fight.

Citing statistics involving tons of coal and boxes of canned goods, one speaker evokes the European relief effort. Whereas a number of entrepreneurs have government contracts to deliver the goods, the necessary ships are not available.

The comments above, together with the absence of any American involvement, imply that the United States had not yet entered the war. This impression is confirmed by a reference to the Preparedness Movement, at the lower left, which advocated military intervention in the conflict. Since the movement ceased to exist when America joined the war on April 6, 1917, the poem must have been written earlier. Despite President Wilson's attempts to remain neutral, the composition demonstrates that the war was on everybody's mind. To the triangle's right a speaker announces that the enemy has captured three more towns. Their soldiers are continuing to advance, someone else adds, while a third customer laments the decline in the rate of exchange. If the visual composition is focused on the triangle, the text is dominated by the message that accompanies it. Extending the length of the hypoteneuse, printed in capital letters, is a quote from Nietzsche predicting that the modern era would be consumed by warfare. "NIETZSCHE a dit," someone declares, "VOICI VENIR LE TEMPS DES GRANDES GUERRES" 'NIETZSCHE said: AN AGE OF GREAT WARS IS UPON US.'[4]

Although the war's shadow looms over the café, it is far from the only topic of conversation. At the lower left Roche lists other issues that interested New York intellectuals in 1917. Besides the Preparedness Movement, for example, the concept of a "single tax" was attracting more and more attention. Like Henry George, who first proposed the idea in *Progress and Poverty* (1879), its proponents argued that government revenues should come from a single tax based upon land values. The proposal attracted considerable support for a while that gradually faded away. The next two items in the list had received a lot of publicity recently. On December 30, 1916, a group of Russian noblemen assassinated the mad monk Rasputin, who exercised a despotic influence over the Tzarina. Birth control was also in the news as Margaret Sanger sought to make contraceptive information readily available. Indicted for breaking the law, she fled to Europe but returned to stand trial in 1916, whereupon the charges were dismissed. Later the same year her family planning clinic was closed by the police and she was convicted of maintaining a public nuisance. The remaining references are much more accessible. Although abstract art was hardly new by 1917, it continued to elicit widespread discussion. Founded in 1879 by Mary Baker Eddy, Christian Science was, if anything, even more controversial. The same was true of psychoanalysis, which some people viewed as a panacea and others as a hoax.

At the upper right, we glimpse a man and a woman having a drink together. "*Il sait qu'un chapeau bleu tourbillonne,*" Roche observes, "*parce que le cocktail était trop réfléchi*" '*He knows that a blue hat is turning round and round because the cocktail was too deliberate.*' How this gnomic utterance is meant to be interpreted is not immediately evident. At first glance, it appears to be little more than an amusing portrait. Upon reflection, it can be seen to exploit two different tropes: synecdoche and metaphor. It is not the woman's hat, one comes to realize, but her head that is whirling around. In other words, she has had too much to drink. Depending on how one translates "réfléchi" (which also means "premeditated"), two scenarios suggest themselves. On the one hand, she may have become inebriated on purpose. On the other, her companion may have fed her one cocktail too many in hopes of seducing her. Significantly, although the situation is described by an omniscient narrator (or viewer), it is filtered through the man's consciousness.

Sandwiched in between the rectangle and the three people discussing the war, another group of customers is discussing modern aesthetics. According to Roche, the group is composed of a painter, a poet, a musician, and a woman with a leopard-skin coat. All we know about the latter is that she likes to drink whiskey and talk about modern art. In addition, the painter jokingly compares her to a manometer, which implies that she is tall and thin. Unexpectedly, these details suffice to identify the woman and her three companions. Since the café was one of Roche's favorite hangouts, she included herself in the picture with Picabia and two other friends. In the first place, we know Roche had taken to drinking whiskey during this period. "Mme J. R. s'homéopathise au Whiskey," Picabia reported in 391, "sous la surveillance de Monsieur A. Gleizes" 'Mme J. R. is taking a homeopathic cure at the Whiskey Club under the supervision of Monsieur A. Gleizes' (Picabia 8). In the second place, we know that Picabia made a mecanomorphic portrait of Roche in 1916 (since lost) that depicted her as a manometer (Camfield 100). This means that the musician in the poem must be Varèse, whose avant-garde compositions were as outrageous as Picabia's paintings. Complaining that the table is too short to explain his musical intervals, he throws up his hands in despair. The fourth member, who proclaims that Mallarmé was merely a mechanic, is an avant-garde poet. Although several possibilities come to mind, this is probably Arensberg, whose poetry was equally outrageous.

In contrast to these jocular exchanges, two people are arguing furiously over by the orchestra. While only a few comments can be heard above the music, one perceives that their views are diametrically opposed. One man, who has an official position of some sort, is defending the status quo. In his opinion, the present socio-economic system works "just fine." "Tout va bien!" he exclaims repeatedly as he lists one advantage after another. Neither the capitalist creed nor the government in Washington deserves to be criticized. Identified simply as "Hippolyte," the other man disagrees vehemently with these statements. "Vive l'anarchie," he interjects at every opportunity. Government is a pernicious institution that only serves to undermine individual freedom. Although he appears briefly, this can only be Hippolyte Havel, who was associated with Emma Goldman and her magazine Mother Earth. "A tiny man with spectacles, a pointed goatee, and ferocious mustaches," according to one source, he "possessed a notable record of incarceration for anarchist activity both in this country and abroad" (Churchill 23).

Since all good things must come to an end, the poem concludes as Roche leaves the café. Pushing open the door, she descends the stairs and pauses for a moment on the sidewalk. That each of these objects is cast in progressively larger type underscores a similar expansion in her field of vision. Emerging from the café, she gazes at Washington Square's dull expanse and feels a pang of nostalgia. A zone of boredom has opened up, she declares, because there are no yellow horse-drawn coaches to enliven the landscape, as there are in Paris. Printed in large boldface capitals, the word "ZONE" marks the end of the visual expansion and acknowledges her debt to Apollinaire, whose poem of the same name (Apollinaire 39-44) inaugurated simultanist poetry. Extending from the circular fan to the area in question, an arrow traces her itinerary and suggests a link between its two poles. Like the fan's dull hum, whose sound resembles snoring, the view of the park is positively soporific. Unlike the latter site, however, the café itself is overflowing with vitality. The contrast between the inside and the outside, between the crowds of people and the desolate square, is finally overwhelming.

The second poem, which for some reason has no title, is more difficult to decipher (Figure 2). Not only do the verbal elements seem much more fragmentary, but they appear to have little relation to one another. At least half the sentences lack a verb or a subject, but even those that are grammatically correct make very little sense. Hoping to shed some light on the poem, the reader searches frantically for some sign of order, but the phrases persist in their isolation. Roche's decision to dispense with a title reminds us how much we normally depend on one to provide an interpretive context. The absence of a convenient signpost reinforces the impression of chaos and forces the reader to look for clues elsewhere. We learn, for instance, that the poem is an example of "idéoplastie" 'ideoplastic composition.' Its visual elements apparently reproduce the author's thought patterns, which are rendered in schematic fashion. Does this mean that the design is purely conceptual, one wonders, or does it include sensory data as well? Is it an abstract composition, or does it contain traces of what Roche sees and hears?

Like the previous work, one eventually discovers, the poem is located at the center of Roche's mental universe. In keeping with simultanist precepts, thoughts are juxtaposed with sense impressions and vice versa. Like the previous work, moreover, the poem evokes one of the author's favorite hangouts. Readers who are familiar with the New York avant-garde will recognize Marcel Duchamp and Henri-Pierre Roché, who are absorbed in one of the frequent games of chess that occupied them during this period. Indeed, Duchamp became so fond of the game that he began to neglect his art. Whereas the chessboard is rendered realistically, the players are simply indicated by their initials. Despite the scarcity of recognizable forms, the scene is almost certainly the Arensbergs' apartment. Judging from the surviving photographs, the poem is situated in the large studio that served as their livingroom. Among other things, the photographs

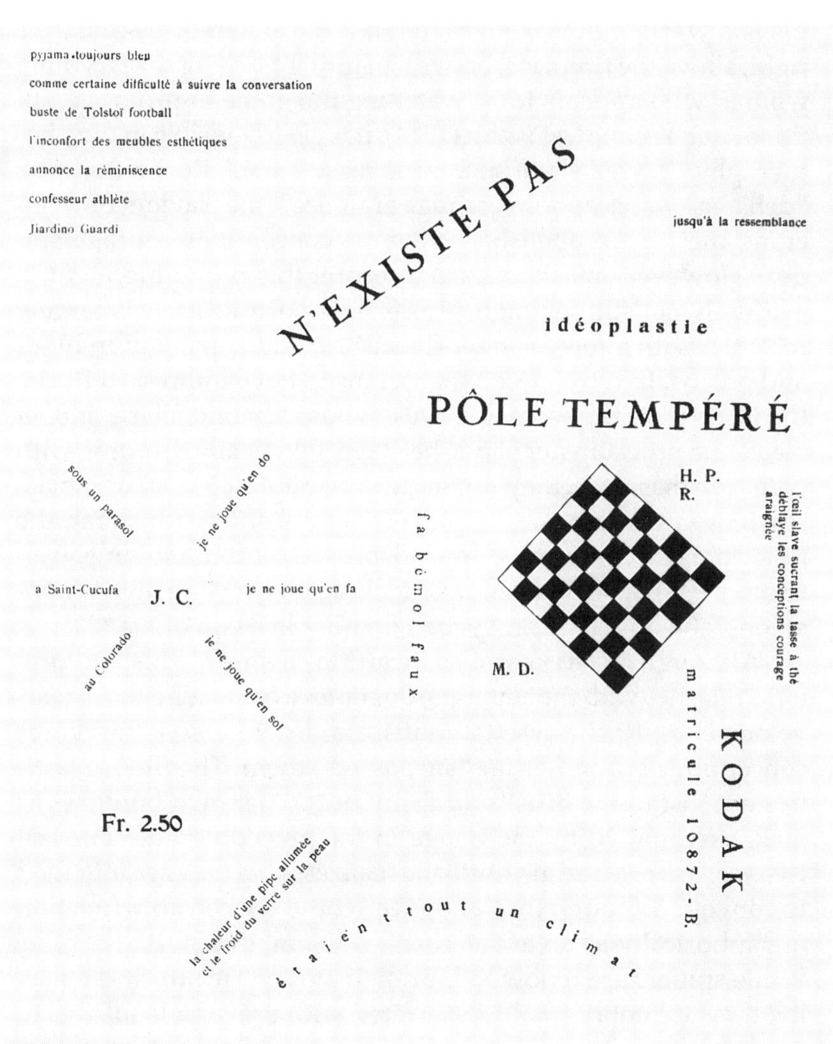

Figure 2. Juliette Roche, untitled. Photograph from *Demi-Cercle*.
Paris: Editions d'Art la "Cible," 1920.

reveal that the room contained a grand piano and that its walls were covered with paintings. On one side, there was a small sitting area with a couch, two armchairs, and a victrola. The opposite wall was lined with more furniture, including a table and two chairs next to the fireplace. The chessboard in the poem is apparently resting on a small table in front of the fireplace.[5]

Elsewhere in the room another visitor — possibly Varèse — is playing a composition on the piano. Distracted momentarily, he plays a wrong note by mistake (an F flat). To the chessboard's right, above the fireplace, hangs a painting by Matisse of a young woman who appears to be watching the game in progress. Entitled *Mlle Yvonne Landsberg* (1914), it is clearly visible in the photographs. "L'Oeil slave sucrant la tasse à thé," Roche declares, "déblaye les conceptions courage araignée" 'the Slavic eye sweetening the teacup abolishes previous conceptions courage spider.' However one chooses to interpret this pronouncement, it evidently constitutes high praise. The portrait itself is largely realistic, with a few abstract flourishes, and is painted in blues and greens. In retrospect, what seems to have impressed Roche the most were the woman's eyes, whose almond shape and jet black hue proclaim her Slavic heritage. Practically dripping with paint (or mascara), they apparently reminded Roche of molasses. Since molasses was employed as a substitute for sugar, the final image represents a logical progression. Following Jean Crotti's lead, who had begun to include glass eyes in his compositions, she imagined an eyeball floating in a cup of tea.[6]

Although *déblayer* can also mean "to clean off," this interpretation clashes with the avant-garde context. In creating those marvelous eyes, Roche asserts, Matisse did not "revive" previous conceptions but rather far "surpassed" them. The phrase testifies not just to the artist's audacity but to her own boldness as well, exemplified by the image in the preceding line. The last two words are puzzling until one realizes what they are intended to convey. Although the "araignée" could conceivably function metaphorically as an avant-garde emblem, this is not the case. While spiders are renowned for their agility, stealth, and tenacity, they are not normally associated with bravery. It suffices to recall Walt Whitman's "A Noiseless Patient Spider," which depicts an archetypal specimen. Indeed Roche's spider appears to be engaged on a similar mission. Glancing at Matisse's painting,

Roche is amused to find that another, more traditional artist is seeking to rival the master. "Du courage" 'Keep on working,' she admonishes the tiny spider who occupies one corner. If the latter persists, these words imply, her web will soon cover the whole canvas.

At this juncture the remaining pieces of the puzzle begin to fall into place. That the poem is set in the Arensbergs' apartment, for example, explains why it has no title. To have labeled it, say, "Chez les Arensberg" would have made the allusions much too transparent. As originally conceived, the work was restricted to a small group of initiates, like the gatherings themselves. Inevitably, with the passing of time and the original participants, the references have become even more obscure. What are we to make of the list at the upper left, for instance, that describes the soirée in more detail? Who was the woman who always wore blue pajamas? What reminiscences are being recounted, and why is the conversation hard to follow? Although no trace remains of the bust of Tolstoy, or the football beside it, one reference is easy to verify. While the Arensbergs were quite wealthy, the photographs reveal that their furniture was somewhat primitive. Unimpressed by the Craftsman aesthetic, which emphasized austere lines and natural materials, Roche denounced "l'inconfort des meubles esthétiques" 'the discomfort of the aesthetic furniture.' The remaining allusions are less easy to pinpoint. Although the "confesseur athlète" could be almost anybody, one thinks of Arthur Cravan, the boxer-poet, whose serious demeanor belied his outrageous behavior. The words "Jiardino Guardi" probably refer to the 18th century Venetian painter Francesco Guardi, who occasionally depicted gardens.[7] The work in question may be hanging on the wall, or it may simply be reproduced in a book that is lying open. Descending the page, one encounters three sentences arranged in a sunburst pattern, centered around the initials "J.C." The design itself was borrowed from Apollinaire's "Lettre-Océan" (Apollinaire 200-01), which juxtaposes two wheel-and-spoke patterns within a postcard framework. The one on the left seems to have served as Roche's model. In all three cases, the design portrays various sounds radiating outward from their point of origin. The three phrases here are uttered by Crotti, another expatriate artist who married Duchamp's sister two years later. Whereas the rest of the poem is filtered through Roche's consciousness, which interprets what it perceives, Crotti's words manage to escape this fate. For better or for worse, they retain their original identity as nonsense statements. Apparently inspired by the pianist, Crotti ascends the musical scale verbally, rhyming each note with a noun ending with the same syllable. Whenever he finds himself beneath a parasol, he proclaims, he only plays in the key of sol (G). Whenever he travels to Colorado or to Saint-Cucufa (just outside Paris), he adopts the key of do (C) and fa (F) respectively. Since each sentence consists of ten syllables, Crotti may be singing the words rather than merely pronouncing them.

At the bottom, we glimpse another guest who holds a pipe in one hand and a drink in the other. Although he is never identified, he seems to have recently arrived from Paris. Someone has returned from France, at any rate, for a nearby object still bears a French price tag. While it could be a book or a bottle of wine, one suspects it is a package of pipe tobacco. Gazing at the anonymous visitor, Roche is struck by a sudden thought: he has succeeded in creating "tout un climat" 'a whole climate' for himself by juggling fire and ice. When he gets too hot he takes a sip of his drink, and when he gets too cold he puffs on his pipe. Why one phrase has a convex shape is difficult to say. Most likely it represents another piece of furniture or perhaps a screen. Existing photographs reveal the presence of a strange, truncated door in this area.

Whatever the explanation, the visual curve directs our attention back to the chessboard and to a statement above it in large boldface capitals. Despite its fragmented condition, it can be reconstructed to read: [IL] N'EXISTE PAS [DE] PÔLE TEMPÉRÉ" '[THERE IS] NO SUCH THING AS [A] TEMPERATE POLE.' Of course not, the reader exclaims, the earth's temperate zones are located far from its poles, which are subject to climatic extremes. Little by little one realizes that this sentence is related to the one at the bottom of the page. Both pronouncements are concerned with extreme temperatures, both are structured around polar oppositions. In a similar vein, one perceives that they contain analogous metaphors. Having come to the Arensbergs' expecting to enjoy herself, Roche is unable to find a temperate (i. e., comfortable) place in which to settle. The basic problem, she complains, is that the company is divided into two opposing groups.

Centered about Crotti, whose clowning they find amusing, one group of visitors takes the warm pipe as its emblem. Quietly observing the chessplayers, whose concentration does not waver, the other gathers under the sign of the cold drink. This group revolves around Marcel Duchamp, whose sang-froid was legendary even then. Thus an opposition exists between exuberance on the one hand and passivity on the other. The gaiety of the first bunch provides a striking contrast to the seriousness of the second. Refusing to choose between them, Roche stations herself in the middle of the room and takes out an imaginary camera. Instead of focusing on one group or the other, she decides to record the entire scene. Seizing her trusty "KODAK," whose serial number 10872-B is recorded at the lower right, she translates her impressions into visual outlines on the page. Although these are largely abstract, they manage to delineate the soirée's salient features. The degree of visual fidelity varies in effect from pure abstraction to total mimesis. In particular, the composition maps out the principal lines of force that structure the gathering. At the same time Roche adds a few realistic touches that represent the actual scene. Besides recording her mental impressions, her ideoplastic method allows her to exploit physical resemblance ("jusqu'à la ressemblance") whenever the occasion warrants.

Notes

[1]The Gleizes resided in New York from September 1915 to May 1916 and from February 1917 to October 1919 (Sanouillet 42-43; 53; 110).

[2]For a reproduction of this poem and an analysis, see Bohn, *Aesthetics* 185-203.

[3]All translations are my own. For a humorous anecdote involving Juliette Roche, Picabia, and Duchamp, see Roché 41.

[4]Roche seems to be referring to a passage in *The Will to Power* where Nietzsche foresaw an "age of tremendous wars, upheavals, explosions" (Nietzsche, *Will*, section 130). See also Nietzsche, *Will*, section 2; Nietzsche, *Science*, section 362. I would like to thank David Parent for this information.

[5]Four photographs taken by Charles Sheeler are included in Naumann. Two more are included in *Arensberg Collection*, n.p.; Stebbins and Keyes 5.

[6]See, for example, Crotti's "Ballade sucrée et oeil de verre" ("Sugary Ballad and Glass Eye") in Camfield and Martin 15.

[7]See Guardi's drawing of the Contarini Garden in Albrizzi and Pool 108-09. The painting that resulted from this study belongs to the Rothermere Collection of the Ashmolean Museum, Oxford University.

Works Cited

Albrizzi, Alessandro and Mary Jane Pool, eds. *The Gardens of Venice.* New York: Rizzoli, 1989.

Apollinaire, Guillaume. *Oeuvres poétiques.* Ed. Marcel Adéma and Michel Décaudin. Paris: Gallimard/Pléiade, 1965.

Arensberg Collection, The Louise and Walter. 20th Century Section. Vol 1. Catalogue compiled by Marianne Winter Martin. Philadelphia: Philadelphia Museum of Art, 1954.

Bohn, Willard. *The Aesthetics of Visual Poetry, 1914-1928.* Cambridge: Cambridge UP, 1986.

Camfield, William A. *Francis Picabia: His Art, Life, and Times.* Princeton: Princeton UP, 1979.

______ and Jean-Hubert Martin, eds. *Tabu Dada: Jean Crotti and Suzanne Duchamp, 1915-1922.* Bern: Kunsthalle Bern, 1983.

Churchill, Allen. *The Improper Bohemians.* New York: Ace, 1959.

Henderson, Linda Dalrymple. *The Fourth Dimension and Non-Euclidean Geometry in Modern Art.* Princeton: Princeton UP, 1983.

Naumann, Francis. "Walter Conrad Arensberg: Poet, Patron, and Participant in the New York Avant-Garde, 1915-1920." *Philadelphia Museum of Art Bulletin* 76 (1980): 2-32.

Nietzsche, Friedrich. *The Gay Science.* Trans. Walter Kaufmann. New York: Vintage, 1974.

______. *The Will to Power.* Trans. Walter Kaufmann and R. J. Hollingsdale. New York: Vintage, 1968.

Picabia, Francis. "New York." *391* 5 (1917).

Roché, Henri-Pierre. *Victor (Marcel Duchamp).* Ed. Danielle Régnier-Bohler and Jean Clair. Paris: Centre Pompidou, 1977.

Sanouillet, Michel. *Francis Picabia et "391."* Vol 2. Paris: Losfeld, 1966.

Stebbins, Theodore E., Jr. and Norman Keyes, Jr. *Charles Sheeler: The Photographs.* Boston: New York Graphic Society, 1987.

Ralentir travaux:
The Second
Surrealist Manifesto

Virginia A. La Charité

> Le chemin vers le haut [qui ascend] et celui
> vers le bas [qui descend] est le même.
> —Heraclitus
>
> The road towards the top [which ascends]
> and the one towards the bottom [which
> decends] is the same.[1]

Surrealist historians and critics consider *Ralentir travaux* (*Slow Down, Road Work*) by André Breton, René Char, and Paul Eluard the best example of surrealist poetic collaboration.[2] The work is usually described as the most collectively written surrealist text—hailed as "un vers de trois mains" 'a poem by three hands' by José Corti (Sebbag 43)—because the volume was written, edited, corrected, proofed, and supervised into print by the three poets themselves. Even Breton later praised *Ralentir travaux* as "une collaboration poétique véritablement intime . . . réalisée à trois mieux qu'à deux, le troisième élément sans cesse variable étant de jonction, de résolution et intervenant auprès des deux autres comme facteur d'*unité*" 'a truly intimate poetic collaboration better produced by three than by two, the third unceasingly variable element being that of junction, of resolution and working with the other two as a factor of *unity*' (Breton 2: 331). For Breton and generations of readers, this short volume of 30 poems captures simultaneously the two poles of human action "entre la conscience de ... autonomie et celle de son étroite dépendence ... pour la libération future de la pensée de l'homme" 'between consciousness of ... autonomy and narrow dependency ... for the future liberation of human thought' (Breton 2: 331).

However, the acceptance of this volume of poetry as a synthesis—unlike that of any other work—of thought and unthought in a single interactive continuum raises questions that go to the very heart of the surrealist endeavor to communicate the true flow of human thought processes and authenticate the poetic space of the surreal. As language reconciles perception and recognition in a single moment of essence, the fusion of motion and stasis into the creative principle of poetry—expressed earlier by Breton in *Nadja* as convulsive beauty—projects desire into a form of its realization. But does *Ralentir travaux* open the road to the surreal by affirming and confirming a singular cosmic surrealist voice? Or is *Ralentir travaux* the virtual poetic counterpart of the *Second Manifeste du Surréalisme* and thereby the linchpin of a surrealist poetics of audience?

The historical circumstances surrounding the composition of *Ralentir travaux* (Breton's "sale temps" 'rotten time' [Breton 1: 1576]) offer insight into the artistic circumstances of the undertaking. By the beginning of 1930 Surrealism found itself in a political, social, moral, and poetic crisis. Severely affected by external events during the years following the *Premier Manifeste* (1924), Breton undertook a *Second Manifeste*, which appeared in December 1929 in the pages of *La Révolution Surréaliste*. It advocated political commitment in the name of social justice and embraced Marxism. It appeared therefore to contradict, if not negate, the non-conformist stance of the *Premier Manifeste* and its clarion call for the "primauté de la pensée sur la matière" 'primacy of thought over matter' as a way to liberate the individual and investigate the sources of human creative activity (Breton 2: 232). For many, support of Marxist dialectical materialism denigrated the Rimbaldian spirit of the *Premier Manifeste*, which extolled the exploration of the dysfunction of reason or Rimbaud's "dérèglement de tous les sens" 'upsetting of all the senses.' Rimbaud's defiance of order in society and politics as well as in poetry and morality seemed challenged by a Marxist emphasis on historical reality. Where the *Premier Manifeste* insisted on an irrational revolt and non-submission, the *Second*

Manifeste demanded a lucid or intellectual revolt of commitment. While the *Premier Manifeste* could be described as an aggressive document that called for a psycho-sexual revolt, the *Second Manifeste* was seen as a defensive statement justifying social revolution. Hence, the artistic protest of 1924 was replaced in 1929-30 by a call for political confrontation.

Reactions to the *Second Manifeste* ranged from overt hostility to exhuberant enthusiasm. While it attracted new members such as Dali, it alienated what can only be seen as the rest of the old guard, those first members who had not already left. With the loyal Benjamin Péret in Brazil, only Eluard of the original inner circle remained physically and philosophically at Breton's side. Furthermore, Eluard shared Breton's deep hurt over the vitriolic denunciation of the *Second Manifeste* which appeared on January 15, 1930 in *Un Cadavre*, signed by 12 former allies and cohorts, and in Robert Desnos's *Troisième Manifeste du Surréalisme*.

With the publication of the original version of the *Second Manifeste* in December 1929, the first phase of the surrealist adventure was definitely and definitively over. The very make-up of the group itself had changed, and even the list of surrealist undertakings underwent alteration, the addition of film to the artistic canon being the major change. Indeed, a retrospective glance at surrealist works of the 1930s reveals a significant increase in non-verbal art as well as the addition of women as full members of the group in artistic terms. [3]

The *Second Manifeste* may then be said to begin the second decade of the surrealist movement, and one of the new members of this second generation was René Char. He had sent a copy of his 1929 *Arsenal* to Paul Eluard in September 1929. This led first to Eluard's visit to Char in Isle-sur-Sorgue, and second to Char's late November 1929 trip to Paris. While there he met the surrealists, especially Breton and Crevel, became a member of the group, and signed the *Second Manifeste*. Char then dedicated his second and considerably revised edition of *Arsenal* to Eluard. This work was published in February 1930 while Char was working on *Tombeau des secrets* (*Tomb of Secrets*), a volume dramatically different from *Arsenal*. [4] Jean-Claude Mathieu has aptly described *Arsenal* as an act of deliverance and *Tombeau des secrets* as an act of knowledge that unmasks the real (127). Not published until April 5, 1930, Char's *Tombeau des secrets* precedes the composition of *Ralentir travaux* and reveals his early surrealist affinities. The volume even contains a collage by Breton and Eluard done at Breton's apartment in Paris, and it is dedicated to Gala and Paul Eluard. Unfortunately, the volume has never been republished; only five of the ten poems were moved by Char to his 1934 edition of *Arsenal* in *Le Marteau sans maître* (*The Hammer without a Master*), and the photographs have never been reproduced.

For Breton and Eluard in 1930, the young Char exemplified the continuity of the surrealist poetic spirit. Uncontaminated by the group struggles within and without the movement, Char's *Arsenal* reflects basic surreal qualities of intellection, not intellectualism. Marked by rebellious convictions and a form of writing that betrays only the minimum of direction, Char's texts in *Arsenal*, especially the second edition, and in *Tombeau des secrets* show a poet who transforms energy into a force of the imagination, humanizes objects, rejects traditional form and forms, finds the concrete irrational, remains by and large non-mimetic, and above all conjures up the visual from the verbal in the reading act of mentalization. The young Char is not unlike the earlier Breton, but he is tempered by exposure to Eluard's lyrical genius, and it is Eluard's poetry that greatly impressed Char. In addition, Char shared especially with Breton the same literary ancestors: Rimbaud, Mallarmé, Lautréamont, Apollinaire, and above all the Marquis de Sade who dominates Char's *Tombeau des secrets*. In fact, Char never overtly broke with Breton when he left the Surrealist group at the end of 1934. [5]

In the early months of 1930, Char was in Vaucluse at his family home in Isle-sur-Sorgue, and it is there that Breton and Eluard decided to go in order to get away from the turmoil of Paris. Not only were Breton and Eluard in the midst of the uproar over the *Second Manifeste*, but both had also been embroiled in tempestuous love affairs. In fact, it seems that the surrealist group worked more cohesively when its members were relatively free from stormy romantic entanglements. At any rate, by mid-March 1930 Breton was divorced from Simone Kahn (late 1929) and had broken with Suzanne Muzard, while Eluard's beloved Gala had taken up with Dali (the Eluard divorce would be finalized in late 1930). Along with Alice Apel, Eluard and Char met Breton in Avignon, and this foursome was joined by a young dancer from the Moulin Rouge.

Dated March 25-30, 1930 in Avignon, *Ralentir travaux* was published on April 20, 1930 by A. Larguier in Nîmes, the same printing firm that had already published Char's *Arsenal* and had just released his *Tombeau des secrets* (April 5, 1930). *Ralentir travaux* carries the "dépôt" 'copyright' of Corti, who had taken over the Editions Surréalistes. However, the first copies of *Ralentir travaux* were published without any contact with Editions Surréalistes; only those copies printed by Larguier in Nîmes in May 1930 were undertaken with Corti's official permission. [6]

The publishing history of *Ralentir travaux* is important to an understanding of the significance of the volume. The establishment of the Editions Surréalistes under the guidance and patronage of José Corti stabilized the problem of surrealist publications and art expositions. At the time that Breton and Eluard visited the Vaucluse region with Char in late March 1930, the term *surrealist* had actually become accepted in artistic circles. Sebbag finds that Corti's directorship of Editions Surréalistes authenticated the movement and became a major factor at the very moment when the movement needed to launch its counteroffensive on "le terrain du multiple" 'the terrain of the multiple' (178). Moreover, Sebbag asserts that the "official" publication of *Ralentir travaux* by Larguier in May 1930 under the surrealist label marks the poetic counterattack of surrealism in the early 1930s (179).

Ralentir travaux is today available in three different formats. The May 1930 edition was republished by Corti in 1968, the same year that the Pléiade edition of Eluard's *Œuvres complètes* appeared. The Eluard volume identifies from the Eluard archives the authorship of each line of poetry in *Ralentir travaux*. It is the first time that the volume was published with the authorship of each line of verse clearly marked. The Breton Pléiade edition in 1988 reproduced this text and authorial identifications from the Eluard edition. Curiously, the Char Pléiade edition in 1983 omits *Ralentir travaux* completely, but Mathieu has found two manuscripts in the Char archives that confirm the Eluard version (Mathieu 91). Nonetheless, there are two "first" publications of the work. Examination of the April 1930 volume and the Eluard version or May 1930 edition shows no changes in the lines of poetry themselves. However, there is a radical difference in the interior design of the two editions.

The differing order of arrangement of the texts of *Ralentir travaux* begins with the fifteenth poem, that is, nearly halfway through the volume. The first 14 poems follow the same order in April 1930 and in May 1930. By numbering the poems 1-30 in either the Eluard or Breton volume of *Œuvres complètes* and then numbering those in the April 1930 edition, the changes in order are as follows: 14 = 14, 15 = 16, 16 = 15, 18 = 17, 17 = 18, 20 = 19, 19 = 20, 22 = 21, 24 = 22, 21 = 23, 26 = 24, 23 = 25, 28 = 26, 25 = 27, 30 = 28, 27 =29, 29 = 30 (Breton 1: 755-74, 1575-83; Eluard 267-87, 1411-12). While most of these changes in the order of the texts may be minor, the significance of the April 1930 arrangement lies in the text of closure. The Eluard edition on which all studies of the text to date are based closes with the text "Je m'écoute encore parler" ("I Still Hear Myself Talking"), an arrangement that has led scholars to find that the volume as a whole is designed to confirm the existence of a collective surrealist voice. However, the original April 1930 order shows an undetected relationship between the volume and the *Premier Manifeste* and reveals the need for poetry to elect Rimbaud over Marx. The end text in the April 1930 edition is the polemical text "L'Enjeu inutile" ("The Useless Bet") written by Breton and Eluard. As the text of closure, it is a pessimistic warning about what will continue without surrealist protest and revolt. However, what should now be referred to as the definitive version of *Ralentir travaux*, that is, the May 1930 version as republished by Corti in 1968 and as reproduced by the Eluard and Breton Pléiade editions, ends with a positive text in which all three poets participated. It expresses the continuum of the surrealist values of freedom, love, and poetry or art. While "Je m'écoute encore parler" affirms surrealist success in pushing back limits and assures a revolt of the open road, an attitude of creative activity, "L'Enjeu inutile" is a text of revolution that sees art as serving social causes. The original poem of closure lucidly separates the subject from its object in its protest against political militancy and its resultant propaganda. In this text, two of the principal original architects of surrealism issue a call to return to experimentation in order to unveil the rich sources of the imagination and fuse existence and essence. In this warning, they subvert the *Second Manifeste* as having artistic import. [7]

It is the original arrangement of April 1930 that shows how surrealist poetry ends contradictions in its affirmation of multiplicity and diversity, and how art, not history, expresses human-kind. The poem is a creative act that revolts in order to reconcile word and thing. It denies limits and constraints as it circulates freely in its incandescent realization of desire and justifies the activity of poetry. Hence, the 30 poems of *Ralentir travaux* have in common a rejection of Marxism and a poetic counterattack for a return to the enthusiasm and exhuberance of the Rimbaldian spirit of the *Premier Manifeste*.

In surrealist history, it was admiration for Rimbaud that initially brought together Breton, Aragon, and Soupault. Among the attacks considered the most bitter against them were those that accused them of betraying Rimbaud. We know that to be a surrealist meant and still means a strong affinity with Rimbaud—not the Rimbaud of *Une Saison en enfer* (*A Season in Hell*), but the Rimbaud whose poetry is a practice of life in the here and now in a purer realm. As Pierre Daix points out, the surrealists knew that this Rimbaud was a myth, but they reveled in that myth (27). It is this very point that Albert Camus later found to be the basic weakness in surrealism. While Camus praised the movement for exalting human innocence, he believed that its election of Rimbaud over Marx was a decision to adhere to a myth of consolation, not action. Marx insisted upon the intellectual attitude of revolution in order to confront and refuse the human historical condition; art gives form to revolt and so brings about a corrective to the world. The surrealists reveled in the absurd; they did not despair over it; consequently, their revolt was not a lucid one (Camus 120-25).

Camus's analysis of the failure of surrealism to choose Marx over Rimbaud focuses on the central problem that surrounded the composition of *Ralentir travaux*. While the *Second Manifeste du Surréalisme* clearly embraces Marx, *Ralentir travaux* is equally explicit in its election of Rimbaud and return to the original spirit of the *Premier Manifeste*. Regardless, the fact remains that personal, philosophical, and esthetic concerns that plagued the surrealist movement in March 1930 directly affected *Ralentir travaux*, and *Ralentir travaux* in turn impacted surrealist poetic activity after the publication of the official version of the *Second Manifeste* in May 1930 by Kra. Where the *Second Manifeste* is on the defensive in its emphasis on political commitment, *Ralentir travaux* is intensely active in its insistence on a psychic non-Marxist reality: what happens, what appears, what seems to be IS. As the text that reorients and renews the original spirit of surrealism, *Ralentir travaux* is the second artistic manifesto of the movement. In this sense, the volume is indeed the poetic counterattack of surrealism. It also marks Breton's return to poetry since *Claire de terre (Earthlight)* (1923); he wrote no poetry between the two manifestoes. [8]

Ralentir travaux is an experiment that investigates collective automatism in order to free poetry from causality. Seeking new links between the particular and the general, Breton, Char, and Eluard emancipate surrealism from its historical present of psychoanalysis, Marxism, and occultism and transport it into an art of life. Ever opposed to relational contexts, the three poets perpetuate the metaphorical function of poetry as a means of knowledge. Each of the poems in the volume assembles experiences and coheres them into an associative texture of sharing that reverses previously held contradictions. [9]

Written in five days, March 25-30, *Ralentir travaux* is the only surrealist volume of verse that proclaims itself to be a work of collaboration. Certainly, collaboration is part and parcel of surrealist life, art, and history. Surrealist insistence on the mental adventure of the collective creative act is in one sense what led to the crisis of 1930, for that crisis focused on the problem of the individual conscience in opposition to collective needs. In fact, every surrealist form of communication is marked in some way by at least one other voice and usually by more than one. From pamphlets, letters of protest, declarations, brochures, editorials, and various tracts and polemical writings usually written by one to express the views of several or many, to all literary genres, the surrealist experience and artistic product depended on exchange at both the personal and artistic levels. The quest to reveal a new poetic space demanded activity in real historical space, a deliberate confrontation with others. In order to translate interiorized perceptions into external recognizable communications, the message of the language is determined by the reactions of others or at least by the reaction and therefore collaboration of one other. Collaboration, for the surrealist, is an act of friendship and cooperation, not an act of artistic fusion.

Surrealist non-intervention—a morality of spontaneity—is never free from conscious correction, revision, or criticism despite avowals to the contrary. The problem of the subject in surrealism is in fact the problem of the object, and the audience is therefore instrumental to that creative act of bringing the subject and object together into one image. Surrealism is always conscious, and it never functions in a vacuum. The random walk is always a planned event that permits unplanned encounters, and these encounters become valid only when testified to or witnessed by another. Even Nadja was a collective fascination and Breton's meetings with her were prearranged. Literally and figuratively momistic, the collective experience and the collaborative undertaking demonstrate that there is no "other world." Each text unerringly captures the essence of real-life existence. Contact with surreality itself, the supreme point of the surreal undertaking, makes the invisible visible, the fictive real, and comes about only through a poetics of audience.

Breton, Char, and Eluard, the three poets of *Ralentir travaux*, requalify their individual experiences and reactions into a collective response, but one that retains discernible traces of their individual psyches. While the names of the three authors always appear in the alphabetical order of imposed procedure, their contributions do not follow this order.[10] The randomness of the composition within each poem is then a deliberate effort to obfuscate each particular voice but at the same time reveal the likenesses of similar difference. The only known surrealist experiment to write a single poem in three voices occurred in 1926 when Aragon, Breton, and Desnos undertook "Le Chapelet des aiguilles" ("The Needle Rosary") based on the rules for the *cadavre exquis* game (Breton 1: 1033-35, 1418-20). However, in that experiment the order of performance was strictly maintained, just as the order of performance is one of the rigid rules in the *cadavre exquis* games both written and plastic. "Le Chapelet des aiguilles" relies upon having the players know each other extremely well, a point emphasized by Eluard and Breton in their 1936 "Note sur la collaboration" in which they explain that only in close friendship do differences become likenesses (Breton 1: 1633); as surrealist close friends they are able to collaborate and draw one upon the other to assert and maintain continuity in the communication (Breton 1: 1635).

Surrealist collaboration is essentially an act of critical listening and reading. Breton and Aragon, for example, forged their friendship in the early months of 1918 by reading Lautréamont's *Chants de Maldoror* (*Songs of Maldoror*) to each other in loud voices while on guard duty and during air raids. Soupault and Breton read *Les Champs magnétiques* (*Magnetic Fields*) to Aragon and had him determine which parts were to be destroyed in what Daix has called "une stratégie de vérification des réactions" 'a strategy for the verification of reactions' (67). Aragon read his *Traité du style* to Breton who in turn read *Nadja* to Aragon. We do not know how much of *Les Champs magnétiques* Aragon rejected, nor do we know how many proverbs Eluard and Péret actually wrote for their *152 Proverbes mis au jour* (*152 Proverbs Brought to Light*) (1925) and why some were retained and others jettisoned. Even Breton's *Vases communicants* (*Communicating Vessels*) (1932) was finalized through his readings to friends. The reaction of another or of others characterized hypnotic seances such as the 1923 verbal collage *Comme il fait beau!* (*What a Lovely Day!*) by Breton, Desnos, and Péret and Char's later note-taking for Breton's dream recitation in 1931.

The practice of collective writing was, then, for the surrealist an accepted component of creative activity. In fact, surrealist history recounts over and over how the surrealist movement cannot be separated from the ambiance of the Parisian café, for surrealists met daily to exchange experiences and update each other on artistic ventures. All their written and plastic work can truly be said to depend on alliances and friendships, on a spirit of amicable give and take—collaboration. And it is this spirit that pervades and characterizes *Ralentir travaux*, for when all is said and done, *Ralentir travaux* is not an authentically collective work. On the contrary, it is a work of discontinuity that the audience validates as a unified creative act.

Using each other as audience, the three poets of *Ralentir travaux* requalify their individual reactions but not through a collective act or communal activity. The three prefaces clearly outline their differences and individual resonances, just as the deliberate arrangement and rearrangement of the texts within the volume reveal this work as an experiment in intellection and communication. As Mathieu points out, there are abrupt shifts within the poems from the voice of one poet to another (92). Each poet has his own agenda and each text reveals individual preoccupations and concerns. Mathieu finds Eluard's lines marked by love and infidelity, a sadness, probably because Gala had taken up with Dali, while Breton's lines are seen as embracing his two major issues, interest in political and social revolution on the one hand, and fascination with the myth of the eternal woman on the other. Mathieu finds Char at a crossroads between the subject of death, or actually anti-death, in *Tombeau des secrets* and his desire for freedom from the poetic heritage of the past, which had led him to adhere to the surrealist group four months earlier (Mathieu 93).

Indeed, the three authors of *Ralentir travaux* are recognizable by distinct individual tones and emphases. The prefaces first establish these differences, subverting the arbitrariness of the alphabetical order imposed on the order of appearance of the prefaces, but at the same time placing the young Char in the literal and figurative middle position as a verbal bridge guaranteeing projection into the future. The content of the three prefaces reveals serious differences with the *Second Manifeste* as they distinguish three individuals from each other in a new personal association and a new artistic relationship. The verbal communications and order of the prefaces become visual through a reading of the texts that follow. Contact is continuity, as Breton's preface is constructed around the image of the "table rase" and the need to expand the function of words. The key Char term in his preface is "engagé" 'committed,' bringing attention to his call for a "utilité collective," a new approach to poetry, and proposing poetic form as the only code for living in the world. For Eluard the main notion is exchange, exchange to vary the vision of what is and its forms of expression. For all three, poetry is the only principle of coherence, not political or social action and revolution.

The 30 texts of *Ralentir travaux* were written quickly, supposedly in the five days proclaimed by the volume itself. It is an example of speed writing that so characterizes much of surrealism, beginning with what is considered the first authentic surreal text, *Les Champs magnétiques* (1918), written in 15 days. Speed writing, rather than automatism, attempts to reduce authorial control to a minimum and to ensure that there are no chronological sequences or spatially logical distinctions in the work at hand. Speed writing categorically rejects habit, routine, and the formalities of procedure; defiance of the constraints of order and form permits free associationism. However, speed writing is not completely free from the notion of work and revision, for it depends on discipline to suppress attachment and yet simulate detachment, the free flow of the thought processes.

At the time of the writing of *Ralentir travaux*, Breton and Eluard were close friends experienced in the art of speed writing. In fact, just after the publication of this work, they spent the summer on *L'Immaculée Conception*, which was published in November, 1930. [11] Char had no prior experience with surrealist experiments, games, communal living, daily reunions, and efforts to experience the surreal in their travels through exterior and interior space. All accounts of surrealist life testify to the spirit of interaction on a personal level that imbued the group and kept it together. Char did not share on a personal level the degree of close intense friendships that had so synthesized (and then dispersed) the first generation of surrealists. In his criticism of *Ralentir travaux*, Rolland de Renéville went so far as to accuse Char of bringing about a loss of the value of the individual by insisting in his preface on the sacrifice of the individual to the idea of a cosmic conscience (Breton 2: 1485). But even Breton's preface to *Ralentir travaux* questions the value and validity of collective art.

The whole surrealist notion of the individual and his relationship to a collective unit or group underlies *Ralentir travaux*. The emphases of the prefaces on expansion, engagement, and exchange belie the non-randomness of the volume. Even if the texts were actually written during the five-day period proclaimed by the volume, the poets themselves did not return to Paris until April 10, eleven days later. Little is known of their activities during that time except that they worked with the A. Larguier printing firm on the volume, made some attempt to create a list of subscribers for the work, and Breton went to Cannes. Most likely, parts of that time period were spent reading and rereading the poems, possibly rejecting some, possibly coming up with appropriate titles. Certainly some attempt was made to make the volume even, or give it the appearance of an authentic collaborative work.

Examination of the nature of the participation of the three poets shows that 15 texts (50% of the volume) were composed by all three; five were composed jointly by Breton and Eluard, five by Eluard and Char, four by Char and Breton, and one, "L'Autre Poème" ("The Other Poem"), by just Eluard. Breton and Char authored lines in 24 texts, while Eluard appears in 26. The distribution of the work effort is too well calculated to result in a work written totally in haste with no regard for the rules of the game at hand. And *Ralentir travaux* is a game, albeit a serious game, in the same way that the artistic forms of collage and montage employ gamesmanship in the play of associative textures. But like collage and montage, *Ralentir travaux* is very much directed by aesthetic and critical principles. Wedding Mallarmé's sense of objectivity to Rimbaud's subjective practice brings about a surrealist marriage, but not a fusion, of expression and experience. Adoption of "Je m'écoute encore parler" as the definitive text of closure is a decision that includes Char in the writing group, and it reinforces the effect of a collective voice, which the volume set out to simulate. The rearrangement of the texts for the May 1930 publication softens the abrupt shifts from voice to voice within each text and reforms the impression of the volume from one of disjointedness to one of homogeneous accord. Part of the effect of creating the impression of an uninterrupted flow may be due to Eluard as the poet of opening (46%), Char as the poet of closure (46%), and Breton as the moderator between the two different styles and tones, idealism and realism.

Conceived, composed, and formalized outside of Paris, *Ralentir travaux* is undertaken under the aegis of displacement, for the three poets are outside their usual location. Free from habit, routine, usual places and people, the volume is supposedly undertaken along the road in an almost carefree schoolboy attitude. However, the 30 texts were not written in Avignon, only revised and arranged in Avignon; rather, the writing occurred in multiple places: Les Nevons, Gordes, Châteauneuf-du-Pape, along the highway, during walks, in the car, in cafés, and in general throughout the Vaucluse. The naming of one place (Avignon) in the volume is a metaphor to unify the many places of inspiration and composition, just as the car trip is not one single trip but an amalgam of many trips. The journey has no beginning, middle, or end — it is and takes place, and believably so because there are three known identified real-life participants whose prefaces authenticate the experience of the trip. The trip takes place in real space and in real time, March 25-30, Avignon, while it simultaneously takes place outside of time and place, for there is no one place and there is no temporal progression. The volume stops time and reverses the usual dimensions of space, but all within the realm of human experience. Inversion is the structuring principle of the work and permits the three poets to convert their lived experiences into a tribute to the cohesiveness of surrealist poetry. Breton, Char, and Eluard transmute the raw material of their individual psyches into a historical document (time, place, witnesses). As disjunction and displacement become through inversion conjunction and pleasure, the ultimate poetic act of assembly testifies that life is faithful to poetry and poetry is faithful to life. There is no separation between existence and the essence of art. Indeed, changing the world is a collective process and collaborative undertaking, and language is its primary matter.

The road sign that is the title of the volume signals contact on the highway that leads towards poetry. It is language in its most visible form as both process and product, for it is a readymade referent of arrangement. Basically immobile and fixed, it stands in direct contrast to the image of the road. Significantly, the title does not explicitly state that a road or car or trip is involved in the volume, but the verbal inspiration of the sign triggers the visual image of an automobile adventure that poeticizes the car and its passengers and the state of mind necessary for following the road. Just as the car is freed from its mechanical properties and utilitarian purpose, so the travelers are freed from scientific maps and geographical location and the road is freed from the logic of its technical construction and known destinations. The ordinary prosaic banal road sign, an object, announces that it is both the functioning subject and the metaphorical image of the journey.

At first glance, the title *Ralentir travaux* seems to be a contradiction of the surrealist adventure. To slow down because of road works ahead negates the essence of the surrealist desire and risk to travel into the unmapped territory of the human psyche, the marvelous atmosphere of everyday phenomena. It is typical of surrealism to take a title from an ordinary sign and real life event. Sebbag's suggestion that Char was instrumental in the choice of the title because *ralentir* contains six of the seven letters of Artine seems somewhat fanciful. Char himself says that the title came from a road sign posted on the Caumont-sur-Durance road, which happened to be near Artine's home (Char 833; see also Sebbag 62 and Mathieu 101, 130). Traveling back along this highway with Tzara some months later, Char found that the sign was still posted. Regardless, it was a real sign on a highway traveled by the three poets in March 1930, and was undoubtedly agreed upon as the overall title for the volume by all three because of its grounding in their experience together and because of its verbal strength to project a visual image.

In *Ralentir travaux*, the image of a moving car on a fixed road is transformed by the road sign, which subverts the order of the experience. The warning of the road sign is an invitation to travel, to adventure, to journey. No rationale for the sign is given; rather, the sign eliminates rational contextuality in a reformation of its own components. A non-human structured reality is surrealistically replaced by a vision of human immanence. As Breton used photographs in *Nadja* and Char used them in *Tombeau des secrets*, the road sign of the title of *Ralentir travaux* transmutes experience into virtual essence and makes the invisible visible.

To slow down, but not to stop, underlines the pleasure of the open road, the open text, the open mind, and the pleasure of exchange. The privileged place and time of existence resides in the negation of historical determinism, in the purifying of language from its practical aspect and causality. The road sign is the sign of a system, here a system of public road works, that announces the negation or breakdown of that system. Hence, the inherent contradiction of the title is necessary in order to grasp how *Ralentir travaux* is the poetic manifesto of surrealism in its subversion of the historical circumstances that surround the text. While the surface theme of the volume may be a wandering or errancy through time and space, reminiscent of Aragon's *Le Paysan de Paris* (*The Peasant of Paris*) and Breton's *Nadja*, the actual subject is the election of living poetry by reenergizing and redirecting the surrealist adventure. The title opens the mind of its viewer/reader/audience to a journey with no restrictions, no limits, and no systematized procedures.

The central image of the volume is its title, *Ralentir travaux*, and it is maintained throughout the volume. Explicitly engaging three voices to detach one, the volume confers value on experimentation and the quest to remake the world by opening it to another order in a perpetual voyage of discovery. The irony of the title is its advocacy of its opposite meaning; rather than signaling a slowing down, it urges a speeding up of the process of rejection of logical causality and practical considerations. Rather than projecting images of road works, the volume testifies to the *trouvailles* (marvelous finds) that come from efforts to change life, if not transform the world. The mental materiality of the road sign of the title stresses the affective value of collective witnessing of the activities that convert real-life events into very human expressions of the unity behind contradictions. Language in its most visible form, the road sign, brings together the verbal and the visual, the static and the dynamic, perception and recognition. It is hope and desire in action, for the texts were not really written in a car going down an open highway with no concern for the outcome of the journey. Poetically defying the appearance of an actual trip, *Ralentir travaux* captures the experience of art as an event, as knowledge of the self and the world. *Ralentir travaux* decelerates the surrealist journey in order to requalify it.

The circumstances of the paratext that the personal quality of the three prefaces validates is a sign to the reading audience to make collective the individual psyches of the individuals who actually wrote the lines of verse. The road sign permits contact with the surreal, a non-mimetic and nonfigural purer realm of existence. As a poetics of audience—the reading audience and the original writing audience—the volume mentalizes, valorizes, and spiritualizes the historical circumstances of mobility that frame the work. Fluid only in mental space, the textual performance of the writing and reading exposes new relationships and unsuspected affinities among disparates. From the multiple layers of the verbal-visual, write-read, organize-materialize processes that envelop *Ralentir travaux*, there emerges the ultimate surrealist hypertext of interchange. Reading the text was a performance for each of the original poets and remains one for the virtual reader. While not a true collective work of collaboration, *Ralentir travaux* is nonetheless an historical realization of the event of the creative act of the poem. The documentary value of the work verifies that event and stands even today as a monument to a surrealist moment in time and place where the same road ascended and descended. The spirit of regeneration that characterizes *Ralentir travaux* and marks it as the countertext to the *Second Manifeste* expresses the continuum of surrealist faith in poetry to better the world and justify life. The very plurality of "travaux" in the title, preceded by the command form of the verb "ralentir," brings together the joint efforts of Breton, Char, and Eluard to transmute desire into hope and negate historical determinism. Breton's final image in the *Second Manifeste* salutes "un feu de salve" 'a salvo' (Breton 1: 828), his call in *Ralentir travaux* for a "table rase" to reverse the world in the surrealist voice of the creative act.

Notes

[1]All translations are my own.

[2]Renée Riese Hubert suggests that the title of Kay Sage's 1940 canvas, *Danger, Construction Ahead,* "provides an accurate if free translation of a key surrealist collaboration, *Ralentir travaux*" (187).

[3]Valentine Hugo is considered the first official woman member of the surrealist group. For a perceptive analysis of women as viable and vital artistic partners in the surrealist venture and a study of their evolution from disciple to primary figure, see Hubert.

[4]Every text of Char's *Arsenal* underwent some sort of revision between the 1929 and 1930 editions. The Char Pléiade edition ignores these numerous changes and does not reproduce at all his *Tombeau des secrets,* much less his first volume of poetry, *Les Cloches sur le cœur (Bells on the Heart)* (1928).

[5]Breton, Char, and Eluard became very close friends after *Ralentir travaux.* Sebbag asserts that the printings of Breton's and Eluard's *Immaculée Conception* on November 24, 1930 and Char's *Artine* on November 25, 1930 were coordinated by the three poets because of their *Ralentir travaux* relationship (62). Char's *Tombeau des secrets* (1930) has an opening quotation by Eluard and contains a poem dedicated to Breton; in December 1930, Breton and Eluard wrote the "Prière d'insérer" 'Publisher's Insert' for Char's *Artine.* In 1931, the three visited Spain together, and Eluard gave Char the manuscript of his *A toute épreuve (Fool-Proof)* during the return voyage; also in 1931, Char dedicated *L'action de la justice est éteinte (The Action of Justice is Extinguished)* to Breton. In 1932, Char wrote the first version of his "Hommage à

Paul Eluard" and undertook the difficult task of editing, revising, and entitling *Paillasse!* (*Whore!*), the surrealist tract that formally ended the disruptive Aragon affair. Breton originally agreed to write the "avant-propos" 'forward' for Char's *Le Marteau sans maître* (1934), although it was eventually written by Tzara. Char and Eluard remained close friends until World War II. Char was even a witness at Eluard's marriage to Nusch on August 21, 1934. Although Eluard's 1934 choice of the title *La Rose publique* for his most surrealist volume of poems was vigorously opposed by Char and Breton, and their opinion did not prevail, Eluard still dedicated the work to Char (Mathieu 271). It should also be noted that Eluard's preface to *Ralentir travaux* is republished as his "Prière d'insérer" for *La Rose publique*.

[6]Writing on *Ralentir travaux*, Sebbag asserts that Corti regretted that Editions Surréalistes was not involved in printing the volume, but the work was already completed and in press in Nîmes when the poets returned to Paris in April (43).

[7]It should be noted that even the "Seconde Prière d'insérer" for the *Second Manifeste* had been written before Breton left for Avignon in late March 1930. In other words, Breton was free from his own efforts to justify the *Second Manifeste*.

[8]It should also be noted that by the time Breton joined Char and Eluard in Avignon in late March 1930, he had written his two personal responses to the attacks in *Un Cadavre*: "Avant/Après" ("Before/After"), and "Prière d'insérer," to be published with the official *Second Manifeste* in press at Kra. The Breton Pléiade edition correctly places *Ralentir travaux* before the *Second Manifeste* because it bases its order on publication dates. However, it is important to note that *Ralentir travaux* was composed at least three months after the *Second Manifeste* and at least one month after Breton finalized revisions of and additions to the *Second Manifeste*.

[9]For an excellent descriptive analysis of *Ralentir travaux*, see Bonnet and Hubert; Mathieu 90-94; Sebbag 42-46, 205-07.

[10]Sebbag states that the order of the names of the poets was changed from the alphabetical order to the following order: Eluard, Breton, Char (45). However, there is no evidence of this change in any of the published forms.

[11]In 1931 Breton wrote *L'Union libre* (*Free Union*) in two days (May 20-21); significantly, this example of speed writing is his first work of poetry after *Ralentir travaux* and his first individual work of poetry since *Clair de terre* (1923).

Works Cited

Bonnet, Marguerite and Etienne-Alain Hubert. "Notice." Breton 1: 1565-74.

Breton, André. *Oeuvres complètes.* 2 vols. Paris: Gallimard, 1988-1992.

_____ and Paul Eluard. "Note sur la collaboration." Breton 1: 1633.

Camus, Albert. *L'Homme révolté.* Paris: Gallimard, 1951.

Char, René. *Oeuvres complètes.* Paris: Gallimard, 1983.

Daix, Pierre. *La Vie quotidienne des surréalistes 1917-1932.* Paris: Hachette, 1993.

Eluard, Paul. *Oeuvres complètes.* Vol. 1. Paris: Gallimard, 1968.

Hubert, Renée Riese. *Magnifying Mirrors: Women, Surrealism, and Painting.* Lincoln: U of Nebraska P, 1994.

Mathieu, Jean-Claude. *La Poésie de René Char ou Le Sel de la splendeur.* Vol. 1: Traversée du surréalisme. Paris: Corti, 1984.

Sebbag, Georges. *Les Editions Surréalistes 1926-1968.* Paris: Institut Mémoires de L'Edition Contemporaine, 1993.

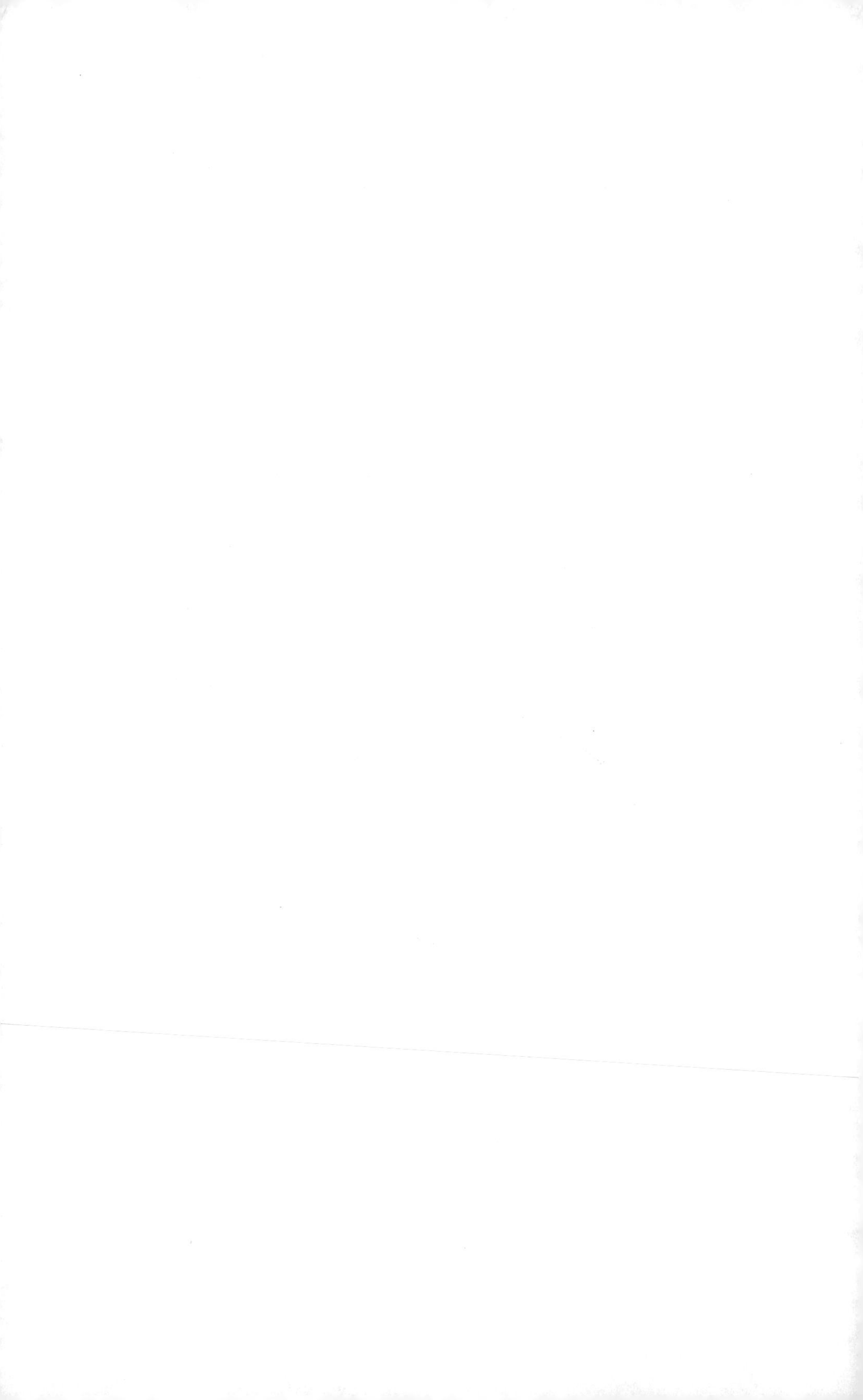

Renée's Biography

Unless you had known Dr. Walther and Dr. Hertha Riese, you might wonder how Renée would some day make her reputation, not in health care, but as a poet and scholar, or how her sister, Beatrice, would become President of the American Abstract Artists. Walther Riese, who practiced medicine and taught at the Medical College of Virginia, was even more interested in ideas than in patients. He published some 15 books and 350 articles in German, French, and English on neurology and psychiatry as well as on the history and philosophy of medicine. Hertha Riese, a poetry enthusiast, became famous in Frankfurt for her pioneering work in family planning. In the racist environment of Richmond in the fifties, she founded and directed a therapy center for threatened black children, publishing the results of her daring project in *Heal the Hurt Child*.

Soon after Walther and Hertha Riese's brief imprisonment in 1933 by the Nazis because of their liberal ideas rather than their Jewish background, the family settled in France, first in Lyon and then in Paris where Renée obtained her Licence-ès-Lettres. The day before the outbreak of war, she travelled to England where supposedly a position as French teacher awaited her. And there she spent the next four years, teaching mainly at a progressive school in the company of pacifist artists and writers. In 1944, after a perilous sea voyage, she finally joined her parents and her sister in the United States. She obtained an M.A. in Comparative Literature and a Ph.D. in French at Columbia University. During this period, she taught first at Wilson College, then at Sarah Lawrence, where she was tenured, and married Judd. When the latter accepted a position at Harvard, she commuted between Cambridge and Bronxville for a year before settling for a position as "Emergency Instructor" at Harvard, apparently becoming the first woman faculty member in the history of that august institution. When the emergency subsided, she moved to Suffolk University as Dean of Women and Assistant Professor of French.

A year after Judd's appointment as Associate Professor at UCLA in 1957, Renée founded the Department of Foreign Languages at what was to become the State University of California, Northridge. In spite of a heavy teaching load and administrative duties, she obtained on the strength of her research in poetry a Guggenheim Fellowship. In 1965, the couple moved to the University of Illinois where, for the first time, Renée could teach graduate courses. Two years later, they moved back to California where the chance of creating a different kind of graduate program, first in French and then in Comparative Literature, proved to be irresistible. At the University of California, Irvine, in addition to creating a wide variety of new courses in French, comparative literature, women's studies, art history, and film, as well as sponsoring a great number of doctoral dissertations and completing many a research project, Renée chaired the Department of French and Italian, directed the program in Comparative Literture, and served as Chair of the Academic Senate. Shortly before her retirement, she was awarded a senior fellowship by the National Endowment for the Humanities.

List of Publications

Renée Riese Hubert

Poetry

La Cité borgne. Paris: Seghers, 1953.

Asymptotes. Paris: Debresse, 1954.

Le Berceau d'Eve. Paris: Minuit, 1957.

Plumes et pinceaux. Paris: Dervy, 1960.

Chants funèbres. Rodez: Subervie, 1964.

Enchaînement. Rodez: Subervie, 1969.

Natures mortes. Honfleur: Oswald, 1972.

A translation by Roger Shattuck of "The Doll" from *Le Berceau d'Eve* appeared in his *Half Tame* (Austin: U of Texas P, 1964). Translations by Raymond Federman and J. D. Hubert were published in such journals as *Mica, Calyx, Uclan Review*.

Critical Studies

The Dreyfus Affair and the French Novel: From Fact to Fiction. New York & Boston: Eagle Enterprises, 1951. [Doctoral Dissertation, Columbia University]

Surrealism and the Book. Berkeley & Los Angeles: U of California P, 1988. 358 pp. [Paperback edition: U of California P, 1992.]

Magnifying Mirrors: Women, Surrealism, and Partnership. Lincoln & London: U of Nebraska P, 1994. 409 pp.

Translation

Louis Aragon, *The Adventures of Telemachus.* Prefaced and translated in collaboration with Judd D. Hubert. Lincoln & London: U of Nebraska P, 1988. 101 pp.

Text Books

*Deux pièces sur la fin d'un monde: Supervielle, **La Belle au bois;** Vian, **Les Bâtisseurs d'empire**.* New York: Macmillan [Modern French Series], 1966.

Anthologie de la poésie française du vingtième siècle [in collaboration with J. D. Hubert]. New York: Appleton Century Crofts, 1971.

Articles

"Three Women Poets." *Yale French Studies* 21 (1958): 40-49.

"Les Mythologies intimes de Supervielle." *Symposium* 3.2 (1959): 300-06.

"The Fleeting World of Humor from Watteau to Fragonard." *Yale French Studies* 23 (1960): 85-92.

"L'Evolution du poème en prose dans l'œuvre de Reverdy." *Modern Language Notes* 25 (1960): 17-24.

"French Notes on Two Italian Painters." *Italian Quarterly* 4 (1961): 17-23.

"L'Elan vers l'humain." *Entretiens* 21 (1962): 94-101. [Special issue on Reverdy]

"Claudel, poète en prose." *French Review* 35 (1962): 369-76.

"Le Langage de la peinture dans le poème en prose." *Revue des Sciences Humaines* (1962): 109-16.

"Julien Gracq et la solution poétique." *Cahiers de L'Association Internationale des Etudes Françaises* 14 (1962): 195-207.

"Patterns in the Antinovel." *Forum* 3.11 (1962): 11-15.

"Jules Supervielle in Stageland." *Yale French Studies* 29 (1962): 102-07.

"The Couple and the Performance in Samuel Beckett's Plays." *L'Esprit Créateur* 3 (1963): 175-81.

"Georges Braque and the French Poets." *Books Abroad* 37 (1963): 385-90.

"L'Amour et la féérie chez Madame d'Aulnoy." *Romanische Forschungen* 75 (1963): 1-10.

"Poetic Humor in Madame d'Aulnoy's Fairy Tales." *L'Esprit Créateur* 3 (1963): 123-29.

"The Cult of the Visible in *Gaspard de la nuit*." *Modern Language Quarterly* 25 (1964): 76-85.

"Miró and Breton." *Yale French Studies* 31 (1964): 52-61.

"The French Avant-Garde Theater in America." *Studi Francesi* (1965): 19-22.

"Julien Gracq, historien du rêve." *French Review* 38 (1965): 630-36.

"Le Théâtre poétique de Jules Supervielle." *Iô* 3 (1965): 4-10.

"Les surréalistes et Picasso." *L'Esprit Créateur* 6 (1966): 45-51.

"La Technique de la peinture dans le poème en prose [XIXème siècle]." *Cahiers de L'Association Internationale des Etudes Françaises* 18 (1966): 169-78.

"Apollinaire et Picasso." *Cahiers du Sud* 53 (1966): 22-27.

"Beckett's *Play* between Poetry and Performance." *Modern Drama* 9 (1966): 339-46.

"Fromentin's *Dominique*: The Confessions of a Man Who Judges Himself." *PMLA* 82 (1967): 634-39.

"Interprétation figurée des *Fables* de La Fontaine." *Kentucky Romance Quarterly* 14 (1967): 177-90.

"Characteristics of an Undefinable Genre: The Surrealist Prose Poem." *Symposium* 22 (1968): 25-34.

"L'Elan vers l'actuel dans la poésie d'Apollinaire et de Breton." *Revue des Lettres Modernes* 183-88 (1968): 195-206.

"The Maids as Children, a Commentary on Genet's *Les Bonnes*." *Romance Notes* 10 (1969): 204-09.

"The Use of Reversals in Rimbaud's *Illuminations*." *L'Esprit Créateur* 9.1 (1969): 9-18.

"The Paradox of Silence: Samuel Beckett's Plays." *Mundus Artium* 2.3 (1969): 82-90.

"The Coherence of Breton's *Nadja*." *Contemporary Literature* 10 (1969): 241-52.

"Collages and Surrealist Genres." *Proceedings of the Comparative Literature Symposium. From Surrealism to the Absurd* (Vol. 3). Ed. Wolodymyr T. Zyla. Lubbock: Interdept. Comm. on Comp. Lit., Texas Tech U, 1970. 163-90.

"Intimacy and Distance in Baudelaire's Prose Poems." *Texas Studies in Literature and Language* 12 (1970): 241-47.

"*L'Archangélique* de Georges Bataille, le jeu de la mort et de la poésie." *Revue des Sciences Humaines* 35 (1970): 603-12.

"André Masson and His Critics." *Comparative Literature Studies* 7 (1970): 480-88.

"Contexts of Twilight in Baudelaire's *Petits poèmes en prose.*" *Orbis Litterarum* 25 (1970): 352-60.

"Limbour et la poétique de Masson." *Romance Notes* 12 (1970): 1-4.

"Lecture de Giacometti." *Revue d'Esthétique* 3 (1971): 75-90.

"Supervielle." *Encyclopedia of XXth Century World Literature* 3 (1971): 264-65.

"Mother Goose in Rags and Riches." *Journal for Popular Culture* (1972): 148-61.

"The Fabulous Fiction of Two Surrealist Artists: Giorgio de Chirico and Max Ernst." *New Literary History* 4 (1972): 151-66.

"*Liberté grande*: La ville comme aventure." *Julien Gracq.* Ed. Jean-Louis Leutrat. Paris: Cahiers de l'Herne, 1972. 136-45.

"Le Sens du voyage dans quelques contes de Madame d'Aulnoy." *French Review* 46 (1973): 931-37.

"Villiers de l'Isle Adam: Le Domaine du fantastique et les limites de la science." *Nineteenth Century French Studies* 1 (1973): 174-81.

"Apollinaire: Le Langage des merveilles et des surprises." *Apollinaire, inventeur de langages.* Ed. Michel Décaudin. Paris: Lettres Modernes, 1973. 70-86.

"Au-delà de *L'Ephémère.*" *SubStance* 5-6 (1973): 117-27.

"Aimé Césaire: French Poet." *Dada/Surrealism* 3 (1973): 53-60.

"L'Universo Fantastico di Alain Lesort." *Pianeta* 56 (1973): 156-57.

"Microtexts: An Aspect of the Work of Beckett, Robbe-Grillet, and Nathalie Sarraute." *International Fiction Review* 1.1 (1974): 9-16.

"Une Collaboration surréaliste: *Les Malheurs des immortels.*" *Surrealismo.* Ed. P. A. Jannini. Rome: Bulzoni, 1974. 205-19. [With Judd D. Hubert]

"Ernst and Eluard, a Model of Surrealist Collaboration." *Kentucky Romance Quarterly* 21 (1974): 113-21.

"The Invasions of Poetry." *Diacritics* 4.1 (1974): 21-25.

"Max Jacob: The Poetics of *Le Cornet à Dés.*" *About French Poetry From Dada to "Tel Quel": Text and Theory.*" Ed. Mary Ann Caws et al. Detroit: Wayne State UP (1974): 99-111.

"Three Eighteenth Century Graphic Interpretations of *Don Quixote.*" *Bulletin du Bibliophile* (1975): 28-41.

"'Trésor des fèves et fleur des pois': A Modern Fairytale." *The French Short Story.* University of South Carolina French Literature Series 2 (1975): 217-20.

"*Aurora*: Adventure in Word and Image." *SubStance* 11-12 (1975): 74-87.

"Literature and the Arts." *Yearbook of Comparative and General Literature* 24 (1975): 40-43.

"L'Image poétique de Michel Leiris." *French Forum* 1 (1976): 68-78.

"Les Contes." *Gustav Meyrink.* Paris: Cahiers de l'Herne, 1976. 55-59.

"Le Triomphe de la mort chez Kubin." *Obliques* 6-7 (1976): 247-53. [Special issue on *L'Expressionisme allemand*]

"A la trace de Bing." *Samuel Beckett*. Ed. Tom Bishop and Raymond Federman. Paris: Cahiers de l'Herne, 1976. 253-59.

"Max Jacob's Bourgeois Voices." *Max Jacob Centennial (1876-1976)*. Ed. Judith Morganroth Schneider. Brockport: Dept. of Foreign Languages, SUNY, 1976. 38-42.

"The Landscape of Desire in *Le Point cardinal*." *Dada/Surrealism* 6 (1976): 31-37.

"*Nadja* depuis la mort de Breton." *Œuvres et Critiques* 2.1 (1977): 93-102.

"Writers as Art Critics: Three Views of the Paintings of Paul Klee." *Contemporary Literature* 18 (1977): 75-92.

"Annie Le Brun et Toyen." *Obliques* 14-15 (1977): 174. [Special issue on *La Femme surréaliste*]

"Henri Michaux et René Magritte." *Stanford French Review* 2 (1978): 61-72.

"Ethique et esthétique dans les utopies de Michaux." *Ethique et esthétique dans la littérature française du vingtième siècle*. Ed. Maurice Cagnon. Saratoga, CA: Anma Libri, 1978. 79-85.

"The Illustrated Book: Text and Image." *New York Literary Forum* 1 (1978): 77-97. [Special issue on intertextuality]

"The Other Worldly Landscapes of E. A. Poe and René Magritte." *SubStance* 21 (1978): 69-78.

"Le Dialogue entre André Malraux et Pablo Picasso." *La Revue des Lettres Modernes* 537-42 (1978): 73-82. [Special issue on "Malraux et l'art"]

"L'Antiportrait surréaliste." *Le Siècle Eclaté* 2 (1978): 67-83.

"Ponge: Visual and Poetic Writing." *Visible Language* 12 (1978): 319-40.

"Michel Deguy's 'Art Poétique.'" *SubStance* 23-24 (1979): 172-76.

"Max Ernst and Romanticism." *Dada/Surrealism* 9 (1979): 48-62.

"Surrealism in the Americas." *Proceedings of the 7th Congress of the International Comparative Literature Association.* Ed. Eva Kushner. Stuttgart, 1979. 237-39.

"Henri Michaux." *Critical Bibliography of French Literature.* Syracuse: Syracuse UP, 1979. 1155-62.

"Michaux, Henri." *Columbia Dictionary of Modern European Literature.* Vol. 2. New York: Columbia UP, 1979. 533-34.

"'Lokis': La Recherche de l'identité et l'énigme fantastique." *Nineteeth Century French Studies* 8 (1980): 228-35.

"Images du criminel et du héros surréalistes." *Mélusine* 1 (1980): 187-98.

"Apollinaire and Dine: A Re-Enactment of the Poet's Assassination." *Symposium* 34 (1980): 333-51.

"Les Fictions déformantes: Une Lecture du *Voleur de Talan.*" *Bousquet, Jouve, Reverdy.* Ed. Charles Bachat et al. Marseille: Sud, 1981. 317-43. [Special issue of *Sud* on Bousquet, Jouve, Reverdy]

"The Encounter of Bertolt Brecht and François Villon: A Commentary on *The Threepenny Opera.*" *The Comparatist* 5 (1981): 47-53.

"Simulacre et mimésis." *Mélusine* 11 (1981): 222-27.

"*L'Alphabet* de Claes Oldenburg." *La Sape* 16 (1981): 54-56.

"Poésie calligrammatique et poésie concrète." *Que-Vlo-Ve?* 9 (1981): 1-17.

"La Présence du théâtre dans *Le Poète assassiné.*" *Papers-in-Romance* 3.1 (1981): 1-10.

"Paul Eluard." *Encyclopedia of World Literature in the XXth Century.* New York: Ungar, 1982. 24-26.

"Le Livre surréaliste" and "Yves Tanguy." *Dictionnaire général du surréalisme.* Freiburg: Office du Livre, 1982. 248-49 and 396-97.

"Sur les traductions." *Recherche et pluridisciplinarité.* Ed. J. Morel et al. Paris: Sorbonne Nouvelle, 1982. 317-19.

"Verhaeren et James Ensor." *Cahiers de L'Association Internationale des Etudes Françaises* 34 (1982): 179-92.

"The Artbook as Poetic Code: Breton's *Yves Tanguy.*" *L'Esprit Créateur* 22.4 (1982): 56-66.

"Livre illustré, culture actuelle." *Cahiers de l'Archipel* 9 (1982): 28-30.

"Miró et le livre surréaliste." *Mélusine* 4 (1983): 22-41.

"Patch and Paradox in Joseph Cornell's Art." *New York Literary Forum* 10-11 (1983): 167-79. [Special issue on collage]

"Art and Perversity: Barlach's and Dali's Views of Walpurgisnacht." *Journal of European Studies* 13 (1983): 75-95.

"The Encounter of Balzac and Picasso." *Dalhousie French Studies* 5 (1983): 38-54.

"Max Ernst: The Displacement of the Visual and the Verbal." *New Literary History* 15.3 (1984): 575-606.

"Graphisme poétique et poésie graphique: Les *Illuminations* de Fernand Léger." *Minute d'éveil: Rimbaud maintenant.* Paris: SEDES, 1984. 149-57.

"Henri Michaux: Illustration and Double Talent." *World Literature Today* 58.2 (1984): 209-15.

"Intertextualité et illustrations: La Poupée de Bellmer et d'Eluard." *Les Mots, la vie*. Ed. Colette Guedj. Publications du Groupe Eluard. Nice: Université de Nice, 1984. 63-71.

"Surrealist Women Painters, Feminist Portraits." *Dada/Surrealism* 13 (1984): 70-83.

"The 'Tableau-poème': Open Work." Tr. Kathryn Aschheim. *Yale French Studies* 67 (1984): 43-56.

"René Char et l'illustration surréaliste." *René Char: Actes du colloque international de l'Université de Tours*. Ed. Daniel Leuwers. Marseille: Sud, 1984. 274-88. [Special issue of *Sud* on René Char]

"Raw and Cooked: An Interpretation of *Ubu roi*." *L'Esprit Créateur* 24.4 (1984): 75-83.

"Du Tableau-poème à la poésie concrète." *Ecritures* 2 (1985): 271-89.

"The Ancient Mariner's Graphic Voyage through Mimesis and Metaphor." *Yearbook of English Studies* 15 (1985): 80-92.

"Satire and Utopia: Robida and Grandville." *The Comparatist* 9 (1985): 47-54.

"La Critique d'art surréaliste: Création et tradition." *Cahiers de L'Association Internationale des Etudes Françaises* 37 (1985): 213-27.

"'Peau pour mon alphabet': Langage et lecture dans *Ouï dire*. " *French Forum* 10.2 (1985): 215-23.

"Readable-Visible: Reflections on the Illustrated Book." *Visible Language* 19.4 (1985): 519-38.

"Paul Klee: Modernism in Art and Literature." *Modernism: Challenges and Perspectives*. Ed. Monique Chefdor et al. Urbana: U of Illinois P, 1986. 212-37.

"*Paix dans les brisements*: Trajectoire verbale et graphique." *L'Esprit Créateur* 26.3 (1986): 72-86. [Special issue on *Henri Michaux*. Ed. Laurie Edson]

"Poe vu par cinq illustrateurs." *Dimensions du merveilleux*. Vol. 3. Oslo: Colloque International, 1986. 134-54.

"Max Ernst entre la bonté et le plaisir." *Du Surréalisme et du plaisir*. Ed. Jacqueline Chénieux-Gendron. Paris: Corti, 1987. 149-59.

"*Ubu roi* and the Surrealist 'Livre de Peintre.'" *Word and Image* 3.4 (1987): 259-78. [Special issue on *The Question of Illustration*. Ed. Eric Haskell and Renée R. Hubert]

"Max Ernst and Samuel Beckett." *Beckett Translating / Translating Beckett*. Ed. Alan Warren Friedman et al. University Park, PA: Pennsylvania State UP, 1987. 199-212.

"Robert Champigny et le récit poétique." *Robert Champigny*. Ed. Hédi Bouraoui. Geneva: Slatkine, 1987. 47-55.

"Proverbes et images dans *Les Pénalités de l'enfer*." *Moi qui suis Robert Desnos: Permanence d'une voix*. Ed. Marie-Claire Dumas. Paris: Corti, 1987. 115-25.

"Gertrude Stein, Cubism and the Postmodern Book." *Genre* 20 (1987): 329-58. [Reprinted in *Postmodern Genres*. Ed. Marjorie Perloff. Norman: U of Oklahoma P, 1989. 96-125]

"The Surrealist Book." *Word and Image* 4.1 (1988): 265-74.

"*Le Calumet*." *André Salmon*. Turin: Quaderni del Novecento Francese, 1988. 77-83.

"Portrait d'Unica Zürn en anagramme." *Pleine Marge* 7 (1988): 60-72.

"The Postmodern Line and the Postmodern Page." *The Line in Postmodern Poetry*. Ed. Robert Joseph Frank and Henry M. Sayre. Urbana: U of Illinois P, 1988. 132-51.

"Francis Ponge and Postmodern Illustration." *Criticism* 30.3 (1988): 375-98. [Special issue on Modern Poetry and the Visual Arts]

"La Fontaine et la famille Vernet." *Ouverture et dialogue*. Ed. Ulrich Doring et al. Tübingen: Gunter Narr Verlag, 1988. 247-62.

"Gertrude Stein and the Making of Frenchmen." *SubStance* 59 (1989): 71-93.

"Women, Gender, Genre." L'Esprit Créateur 29.3 (1989): 3-10. [Guest Editor's preface]

"The Postmodern Book and the Example of Michel Butor." *Postmodernism and Beyond: Architecture as the Critical Art of Contemporary Culture*. Irvine: U of California Regents, 1989. 7-12.

"The Books of Fernand Léger: Illustration and Inscription." *Visible Language* 23 (1989): 255-79. [Special issue on Inscriptions in Painting]

"Fernand Léger, lecteur de Malraux." *Revue André Malraux* 21-22 (1989-90): 92-103. [Special issue on Metamorphosis and the Creative Process]

"Le Rôle du couple dans la peinture surréaliste." *Mélusine* 11 (1990): 249-62. [Special issue on History, Historiography]

"From *Déjeuner en fourrure* to *Caroline*: Meret Oppenheim's Chronicle of Surrealism." *Dada/Surrealism* 18 (1990): 37-49. [Special issue on Women and Surrealism; reprinted by M.I.T. Press]

"Masson's and Mallarmé's *Un Coup de dés*: An Esthetic Comparison." *Nineteenth Century French Studies* 18 (1990): 508-23. [In collaboration with J. D. Hubert]

"Gender, Genre and Partnership: A Study of Valentine Penrose." *The Other Perspective in Gender and Culture: Rewriting Women and the Symbolic*. Ed. Juliet Flower MacCannell. New York: Columbia UP, 1990. 117-42.

"Max Ernst: Die Verdrängung des Visuellen und des Verbalen." *Bildlichkeit*. Ed. Volker Bohn. Frankfurt: Suhrkamp, 1990. 192-229. [Translation of article in *New Literary History* 15.3 (1984)]

"Leonora Carrington and Max Ernst: Artistic Partnership and Feminist Liberation." *New Literary History* 22 (1991): 715-47.

"Wolfgang Paalen et ses familiers: L'Itinéraire visuel et verbal de *Dyn* à *Dynaton*." *Mélusine* 12 (1991): 129-45.

"Traces of Transcendence: Masson, Ernst, Tàpies." *Word and Image* 7. 2 (1991): 165-76.

"Unica Zürn and Hans Bellmer." *Sulfur* 29 (1991): 98-104.

"Antoni Tàpies: Between History and Mysticism." *Dalhousie French Studies* 21 (1991): 101-11. [Special issue on Art Criticism by French Poets since World War II]

"Introduction." *The Artist's Book: The Text and its Rivals*. Ed. Renée Riese Hubert. *Visible Language* 25 (1992): 117-136.

"Soupault et Alexéïef." *Philippe Soupault le poète*. Ed. Jacqueline Chénieux-Gendron. Paris: Klincksieck, 1992. 149-61.

"The Four Dimensional Book." *Word & Image Interactions*. Ed. Martin Heusser. Basel: Wiese Verlag, 1993. 85-95.

"Romantic Intertextuality: Meret Oppenheim's Verbal and Visual Works." *Intertextuality: German Literature and Visual Art from the Renaissance to the Twentieth Century*. Ed. Ingeborg Hoesterey and Ulrich Weisstein. Columbia, SC: Camden House, 1993. 100-17.

"L'Après-coup de l'amour fou: Joyce Mansour et Annie Le Brun." *Carrefour de cultures; Mélanges offerts à Jacqueline Leiner*. Ed. Régis Antoine. Tübingen: Gunter Narr Verlag, 1993. 227-36.

"Derrida, Dupin, Adami: Il faut être plusieurs pour écrire." *Boundaries: Writing and Drawing*. Ed. Martine Reid. *Yale French Studies* 84 (1993): 242-64.

"Sophie Taeuber and Hans Arp: A Community of Two." *Art Journal* 52.4 (1993): 25-32.

"Ania Staritsky." *Pleine Marge* 20 (1994): 93-115. [In collaboration with J. D. Hubert]

"Bertrand Dorny at the Musée Pompidou" and "The Book Fair of Saint-Yrieix." *Journal of Artists' Books* 4 (1995): 21-22.

"Notes de lecture sur la poésie d'André Marissel." *Cahiers de l'Archipel* 32 (1995): 15-19. [In collaboration with J. D. Hubert]

"Kokoschka, Kandinsky and the Art of the Expressionist Book." *Forum for Modern Language Studies* 32.2 (1996): 166-83.

[Some sixty book reviews not listed]

Contributors

Willard Bohn is Professor of French at Illinois State University. He is the author of some seventy articles and five books, including *Apollinaire and the Faceless Man, The Aesthetics of Visual Poetry,* and *Apollinaire and the International Avant-Garde.*

Joan Brandt teaches French in the Cooperative Program in Modern Languages at Scripps College, Claremont University Center. She has published numerous articles on contemporary French literature and critical theory, and her book, *Geopoetics: The Politics of Mimesis in Poststructuralist French Poetry and Theory,* is forthcoming in 1997 from Stanford University Press.

Roger Cardinal is Professor of Literary and Visual Studies at the University of Kent at Canterbury, where he directs the Comparative Literary Studies program. He has written widely on Dada and Surrealism (*Surrealism: Permanent Revelation,* with R. Short, 1970; *The Landscape Vision of Paul Nash,* 1989) and on modern poetry (*Figures of Reality,* 1981).

Anne-Marie Christin is Professor at the University of Paris VII-Denis Diderot and Director of the Centre d'étude de l'écriture at the CNRS. She has written numerous articles and has edited several collections on visual forms of writing: *L'Espace et la lettre* (1977), *Ecritures* (1982), *Ecritures II* (1985), and *Ecritures III* (1989). She is also the author of *L'Image écrite ou la déraison graphique* (1995).

Michel Deguy is one of France's most important poets and essayists, and teaches philosophy at the University of Paris-Vincennes. He has published numerous collections, the most recent of which include *Gisants: poèmes* (1985), *Brevets* (1986), *Arrêts fréquents* (1990), *Aux heures d'affluence: poèmes et proses* (1993), *A ce qui n'en finit pas: thrène* (1995). His 1981 collection, *Donnant, donnant,* was translated by Clayton Eshleman and published as *Given giving* (U of California P, 1984). He has made frequent lecture tours in the United States.

Bertrand Dorny, sculptor, graphic artist, and book artist, lives in Paris. He has collaborated with such major writers as Michel Deguy, Bernard Noël, Michel Butor, Eugène Guillevic, Ron Padgett, and William Jay Smith. He has created close to one hundred books, highly experimental in form, of which he is simultaneously the artist and publisher. He has had over one hundred shows, including a recent exhibition at the Centre Georges Pompidou in Paris, with a simultaneous colloquium devoted to his work. His works can be seen in many major museums and rare book collections in Europe and North America.

Laurie Edson is Professor of Comparative Literature and French at San Diego State University. She is the author of *Henri Michaux and the Poetics of Movement* (1985), the guest editor of a special issue of *L'Esprit Créateur* on Henri Michaux (1986), the guest editor of a special issue of *Studies in Twentieth Century Literature* on *Contemporary Feminist Writing in French: A Multicultural Perspective* (1993), and the translator (with critical afterword) of Jeanne Hyvrard's *Mother Death* (1988). She has just completed a book manuscript on literature and visual art.

Claude Gandelman is Professor of French and Comparative Literature at Haifa University, Israel, and the author of *Le Regard dans le texte: Image, écriture du Quattrocento au XXe siècle* (1986) and *Reading Pictures, Viewing Texts* (1991).

Robert W. Greene is Professor of French at the State University of New York, Albany, and author of *The Poetic Theory of Pierre Reverdy, Six French Poets of Our Time,* and *Just Words: Moralism and Metalanguage in Twentieth-Century French Fiction.* He edited

Dalhousie French Studies 21, devoted to "Art Criticism by French Poets Since World War II," and is currently writing a book on Yves Bonnefoy's art criticism.

Eric T. Haskell is Professor of French and Humanities at Scripps College, Claremont University Center, where he is also Director of the Clark Humanities Museum. The focus of his research and writing is image-text inquiry. He has published articles on Baudelaire, Flaubert, Huysmans, Nerval, Rimbaud, and Wilde. He has also curated several exhibitions on the book arts including *The Image and the Text, Transcending Mimesis: The French Illustrated Book,* and *Twentieth-Century Illustrated Books from the Hubert Collection.*

Judd D. Hubert is Professor Emeritus at the University of California, Irvine. He is author of *L'Esthétique des Fleurs du mal* (Cailler, 1953); *Essai d'exégèse racinienne* (Nizet, 1956); *Molière and the Comedy of Intellect* (U of California P, 1962); *Metatheater: The Example of Shakespeare* (U of Nebaraska P, 1991); and *Corneille's Performative Metaphors* (forthcoming, EMF Monographs, Rookwood, 1997). He is presently collaborating with Renée Riese Hubert on a book entitled *On the Cutting Edge of Reading: The Artist's Book.*

Georgette James is a poet, freelance interpreter, and translator for Spanish, French, and Portuguese. She has published her own poetry, and teaches creative writing, literature, and composition part-time at San Diego State University. She has also collaborated on a translation of the early poetry of Borges.

Virginia A. La Charité is Professor of French at the University of Kentucky. Co-founder and co-editor of *French Forum* since 1976, she is the author of five books on modern French poetry and numerous articles concerning nineteenth- and twentieth-century writers. Her most recent book, *Twentieth-Century French Avant-Garde Poetry, 1907-1990,* was published by French Forum.

Sydney Lévy is Professor of French at the University of California, Santa Barbara. He is the co-founder and co-editor of *SubStance: A Review of Theory and Literary Criticism,* the author of *The Play of the Text: Max Jacob's Le Cornet à Dés* (1983), and the author of numerous articles on contemporary poetry and literary theory. He is currently working on a book on Ponge's epistemology.

Breon Mitchell is Professor of Germanic Studies and Comparative Literature at Indiana University in Bloomington, where he also serves as Director of the Wells Scholars Program. He has written extensively on modern literature and the illustrated book, including *Beyond Illustation: The Livre d'artiste in the Twentieth Century*, and is currently retranslating Franz Kafka's *The Trial* for Schocken Books.

Marjorie Perloff is Sadie Dernham Patek Professor of Humanities at Stanford University. She is the editor of *Postmodern Genres* (1989), and her most recent books are *The Futurist Moment: Avant-Garde, Avant-Guerre, and the Language of Rupture* (1986), *Poetic License: Essays on Modernist and Postmodernist Lyric* (1990), *Radical Artifice: Writing Poetry in the Age of Media* (1991), and *Wittgenstein's Ladder: Poetic Language and the Strangeness of the Ordinary* (forthcoming 1996).

Judith Preckshot teaches modern French literature and culture at the University of Minnesota-Twin Cities. Her publications and research focus on twentieth-century poets and poetics, francophone literature, and immigration and cultural diversity in France.

Georges Roques is a researcher at the Centre National de la Recherche Scientifique in Paris, and is currently a visiting scholar at the Instituto de Investigaciones Estéticas of the Universidad Nacional Autónoma de México (UNAM). He has published several volumes, including *Ceci n'est pas un Magritte*, and his *Art et science de la couleur: Chevreul et les peintres* is forthcoming.

Roger Shattuck is the author of *The Banquet Years*, two books on Proust (one of which won a National Book Award), a volume of poems, a study of the Wild Boy of Aveyron, and *The Innocent Eye*, a collection of essays. *Forbidden Knowledge: From Prometheus to Pornography* will appear in 1996. He teaches at Boston University and is the current president of the Association of Literary Scholars and Critics.

Richard Vernier, Professor Emeritus at Wayne State University, now lives and writes near Seattle and Mount Rainier. In addition to numerous articles on French literature, he has published *Poésie ininterrompue et la poétique de Paul Eluard* (1971), *Yves Bonnefoy, ou, Les mots comme le ciel* (1985), *Un parcours américain: récits* (1991), and collaborated on a translation, *Winds of the People: Poetry of the Spanish Civil War* (1986). His most recent work is *Naufrage à Munising*, a novel.

Harriett Watts is Associate Director of the Lionel Feininger Museum in Quedlinburg, Germany. She is the author of *Chance: A Perspective on Dada* (UMI Press, 1975, 1980), and the translator (with introduction) of *Arp, Schwitters, Klee: Three Painter-Poets* (Penguin, 1974). She also wrote the text for a catalog on Antoni Tàpies as a book artist (*Die Bildzeichen und das Buch,* 1988), as well as the text for a catalog of the *livre de peintre* (*Das Buch des Künstlers,* 1989).

Steven Winspur is Professor of French at the University of Wisconsin, Madison. He has published *Saint-John Perse and the Imaginary Reader, Bernard Noël,* and edited a volume of essays entitled *Mallarmé, Theorist of Our Times.* A book that he has co-authored with Jean-Jacques Thomas on contemporary French poetry will appear shortly.